German in the World

Studies in German Literature, Linguistics, and Culture

German in the World

The Transnational and Global Contexts of German Studies

Edited by
James Hodkinson and
Benedict Schofield

CAMDEN HOUSE
Rochester, New York

This project was supported by the Arts and
Humanities Research Council (AHRC).

The Arts and Humanities Research Council (AHRC) funds world-class, independent researchers in a wide range of subjects: history, archaeology, digital content, philosophy, languages, design, heritage, area studies, the creative and performing arts, and much more. This financial year the AHRC will spend approximately £98 million to fund research and postgraduate training, in collaboration with a number of partners. The quality and range of research supported by this investment of public funds not only provides social and cultural benefits and contributes to the economic success of the UK but also to the culture and welfare of societies around the globe.
For further information on the AHRC, please go to: www.ahrc.ac.uk.

Copyright © 2020 by the Editors and Contributors

All Rights Reserved. Except as permitted under current legislation, no part of this work may be photocopied, stored in a retrieval system, published, performed in public, adapted, broadcast, transmitted, recorded, or reproduced in any form or by any means, without the prior permission of the copyright owner.

First published 2020
by Camden House

Camden House is an imprint of Boydell & Brewer Inc.
668 Mt. Hope Avenue, Rochester, NY 14620, USA
www.camden-house.com
and of Boydell & Brewer Limited
PO Box 9, Woodbridge, Suffolk IP12 3DF, UK
www.boydellandbrewer.com

ISBN-13: 978-1-64014-033-2
ISBN-10: 1-64014-033-X

Library of Congress Cataloging-in-Publication Data

Names: Hodkinson, James R., 1973– editor. | Schofield, Benedict, editor.
Title: German in the world : the transnational and global contexts of German studies / edited by James Hodkinson and Benedict Schofield.
Description: Rochester : Camden House, 2020. | Series: Studies in German literature linguistics and culture | Includes bibliographical references and index.
Identifiers: LCCN 2020002977 | ISBN 9781640140332 (hardback) | ISBN 9781787446847 (pdf)
Subjects: LCSH: Germany—Civilization—Study and teaching. | German language—Study and teaching (Higher) | Transnationalism.
Classification: LCC DD67 .G485 2020 | DDC 943—dc23
LC record available at https://lccn.loc.gov/2020002977

This publication is printed on acid-free paper.
Printed in the United States of America.

Contents

Acknowledgments vii

Introduction: German in Its Worlds 1
   James Hodkinson and Benedict Schofield

Part I. The World in German Culture

Introduction to Part I: The World in German Culture . . . 17
   James Hodkinson and Benedict Schofield

1: Goethe's World 22
   John K. Noyes

2: Embodying and Distributing World Literature: Goethe's
   Novelle in the Context of the 1820s 34
   Ben Morgan

3: *Weltdeutschtum*: On the Notion of a German World
   Community from Schiller to Thomas Mann 58
   Tobias Boes

4: Nineteenth-Century German Travelers to Wales: Text,
   Translation, and the Manipulation of Identity 74
   Carol Tully

5: "Weltliteratur aus der Uckermark": Regionalism and
   Transnationalism in Saša Stanišić's *Vor dem Fest* . . 91
   Frauke Matthes

6: Postcolonial Studies in International German Studies:
   Postcolonial Concerns in Contemporary German Literature . . 109
   Dirk Göttsche

Part II. German in World Locales

Introduction to Part II: German in World Locales 135
   James Hodkinson and Benedict Schofield

7: German in a South African Context: From Colony to
   Decolonization   138
   Carlotta von Maltzan

8: From German Studies to Environmental Humanities (and
   Back Again): A Journey across Continents and Disciplines   155
   Kate Rigby

9: A Philo-Selfie Approach to German-Indian Studies   170
   Sai Bhatawadekar

Part III. German Worlds beyond the Academy

Introduction to Part III: German Worlds beyond the Academy   191
James Hodkinson and Benedict Schofield

10: Towards a Socially Engaged Academy: Islam in German
    History and Its Relevance for Nonacademic Publics   194
    James Hodkinson

11: Theater without Borders? Tracing the Transnational Value of
    German Theater beyond Germany: A UK Case Study   219
    Benedict Schofield

12: Tuning in to Germany: The BBC German Service and the
    British Occupation   239
    Emily Oliver

13: Reterritorializing German Pop: Kraftwerk's *Industrielle
    Volksmusik* as a Transnational Phenomenon   257
    Uwe Schütte

Notes on the Contributors   281

Index   285

Acknowledgments

THE EDITORS WISH to acknowledge and thank a number of individuals and organizations for helping to conceive and bring this volume to fruition. The collection has grown, changed, and taken on a global life of its own over the last five years. Nonetheless, it was born at a series of meetings and events in the United Kingdom. First, then, we thank the colleagues who participated in the annual meeting of university Heads of German (HOGMeet) in 2013, especially Dr. Robert Gillet and Dr. Katerina Somers, for helping to spawn the idea of an event surveying our field of study and its ongoing global diversity and value. For their work in conceiving, planning, and delivering the main event, held in London in the summer of 2014 and entitled "German in the World," we thank Professor Erica Carter, Professor Sarah Colvin, Dr. Robert Gillett, and Dr. Godela Weiss-Sussex, and also Dr. Anne Simon, and Dr. Andreas Hoeschen of the German Academic Exchange Service, as well as Jane Lewin and the Institute for Modern Languages Research in London for their support as hosting venue.

As the volume evolved, we gained new contributors, several of whom were not present at the London event but nonetheless gave of themselves to write for the volume, often under time pressure, and have done so in a spirit of collegiality and conviction. The editors thank all contributors most sincerely, especially those who came on board later in this process.

James Hodkinson would like to thank the School of Modern Languages and Cultures, the Humanities Research Fund, and the "Connecting Cultures" Global Research Priority fund, all at Warwick University, for their financial support, Cecilia Scott of St. Catherine's School, especially, and his colleagues and family.

Ben Schofield would like to thank the Faculty of Arts and Humanities at King's College London for their generous financial support of this volume. Additionally, he would like to thank his colleagues in the German Department at King's College London, where "German in the World" has been a core teaching and research theme since 2011, and above all Professor Erica Carter, who has offered unstinting, and much valued, support for this project from the outset. He would also like to thank the 2019 "Transnational German Studies" workshop team—a postgraduate research network involving students and colleagues from Amherst College, King's College London, Michigan State University, the University of Massachusetts Amherst, and the University of Michigan-Ann Arbor, and initiated by colleagues at Warwick University—who provided valuable feedback on this project in its final stages.

Finally, both editors wish to thank all at Camden House for their time, expertise, and support in the production of the volume, not least Jim Walker, Mary Petrusewicz, Jane Best, Julia Cook, Sue Smith, and Rio Hartwell, as well as our anonymous peer reviewers for their detailed feedback and support.

Introduction: German in Its Worlds

James Hodkinson and Benedict Schofield

What is the state of German studies as an academic discipline in its national and global contexts as we move deeper into the twenty-first century? What future does it face, how does this relate to its past, and how are Germanists of diverse origins and persuasions around the world responding to such issues? These questions form the nexus of this volume. They are questions that demand we consider even larger topics: not just the status of our discipline but of interdisciplinarity as a model for the arts and humanities; not just the role of the canon but the decolonization of that canon; and not just the linguistic and geographic boundaries that we have traditionally used to contour German studies but also the temporal and disciplinary boundaries we use to determine (and limit) the scope of our work as Germanists. However influential in the world the German-speaking nations have been, and might still be, German language and culture, and their academic study, increasingly seem to be at the mercy of tectonic shifts (some required and sought, others not)—from changes in the way our universities are structured and funded to the reshaping of cultural and political discourse under the geopolitical forces of nationalism and globalization.

The question of how we can define and evaluate a specifically German-language culture in such a global context is thus a fraught one. In the wake of the so-called global financial crisis of 2008, and also of large migrational population shifts that saw communities moving in truly unprecedented numbers to cross borders into safer and more prosperous territory, driven by war, famine, and poverty, positively connoted narratives of globalization have fallen out of favor in many quarters. As the former British Prime Minister Theresa May's 2017 comment that "a citizen of the world is a citizen of nowhere" demonstrates, global thinking has been increasingly rejected in favor of resurgent nation-centered thinking. In the United Kingdom, the 2016 European Union Membership Referendum rapidly became about much more than Europe's future, and "Brexit" developed into a protest vote against globalization and its manifestations. Simultaneously, Donald Trump proposed the building of a wall along the US-Mexican border and made his wish to replace America's "globalism" with a more isolationist "America-first" policy the cornerstone of a successful presidential campaign. In Germany itself there has been a rise in nation-centered politics, with the Alternative für Deutschland (Alternative for Germany) Party, campaigning on an anti-immigration, anti-multiculturalism, anti-Islam platform, narrowly missing election to the German Parliament in the 2013 federal elections and remaining a significant presence ever since. "Britain First," "America First," "Mut zu Deutschland" (Courage [to stand up] for Germany)—so the slogans now run, challenging the long-held coexistence of the global and the local by placing the nation at the forefront once again; these are part and parcel of the rhetorical (and real) resurgence of nationalism in populist political discourse.

In this context, scholarly concern about the specific or unique qualities and values of a certain language (like German), and of the culture flowing from it, can easily find itself an unwitting and uneasy bedfellow with exclusivist, nationalist, and territorial thinking. As scholars of German-language cultures we find ourselves caught in a field of tension between our work on national traditions on the one hand, and our exploration of the transnational and global on the other. When thinking about the size, shape, and future of our discipline, then, it seems we need to find ways to define the continuing roles for both national cultures and transnational perspectives within them. In seeking to engage with and shape this debate, this volume thus considers how German culture has migrated geographically and culturally and how it has transformed, adapted, and responded to the world in differing locations and in both contemporary and historical contexts. In turn, it seeks to track the ways in which our academic field has diversified to capture and express the vibrant multiplicity of what it is now possible to study and teach under the rubric of German studies—a field that has expanded radically over the past decades to embrace a more global sense of the value of "the German," broadly conceived. Many works have already contributed to this area, such as the groundbreaking 1997 volume *A User's Guide to German Cultural Studies*, edited by Scott Denham, Irene Kacandes, and Jonathan Petropoulos, which persuasively made the case for the expansion of the German studies curriculum.[1] The American context has also produced several crucial accounts of the development of the discipline, which both look back historically and propose broader and more responsive models for a future form of German studies, such as George F. Peter's *Teaching German in America: Past Progress and Future Promise; A Handbook for Teaching and Research*, Peter Uwe Hohendahl's *German Studies in the United States: A Historical Handbook*, and, most recently, *Taking Stock of German Studies in the United States: The New Millennium*, edited by Rachel J. Halverson and Carol Anne Costabile-Heming.[2]

Of course, the expansion of German studies beyond its traditional roots in *Germanistik* (literary German studies) has the potential to be both invigorating and disorientating in equal measure. If we begin to question the geographic, linguistic, and temporal boundaries that have traditionally been used to prescribe German-language culture—if, in other words, German can now be anywhere and everywhere, and at any time—how do we approach this radically expanded disciplinary area methodologically? If we accept a broader vision of German studies rooted in the idea of German in its "wider worlds," how do we articulate this breadth and depth to our core constituencies (to our students in the classroom and to fellow academic colleagues) and also more broadly to our institutions, funders, and the world beyond academe? These are concerns that have been addressed in exciting and innovative ways by the discipline in recent years and they are the central concerns of this book.

Tracing a "Transnational Turn"

One recent innovation, to which this current volume both contributes and responds, has been the "transnational turn" in German studies. As Celia Applegate and Frank Trommler stress in their 2016 survey of disciplinary developments in German studies (written to mark the fortieth anniversary of the German Studies Association) this "turn" has had a transformative impact on the discipline, with "scholars of all time periods, historians, *Germanisten/innen* [German studies scholars] alike ... exploring a great range of topics concerning networks, cultural transfers, migrations of peoples, goods, and services, in short global movements and displacements of every kind, through which German history and culture could be studied everywhere, dismantled and reconstructed in multiple ways, and refracted through infinite points of view."[3] Here, Applegate and Trommler usefully gloss some of the key concepts or approaches that have been brought together under the term "transnational," such as network theory, migration studies, and postcolonialism, and emphasize the special relationship of transnationalism to the forces of globalization. While strongly in favor of the disciplinary enrichment this has wrought, they too note the disciplinary stretch (those "infinite points of view") that can be the result of a focus on the transnational.

This growth of the transnational as a paradigm within German studies has, of course, not taken place in isolation but has been part of a much wider "turn" to the transnational across the modern languages, the arts and humanities, and the social sciences. Konrad H. Jarausch notes in particular the impulses that German studies has taken from history, where the transnational has uncovered the global dimensions of the German past—dimensions that had traditionally been "largely invisible due to the lateness of [German] unification and the even later acquisition of colonies," and has thus obscured a much longer German history of colonization, settlement, exploration, and trade.[4] Such an approach to "global history" not only reveals the previously unseen but ultimately also asks us to "question our reliance on the nation as the container of histories, societies, and cultures," as Applegate and Trommler also stress.[5]

In English studies, too, the transnational has become a dominant paradigm, one shaped by passionate ideological discussions, in particular around the question of disciplinary diffusion. As Paul Jay outlines, "one claim that is often made against the changes ushered in by the transnational turn in literary studies is that it has led to a debilitating fragmentation, [with] principles of coherence that have guided the field for decades [giving] way to a focus on pluralities, differences, hybrid identities, and complicated transnational geographies that are seemingly incoherent and unmanageable."[6] Alongside its potential for expanding and enriching a field of study, the transnational, as we noted at the start of this introduction, thus raises complex disciplinary and methodological questions. What is the difference between a "transnationalized" English studies curriculum and the methodological modes of inquiry of comparative literature, for instance? What role does linguistic competence and the study of literatures in translation play when English studies is transnationalized, and how can we account for the continued Anglophone dominance of world literature, despite the fact that, as Russell A. Berman has stressed, "globalization is not an 'English-only' process"?[7]

Iterations of these questions and anxieties also arise when the modern languages as a discipline engages with the transnational. What place is there, for example, for a "German" contribution to a transnational modern languages? Which disciplinary and methodological specificities of German studies need to be adhered to (and which overcome) when thinking about a "transnational" form of German—indeed, put more provocatively, is there anything distinctive about the approach of traditional German studies? How does German studies differ, say, from French studies, with its clearer sense of a (post)colonial "global French"[8] and a *Francophonie*, or its ability to place France confidently at the heart of what Pascale Casanova influentially called the "world republic of letters"?[9] What does German have to offer in contrast to a transnational Spanish or Portuguese studies, which, given the linguistic reach and colonial histories of both languages, might be considered to be transnational per se? Against this background, perhaps the question really becomes how we might still study the particularities of German-language culture while embracing an enriching transnational framework, without reinscribing what Ulrich Beck succinctly and powerfully termed the "methodological nationalism"[10] inherent to all iterations of area studies.

One area in German studies in which the transnational has clearly overcome such methodological nationalism has been in its focus on literatures of diaspora, on migration and exile, and on questions of hybridity and cultural transfer. These approaches, not least those derived and inspired from the Turkish and Eastern "turns" outlined in influential studies by Yasmin Yildiz, Brigid Haines, and others,[11] have helped displace and decolonize a largely white, male canon and have enabled instead what David Gramling has called "a progressive, multiethnic conception of 'German-language literature' as opposed to the ethnically conceived 'German literature' of previous eras."[12] For Gramling, this gestures towards yet another potential "turn," or at least a partner for the transnational turn: what he calls a "multilingual" or perhaps even a "translingual" one, which recognizes that "even in the deepest recesses of nationalism and totalitarianism, we ... have never been monolingual."[13] For scholars of the translingual such as Dirk Weissmann, the existence of multilingual or translingual authors in the German context reveals (at its most positive) how "German is not a language of national community, but an open, hospitable language that enriches itself with foreign identities, experiences and idioms," and, at the very least, has required us as a discipline to "replace the traditional binary categories (native/foreign, national/foreign, native language/foreign language) [with] more nuanced and open concepts."[14] These debates are reflected in this volume, for instance in Frauke Matthes's exploration of translingual voices, and the challenges faced when these "transnational" authors enter into what is still often a nationally defined German book market; and in Dirk Göttsche's comprehensive survey of the ways in which a postcolonial German studies has sought to engage critically with Germany's colonial past and its legacy.

While acknowledging the crucial enrichment that this focus on multilingualism, migration, and the postcolonial has engendered, Elisabeth Herrmann, Carrie Smith-Prei, and Stuart Taberner have, however, recently encouraged German studies to broaden its conceptualization of transnationalism even further. Suggesting we move "beyond a focus on diasporic formations, hybridity, or notions of center and periphery," they stress an increasing need to acknowledge what they see as "transnationalism's characteristic multidirectionality and saturation of all aspects of everyday life, from consumption to culture," and how this ultimately "impacts everyone."[15] For Herrmann, in particular, this broader sense of transnationalism allows us to consider "a new collective life experience, namely the manifestation of globalization through the phenomenon of transnationalism."[16] Herrmann sees this as "a new significant 'pillar' within contemporary German literature," in which the transnational is both a theme (for instance, Herrmann notes an increasing thematic focus on overseas settings and, at the same time, attempts to engage with histories beyond the immediate German national context, drawing on authors such as Felicitas Hoppe, Daniel Kehlmann, Christian Kracht, Illija

Trojanow, and Dan Vyleta) and an aesthetic mode (characterized, for instance, by intertextual references to world literature, the use of irony, or postmodern games with authorial identity).[17] Anke S. Biendarra has similarly stressed the significance of globalization for a contemporary transnational German literature. Drawing on Ulrich Beck's argument that the "shock of globalization" forced Germans to move on from a largely internal-facing "negotiation [of] competing versions of a new normality" after German reunification in 1989,[18] Biendarra argues that a range of transnational issues, including the "neo-liberal work world, global travel, and the aftermath of 09.11" have become dominant features of a contemporary German culture that both reflects and is the product of the "ever denser network of interconnections and interdependencies that characterize modern life."[19]

What cuts across these approaches to "worlding" German is their shared understanding of the transnational as a *contemporary* phenomenon: one that has occurred alongside, or is even a direct consequence of, globalization. This is a stance shared by the social sciences, which indeed led the way in first proposing the transnational as a crucial methodology for mapping and analyzing what the leading political theorist of the transnational, Steven Vertovec, calls the "sustained cross-border relationships, patterns of exchange, affiliations and social formations spanning nation states."[20] While Vertovec does acknowledge that such connections have always existed—in other words, that we can trace global flows of trade and migration historically—he nevertheless argues for the contemporaneity of the "transnational turn," which differs (in his view) from earlier periods due to "the extensiveness, intensity and velocity of networked flows of information and resources" in the wake of twentieth-century globalization.[21]

Numerous studies of the transnational have, however, attempted to problematize any easy relationship between the transnational and globalization. Randall Halle, for instance, in his work on transnational German cinema, insists that "while interrelated, we must distinguish globalization, as primarily an economic process, from transnationalism, as an affiliative and ideational network. . . . Globalization alters monetary flows and economic funding of all commodity relations. Transnationalism organizes and mediates public spheres; it offers new imaginings of community."[22] Ulf Hannerz has similarly noted his discomfort with "the rather prodigious use of the term globalization to describe just about any process or relationship that somehow crosses state boundaries," and suggests that the transnational as a term is "in a way more humble, and often a more adequate label for phenomena which can be of quite variable scale and distribution."[23] Crucial to Hannerz's argument is the notion that when we use the concepts of "globalization" and "transnationalism" in Cultural or Anthropological studies, we are in fact no longer strictly speaking of "nations ... as corporate actors." Instead, our focus has undertaken a small but significant shift: "in the transnational arena, the actors may now be individuals, groups, movements."[24] This shift is reflected in the approach we have taken in this volume, where we consider not only individual authors but also bodies of work, including the canon (in the contributions to Part 1); not only individual academic journeys but also the wider construction of the discipline of German studies as it circulates around the world (in Part 2); and individual cultural practitioners, their relationship to wider transnational networks, and the role of cultural organizations entirely outside the academy (in Part 3). For this current volume, these are all equally important manifestations of where German might be found "in the world."

It is not only transnational German studies that has questioned the place of German culture in the world, though. World literature has also focused on Germany; indeed, it now is something of a cliché that you can't "do world literature" without recourse to Goethe. David Damrosch's seminal *What Is World Literature?* opens with the image of Goethe purportedly coining the very phrase *Weltliteratur* (world literature) in 1827.[25] In shifting our focus back (at least) to the early nineteenth century, world literature indeed marks a very important approach to thinking about "German in the world," since it demands we broaden the temporal range of our inquiry beyond the immediate present. As Damrosch notes, Goethe was already, over two hundred years ago, articulating "a literary perspective, and a new cultural awareness, a sense of an arising global modernity, whose epoch ... we now inhabit."[26]

World literature also asks us to think about the global positioning of German-language culture more structurally, in terms of networks, flows, and literary systems, and the people that power those systems: authors, translators, publishers, as well as texts and their contexts. Thomas Oliver Beebee's significant work in this field thus stresses the importance of "processes of translation, dialogue and rewriting that create the worldwide web of literary intertextuality."[27] For Beebee, this "global" web reveals how German-language literature is—and, crucially, has always been—"imbricated in other cultural traditions," and has "ventriloquized other cultures, and translated and transadapted their texts" (and vice versa).[28] Given that the "foundational" moment for "world literature" as a concept can be traced back to German studies and (supposedly) to no less a figure than Goethe, it is perhaps unsurprising that Goethe's works and his concept of *Weltliteratur* are the subject of several contributions to this volume, such as those by John Noyes and Ben Morgan, both of whom interrogate Goethe's concept and its legacy.

Locating the German

Although this book is not intended to focus specifically on theories of the transnational or world literature, its focus on "German in the world" clearly requires that it reflect and respond to the many approaches that the debates outlined above have given us. At the same time, however, it asks a question that at first glance might appear to jar with, even contradict, the transnational and world literature, and their predominantly progressive impulse to gesture beyond the nation. The question is this: Can we still articulate the value of something specifically "German" or "Germanophone" today? Indeed, can we even ask this question without it being a retrograde one, too easily seen as an attempt to reinscribe an exclusive (white, male) canon and reinforce a set of geopolitical and linguistic limits on German studies that could potentially promote an essentializing view of German-language culture?

As outlined at the very start of this introduction, this is an inescapable and crucial question for the discipline, not least because however much we increasingly dispense with and dismantle an ossified model of German studies as a *Nationalphilologie* (national philology), and the elitist and exclusive canons and methodologies that this implies, the discipline still feels driven to seek the place of something "German" in the world: this "Germanness," even when very broadly defined, remaining a common point of focus in our studies, our teaching, and our research. In answering this question, then, this volume tries to place itself on the pivot between the national and the transnational, echoing Hannerz's sense that the transnational should enable us to become both "guardians of continuity [and] agents of change" between the local and the global.[29] We thus seek to broaden our understanding of the value of the particularities of German studies as a field of critical cultural discourse within a globalized public sphere, and argue that interrogating the value of German-language culture around the world requires us to look both at the value of the "specifically German," and its "multiple beyonds," including beyond the academy in the cultural sphere (an approach undertaken in the contributions to this volume by Uwe Schütte and Benedict Schofield). It requires us to grasp that while German-language culture can always be historically, linguistically, and geographically contextualized, its value, legacy and impact can never be entirely constrained by those temporal, linguistic, and geographic borders. It is a model of German studies where the "local" particularities of a culture are still important (something revealed, for instance, in the contributions by Carol Tully, Carlotta von Maltzan, and Emily Oliver), but the productive boundary transgressions of any culture are multiple and are an equally important site of critical inquiry, as shown in Tobias Boes's assessment of *Weltdeutschtum* (cosmopolitan Germanness), and in Sai Bhatawadekar's and Kate Rigby's accounts of their own geographic and disciplinary boundary crossings throughout their careers in German studies.

In focusing on these productive boundary crossings, we thus echo Steven Clingman's conception of the transnational boundary. For Clingman, central to the transnational is the notion of "navigation across boundaries," both real and imagined (or even imaginative). These boundaries "exist everywhere and in every way,"[30] Clingman argues, but "what matters just as much as the existence of the boundary is the nature of the boundary navigation: how navigation can, in effect, transform the nature of the boundary—the effect becoming the cause."[31] This transformative potential does not negate "the painful side of displacement—pre-eminently as it effects those for whom the 'transnational' is not a matter of choice."[32] But it does force us to acknowledge, as we have repeatedly stressed throughout this introduction, that even at their most national, German-language cultures are, as Françoise Lionnet and Shu-mei Shih have persuasively argued of all cultures, "products of transmigrations and multiple encounters" and are thus "already mixed, hybrid and relational."[33]

Broadening the Global: The World, the Academy, and "Porosity"

One wing of our project involves us widening our concept of the "global" to think of it not only as some version of an overarching geographical or cultural totality but also in terms of how culture and its study intersect with other spheres of our complex world: how it enmeshes with and contributes to nonacademic contexts, to wider society, to political discourse and activity, and to our national and global economies. Certain of the chapters in this volume, for instance James Hodkinson's contribution, attempt to consider the value of the discipline of German studies within the teaching and research agendas of contemporary educational systems, not only in higher education but also in schools, both in the English-speaking world and further afield. At the same time, the value of German studies, though, need not merely be measured in how it reaches beyond its own disciplinary boundaries within education. An informative point of departure here is the UK scenario, where, for better or for worse, academics are today compelled to track and evaluate both the academic quality and the nonacademic reach of their work as part of the Research Excellence Framework (REF).[34]

Perhaps the best-known and most infamous measure of the extraacademic reach of research in this context is that of "impact." UK academic institutions need, as part of their submissions to the REF, to enter "impact case studies" chronicling and evaluating what kinds of benefit their research has brought. Probably the most familiar definition of impact is that used by the Arts and Humanities Research Council (AHRC), who refer to it in terms of the "direct and indirect social and economic benefits" research in the arts can bring to wider society,[35] while the UK Research and Innovation (UKRI) think tank further specifies "pathways" along which impact can be measured, which include:

- fostering global economic performance, and specifically the economic competitiveness of the United Kingdom
- increasing the effectiveness of public services and policy
- enhancing quality of life, health, and creative output[36]

The relative infamy of impact among scholars of the arts and humanities stems not least from the fact that funding bodies such as the AHRC quite openly announce their remit as answering "key questions posed by the Department for Business, Energy and Industrial Strategy (BEIS)" to assist in "demonstrating the value of arts and humanities research" and justifying "why it should be funded by the taxpayer," thus rendering funding applications for research in the arts "assessible" within a framework that appeals to social and economic merit, and thus not to a purer sense of subject-specific intellectual value.[37] This culture and practice of charting academic value beyond the academy is not, of course, limited to the United Kingdom; in the anglophone context of Australian academia, it forms part of the Excellence in Research Australia (ERA) program, and impact is also now increasingly an outcome that has to be planned for as part of bids for academic funding within the European Union.[38]

It is not the task of this volume to make a case for or against any political policy or particular model of extending academic benefit to the wider society, but a number of our chapters refer, in various levels of detail, to impact work and public engagement in the area of German studies.[39] These frame engagement and impact work within a wider set of developments that have in part been triggered by political developments, but that have, certainly for the generation of scholars entering the profession after 2010, superseded such concerns and become a meaningful part of accepted academic practice. Certain of the chapters in this volume testify not only to the benefits, professional and institutional, that outreach work can bring, but also describe the positively transformative working experiences whereby encounters between academic researchers and arts practitioners, secondary schools, educationalists, and socially and ethnically diverse communities have been genuinely transformative of research foci, methods, and outcomes in a way that is demonstrably beneficial to all concerned. In outlining such developments, the volume is not advocating for a wholesale shift away from traditional academic research methods, publishing, and teaching, but illuminating yet another strand by which the discipline of German studies has adapted and restated its value.

However ambivalent the drivers of such change, which are in part compulsion, in part natural evolution, that change marks a process by which knowledge, skills, agendas, and methods are now thought of as flowing bilaterally between the academy and wider society—at times as the result of consciously reflective practice, and at times because activity, practice, and scholarship always were part of a continuum. In light of this discussion, these chapters will be referring to, tracing, and evaluating what we call the "porous" relationship, the two-way productive interplay between German culture, its study, and the nonacademic world, both historically and today.

Departing for the World

In addressing our theme of "German in the world," we thus want to avoid reinscribing any simplistic sense of German-language culture as easily located or defined. Throughout this book, this involves a form of deterritorialization of German studies: a palindromic tactic that both acknowledges the national in different senses and gestures beyond it. Indeed, our volume as a whole argues that our area of study can and should exist precisely in a field of tension between a notion of the specific contributions made from within a linguistically bound notion of "German culture" on the one hand, and the idea that all culture is and always was enmeshed within and overlapping with other cultures, on the other. What comes out the other side of this debate is not a discipline undone but a discipline transfigured: it is thus above all about the enrichment of German studies.

The first part of this volume, "The World in German Culture," thus explores the ways in which German-language literature, from the eighteenth century to the contemporary period, has sought to grapple with the themes of world culture, both historically and through its reconfiguration for a postcolonial present. In the second part, "German in World Locales," the focus shifts beyond the European German-speaking countries and traces how German studies has mapped itself institutionally around the world, and the ways in which transnational scholars of German act as transient, culturally hybrid practitioners. The third and final part, "German Worlds beyond the Academy," looks even further afield and questions what the world beyond the academy needs and takes from the world of German culture: what language, which traditions, and which intellectual insights? Cutting across these parts is thus a concern with how we construct German culture and how we might reframe, research, and teach German studies differently, in ways that still allow those studies to be a coherent experience. After all, at its best, German culture has always been concerned with looking beyond its own parochial needs and values, and it continues to thrive in the world culturally, intellectually, and in the work of countless sectors beyond academe. We aim to capture this abundance, developing as we do so a more mobile idea of a "German-language culture" that continues to fascinate us as scholars, both in its particularities and in its ability to gesture continuously beyond itself.

Notes

[1] Scott Denham, Irene Kacandes, and Jonathan Petropoulos, eds., *A User's Guide to German Cultural Studies* (Ann Arbor: University of Michigan Press, 1997).

[2] See George F. Peters, ed., *Teaching German in America: Past Progress and Future Promise; A Handbook for Teaching and Research* (Cherry Hill, NJ: AATG, 2003); Peter Uwe Hohendahl, ed., *German Studies in the United States: A Historical Handbook* (New York: Modern Languages Association of America, 2003); and Rachel J. Halverson and Carol Anne Costabile-Heming, eds., *Taking Stock of German Studies in the United States: The New Millennium* (Rochester, NY: Camden House, 2015).

[3] Celia Applegate and Frank Trommler, "The Project of German Studies: Disciplinary Strategies and Intellectual Practices," *German Studies Review* 39, no. 3 (2016): 471–92 (489).

[4] Konrad H. Jarausch, "From National to Transnational German Studies: Some Historical Reflections, 1977–2017," *German Studies Review* 39, no. 3 (2016): 493–503 (500).

[5] Applegate and Trommler, "The Project of German Studies," 489.

[6] Paul Jay, *Global Matters: The Transnational Turn in Literary Studies* (Ithaca, NY: Cornell University Press, 2010), 4.

[7] Russell A. Bermann, "The Real Language Crisis," *Academe* (Sept.–Oct. 2011), https://www.aaup.org/article/real-language-crisis#.XQaoEy2ZPOQ.

[8] Christie McDonald and Susan Ruben Suleiman, *French Global: A New Approach to Literary History* (New York: Columbia University Press, 2010).

[9] See Pascale Casanova, *The World Republic of Letters* (Cambridge, MA: Harvard University Press, 2009).

[10] Ulrich Beck, "The Cosmopolitan Condition: Why Methodological Nationalism Fails," *Theory, Culture & Society* 24, nos. 7–8 (2007): 286–90.

[11] See Yasemin Yildiz, *Beyond the Mother Tongue: The Postmonolingual Condition* (New York: Fordham University Press, 2012); and Brigid Haines, ed., *The Eastern European Turn in Contemporary German-Language Literature*, special issue of *German Life and Letters* 68, no. 2 (2015).

[12] David Gramling, "Researching Multilingually in German Studies: A Brief Retrospective," *German Studies Review* 39, no. 3 (2016): 529–40 (530).

[13] Gramling, "Researching Multilingually," 532.

[14] Dirk Weissmann, "German Writers from Abroad: Translingualism, Hybrid Languages, 'Broken' Germans," in *Transnational German Studies*, ed. Rebecca

Braun and Benedict Schofield (Liverpool: Liverpool University Press, forthcoming, 2020), 75.

[15] Elisabeth Herrmann, Carrie Smith-Prei, and Stuart Taberner, eds., *Transnationalism in Contemporary German-Language Literature* (Rochester, NY: Camden House, 2015), 1.

[16] Elisabeth Herrmann, "How does Transnationalism Redefine Contemporary Literature?" in Herrmann, Smith-Prei, and Taberner, *Transnationalism in Contemporary German-Language Literature*, 37.

[17] Herrmann, "How does Transnationalism Redefine Contemporary Literature?" 36.

[18] Anke S. Biendarra, *Germans Going Global: Contemporary Literature and Cultural Globalization* (Berlin: de Gruyter, 2012), 2.

[19] Biendarra, *Germans Going Global*, 6.

[20] Steven Vertovec, *Transnationalism* (Abingdon: Routledge, 2009), 1–2.

[21] Vertovec, *Transnationalism*, 23.

[22] Randall Halle, *German Film after German: Toward a Transnational Aesthetic* (Urbana: University of Illinois Press, 2008), 28.

[23] Ulf Hannerz, *Transnational Connections: Culture, People, Places* (London: Routledge, 1996), 6.

[24] Hannerz, *Transnational Connections*, 6.

[25] David Damrosch, *What Is World Literature?* (Princeton, NJ: Princeton University Press, 2003). Rebecca Braun has noted that *Weltliteratur* was not actually Goethe's "coinage and was already in isolated use some twenty years earlier by Christoph Martin Wieland and other contemporaries at Anna Amalia's court in Weimar." See Rebecca Braun, "Networks and World Literature: The Practice of Putting German Authors in their Place," in Braun and Schofield, *Transnational German Studies*, 97.

[26] Damrosch, *What Is World Literature?*, 1.

[27] Thomas Oliver Beebee, *German Literature as World Literature* (London: Bloomsbury Publishing, 2014), 5.

[28] Beebee, *German Literature as World Literature*, 5.

[29] Hannerz, *Transnational Connections*, 28.

[30] Stephen Clingman, *The Grammar of Identity: Transnational Fiction and the Nature of the Boundary* (Oxford: Oxford University Press, 2009), 21.

[31] Clingman, *The Grammar of Identity*, 22.

[32] Clingman, *The Grammar of Identity*, 22.

[33] Françoise Lionnet and Shu-mei Shih, eds., *Minor Transnationalism* (Durham, NC: Duke University Press, 2005), 10.

[34] See https://www.ref.ac.uk/, accessed November 29, 2019.

[35] See https://ahrc.ukri.org/research/impact, accessed November 29, 2019. The practice and measuring of impact is part of an attempt to capture the relationship between the academy and the wider world; these include the broader

notion of "public engagement" (see https://www.publicengagement.ac.uk/about-engagement/what-public-engagement) and the more economically orientated notion of "shared knowledge production," or "knowledge exchange" (see https://www.vitae.ac.uk/doing-research/leadership-development-for-principal-investigators-pis/intellectual-leadership/demonstrating-research-impact/knowledge-exchange).

[36] See the UK Research and Innovation website: https://www.ukri.org/innovation/excellence-with-impact/pathways-to-impact/, accessed November 29, 2019.

[37] See again https://ahrc.ukri.org/research/impact/.

[38] See the Australian Research Council's ongoing consultation on impact: https://www.arc.gov.au/engagement-and-impact-assessment, and the European Research Council's definition of impact: https://erc.europa.eu/news/how-define-research-impact, both accessed November 29, 2019.

[39] See Rebecca Braun and Lyn Marven, eds., *Cultural Impact in the German Context* (Rochester, NY: Camden House, 2010).

Part I

The World in German Culture

Introduction to Part I: The World in German Culture

James Hodkinson and Benedict Schofield

THE PROJECT OF tracing the legacy, influence, and value of German culture across national, linguistic, and historical contexts might imply that scholars need to look away from the traditional exemplars of German culture. That might involve, one might think, shifting our contemporary research and teaching priorities away from German writing and cinema, now the traditional stuff of German studies, attending instead to a wider range of cultural products that may have been forgotten, marginalized, overlooked, or are simply not contained within obviously Germanophone contexts, and examining these through an appropriately expanded set of methodologies. This volume seeks to map and promote this process of expansion, and the chapters as a whole testify to how far such developments have already come within different iterations of German studies around the globe. However, this collection does not shy away from returning to the traditional core of our discipline. Key to our project is a process of viewing canonical texts afresh and reviewing how we read them—opening out interrogations of how contemporary and historical Germanophone culture speaks to models of the "world" as a complex shifting entity that is cultural, political, economic, and the object of scientific inquiry.

One fascinating and invaluable characteristic of much pre-twentieth-century German literary and philosophical production, particularly from the period around 1800, is the fact that it not only wrestled with questions of Germany's identity as a nation but also explored, often quite explicitly, such notions as "world culture," "world consciousness," or "world belonging." The first part of this volume seeks to continue a process of refocusing the products of German culture, taken from that period and indeed the epoch, to show how they can be used to explore matters of transnational and worldly concern. It begins with a cluster of chapters that revisit a sequence of what might be termed "older" canonical writers. John Noyes offers one of several contributions in the volume that draw on Goethe. Noyes seeks to "sketch the dimensions of *Welt* as Goethe explored it" in *Faust*, in the writings on *Weltliteratur* (world literature), and in the methodological considerations of his *Farbenlehre* (Theory of Colors, 1810). Across these writings, argues Noyes, Goethe appears to reconstruct a layered and complex understanding of what "world" means. Faust leaves his "world" of learning behind him, one world of many, and his journey takes him into complex experiences of numerous worlds, social, cultural, scientific, contemporary, and historical. Writing about such experiences, contends Noyes, allows Goethe to explore tensions between the necessarily finite, subjective, and culturally and historically determined position of the individual and the limited vision of world that they experience, and the potentially infinite physical, social, and cultural diversity of the context that individual shares with all of humanity. In this context, Goethe's definition of *Weltliteratur* does not, for Noyes, describe a culturally centered definition of great literature or a pantheon of great writers from distinct and disconnected cultures but a remarkably modern attempt to work across discursive representational modes, both scientific and cultural, to map out a "shared world identity" and promote a "collective consciousness of shared representations" that attempts to make sense of a diverse and shifting notion of "world."

Ben Morgan's chapter continues the focus on *Weltliteratur*. Morgan considers a range of primary texts by Goethe, including, though stretching beyond, the well-known conversations with Eckermann. His aim is "to get a clearer sense of the specific literary practices" that make up Goethe's pursuit of world literature. These express themselves in Goethe's attempt, in the 1827 edition of his journal *Über Kunst und Altertum* (On Art and Antiquity) to provide contrasting views, one critical the other more laudatory, on a French reworking of his 1790 play *Torquato Tasso*. Goethe's consciously cultivated, culturally plural juxtaposition of views expresses his understanding that world literary practice has necessarily to reflect critically on and decenter any one writer's culturally determined position, and the judgments that emanate from it, and give way to a rhetorical process of self-questioning that leads ultimately to a "transnational discussion." The enigmatic *Novelle* (Novella, 1827) also cultivates differing narrative perspectives on a common thread of events centering around two fictional excursions in a European provincial setting—one a touristic visit, the other a hunt—and thus thematizes and reminds the reader of the "mediated" and thus limited nature of their experience of the world. The perspectival experimentalism parallels, Morgan contends, Goethe's attempt to provoke contrasting emotional and body-centered responses in his readership, not in the naïve belief that this helps us better understand others or other cultures but in order that we might, again, gain critical perspective on our own conditioned responses to the world around us. Thus Goethe produces "techniques that immerse us, while helping us reflect on our propensity to immersion, assisted by the ongoing, multiperspectival conversation that constitutes global literary debate." This remarkably modern program of theories and practices pursued by Goethe is significant, writes Morgan, not merely because they are so multilayered but because the critical self-reflexivity of his envisioned practices serves as an intervention into many contemporary anglophone discussions of world literature that can remain ironically unaware of their own cultural centeredness.

Tobias Boes traverses the long nineteenth century to consider how Thomas Mann's idea of *Weltdeutschtum*, essentially a deterritorialized German-speaking community, or a cosmopolitan Germanness, actually represents a reworking of an intellectual tradition that, first in the sentiments of Schiller's lyrical poetry, elevates German "greatness" to a spiritual rather than a political value and then, in the perhaps unlikely form of Fichte's *Reden an die deutsche Nation* (Addresses to the German Nation, 1808), makes Germanness a characteristic to which people of nations can aspire and share in. This tradition, shows Boes, resonated in turn around certain strains of Germanophone historiography and cultural production before it made its way to Mann, who first laid out the notion in his famous and provocative 1945 address to the Library of Congress in the United States.

Taking forward the idea of literature's power to articulate a complex world, there follow two chapters focusing on how German literary texts, in the nineteenth century and the present, problematize the relationship between cultural identity, language, and physical and cultural notions of "territory." Carol Tully's contribution surveys nineteenth-century Germanophone travelogues produced during travels to Great Britain, including works by lesser-known figures such as Christian August Gottlieb Goede, Samuel Heinrich Spiker, Johann Georg Kohl, and Julius Rodenberg, though also better-known travel writers such as Hermann von Pückler-Muskau. The travelogues tend, according to Tully, to reflect a variously inflected though usually heightened sense of the traveler's own Germanness, which in turn plays into the travelers' reflections on the relationship between the culturally and politically hegemonic nation of England and its relationships to the "peripheral" Celtic nations within the structure of Great Britain, with a particular focus on Wales. As certain of these travelogues were later translated into English, and edited in the process to remove German writers' criticism of English attitudes towards Wales, so the constellation of texts shows how writing about Wales becomes the site of a struggle for cultural and ethical superiority by Germans and British publishers and serves as both "an assertion and a critique of German influence on the world stage at a time when an emergent German nation-state found itself in direct competition for economic and colonial power with a British imperial force that had both the benefit of longevity and scope."

In her chapter, Frauke Matthes examines how notions of "regionalism" and "transnationalism" are intertwined in one of the most acclaimed novels of recent years by Saša Stanišić, the winner of the 2019 German Book Prize. Matthes shows how the positive reception of Stanišić's 2014 novel, *Vor dem Fest*, was framed in terms of its aesthetic strategies and narrative "musicality," which is significant as it shows how Stanišić no longer needs to tell the story of his migration to Germany but can tell local and national stories of memory and the past, flight and migration, legends and their archiving, and contribute to his work's reception as transnational rather than underwriting a prefabricated authorial persona that neatly fits the restrictive and, as Matthes notes, often essentializing category of *Migrantenliteratur*. Matthes shows how his aesthetically engaging treatment of a specific part of Germany allows him to pursue literary avenues that lead him towards world literature, in turn highlighting how his work has required scholars of German studies to think critically in new categories and has helped to expand the discipline's notion of who can write world literary texts in German.

Our first part closes with Dirk Göttsche's rich and detailed reconstruction of postcolonial themes in German culture. Göttsche's chapter combines a representative survey of postcolonial literary writing in German, especially from the 1990s onwards, with a history of its scholarly reception, and thus an overview of how postcolonial studies established itself in German studies. As well as offering an overview of how key concepts from international postcolonial studies—such as the "postcolonial gaze"—both shaped and were further developed by German studies scholars, the survey examines postcolonial iterations of such literary genres as historical novels, family novels, metafiction and crime fiction, and looks, in the context of multicultural Germany, at African migrants' writing, black German literature, and cultural treatment of the African diaspora in light of memory studies. Thus, although postcolonial studies came late to German culture and its study, not least due to "the early end of Germany's colonial empire, the lack of significant postcolonial immigration, the limited global status of the German language," and "the primacy of National Socialism and the Holocaust in Germany's politics of memory," Göttsche shows how this field of study can serve not only to rethink the position of Germany, Austria, and Switzerland in the world but how that process, in turn, can also contribute to a global critical consciousness of the legacy of empire.

This first part, then, places German-language literature at the center of its considerations: both historical and contemporary writing; both canonical and little-known texts. These chapters testify to the ongoing range and flexibility of German culture and its study, and the multiple ways in which it proves anew its value in contemporary discussions. It offers remarkably modern, self-reflexive traditions that consider the specifics of German culture within sophisticated and evolving notions of the "worldly" and the "transnational"; it models critical notions of German community and culture that are not territorialized or plagued entirely by proprietorial concerns; and it offers examples both of the frailties of literary practices and paradigms that seek to frame and represent other cultures in their own monocultural terms and demonstrates how cultural and literary traditions can be opened out, become inclusive and diverse and afford expressive space to cultural producers ostensibly from outside those traditions. By including these chapters we hope to not only show the expanding boundaries of what can be deemed and analyzed as "German culture" but also repurpose and thus reinvigorate inquiry into its traditional core, thus testifying to the value of both its margins and its centers, which are themselves always multiple.

1: Goethe's World

John K. Noyes

What Is *World*?

WHAT DO WE MEAN when we say the word "world"? Or more precisely, when we say the word *Welt*? *Welt*, or "world," is a key concept in modernity, and the way we think about it is inseparable from the way we think about what it means to be human and to relate to other humans, to the imagined environment, and to the physical environment. Modernity's struggle with the network of relationships humanity has established is encompassed in the question, what is world? Barbara Cassin's *Dictionary of Untranslatables* (2014) gives *Welt* a full seven and a half pages, noting how it separates "the cosmological concept of the world, of which I am but a tiny part," from the "phenomenological conception—that within which the human being deploys his being, according to a triple determination: cosmological, anthropological and ontological."[1] This dividing function is a concise description of the ground Johann Wolfgang Goethe covers in his poetic and scientific works. To understand what the work of this concept has been in modernity, it is worth investigating what the term meant for Goethe, not as a unified concept that was carried through into subsequent discussions of what *Welt* might mean, but as a series of explorations in various discourses whose aim was a unified experience of life.[2] The purpose of this chapter is to sketch the dimensions of *Welt* as Goethe explored it, and the analysis is framed by the assumption that the tensions he attached to the concept are defining tensions of modernity with which we continue to live. It is possible to read almost any text of Goethe's in this way—and to do so profitably. This chapter confines itself to *Faust*, the writings on *Weltliteratur* (world literature), and the methodological considerations in *Farbenlehre* (Theory of Colors, 1810).

In keeping with the theme of this volume, the understanding of German as a language and a culture in the world points to a multilayered mapping of linguistic and cultural processes onto territory. The practical dimension involved here was of interest to Goethe, and he noted it in such everyday experiences as the informal dissemination of information, navigating the built world, assimilating global news, tending libraries, cultivating friendships, and so on.[3] Part of the richness of the concept "world" emerges from Goethe's interest in how various forms of representation create and preserve the transcendental dimension of experiences like the ones just mentioned, but also how these forms call into question the universality of experience. This is why the singularity or plurality of (the) world as it relates to human life matters.

Although the problems he engages with persist, there are some serious obstacles to understanding Goethe's conception of "world" in today's context. Most important, it is necessary to untangle the similarities and differences in the world-creating phenomena of modernity that the twenty-first century shares with the eighteenth, such as global trade, the circulation of information, the world stage of political conflict, the expanding reach of the public sphere, and more. This is probably nowhere as evident as in the term *Weltliteratur*, which has arguably become Goethe's most well-loved and—as this discussion will show—most widely misunderstood expression.[4]

Hybrid Representation: *Welt* and *Literatur*

A look at the idea of *Weltliteratur* can serve to illustrate the problems that arise when this work of untangling is not performed carefully enough. In the context of postcolonialism, *Weltliteratur* has come to be identified with what Emily Apter calls "the Goethean/Auerbachian heritage in the humanities," namely the global imposition of a Western literary canon. Apter writes: "World literature is a cosmopolitan project better suited to privileged émigrés then to immigrant, second-generation minority cultures. World fiction uses *métissage* as yet another Occidental foil for inattention to cultural and historical particularism. World Literature inadequately takes stock of the impact of colonialism and decolonization on literary history." And world literature "either reinforces old national, regional, and ethnic literary alignments or projects a denationalized planetary screen that ignores the deep structures of national belonging and economic interest contouring the international culture industry."[5] This view of *Weltliteratur* justifies the "serious reservations" Apter expresses about its "reflexive endorsement of cultural equivalence and substitutability" and "celebration of nationally and ethnically branded 'differences' that have been niche-marketed as commercialized 'identities.'"[6]

This critique in not new.[7] Nevertheless, it is safe to say that, at least in anglophone comparatist and postcolonial discussions, *Weltliteratur* has allowed a critique of economic universalism to attach in vague ways to a critique of Goethe's purported cultural universalism. Apter's observations are certainly a justified critique of the world market in literary translation, but to attach this critique to Goethe's concept is problematic to say the least.[8] This matters not just in philological terms as a way to stay true to one scholar's concepts, but because what Goethe wanted to talk about runs deeper than Apter's critique of the literary marketplace. As I will explain below, Goethe wanted to talk about mechanisms for communicating across diverse epistemological models and discourses. He wanted to reflect on how the writing subject is positioned within spatio-temporal systems (*Welt*) and discourses (*Literatur*). The resultant compound combines two concepts that may appear familiar to us but that are easily misunderstood or at least misplaced.

Apter's *Weltliteratur* is a misapprehension of the role the aesthetic is supposed to play in negotiating the changed space and time of modernity. The aesthetic as Goethe understands it does not enable modernity by smoothing the space of the world, as many readings of *Weltliteratur* would seem to imply. On the contrary, it resists this process.[9] This resistance makes the concept a part of a larger project of positioning subjectivity in the changing world of modernity through the investigations of various natural phenomena. In apprehending natural phenomena in representation, the subject is acting in humanity's most creative capacity—as scientist, poet, and historian, in other words acting to find adequate representations for universal natural processes. This leads Goethe to adopt the position that the objective processes that allow him to speak of "world" are not easily distinguishable from the subjective processes that give rise to the question, what is world? For Goethe, literature negotiates the boundary of these processes.

Most discussions of *Weltliteratur* assume that it refers to what is taught in university departments of literature, or what is offered in the fiction section of better bookstores. This is an impoverishment of what Goethe meant when he spoke of *Litteratur*. This is not a problem of translation, it is the wider problem, discussed by Spivak, of the discursive register chosen to imagine different forms of the world.[10] But it is necessary to go beyond this. In lexical terms, Goethe's *Litteratur* expressed a fundamental fluidity between the discourses. *Literatur* isn't to be found in the standard lexical reference works of the time. Neither *Grimms Wörterbuch* (Grimm's Dictionary), nor *Zedlers Universal-Lexicon* (Zedler's Universal Lexicon) have entries for *Literatur* or *Litteratur,* nor did Diderot and D'Alembert see fit to include *littérature* in their *Encyclopédie* (Encyclopedia). If we take a look at the articles published in any of the journals that announced themselves as a forum for the dissemination of "literature"—Bertuch's *Allgemeine Literatur Zeitung* (General Journal of Literature), Meusel's *Historisch-Litterarisches Magazin* (Historical-Literary Magazine), Archenholz's *Litteratur- und Völkerkunde* (Literature and Ethnography, 1782–1786), and then *Neue Litteratur und Völkerkunde* (New Literature and Ethnography), Goethe's own *Jenaische Allgemeine Literatur-Zeitung* (Jena Journal of Literature), just to name a few—we discover that it provided a way of talking about writing without deciding how to categorize it institutionally, epistemologically, or aesthetically.

The semantic and discursive fuzziness of the word *Litteratur* is central to Goethe's view of the world, since it reflects his project of foregrounding the representational strategies chosen to understand the world. Goethe, for the most part, uses the word as a designation for *belle lettres*, but his awareness of its wide semantic field is always apparent. The constant references to the literary journals, some of which are mentioned above, in the *Xenien* is just one example. And so are the discussions of *Weltliteratur*, which clearly delineate it as (to repeat Anne Bohnenkamp's insight) a process of exchange and of conversation, or what he referred to as a "free trade in concepts and feelings," whose fundamental importance enables the crossing of boundaries—linguistic and otherwise.[11] This is why an adequate comprehension of the discursive complexity of *Litteratur* is essential for appreciating the complexity of *Welt*.

The same holds true for any of the numerous compound nouns constructed on the word *Welt*, which were proliferating at the time, and whose diversity Goethe happily exploited—*Weltgeschichte, Weltseele, Weltgeist, Weltensumpf, Welthistorie, Weltregiment, Weltwirrwesen, Weltenschöpfer, Weltbürger* (respectively, world history, world soul, world spirit, the world's mire, world history, world regiment or order, chaotic world essence, creator of worlds, citizen of the world) and more.[12] In any of them, we can witness Goethe thinking of *Welt-* together with other networks that navigate the transformational intersections of science and literature, and trying to think of this intersection in relationship to the economic sphere, where much of the impetus for neologisms around "world" was originating.[13] Goethe uses the word *Welt* repeatedly in his writing, especially in his poetry, singularly and in compounds, and almost every time he does, he uses it in this way. To explore this exhaustively would exceed the bounds of this chapter, but it is worth pointing to the richness of the resulting constellation of world, nature, divinity and subjectivity, managed discursively in the intersection of economics, science and literature.[14]

The nuances given to *Weltliteratur* by its discursive overdetermination make misunderstanding almost a necessary part of this concept.[15] The combined scientific and literary direction in the concept of *Weltliteratur* is important because, throughout his life, Goethe pursued adequate representational strategies for phenomena by attempting to combine scientific and literary methods. *Faust* is a perfect example, but so is *Wahlverwandtschaften* (Elective Affinities, 1809), as is "Metamorphose der Pflanzen" (Metamorphosis of Plants, 1798) as both a morphological study and a poem, and so on. The repositioning of human action in the world context requires scientific and literary discourse to assert their control over natural processes that appeared to be coming ever more under the sway of economics. This is played out, for example in the descriptions of the production of paper money in the first act of *Faust II*.[16] The entanglement of natural processes and economic principles was complicated by the ever-widening suspicion that humans are by nature *homo economicus*, a matter explored throughout the *Wilhelm Meister* novels.[17]

The idea that the essence of nature is best unlocked in acts of representation defines Goethe's world in another way. Human activity becomes a world-seeking and world-forming activity, whereby nature is represented via sensory stimulus and given form in scientific and aesthetic representation. This process grants human activity a generality, making it possible to speak of world citizenship. Since the human task of unlocking nature's phenomena is something that binds the citizens of various European nations (Goethe doesn't appear to have been looking beyond Europe when considering this unity), art and science form the ground for world citizenship. In the introductory article (1798) of his journal *Die Propyläen* (The Propylaea), he proposes that art and science can bind inquisitive investigators together in a world citizenship that compensates for the loss of antiquity.[18] The reconstruction of a sense of shared world identity is to take place via a collective consciousness of shared representations, allowing for a modernized *Respublica literaria*.

Progress: The Spatio-Temporal World

Alongside this conceptualization of "world," which balanced economics, science, and aesthetics, Goethe was interested in world as the spatio-temporal unfolding of a fundamental principle of life—the morphological development from primary phenomena to diverse manifestations.[19] This constitutes the importance, which Pheng Cheah notes, of seeing the world as "a dynamic process with a practical-actional dimension instead of a spatio-geographical category or only in terms of global flows, even if the latter constitutes an important material condition of a world."[20] This morphological principle unifies the world as a place of diversity, according to one of nature's fundamental laws. Goethe probably retained this idea from his early interactions with Herder, for whom it was one of the most basic principles of life. This morphological understanding of development also brought with it a problematic relationship to what might be called "world temporality." The geographically unified world could not be conceptualized in the way it has come to be without a struggle over world temporality and world history—in other words over the concept of "progress."[21] As Reinhart Koselleck noted, unlike decline (*Niedergang*), progress (*Fortschritt*) is "eine modern Kategorie, deren Erfahrungsgehalt und deren Erwartungsüberschuß vor dem 18. Jahrhundert nicht gegeben war."[22] The eighteenth-century concept of "progress" responded to sudden changes in the way humans related to the world, most immediately through the new forms of movement and the accompanying expansion in the horizons of possibility for experiencing the world. Progress (and even more clearly the German word *Fortschritt*) has both a spatial and a temporal meaning.[23] Furthermore, the radical nature of world exploration linked the process of imagining a better future to what Guthke calls "die große Öffnung in die weite Welt."[24] This ideological and practical opening of time and space can be traced in a number of important areas of life in Goethe's time, including world trade and the changing relationship between the economy and sovereignty, labor and slavery, world exploration, communication, and many more.[25]

In German, the idea of progress as a spatialized concept was underlined by the spatial origins of the word *Fortschritt*. To think of progress was to imagine a spatial movement that lent itself well to the advance of armies or the passing of time through the revolution of the earth.[26] Revolution, as Koselleck notes, had a spatial meaning before it was given its political and temporal meaning, and writers sympathetic to the revolution reminded its critics of this point.[27] This also had far-reaching consequences for the all-pervasive attempts to relate the history of the world to the question of individual development, or *Bildung*. The growing awareness of the diverse histories of different peoples made it increasingly difficult to speak of history as a single global story of progress analogous to the learning processes of human education. And conversely, the idea of human development required an increasing exposure (at least in the imagination) not only to the entirety of history but to an open world. This is clearly visible in Act 2 of *Faust II*, where Homunculus recognizes that if a humanoid conceived in idealism is to become human it must first of all expand into the world because all natural organisms must find their place in the world, or as he puts it: "what is natural takes almost endless space, / while what is not, requires a container."[28] The individual organism must also find its relation to the representation of history, going all the way back to the origins of life, which are accessible, as Goethe demonstrates at the end of Act 2 of *Faust II*, only via mythology.

Representation and World Progress

By placing the question of representation at the center of the problem of progress and world, Goethe is paving the way for a novel solution to the question of world progress. Where Goethe holds great mistrust for the various technologies and economies he sees driving historical change and shaping the geography of power on a global scale,[29] there is one practice (perhaps it can even be called a "technology") that holds promise as a means of establishing agency in the way history relates to geography. This is writing as a gestural, subjective, symbolic act.

There is a close connection between Goethe's fundamental mistrust of the idea of global progress and his insistence on foregrounding representation, whether this be scientific or artistic representation.[30] The grounds for this connection are to found in Goethe's studies in the changing forms of natural phenomena—his morphology.[31] As a scientific concept, morphology allowed him to adopt Leibniz's concept of "development," but without the notion that there was a preordained direction towards perfection, and without taking the Kantian step that linked moral universalism to the concept of "historical progress." Instead, progress is a natural morphological operation, driven by the forces of nature and expressed on an individual level in acts of representation. The morphology of representational progress carries over into the act of writing. It is in writing that Goethe most noticeably employs the concept of "progress," as is evident from his letters. Here he refers repeatedly to progress in the writing of literary works, but also in his scientific studies. This use of the word may seem trivial enough to not warrant comment, but the point is that, even in his casual use of a more or less unexamined concept, we see a broad semantic field that links writing projects to scientific knowledge within a context of personal development and of the physical progression of words on the page or the making of a book. For Goethe, it is in writing that the idea of a physical link with an open world is tied to the idea of "temporal processes." This intersection of temporality and spatiality in writing positions the individual in the world.

Goethe's view on science posits a unitary model of human life, for it is only within this totality that at any one moment in history there will be either a solo or a polyphonic expression of appreciation for the mysteries of nature. This expression of appreciation is neither the domain of science nor of poetry, and its past is not to be unlocked by history or mythology alone ("For the historian, the point where history meets legend is an extremely attractive challenge. It is generally the loveliest of all historical tradition").[32] It is in the nature of creation that it requires a polyphonic representational response from humanity.[33] Goethe intends this model of polyphonic representation to carry the idea of "diversity" in expression, location, and development of both individuals and cultures, and this leads him to a different model of history than the narrative of collective linear development. In *Farbenlehre* he speaks of "two moments in world history that are revealed in individuals and peoples. They are at times subsequent, at times simultaneous; at times they are singular and separate, at times intertwined in the greatest measure."[34] What he has in mind regarding these two moments or epochs or tendencies appears to be the distinction between, on the one hand, intellectual pursuit aimed at understanding and representing the world for the sake of the process alone (it is tempting to think of this as the beauty of intellectual pursuit in the Kantian sense), and on the other hand the instrumental use of knowledge. The first epoch is one "in which individuals develop freely alongside one another. This is the era of becoming, of peace, of nourishment, the arts and sciences, of *Gemütlichkeit*, of reason."[35] The second is the epoch "of utility, of war, consumption, technology, knowledge, understanding. All effects are externally oriented. Under certain conditions, this point in time offers continuity and enjoyment in the most lofty and beautiful sense."[36] These are conceived not in terms of a cyclical advance of humanity but of a temporally and spatially coordinated rhythm of development and decline, in the tradition of Diderot and Voltaire.[37] Thus Goethe identifies in each of these developmental epochs an internal tendency to self-destruction. The epoch of scientific purity will, he observes, give way to "partisanship and anarchy," while the epoch of scientific instrumentality tends to degenerate into "self-interest and tyranny."[38]

If there are social processes at work that tend to undo scientific advances, or at least to translate scientific insights into detrimental social arrangements, then Goethe ascribes to the individual the task of retaining some connection to these advances, lending them continuity: "There is a tenuous thread drawn from the often-broad fabric of knowledge and science that extends uninterrupted through all times, even the darkest and most confused, and it is drawn by individuals."[39]

This work of scientific continuity is representational work, since it allows the processes of collection, isolation, organization, and unification described here: "The conflict of the individual with unmediated experience and with mediated tradition is actually the history of the sciences, since that which takes place within the masses and for them relies in the final instance on a capable individual who collects, separates, arranges, and combines the whole."[40] Goethe understood that the burden that this places on the individual is a burden that the individual can scarcely bear. This leads him to repeated encounters with imaginary individuals, whose struggle to retain a sense of personal development is at the same time a struggle for a larger truth. This is played out on both a temporal scale, where the development of the individual is connected to historical events—for example in *Hermann und Dorothea*, *Egmont*, and *Götz von Berlichingen*—and a spatial scale, whereby the life story of the individual is grasped as a trajectory out into the wider world—as laid out in the moments in *Wilhelm Meisters Lehrjahre* (Wilhelm Meister's Apprenticeship, 1795/96) and *Wilhelm Meisters Wanderjahre* (Wilhelm Meister's Journeyman Years, 1821/29), where the actions of the European protagonists open up a theater of possibilities that extends to the new world. This is also the trajectory that Goethe uses to contextualize the Faust story in the *Vorspiel auf dem Theater* (Prelude on the Stage) when he has the director introduce the *Prolog im Himmel* (Prologue in Heaven) with the words:

> So now upon our modest stage act out
> creation in its every aspect,
> and move with all deliberate haste
> from heaven, through the world, to hell![41]

Conclusion: Goethe's World

Goethe's world is an extension of this world of the theater, and it coexists with it. It is a multilayered, discursively organized world that serves as the testing ground for the modern subject's wager with life: that it is possible to imagine an individual life developing according to a plan, and to act in keeping with this, while realizing all along that this conception of life and of the individual's place in time and space is played out in representation. The multiple nature of this discursive organization makes it difficult to find a point at which to criticize the concept of *Weltliteratur*, whether this might be by tying it to global markets or by asserting (as Cheah does) a blindness "to the way literary processes of world formation are imbricated in power relations."[42] All of *Faust II* is built upon the premise that power relations require literary processes of world formation—as long as we take literature in the broad sense outlined above. But it is also in literary processes that world formations of power can be opened to critique. When we consider the nature of *Welt*, it is important to follow the structure of *Faust*, where anything that can be shown to be true about the world is already contexualized within another discourse, which dramatizes the discursive quality of the act of showing. This serves to remind us of the key insight that *Welt* cannot be spoken of without political qualification.

Notes

[1] Pascal David, "Welt," in *Dictionary of Untranslatables: A Philosophical Lexicon*, ed. Barbara Cassin, trans. Steven Rendell et al. (Princeton, NJ: Princeton University Press, 2014), 1217.

[2] See David Seamon, "Goethe, Nature, and Phenomenology: An Introduction," in *Goethe's Way of Science: A Phenomenology of Nature*, ed. David Seamon and Arthur Zajonc (Albany: State University of New York Press, 1998).

[3] See Birgit Tautz, *Translating the World: Toward a New History of German Literature around 1800* (University Park: The Pennsylvania State University Press, 2018), particularly chapter 4.

[4] The past few decades have seen a resurgence in discussions in the English-speaking world of the meaning and usefulness of the term *Weltliteratur*. Just to name a couple of works, see John Pizer, *The Idea of World Literature: History and Pedagogical Practice* (Baton Rouge: Louisiana State University Press, 2006); David Damrosch, *What Is World Literature?* (Princeton, NJ: Princeton University Press, 2003); and B. Venkat Mani, *Recoding World Literature: Libraries, Print Culture, and Germany's Pact with Books* (New York: Fordham University Press, 2017).

[5] Emily Apter, *Against World Literature: On the Politics of Untranslatability* (London: Verso, 2013), 177.

[6] Apter, *Against World Literature*, 2.

[7] See the comments in the introduction to Manfred Koch, *Weimaraner Weltbewohner: Zur Genese von Goethes Begriff "Weltliteratur"* (Tübingen: Niemeyer, 2002).

[8] See my discussion in John K. Noyes, "Writing the Dialectical Structure of the Modern Subject: Goethe on World Literature and World Citizenship," *Seminar* 51, no. 2 (2015): 100–114.

[9] See my discussion in Noyes, "Writing the Dialectical Structure of the Modern Subject."

[10] Gayatri Chakravorty Spivak, "The Stakes of a World Literature," in *An Aesthetic Education in the Era of Globalization* (Cambridge, MA: Harvard University Press, 2012), 455–66.

[11] Anne Bohnenkamp, "'Versucht's zusammen eine Strecke': Goethes Konzept einer Weltliteratur als Form europäischer Geselligkeit?" in *Einsamkeit und Geselligkeit um 1800*, ed. Susanne Schmidt (Heidelberg: Winter, 2008), 177–91, here 186.

[12] The translations are my own, J.K.N.

[13] Koch, *Weimarer Weltbewohner*, 2.

[14] Pheng Cheah points to the way Goethe uses "metaphors of mercantile and evangelical activity" to elucidate the "dynamic universality" of translation. Pheng Cheah, "What Is a World?: On World Literature as World-Making Activity," *Daedalus* 137, no. 3 (2008): 26–38, here 27–28.

[15] See Koch, *Weimarer Weltbewohner*, 2–3.

[16] See Jochen Schmidt, *Goethes Faust erster und zweiter Teil: Grundlagen, Werk, Wirkung* (Munich: Beck, 1999). See also Gernot Böhme, *Goethes Faust als philosophischer Text* (Zug, Switzerland: Die Graue Edition, 2005), 184–86, 190; and Michael Jaeger, *Fausts Kolonie: Goethes kritische Phänomenologie der Moderne* (Würzburg: Königshausen & Neumann, 2004), 289–307.

[17] Adorno and Horkheimer's description of Odysseus and Robinson Crusoe as *homo economicus* lays out the ground tested by Wilhelm Meister. See Theodor W. Adorno and Max Horkheimer, *Dialektik der Aufklärung* (Frankfurt: Fischer, 2006), 68–69.

[18] Johann Wolfgang von Goethe, *Einleitung in die Propyläen* (Introduction to the Propyläen, 1798), in *Poetische Werke: Kunsttheoretische Schriften und Übersetzungen* (Berlin & Weimar, 1960–78), vol. 19, 193–94.

[19] See Karl J. Fink, *Goethe's History of Science* (Cambridge: Cambridge University Press 1991), 35, 40–41.

[20] Cheah, "What Is a World?" 35.

[21] See Amy Allen, *The End of Progress: Decolonizing the Normative Foundations of Critical Theory* (New York: Columbia University Press, 2016).

[22] Reinhart Koselleck, *Begriffsgeschichten: Studien zur Semantik und Pragmatik der politischen und sozialen Sprache* (Frankfurt: Suhrkamp, 2010), 160.

[23] Koselleck, *Begriffsgeschichten*, 161.

[24] Karl S. Guthke, *Goethes Weimar und "Die große Öffnung in die weite Welt,"* Wolfenbütteler Forschungen 93 (Wiesbaden: Harrassowitz, 2001).

[25] Just to name a few relevant studies, see Immanuel Wallerstein, *The Modern World-System*, vol. 3, *The Second Era of Great Expansion of the Capitalist World-Economy, 1730–1840s* (San Diego, CA: Academic Press, 1989); Istvan Hont, *Jealousy of Trade: International Competition and the Nation-State in Historical Perspective* (Cambridge, MA: Belknap Press, 2005); Joseph Vogl, *The Spectre of Capital*, trans. Joachim Redner and Robert Savage (Stanford, CA: Stanford University Press, 2014); Joseph Vogl, *The Ascendency of Finance* (Cambridge, UK: Polity Press, 2017); Kenneth Pommeranz, *The Great Divergence: China, Europe, and the Making of the Modern World Economy* (Princeton, NJ: Princeton University Press, 2000); and John M. Headley, *The Europeanization of the World: On the Origins of Human Rights and Democracy* (Princeton, NJ: Princeton University Press, 2008).

[26] Thus Goethe writes in May 1796 to Wilhelm von Humboldt: "I am concerned in no small measure about the latest advances of the French in Italy." Johann Wolfgang von Goethe, *Goethes Werke*, herausgegeben im Auftrage der Großherzogin Sophie von Sachsen (Munich: Deutscher Taschenbuch Verlag 1987), part 4, vol. 11, 78.

[27] Koselleck, *Begriffsgeschichten*, 162. This is precisely the point made by Herder in his unpublished notes on the concept of "revolution," which he wrote for the section of *Ideen* dealing with the present. See Johann Gottfried Herder, *Sämtliche Werke*, ed. Bernhard Suphan (Hildesheim: G. Olms, 1967–68), vol. 14, 648–51.

[28] Johann Wolfgang von Goethe, *Faust*, *Werke*, ed. Erich Trunz et al. (Hamburg: C. Wegner, 1961–64), vol. 3, 211.

[29] This is well described by Jaeger in *Fausts Kolonie*.

[30] Thus, for example, Albrecht Schöne observes that, in designating *Faust* a tragedy, Goethe is, from the outset, obstructing any attempt to read the play as a statement of historical optimism built upon a teleology of Faust's development. Johann Wolfgang Goethe, *Faust, Kommentare*, ed. Albrecht Schöne (Frankfurt: Deutscher Klassiker Verlag 2005), 17. Géza von Molnár argues that if there is a teleology in Faust, it is subject to the limitations Kant described in the Third Critique. Géza von Molnár, "Hidden in Plain View: Another Look at Goethe's Faust," *Eighteenth-Century Studies* 35, no. 3 (2002): 469–96, here 483.

[31] See Goethe, *Morphologie*, *Werke*, vol. 13, ed. Erich Trunz (Hamburg: Wegner, 1966), 53–197.

[32] Goethe, *Zur Farbenlehre*, *Gedenkausgabe*, vol. 16, 340. All translations from this edition are my own, J.K.N.

[33] This has been explored with regard to Novalis by James Hodkinson. See Hodkinson, *Women and Writing in the Works of Novalis: Transformation Beyond Measure?* (Rochester, NY: Camden House 2007), in particular, chapter 4: "Music and the Manifold of Voices: The Subject and the Theory of 'Polyphony,' 1797–99," 134–67.

[34] Goethe, *Zur Farbenlehre*, vol. 16, 341.

[35] Goethe, *Zur Farbenlehre*, vol. 16, 341.

[36] Goethe, *Zur Farbenlehre*, vol. 16, 341.
[37] See Koselleck, *Begriffsgeschichten*, 176.
[38] Goethe, *Zur Farbenlehre*, vol. 16, 341.
[39] Goethe, *Zur Farbenlehre*, vol. 16, 341.
[40] Goethe, *Zur Farbenlehre*, vol. 16, 343.
[41] Goethe, *Faust*, 15.
[42] Cheah, "What Is a World?" 31.

2: Embodying and Distributing World Literature: Goethe's *Novelle* in the Context of the 1820s

Ben Morgan

World Literature Redistributed

THIS ESSAY RETURNS to Goethe's original elaboration of a model of world literature in the late 1820s and early 1830s to get a clearer sense of the specific literary practices he conceived as contributing to the project. Paying attention to the techniques that might distinguish world literature has not been a focus in early twenty-first century debates on the topic. Indeed, David Damrosch, in his seminal study *What Is World Literature?* (2003), doubts that we could define the specifically literary aspect of world literature: "Any global perspective on literature must acknowledge the tremendous variability in what has counted as literature from one place to another and from one era to another."[1] Consequently, as Elleke Boehmer has recently noted, "We look in vain to world literature studies to learn more about the poetics of this writing—about, say, its rhetoric of address, tropes of identity, or paradigms of worldliness."[2] Boehmer has responded by elaborating her own postcolonial poetics, exploring how readers, "invited by the writing's shaped substance, or by its poetics, ... step forward to gather in the intensified knowledge or awareness" that postcolonial writing offers of the distinctive, often unfamiliar context in which it was written.[3] Returning to the full range of relevant texts by Goethe before and after the famous conversations on world literature with Johann Peter Eckermann in January and July 1827 (*FA*, 39, 223–28, 255–57) allows us to construct a fuller and, where necessary, critical picture of the literary practices through which the ideal was originally promulgated.[4] A key element in my argument will be a reading of Goethe's short *Novelle* (Novella, 1828) (*FA*, 8, 531–55), which can be read as a founding document of world literature.[5] It was written, discussed, and rewritten in late 1826 and early 1827 (*FA*, 8, 1054–60), accompanying other important moments in the articulation of the idea: the 1827 issue of Goethe's journal *Über Kunst und Altertum* (On Art and Antiquity) in which Goethe first used the term "world literature" in print (*FA*, 22, 356); the poetry volumes of the ongoing new edition of his works that Goethe and Eckermann prepared for publication in 1827, including Goethe's translations of Byron and Manzoni under the rubric "Aus fremden Sprachen" (From Foreign Languages, *FA*, 2, 53–72); the 1827 revised edition of the *West-östlicher Divan*; and the short cycle of poems *Chinesisch-Deutsche Jahres- und Tageszeiten* (Chinese-German Seasons and Hours) that Goethe wrote in the summer of the same year (*FA*, 2, 695–99).[6] The *Novelle*, with its intentionally unresolved ending and its pointed manipulation of perspective, will stand as an example of what Boehmer calls the "rhetoric of address" of world literature, and so allow a study of the bodily or "kinesic" effects that world literature occasions, insofar as it adopts such a rhetoric.[7] My analysis of Goethean world literature as an embodied practice will be shown to have implications for an understanding of the functioning of culture both in the 1820s and the present. Read as a self-consciously fashioned instantiation of world literature, the *Novelle* illustrates how world literature was deployed by Goethe as a cultural tool to further what he believed to be his major legacy, formulated in his anti-Newtonian *Farbenlehre* (1810) (*FA*, 23.1, 1061): that of resisting a narrowly scientific understanding of the world. World literature, in this respect, takes over the role played by *Bildung*, or an ideal of universal education, that Goethe articulated in the 1790s in his discourse-founding *Bildungsroman*, *Wilhelm Meisters Lehrjahre* (Wilhelm Meister's Apprenticeship) (1795/96).[8] The interactive and internationally distributed project of "world literature" enriches and resituates *Bildung* as it was individualistically first conceived in the 1790s, complementing the rethinking of the figure of Wilhelm Meister that was another concern of Goethe's in the later 1820s (the sequel to Goethe's first *Bildungsroman*, *Wilhelm Meisters Wanderjahre* (Wilhelm Meister's Journeyman Years), was expanded and reworked for a second edition between June 1825 and February 1829) (*FA*, 10, 790–94). This essay will explore what has been lost and what has been gained in the process of transformation from individual self-fashioning to a literary practice of distributed cognition.

The first step in my argument will be a brief discussion of Erich Auerbach's famous essay "The Philology of World Literature" (1952). There are two reasons to start with Auerbach's essay. The first is the foundational role it has played in establishing twentieth-century discourses of comparative literature: contemporary debates are still shaped by Auerbach's arguments.[9] The second is the astute way in which the essay makes explicit the cognitive context to which the project of world literature is a response and so helps us understand the cultural work that world literature can do when its embodied and distributed aspects are actively taken into account.

Resituating Auerbach's Profane Illuminations

From the very first sentence of the essay, it is clear that Auerbach understands himself to be continuing and deepening the Goethean project of world literature.[10] Underlying his version of the project is a particular anthropology according to which human existence is emphatically historical: "For only in history do human beings appear before us in the fullness of their lives."[11] "What we are we have become in the course of our history, and it is only in history that we can remain what we are, and develop."[12] By the mid-twentieth century, when Auerbach was writing, grasping the wider historical context in which a human life becomes meaningful had become increasingly difficult for two reasons. The first is the sheer wealth of material that must be coherently articulated once all the world's cultures have been acknowledged to belong to the undertaking, not just a European canon, and once the study of literary culture is understood to involve attention to "the religious, philosophical, political and economic circumstances," as well as to cultural expressions over and beyond literature.[13] The second difficulty is that in a world of increasing cultural standardization, the very historical and cultural differences that world literature might articulate and reflect on are being eroded, leaving the prospect of a global monoculture in which "the idea of world literature would simultaneously be realized and destroyed."[14] The philology of world literature will not only register but also nurture cultural differences.

Auerbach believes himself to be writing at a moment when a sense of shared humanity still exists in all its plurality, but new tools must be found if we are dynamically to disclose this plurality to ourselves and participate in it. We cannot simply catalogue the vast array of cultural material and reduce it to terms we have prepared in advance: "The traditional categories, e.g., chronology, geography, and genre, are indispensable for the preparatory steps. But they are not—or are no longer—conducive to a procedure that is dynamic and unifying."[15] Instead, "the place from which one should approach the material" (*Ansatzpunkt*) will be "a product of personal intuition."[16] Auerbach is articulating a method similar to that elaborated by his exact contemporary and correspondent, Walter Benjamin, in his essay on surrealism (1929). Auerbach's *Ansatzpunkt* functions in the same way as Benjamin's profane illumination: in a first step, the attention of the cultural critic is arrested by a detail, an anomaly or other phenomenon that prompts an analytic hunch that, in a second step, is unpacked, situated, and further explored.[17] This analysis, for Auerbach, requires specialist knowledge: "But it is not the specialization that relies on inherited ways of classifying one's material. Rather it is always matched to the specific object at hand. As such, it must itself always be invented anew. . . . The things themselves should be allowed to speak."[18] David Damrosch has argued that "to understand the workings of world literature, we need more a phenomenology than an ontology of the work of art."[19] Auerbach's intuitively guided philology aspires to be just such a phenomenology, flexibly deploying cultural expertise to disclose and participate in "the dynamic movement of the whole," of which the details analyzed and resituated are a part.[20]

Auerbach's vision of a philologically guided, lived reappropriation of a global culture pluralistically conceived is appealing. But it all turns on the *Ansatzpunkt*. If we don't share Auerbach's deep, humanist education, how can our interpretative hunches be unpacked in the inclusive globally oriented way he imagines, given that even his own massive learning can in retrospect itself appear provincially Eurocentric.[21] It seems the *Ansatzpunkt* is doomed to remain opaque to itself, blind to the partiality of its own limited perspective, even where it aspires to connect to the wider whole.

This problem might seem to attend any perspectivism. When Nietzsche, in *The Genealogy of Morals*, declares that only perspective-bound knowledge of the world is possible, and that we should therefore aim to multiply, maximize, and marshal the perspectives to which we have access, his own assertion seems to undermine itself by laying claim to a wider truth to which its own necessarily limited perspective must simultaneously give the lie.[22] For Alexander Nehamas, Nietzsche's solution to this problem is his literary and self-consciously hyperbolic style, which draws attention to the contingency and partiality of the claims even as it formulates them.[23] Nehamas thus suggests that one solution to the (apparent) paradox of a perspectivist approach lies in literary style. Auerbach himself argues that the successful historical synthesis developed from the *Ansatzpunkt* will appear to its reader as a "work of art."[24] Thus it turns out that what Elleke Boehmer termed the "rhetoric of address" is fundamental to the whole project of world literature if we are to articulate a fuller picture of the global context in which we are situated without inadvertently indulging in a kind of vainglorious and self-deluded provincialism.

Goethe's original explorations of the idea of "world literature" are themselves characterized by an attention to rhetoric and perspective. Damrosch notes how Goethe's awareness of the peripheral and provincial state of German letters in the 1820s prevents his cosmopolitanism from collapsing "into a self-confirming narcissism."[25] However, the attention to the perspective is more far reaching. If we return to Goethe's writings of the 1820s, informed as they are by his engagement with Scott, as with other writers whom he considered to be participating in the ongoing project of world literature, such as James Fenimore Cooper, Byron, Manzoni, or the Chinese poets translated into English by Peter Perring Thoms in 1824, then we find that, even as Goethe strives for the formulation of what Lukács called a "distilled social-human essence," he is simultaneously aware of the partial nature of any such formulation and finds a means of reflecting on, and indeed mobilizing, the perspectivicity of any perspective as part of his literary project.[26]

Perspectives on and in World Literature: Goethe's Writings of the 1820s

A reflection on the plurality of voices on which the project of global literary culture is founded is included in the essay in which Goethe first publicly uses the term "world literature."[27] The occasion is an account by Goethe, in the 1827 issue of his journal *Über Kunst und Altertum*, of two contrasting reviews of a French play indebted to his own drama *Torquato Tasso* (1790). Goethe's play, fittingly enough, while drawing on the biography of the sixteenth-century Italian writer Tasso (*FA*, 5, 1391–98), presents a tragic tension between opposed but necessarily complementary attitudes to the world, and closes with a final tableau of Tasso, driven mad by a paranoid distrust of people, being physically supported by the very man with whom he has so devastatingly come into conflict (*FA*, 5, 831–34). Goethe's essay presents a similar, if less extreme, conflict of views, one review praising, the other strongly criticizing, the French reworking of Goethe's play. Furthermore, the essay encourages German readers to profit by, and contribute to, the international literary debates of which this French disagreement is an example, even where they believe the views of other contributors to be misguided. Indeed, Goethe suggests the very errors of participants are part of the process of world literary debate:

> [Ich will doch] von meiner Seite meine Freunde aufmerksam machen, daß ich überzeugt sei, es bilde sich eine allgemeine Weltliteratur, worin uns Deutschen eine ehrenvolle Rolle vorbehalten ist. Alle Nationen schauen sich nach uns um, sie loben, sie tadlen, nehmen auf und verwerfen, ahmen nach und entstellen, verstehen oder mißverstehen uns, eröffnen oder verschließen ihre Herzen: dieß alles müssen wir gleichmütig aufnehmen, indem uns das Ganze von großem Werth ist.
>
> [I shall merely acquaint my friends with my conviction that there is being formed a universal world literature, in which an honorable role is reserved for us Germans. All the nations review our work; they praise, censure, accept, and reject, imitate and misrepresent us, open or close their hearts to us. All this we must accept with great equanimity, since this attitude, taken as a whole, is of great value to us.] (*FA*, 22, 356–57)[28]

World literature, for Goethe, is thus a process of contestation, critique, and adaptation. Moreover, the nations contributing to this debate are not themselves uniform or monolithic. "We Germans" may, in Goethe's view, have an honorable role to play. However, it emerges in the final paragraph of the essay that whatever German literary culture as a whole may be it is very much a work in progress and arises from a heterogeneous group of talents and dispositions undertaking their different activities, judging in their own particular ways, and united only by the fact that they write in German (*FA*, 22, 357). As well as being productively fragmented, Goethe further suggests, in a comment recorded by Eckermann in July 1827, that one literary tradition often benefits from the assessments of critics based in another: Carlyle evaluates Schiller in a more balanced way than German critics, while in return, German critics assess Shakespeare and Byron more lucidly than their English counterparts (*FA*, 39, 257). Carlyle's biography of Schiller was the object of Goethe's final notes on world literature penned three years later as he wrote a preface to its German translation (*FA*, 22, 865–83). In these notes, Goethe makes explicit that the mutual exchange, of which Carlyle's early work is an example, does not produce a single monolithic discourse but rather promotes cultural practices that acknowledge difference without abolishing it (*FA*, 22, 868). Drawing on these notes, Homi Bhabha concludes: "The study of world literature might be the study of the way in which cultures recognize themselves through their projections of 'otherness.'"[29]

Goethe's insistence on the plurality of viewpoints that constitute world literature as both a national and a transnational discussion contrasts markedly with another aspect of the idea that we've already seen in Auerbach, and that is also part of the original Goethean formulation: the idea that "the human spirit itself is not national."[30] The famous discussion with Eckermann of January 31, 1827 begins with Goethe's remarks about a Chinese novel in verse, *Chinese Courtship* (*FA*, 39, 223).[31] Goethe is surprised to find commonalities in the treatment of emotions between the Chinese novel and his own epic poem *Hermann und Dorothea* (1797) or Samuel Richardson's novels (*FA*, 39, 223). Inspired by the novel, Goethe declares that poetry is not a national but a general human good (*FA*, 39, 224). A similar idea had already been formulated in a note from the summer of 1826 in which Goethe imagines genuine poetry as a skill anyone who feels themselves to be a true human might practice (*FA*, 22, 287). Goethe's conception of world literature thus pulls productively in two directions. On the one hand, there is an affirmation of a plurality of perspectives, with the accompanying awareness of the social practices of personal and intercultural exchange needed to sustain them.[32] On the other hand, there is sense of a shared human disposition differently disclosed but nevertheless common to all human cultures.

This shared disposition, viewed now from the perspective of cultural artefacts rather than of the poetically endowed human individual, is the topic of conversation between Eckermann and Goethe on February 1,

1827, the day after the celebrated discussion of world literature. When Eckermann arrives, Goethe has a copy of his *Farbenlehre* in front of him, and the resulting discussion of the "Gesetz des forderten Wechsels" (law of necessary alternation) that, in Goethe's view, underpins all cognition but is especially evident in vision, leads to a wider consideration of the rhythm of changing stimuli that constitute successful music, literary style, and indeed dramatic form, as evidenced by the movement between moments of high drama and comedy in Shakespeare's plays (*FA*, 39, 229–30). Goethe thus predicates perceptual regularities that cultural artefacts exploit in their successful communication. Intercultural exchange can help disclose such regularities, as the commonalities between, say, poetic traditions allow a clearer sense of the deeper structures behind or beyond the culturally specific techniques employed by the individual poet.

The short cycle of poems *Chinesisch-Deutsche Jahres- und Tageszeiten* that Goethe wrote in the summer of 1827 can be seen as just such a work of distillation that directly addresses the cognitive questions raised by Goethe's model of world literature. The poems are narrated from the perspective of "uns Mandarinen" (we mandarins, *FA*, 2, 695) and deploy the pared-down tropes of nature that Goethe encountered in the poems included in Peter Perring Thoms's *Chinese Courtship*: flowers, birds, clouds, and the moon.[33] At the same time, the garden in which the encounter with the beloved is remembered is Westernized: the nightingale, cuckoo, nettle, and rose have replaced the peach flower that featured in Goethe's translations of sections of Thoms's text that he published in *Über Kunst und Altertum* under the rubric "Chinesisches" in 1827 (*FA*, 22, 371) and that Thoms drew attention to as a topos of Chinese poetry unfamiliar to Western readers.[34]

For Daniel Purdy, this mixed voice is the particular achievement of the cycle of poems.[35] But Goethe puts the mixed voice to a particular use. In this universalizing setting, Goethe stages a drama of cognition itself. A single, late rose metonymically represents the retrospective knowledge that we can attain: of roses when the season of blooming is over (*FA*, 2, 698) and, by extension, of past relationships. A complete, intuitive knowledge of the rose, and of human relations, is then contrasted with restless, incomplete empirical investigations (*FA* 2, 698). The cycle of poems holds these two approaches in tension: on the one hand, the necessary scientific investigation of the mechanisms of the natural world, and on the other, an intuitive sense of the whole to which they belong. Having formulated this contrast, the speaking voice is interrupted by the arrival of others in the garden, whom he dismisses as he savors his lived understanding of life's deeper connections: "Mit andern kann man sich belehren, / Begeistert wird man nur allein" (One can learn with other, / one can only be inspired on one's own, *FA*, 2, 699). However, the cycle does not end on this lonely, contemplative note. As the companions, like the readers, leave the poetic subject to his musings, they are given a final admonition to focus on practical engagement with their immediate environment (*FA*, 2, 699). The sentiments that close the cycle echo aphorisms from the second edition of *Wilhelm Meisters Wanderjahre*, written at the same stage of Goethe's thinking, which make explicit what lies behind the exhortation to practice in the present: "Wie kann man sich selbst kennenlernen? Durch Betrachten niemals, wohl aber durch Handeln. Versuche deine Pflicht zu tun, und du weißt gleich was an dir ist. / Was aber ist deine Pflicht? Die Forderung des Tages" (How can one come to know oneself? Through contemplation never; more likely through action. Try to do your duty, and you shall know at once what you are. / But what is your duty? What the day demands, *FA* 10, 557 [§§ 2–3]).[36]

Goethe's "Chinese-German" poems thus take readers to a stylized, transcultural space of contemplation, but they do so the better to launch us back into the here and now (*FA* 2, 699). Our access to the cognitive realm that the poem holds in productive tension with empirical investigation is achieved, it turns out, not through poetry so much as through practical immersion in the world, just as Wilhelm's friend and mentor Jarno suggested when explaining the necessity of specialization in *Wilhelm Meisters Wanderjahre* (*FA* 10, 295).

It might seem inconsistent that Goethe should use a poem to encourage his readers to leave contemplation behind, but only if we overlook the fact that Goethe approaches world literature as itself a form of craft, a skilled engagement with an immediate task rather than a detached form of universal overview. His comments on the works he admires as examples of world literature often focus on specific techniques as much as on the content of the works. This is true of his reaction to *Chinese Courtship*. Goethe adds to the observation of similarities in "denken handeln und empfinden" also expressed in Western novels an analysis of the literary techniques by which, in the Chinese novel, the characters' lives are situated in relation to their natural and domestic environment (*FA*, 39, 223).[37] Similarly, Goethe observes how Byron's formal control allows his poetry to create the vivid effect of improvisation (*FA*, 39, 249), and he adds to his own translation of the first five stanzas of *Don Juan* brief comments on the specific practices that a collective of translators would need to adopt if they were successfully to translate the whole poem (*FA*, 21, 53). Manzoni's great historical novel *I Promessi Sposi* (The Betrothed, 1827), in Goethe's view, balances astute psychological observation with an impressive precision in the presentation of specific localities (*FA*, 39, 257). Finally, although he is critical of the manner in which Scott takes up and adapts the figure of Mignon in the novel *Peveril of the Peak* (1822) (*FA*, 39, 228), Goethe comes to admire Scott's narrative technique (*FA*, 39, 459).

When Eckermann suggests that Goethe write an essay on Scott's formal achievements, Goethe demurs, saying that it is difficult to make any publishable statement about such technical mastery (*FA*, 39, 462). Nevertheless, Goethe made private notes on the craftsmanship of his novelist contemporaries. When he started to reread Cooper's *The Pioneers* on October 1, 1826, his diary records how his attention was particularly directed to the formal mastery that the novel exhibits: "Den Cooperischen Roman zum zweitenmal angefangen und die Personen ausgeschrieben. Auch das Kunstreiche daran näher betrachtet, geordnet und fortgesetzt" (Started Cooper's novel for a second time and wrote out a list of characters. Also studied its artistry, ordered it and continued, *FA* 37, 419). Thus impressed by Cooper's narrative technique, Goethe read *The Last of the Mohicans* (1826), *The Spy* (1821), and *The Pilot* (1824) in quick succession (*FA* 37, 998). The final word of his response to Cooper is especially intriguing, since it raises the question of what it would mean to "continue" the American novelist's artistry. It might mean simply to continue taking note of them. But it also suggests Goethe himself refining and extending in his own prose the techniques we find in the novel.

The *Novelle* can be read as just such a continuation. In early October 1826, Goethe wrote sketches for a prose version of a tale focused on a hunt, which he had originally planned as a verse epic in the mode of *Hermann und Dorothea* in the 1790s (*FA*, 8, 1054–55). The new sketches show the direct influence of Cooper's novel. A key scene in the novel involves the heiress Elizabeth Temple and her friend Louisa Grant unexpectedly confronting "the fierce front and glaring eyes of a female panther" in the forests of a newly settled county in upstate New York.[38] Goethe adapts this sequence in the *Novelle*, and although the final version involves an escaped tiger and an escaped lion, his first plan still imagines a confrontation with a panther (*FA*, 8, 1055).

Before we analyze the formal techniques of the *Novelle* in more detail to establish how Goethe "continues" Cooper's skill in the specialist endeavor to convey a wider intuitive whole with literary means, a brief look at a moment when Goethe comments on an excessive aspect of Scott's otherwise masterful command of detail will clarify which aspects of narrative technique were especially important to him. Goethe read *Ivanhoe* (1820) in 1831, and it was this novel that was the occasion of his discovering a "whole new art" in Scott's craft (*FA*, 39, 458). At the same time, he took issue with a particular scene in the novel in which the very attention to detail led Scott astray:

> So kommt in Ivanhoe eine Szene vor, wo man Nachts in der Halle eines Schlosses zu Tische sitzt, und ein Fremder hereintritt. Nun ist es zwar recht, daß er den Fremden von oben herab beschrieben hat, wie er aussieht und wie er gekleidet ist, allein es ist ein Fehler, daß er auch seine Füße, seine Schuhe und Strümpfe beschreibt. Wenn man Abends am Tische sitzt und jemand hereintritt, so sieht

man nur seinen obern Körper. Beschreibe ich aber die Füße, so tritt sogleich das Licht des Tages herein, und die Szene verliert ihren nächtlichen Charakter.

[There is a nighttime scene in Ivanhoe where people are gathered at table in the great hall of a castle and a stranger comes in. It is of course right that Scott describes the stranger from top to bottom, saying how he looks and what he is wearing. Yet it is a mistake that he also describes his feet, his shoes, and his stockings. When you're sitting at table of an evening and someone enters, you see only his upper body. If I describe his feet, then daylight immediately streams in and the scene loses its nocturnal aspect.] (*FA*, 39, 462)

Goethe's comments focus on how the narrative aligns the reader with a particular point of view, in this case that of the Saxon and Norman guests in the great hall of Rotherwood at the moment when the Jewish character Isaac of York enters the narrative.[39] The sequence is a key part of a novel that explicitly reflects on conflicting and competing perspectives—of nations (Norman, Saxon, Jewish), of classes (feudal lord and bondsman, king and outlaw), of gender, and of the different generations. Yet Goethe does not comment on Scott's nuanced staging of social groupings struggling to understand motives unfamiliar to them, although, as we have seen, it is precisely just such a struggle to which he hopes the practices and institutions of world literature will contribute (*FA*, 22, 868). Instead, he focuses on the formal techniques that briefly interrupt the reader's narrative immersion in a scene unfolding from a particular point of view. Goethe's positive standard, in these comments, is a narrative technique that consistently aligns the reader with perspectives inside the narrative. He censures Scott when his narrator briefly adopts a perspective at odds with the situation being presented. In other words, Goethe's attention, as narrative craftsman, falls on the narrative construction of perspective in a scene in which the limitations of perspective—that is to say, perspectivicity itself—is at issue. For the scene to work, in Goethe's view, we must be immersed in the very perspective whose limits the narrative is critically questioning, and not become suddenly aware of the scene as a literary construct. The narrative, insofar as it is itself a product of craft, should not interfere with the process by which, from inside a particular viewpoint, we are led to understand that very perspective's constraints and partiality.

It is I hope now clear why, before introducing Goethe's writings of the 1820s, I wanted to remind readers of the Auerbachian *Ansatzpunkt*. For we can see how Goethe was already reflecting on a problem that Auerbach faced in the 1950s and that the discipline of comparative literature continues to face today: namely, that of synthetically imagining a whole to which the conscious labor of empirical investigation—striving to understand the "why" and the "how" (*FA*, 2, 698)—will never have access. Consistent with the doctrines of the *Wanderjahre*, Goethe's preferred solution is a form of specialization: the mastery of certain aesthetic techniques. He cannot see, or himself represent, the totality of human culture that the practices of world literature nurture and disseminate. Instead, Goethe devotes his skill to the concrete problems of narrative perspective and reader immersion.[40] This insight could be applied to the fragmented, mysterious, and polyphonic text of *Wilhelm Meisters Wanderjahre* to show how, in addition to its European reflections on the colonial project of the United States of America, the text engages with world literature in the way it abstracts from the historical details of the 1820s to question the very narratability of a developing human life.[41] However, the shorter *Novelle*, with its limited scope and its clear intertexts in Cooper's *The Pioneers* and *The Last of the Mohicans* (*FA*, 8, 1080–81), better lends itself to a first, perspicuous overview of Goethe's confrontation with the perspectivity of narrative perspective, allowing the formulation of hypotheses that could then be tested on the longer work.[42]

Participatory Perspectives in Goethe's *Novelle*

The *Novelle*, set in an unspecified contemporary European principality, tells the story of two parallel expeditions—the prince hunting and the princess visiting the marketplace and a ruined castle—both of which get interrupted when the market catches fire. As the prince and his entourage ride back to oversee the firefighting, they come across the princess and her equerry standing by a dead tiger that the equerry has just shot, and being addressed by a brightly clothed, foreign family to whom the animal belonged. The family mourns the animal's death, and let it be known that they are also in search of the lion that has similarly escaped their care as a result of the fire. They persuade the prince not to set the hunting party in pursuit of the lion, but rather to let mother and son lure the animal back to captivity with the music of the young boy's flute. The narrative stops with the image of the boy singing, as the lion rests an injured paw on his lap: "nicht wie der Überwundene, denn seine Kraft blieb in ihm verborgen, aber doch wie der Gezähmte, wie der dem eigenen Willen anheimgegebene" (not so much vanquished—for his strength, though concealed, was still in him—as tamed and surrendered to his own peaceful will, *FA* 8, 555).[43]

For Andrew Piper (2010), the *Novelle* continues literary experiments that Goethe began with *Die Wahlverwandtschaften* (Elective Affinities, 1809) and *Der Mann von funfzig Jahren* (The Man of Fifty Years, 1818), aiming to transform the relation between reader and text into a form of active engagement. The guiding thread of Piper's reading is paraphrase. Just as Goethe paraphrases an original idea for an epic poem as carefully numbered plans and then again as the finished prose text, so the reader reappropriates the text for his or her own life in a form of paraphrase: "Paraphrase enacts a reading experience based not on individuation, but *incorporation*."[44] In my own reading, I want to take up Piper's metaphor of a bodily form of reading (incorporation)—that is, to look more closely at how the text positions and mobilizes the actual bodies of readers in ways they do not fully control but that leads to the direct somatic experience of perspectival constraint. My reading will take up the careful analyses of forms of mediated vision in the *Novelle* by Rosemary Balfour (1976) and Reinhard Heinritz (1992), connecting them to a wider reflection on the distributed and embodied processes that Goethe understands to be the vehicle of the intercultural project of world literature.[45]

The opening paragraph of the *Novelle* can itself be read as a short essay in perspective. The narrative voice positions us with a narrator who knows the extent of the princely palace that is the opening location of the tale; we share his expertise. At the same time, we are placed among the group preparing to hunt: "Ein dichter Herbstnebel verhüllte noch in der Frühe die weiten Räume des fürstlichen Schloßhofes, als man mehr oder weniger durch den sich lichtenden Schleier die ganze Jägerei zu Pferde und zu Fuß durch einander bewegt sah" (The heavy mist of an autumn morning veiled the spacious court of the prince's castle, but gradually, through the rising haze, the hunting party could more or less be clearly discerned, moving about on horseback and on foot, *FA*, 8, 533 / Trans., 265). We catch glimpses of stirrups being shortened, hounds straining on their leashes, and restless horses. This last detail is of particular importance to the treatment of perspective in the text: "Auch hie und da gebärdete ein Pferd sich mutiger, von feuriger Natur getrieben oder von dem Sporn des Reiters angeregt, der selbst hier in der Halbhelle eine gewisse Eitelkeit sich zu zeigen nicht verleugnen konnte" (Here and there, too, a horse pranced, driven by its own fiery nature or excited by the spur of its rider, who, even in the half light of dawn, could not resist showing off, *FA*, 8, 533 / Trans., 265). Some of the riders cannot resist the temptation of pointlessly spurring their horses, as if to draw attention to themselves despite the fact that no one, the narrator and readers included, can see clearly through the fog. Consistent with the way it has hitherto confined the viewpoint of readers within the misty courtyard, the narrative does not show us the individuals, who are thus needlessly showing off in their individuality. Nevertheless, as with the straining of the dogs, the restless horses will prompt an embodied response from the reader, drawing on the kinesic intelligence of our sensory-motor system. Many readers will likely somatically echo the restiveness of hound and horse.[46] Our alignment in the first paragraph is thus multilayered: we are included in the knowledge of the narrator, and thus situated in the action, and at the same time involuntarily implicated in the vanity of the self-advertising riders by our bodily echo of their horses' reactions.

The novella then proceeds to thematize the mediated nature of our involvement in the world. After the hunting party has left, the princess views the party through "das treffliche Teleskop" (the fine telescope, *FA*, 8, 534 / Trans., 266). Her knowledge of the environment and her husband's habits allows her to predict where she will be able to locate the group with the magnifying device. But her conscious understanding of the situation does not prevent her from then waving at people who are too distant to possibly see her when she believes she can discern a hesitation in her husband's progress (*FA*, 8, 535 / Trans., 266). The telescope and microscope are said, in the *Wanderjahre*, to confuse our everyday engagement with the world (*FA*, 10, 567).[47] Certainly the telescope prompts a momentary failure of self-control in the princess (*FA*, 8, 535 / Trans., 266). Indeed, the very clarity of the image seems to encourage a projection of expectations onto the situation the instrument is supposed objectively to reveal to us.[48] Just as some readers will echo the pointless movement of the restless animals, so they might also wave uselessly with the princess, participating vicariously in an action understood simultaneously to be misguided.

The narrative thus draws attention to the errors prompted by a mediated vision, but the alternative to the telescope is not a pure seeing. The princess is shown drawings of the ruined castle that people at court viewed the evening before through the telescope. The drawings show how the ruin has been tactfully altered so as to offer a spectacle of the eternal struggle between nature and human shaping (*FA*, 8, 536 / Trans., 267). When the drawings are displayed in the garden room of the palace, they will prompt the spectator to want to leave behind its horticultural formality so as to be able directly to enjoy what we have been told is the artfully constructed representation of opposing forces (*FA*, 8, 537 / Trans., 267). However, it transpires, when the princess herself is thus prompted to ride out to the ruin, that the work depicted in the drawings has yet to be completed (*FA*, 8, 537 / Trans., 268). The uplifting and immersive effect of the draftsman's art, like the telescope, prompts an inappropriate reaction because it shows us something not (yet) grounded in reality.

Having presented the flawed perceptions encouraged by technological and aesthetic mediation, the narrative turns to a further mediating social practice. The market square seems to offer the princess a more reliable microcosm of the world over which the prince presides (*FA*, 8, 537 / Trans., 268). As a focusing institution, the market, like the telescope, brings to light that which we would not otherwise see. Moreover, within the narrative itself, its juxtaposition with visual technology and the aesthetics of architectural preservation suggests by association how the technologically, aesthetically, and economically assisted forms of observation are alike all based on complex forms of social interaction: the market draws attention to the social practices also underpinning scientific and artistic representations of the world. At the same time, the market itself turns out to be a place of images. It is overlaid by memories of a fire the uncle has previously had the misfortune to experience (*FA*, 8, 538 / Trans., 268). Moreover, the market itself peddles in images. When they see the princess, the people there feel a special "satisfaction," or *Behagen*, at the way she unites power and beauty: an aesthetic confirmation of social hierarchy (*FA*, 8, 539 / Trans., 269). On the edge of the market there is a building for the display of wild animals, but we do not directly see the creatures themselves. We hear the deafening roar of a lion, which the princess and her entourage call "der König der Einöde" (king of the wilderness, *FA*, 8, 539 / Trans., 269), and we have a brief description of the huge, bright paintings outside the building: "Der grimmig ungeheure Tiger sprang auf einen Mohren los, im Begriff ihn zu zerreißen; ein Löwe stand ernsthaft majestätisch, als wenn er keine Beute seiner würdig vor sich sähe" (A tremendous, fierce tiger attacked a Negro, and was about to tear him to pieces; a lion stood in solemn majesty, as if he could find no prey worthy of him, *FA*, 8, 539–40 / Trans., 269). The animals are present only at one remove, as auditory and visual images of themselves.

This very scene is discussed at the end of Goethe and Eckermann's first conversation on world literature on January 3, 1827. While revising the text, Goethe has decided to add the lion's roar and "einige gute Reflexionen über die Furchtbarkeit dieses gewaltigen Tieres" (some good remarks on the formidable nature of this mighty beast, *FA*, 39, 227).[49] The effect of this late emendation is not only to reinforce the degree to which the animals, when they appear later in the tale, are grasped by the characters in terms borrowed from their experiences at the market stall. The roar can equally activate the reader's physical reactions to the animal, once again mobilizing the sensory-motor responses to encourage our participation in the forms of misguided representation that the novella simultaneously subjects to narrative critique.

Following on from this comment on his own process of revision and rewriting, the conversation finishes with an observation on Scott's, in Goethe's view, unsuccessful reworking of the figure of Mignon in his *Peveril of the Peak* (*FA*, 39, 228).[50] The observation might read like a non sequitur, given that Goethe has, up to this point, been discussing his revisions of his own text. However, the comment can be read in relation to Goethe's own rewriting of his *Novelle*. The final statement on what counts as a good adaptation can then be applied to Goethe's refinement of the motif of the wild animal: "Diese Art zu ändern und zu bessern, sagte Goethe, ist nun die rechte, wo man ein noch Unvollkommenes durch fortgesetzte Erfindungen zum Vollendeten steigert" (This mode of altering and improving, said Goethe, where by continued invention the imperfect is heightened to the perfect, is the right one, *FA*, 39, 227–28).[51]

The text that Goethe is at this point adapting is, as we have seen, Cooper's *The Pioneers*. Goethe thus suggests that the *Novelle* takes up an as yet incomplete motif from Cooper's novel and completes it. In what does this completion consist? The natural environment in Cooper's novel can be unpredictably hostile. A tree falls unexpectedly in the forest, almost killing two characters (*Pioneers*, 239–40). The panther straying near settled territory is another such threatening event. The family mastiff fights the panther: "But age, and his pampered life, greatly disqualified the noble mastiff for such a struggle" (*Pioneers*, 308). The dog is killed, as would Elizabeth Temple have been if not for the fortunate intervention of the hunter, Natty Bumppo. The American landscape before the advent of human settlement is thus, in the novel, unspoiled but also ferocious. Nevertheless, the panther briefly hesitates when directly confronted with Elizabeth, for: "There is said to be something in the front of the image of the Maker that daunts the hearts of the inferior being of his creation" (*Pioneers*, 308).

With the falling tree and the panther, Cooper's narrator aspires directly to present the naturalness of nature. In Goethe's text, by contrast, the ferocity of nature is acknowledged as itself an image cultivated by humans. Indeed, the reader is directly shown how the reactions of the princess and even more so of the equerry Honorio, primed by the images of the market stall, provoke the tiger out of its more usual passivity (*FA*, 8, 544 / Trans., 272). Similarly, Cooper's topos of an animal hesitating before a human being made in the image of God is taken up and reworked in the rhapsodic statement by the bereaved father about the taming of wild animals (*FA*, 8, 550 / Trans., 277). Thus, where Cooper's text mobilizes a particular version of the natural environment to stage its drama of conflicting rights and attitudes to the American landscape, Goethe self-consciously juxtaposes images, all of which are presented as images, even those that overturn the projections and misconceptions first imposed on the tiger. The very ruined castle in which the lion is tamed by the boy's music is described as a theatrical arena (*FA*, 8, 553–54 / Trans., 279), and the mother has to be forcibly restrained from applauding when the boy is successful (*FA*, 8, 555 / Trans., 280).

Goethe completes the motif of the wild animal from *The Pioneers* by framing it *as* a motif. A similar transformation is evident in the treatment of the topos of the calming effects of music that Goethe adapts from *The Last of the Mohicans*. In Cooper's novel, the character David Gamut believes that his psalmody might calm the frenzy of a massacre (*Mohicans*, 177), and we do see that his singing has a beneficial emotional effect other characters (*Mohicans*, 59, 84). Nevertheless, his singing protects him on the battlefield only because the Native Americans are astonished by it (*Mohicans*, 177). On the occasion when his psalms seem most effective, causing a bear to repeat "in a sort of low growl, sounds, if not words, which bore some slight resemblance to the melody of the singer" (*Mohicans*, 254), the effect is comically overturned when we learn that the animal is in fact the hunter, Natty Bumppo, in disguise. Nevertheless, at the final funeral, the incantations of the Native American women and the psalmody of David Gamut cross cultural barriers, each being moved by the clear emotional expression of a song whose words they cannot understand (*Mohicans*, 344–46).[52]

Music, in Cooper's novel, establishes communication between cultures. In Goethe's novel, the self-consciously painterly vision of the boy sitting in the ruin bathed in the evening sun "wie verklärt" (as if transfigured, *FA*, 8, 554 / Trans., 279) and singing his calming song with the lion's paw resting in his lap presents the topos as topos. At the same time, as we have seen, Goethe writes in such a way that his text potentially prompts bodily reactions in its readers: straining with the leashed dogs, waving mistakenly with the princess, or indeed, feeling the heavy paw resting on our leg (*FA*, 8, 554 / Trans., 280). The self-conscious reflection on images in the text is not meant to prevent the text from having a bodily effect altogether. Rather, it might provoke in us a particular sort of response to our own labile somatic reactions to the textual cues; a response to our responsiveness. Goethe explicitly reflected on how an audience might react to their own bodily reactions to a work of art in the brief discussion of Aristotle's *Poetics* that he included in the volume of *Über Kunst und Altertum* that also contained his first published discussion of world literature (*FA*, 22, 335–38). The text on Aristotle might justly be called the first poetics of world literature, reflecting as it does on what Elleke Boehmer called the "rhetoric of address" of a work of art. Having reread Aristotle's *Poetics* in 1826 (*FA*, 22, 1158), Goethe undertook a revision of the idea of "aesthetic catharsis," suggesting that the term refers first and foremost to the resolution of aesthetic tensions in the work of art rather than to the purging of audience emotions of fear and pity. If the writer has done what needs to be done, the resolution of aesthetic tensions will transport the audience predictably with the arc of the narrative. The viewer will return home as they left it before the performance. But if they are of an ascetic and attentive disposition they might be prompted to reflect on this very tendency to be moved by the developing arc of the work of art (*FA*, 22, 338).

In Goethe's view, the embodied responses prompted by works of art are not a vehicle for better understanding others (as incantations are in Cooper's novel). Goethe is too aware of the projections and misperceptions that can inform and distort our involuntary reactions (as with imagining a response in what we see through the telescope; or the responses to the fire and the tiger). Instead, he involves us in reactions in the hope that they might prompt a reflection on our very reactivity after the fact. This requires a reader who is "ascetisch aufmerksam genug" (sufficiently ascetic and attentive, *FA*, 22, 338)—that is to say, who cultivates habits of reflection and self-scrutiny. Meanwhile, Goethe's skill as the specialist craftsman of narrative perspective can foster, though not force, this reflection by the way he draws attention to the factors shaping and limiting perception, even as he simultaneously encourages an embodied resonance with the very perspectives called in question.

Goethe's critique of the shift of viewpoint in *Ivanhoe* now makes sense, for his technique requires readerly immersion, the better to prepare for post hoc reflection. This retrospective analysis can be supported in two ways: by a further aspect of the text's form, and by the practices associated with a particular kind of reading. The further formal device, in addition to the self-conscious management of perspective, is the structure of the ending. When Eckermann first finished reading the *Novelle* on January 18, 1827, he was dissatisfied: the ending was too idealizing, too lyrical, and did not sufficiently tie up the threads (*FA*, 39, 208). Goethe explains that much of the subsequent action that we can imagine is already in train and does not need to be made explicit. Moreover, the ending is meant to be a surprising intensification, like the flower that emerges from the roots and stem of a plant (*FA*, 39, 209). The careful depiction of locality with which the novella begins gives way to the unexpectedly idealizing ending (*FA*, 39, 210–11). A further discussion of the *Novelle* on January 29, 1827 includes a brief comment on the ending of another work, the translation of a Serbian poem, which captures what Goethe thinks an ending can achieve. Eckermann is once again dissatisfied with how the poem finishes. "'Das ist,' sagte Goethe, 'eben das Schöne; denn dadurch läßt es einen Stachel im Herzen zurück und die Phantasie des Lesers ist angeregt, sich selbst alle Möglichkeiten auszubilden, die nun folgen können'" ("That," said Goethe, "is the beauty of it; for thus it leaves a sting in the heart, and the imagination of the reader is excited to devise every possible case to follow," *FA*, 39, 221).[53] The ending of a work is formally closed but emotionally open, prompting engagement, which, in the reader with an appropriately ascetic and reflective disposition, will include engagement with the very emotionality of readerly responses.

Goethe is aware that readers left to their own devices won't necessarily achieve this level of reflection (*FA*, 22, 866). As we've already seen in the aphorisms in the *Wanderjahre*, Goethe in any case doubts whether contemplation can lead to self-knowledge (*FA*, 10, 557).[54] Moreover, the vanity with which some riders at the start of the *Novelle* spur their horses in the mist shows Goethe ironically reflecting on a deluded sense of agency and importance. These obstacles to self-knowledge explain Goethe's interest in the reading practices of a shared debate. As we saw in the comments on the *Tasso* plays, being right isn't itself the issue. The very process of transnational conversation itself offers opportunities for recalibration and correction (*FA*, 22, 356–57; *FA*, 39, 257). To the literary techniques of somatically immersing readers in perspectives that are simultaneously questioned, and an ending that acts as an emotional prompt or "Stachel im Herzen" (sting in the heart, *FA* 39, 221), Goethe adds what Martin Puchner has termed the ongoing, future-oriented practice of world literary debate: the permanent process of constituting and nurturing a community.[55] Goethe's model of world literature thus works with productive tensions. His conception of humanity combines underlying communalities with the diverging local practices through which they are disclosed. His understanding of the literary practice insists both on the specialist expertise of authors themselves, honing their techniques to prompt reflections on perspectivity while simultaneously looking beyond individual effort, and individual self-knowledge to a wider dialogue that the awareness of perspectives can help us participate in more fully. These cultural practices don't replace the patient, academic study of forms of difference. But the successful individual work that prompts us to take part in the shared reflective process grants us thereby an intuition of the wider global exchange in which we participate. If there is a metaphysical assumption underpinning Goethe's model of world literature, it is the conviction that the specialist labor, both of writing and of reading well, can connect to the wider whole: to intuitions of completeness, such as that granted to the mandarin contemplating the last rose in the Chinese-German garden. The aspiration to this special kind of knowledge is grounded in Goethe's reading of Spinoza's *Ethics* and the higher knowledge termed *scientia intuitiva*: a direct intimation of the deep structures of the world.[56] But the pursuit of this deeper knowledge is accompanied by the ironic awareness of the fallibility of human endeavors. Accordingly, as we have seen, the speaker in the *Chinese-German* cycle chases readers back to direct engagement with the specific details of their own environment (*FA*, 2, 699).

Conclusions: World Literature as Distributed Practice

Goethe's *Novelle* can be read as an example of world literature in practice. Reading it in the context of his developing thoughts on the new global literary culture, we can see how the text reflects Goethe's expert engagement with questions of literary form. He evinces a special interest in the management of narrative perspective, and in ways of generating openness, in manner that is at once aesthetically coherent and emotionally resonant. We have seen how recent work on the somatic aspects of readers' responses helps to explain the immersive effect of Goethe's literary devices. At the same time, Goethe's text contributes to debates about the moral effects of such literary bodily attunement. Naomi Rokotnitz has studied how our involuntary bodily reactions, such as disgust, can be mobilized in ways of which, were we conscious of the manipulation, we would disapprove.[57] Bodily attunement is not a good in its own right.[58] Goethe develops literary techniques that immerse us while helping us reflect on our propensity to immersion, assisted by the ongoing, multiperspectival conversation that constitutes global literary debate. The endpoint will not be an overcoming of our bodily involvement. *Wilhelm Meisters Lehrjahre* (1795–96) showed how a full, embodied life, even where it entails mistakes and forms of self-deception, is nevertheless an integral part of psychological and spiritual growth.[59] Goethe's work of the 1820s is no less committed to our embodied existence. But in his specialist attention to forms of literary immersion, he develops a passionate reflection on our inevitable involvedness, which takes us beyond ourselves by allowing us to discover that our relation to the world was always mediated in the first place by our relations with others, and by our activity: "Sage mir, mit dem du umgehst, so sage ich dir, wer du bist; weiß ich, womit du dich beschäftigst, so weiß ich, was aus dir werden kann" (Tell me with whom you associate, and I will tell you who you are. Once I know with what you occupy yourself, I know what you can become, *FA*, 10, 560).[60]

This heightening and questioning of perspective also distributes it beyond us: our very perspective on the world turns out not to be ours in any simple way. As a form of attunement with others, as a culturally learned habit, and as a technologically mediated way of seeing it is always more than an individual take on the world. The distributed nature of cultural involvement changes the nature of *Bildung* or spiritual growth itself. What must be fostered is not so much individuals as the wider culture in and through which development is supported. But, in Goethe's view, we will never have an overview of this wider culture. So instead we must face the particular demands of our situation (*FA*, 10, 557).[61] Moreover, since our grasp of our immediate situation will itself always be mediated, dialogue and a sense of irony will always be necessary, lest we come to take our parochial positioning too seriously. Cooper's narrator could allow himself to step back from his initial sketch of the area around Lake Otsego and make something like a general political declaration: "In short, the whole district is hourly exhibiting how much can be done, in even a rugged country, and with a severe climate, under the dominion of mild laws, and where every man feels a direct interest in the prosperity of a commonwealth of which he knows himself to form a part" (*Pioneers*, 15–16). In contrast, in Goethe's view, despite our shared, poetic humanity, the commonwealth, as commonwealth, can never be visible. As an exemplary experiment in world literature, he instead creates the self-consciously tiny principality of his *Novelle*, ironically and indirectly prompting his readers to imagine, and participate in, the wider literary world of which it is but a knowing fragment.

Notes

Uncredited translations are my own.

[1] David Damrosch, *What Is World Literature?* (Princeton, NJ: Princeton University Press, 2003), 14.

[2] Elleke Boehmer, *Postcolonial Poetics: 21st-Century Critical Readings* (Cham, Switzerland: Palgrave Macmillan, 2018), 147.

[3] Boehmer, *Postcolonial Poetics*, 10.

[4] Goethe texts will be cited using the "Frankfurter Ausgabe" published by the Deutscher Klassiker Verlag. Johann Wolfgang Goethe, *Sämtliche Werke: Briefe, Tagebücher und Gespräche*, ed. Friedmar Apel et al., 40 vols. (Frankfurt am Main: Deutscher Klassiker Verlag, 1987–2013). References will be given parenthetically in the text using the abbreviation *FA* and the volume and page numbers.

[5] Damrosch notes that Goethe "himself was writing a novella at this time [i.e., January 31, 1827] and struggling to find an appropriate ending." Damrosch, *What Is World Literature?*, 11. However, he doesn't explore further the fact that the novella was written in parallel with Goethe's developing thoughts on world literature.

[6] For an exemplary overview of Goethe's writings on, and practices in relation to, world literature in the 1820s, see Hendrik Birus's account, which lays particular stress on the role that the work on the 1827 volumes of *Über Kunst und Alterthum* had for the development of Goethe's ideas. Hendrik Birus, "Goethes Idee der Weltliteratur: Eine historische Vergegenwärtigung," in *Weltliteratur Heute: Konzepte und Perspektiven*, ed. Manfred Schmeling (Würzburg: Königshausen & Neumann, 1995), 5–28; and Birus, "Goethes Zeitschrift 'Ueber Kunst und Alterthum' als Kontext seiner Idee der Weltliteratur," *Goethe-Jahrbuch* 134 (2017): 90–98.

[7] The idea of "kinesic intelligence" was first formulated in a discussion of painting in Ellen Spolsky, "Iconotropism, or Representational Hunger: Raphael and Titian," in *Iconotropism, or Turning toward Pictures*, ed. Ellen Spolsky (Lewisburg, PA: Bucknell University Press, 2004), 23–36. The notion has been taken up and extensively applied to literature in Guillemette Bolens, *The Style of Gestures: Embodiment and Cognition in Literary Narrative* (Baltimore, MD: Johns Hopkins University Press, 2012); and Terence Cave, *Thinking with Literature: Towards a Cognitive Criticism* (Oxford: Oxford University Press, 2016). The ethical implications of our involuntary bodily responses to literary texts have been explored in Naomi Rokotnitz, "Goosebumps, Shivers, Visualization, and Embodied Resonance in the Reading Experience: *The God of Small Things*," *Poetics Today* 38, no. 2 (2017): 273–93; and Rokotnitz, "Fairy Tales, Folk-Psychology, and Learning Intersubjective Competency through Embodied Resonance: A Contribution to Debates on Cultural Evolution, the Extended Mind, and Morality," *Journal of Literature and Science* 11, no. 2 (2018): 20–39. Elleke Boehmer herself explores the kinesic effects of poetry and other short texts: Boehmer, *Postcolonial Poetics*, 173–79. Charlotte Lee has recently explored the role of "kinaesthetic empathy" in Goethe's *Märchen* (1795). Charlotte Lee, "Cognition in Action: Goethe's *Märchen*," *Publications of the English Goethe Society* 87, no. 3 (2018): 212–30.

[8] On the early discourse of the *Bildungsroman*, see Ben Morgan, "Embodied Cognition and the Project of the Bildungsroman: *Wilhelm Meister's Apprenticeship* and *Daniel Deronda*," *Poetics Today* 38, no. 2 (2017): 341–62.

[9] The essay is, for instance, anthologized in David Damrosch, Natalie Melas, and Mbongiseni Buthelezi, eds., *The Princeton Sourcebook in Comparative Literature: From the European Enlightenment to the Global Present* (Princeton, NJ: Princeton University Press, 2009), 125–38.

[10] "The time has come to ask what meaning the phrase 'world literature' can still have if we take it, as Goethe did, to refer both to the present and to what we can expect in the future." Erich Auerbach, *Time, History and Literature: Selected Essays of Erich Auerbach*, trans. Jane O. Newman (Princeton, NJ: Princeton University Press, 2014), 253. As Emily Apter points out, Auerbach continues the Goethean project to resist what he understands to be the "un-Goethean" tendencies of the 1950s. Emily Apter, *Against World Literature: On the Politics of Untranslatability* (London: Verso, 2013), 195–96.

[11] Auerbach, *Time, History and Literature*, 255.

[12] Auerbach, *Time, History and Literature*, 256.

[13] Auerbach, *Time, History and Literature*, 258.

[14] Auerbach, *Time, History and Literature*, 254.

[15] Auerbach, *Time, History and Literature*, 261.

[16] Auerbach, *Time, History and Literature*, 260.

[17] Walter Benjamin, *Selected Writings*, ed. Michael W. Jennings (Cambridge, MA: Harvard University Press, 1996–2003), vol. 2.1, 207–21. Confirming the closeness of the two men's thinking, Benjamin quotes Auerbach's study of Dante, 210.

[18] Auerbach, *Time, History and Literature*, 263.

[19] Damrosch, *What Is World Literature?*, 6.

[20] Auerbach, *Time, History and Literature*, 264.

[21] Edward Said, "Erich Auerbach, Critic of the Earthly World," *boundary 2* 31, no. 2 (2004): 11–35, here 18.

[22] Friedrich Nietzsche, *Zur Genealogie der Moral*, ed. Giorgio Colli and Mazzino Montinari, vol. 5, *Kritische Studienausgabe* (Munich: Deutscher Taschenbuch Verlag, 1988), 365 [III.12]. R. Lanier Anderson claims that Nietzsche can avoid appealing to "aperspectival criteria," in R. Lanier Anderson, "Truth and Objectivity in Perspectivism," *Synthese* 115 (1998): 1–32.

[23] Alexander Nehamas, *Nietzsche: Life as Literature* (Cambridge, MA: Harvard University Press, 1985).

[24] Auerbach, *Time, History and Literature*, 60.

[25] Damrosch, *What Is World Literature?*, 8. For a defence of Goethe's intercultural project, see Fawzi Boubia, "Universal Literature and Otherness," *Diogenes* 36 (1988): 76–101.

[26] Georg Lukács, *The Historical Novel*, trans. Hannah Mitchell and Stanley Mitchell (London: Merlin Press, 1962), 66.

[27] In using the term *Weltliteratur*, Goethe was preceded by his contemporary Christoph Martin Wieland in the early 1810s, and before that by the little-known German literary historian August Ludwig Schlözer, writing on Icelandic literature in 1773. Hans J. Weitz, "Weltliteratur zuerst bei Wieland," *Arcadia* 22, no. 2 (1987): 206–8. Wolfgang Schamoni, "'Weltliteratur'—Zuerst 1773 bei August Ludwig Schlözer," *Arcadia* 43 (2008): 288–98. Peter Goßens, *Weltliteratur: Modelle Transnationaler Literaturwahrnehmung im 19. Jahrhundert* (Stuttgart: J. B. Metzler, 2011), 83–86.

[28] Translation: Hans-Joachim Schulz and Phillip H. Rhein, eds., *Comparative Literature: The Early Years* (Chapel Hill: University of North Carolina Press, 1973), 5.

[29] Homi Bhabha, *The Location of Culture* (London: Routledge, 1994), 12.

[30] Auerbach, *Time, History and Literature*, 264. For a clear account of the difference-respecting versus the universalist aspects of Goethe's model of *Weltliteratur*, see John Pizer, "Cosmopolitanism and Weltliteratur," *Goethe Yearbook* 13 (2005): 165–79.

[31] Peter Perring Thoms, *Chinese Courtship: In Verse* (London: Parbury, Allen and Kingsbury, 1824).

[32] For Goethe's awareness of the practical infrastructure that supports the project of world literature, see Birus, "Goethes Idee der Weltliteratur," 5–28.

[33] Thoms, *Chinese Courtship*, 249–80.

[34] Thoms, *Chinese Courtship*, 263.

[35] "Rather than just disappearing into a simulated China, the late Goethe incorporates the few Chinese motifs familiar to Europeans into his own voice." Daniel Purdy, "Goethe, Rémusat, and the Chinese Novel: Translation and the Circulation of World Literature," in *German Literature as World Literature*, ed. Thomas Oliver Beebee (London: Bloomsbury, 2014), 43–60, here 46.

[36] Translation: Johann Wolfgang Goethe, *Goethe's Collected Works*, vol. 10, *Conversations of German Refugees; Wilhelm Meister's Journeyman Years, or the Renunciants*, ed. Victor Lange, Eric Blackall, and Cyrus Hamlin, trans. Jan van Heurck, Jane K. Brown, and Krishna Winston (Princeton, NJ: Princeton University Press, 1989), 294.

[37] For a fuller discussion of Goethe's response to the Chinese novel, see Purdy, "Goethe, Rémusat, and the Chinese Novel," 43–46, 56–60.

[38] James Fenimore Cooper, *The Pioneers* (London: Penguin, 1988), 307. Further references will be given parenthetically in the text.

[39] Walter Scott, *Ivanhoe* (Oxford: Oxford University Press, 1996), 63–64.

[40] Goethe prefigures in practice Adorno's theory of the different demands made by the aesthetic material to each generation of artists. Theodor W. Adorno, *Ästhetische Theorie* (Frankfurt am Main: Suhrkamp, 1973), 248–50. For a brief critique of Adorno's position, see Andrew Bowie, *Adorno and the Ends of Philosophy* (Cambridge, UK: Polity Press, 2013), 138.

[41] A topic for a future article. For the novel's relation to America, see Nicholas Saul, "Goethe and Colonisation: The *Wanderjahre* and Cooper," in *Goethe and*

the English-Speaking World: Essays from the Cambridge Symposium for His 250th Anniversary, ed. Nicholas Boyle and John Guthrie (Rochester, NY: Camden House, 2002), 85–98. In Andrew Piper's reading of the *Wanderjahre*, the specific issue that Goethe confronts is a problematization of the very medium in which the work was published, namely, that of the definitive complete works: "When taken together, Goethe's uses of print, publication, and narrative, far from establishing and solidifying the regulatory system that was emerging in the nineteenth century, in fact strongly resisted this program. The values of personality, sovereignty, nationality, totality, and permanence that suffused the Weimar edition and that were at the heart of literature's classificatory system in the nineteenth century were, in Goethe's own collected edition, distinctly posited as problem." Andrew Piper, "Rethinking the Print Object: Goethe and the Book of Everything," *PMLA* 121, no. 1 (2006): 124–39, here 27. For John K. Noyes, the problem the novel confronts is that of the necessary fragility of narrative representations of a shared world, if they are not to degenerate into forms of ideological deception. John K. Noyes, "Writing the Dialectical Structure of the Modern Subject: Goethe on World Literature and World Citizenship," *Seminar: A Journal of Germanic Studies* 51, no. 2 (2015): 100–114.

[42] James Fenimore Cooper, *The Last of the Mohicans* (London: Penguin, 1986). Further references will be given parenthetically in the text.

[43] Translation: Johann Wolfgang Goethe, *Goethe's Collected Works*, vol. 11, *The Sorrows of Young Werther, Elective Affinities, Novella*, ed. Victor Lange, Eric Blackall, and Cyrus Hamlin, trans. Victor Lange and Judith Ryan (Princeton, NJ: Princeton University Press, 1988), 280. Further references to this translation will be given parenthetically in the text using the abbreviation "Trans."

[44] Andrew Piper, "Paraphrasis: Goethe, the Novella, and Forms of Translational Knowledge," *Goethe Yearbook* 17 (2010): 179–201, here 197.

[45] Rosemary Picozzi Balfour, "The Field of View in Goethe's *Novelle*," *Seminar: A Journal of Germanic Studies* 12, no. 2 (1976): 63–72; and Reinhard Heinritz, "Teleskop und Erzählperspektive," *Poetica: Zeitschrift für Sprach- und Literaturwissenschaft* 24, nos. 3–4 (1992): 341–55.

[46] For a recent review of embodied responses to literary style, see Arthur M. Jacobs and Roel M. Willems, "The Fictive Brain: Neurocognitive Correlates of Engagement in Literature," *Review of General Psychology* 22, no. 2 (2018): 147–60.

[47] Goethe, *Conversations of German Refugees*, 301.

[48] On Goethe's treatment of the telescope in the 1820s, see Heinritz, "Teleskop und Erzählperspektive," 342–45.

[49] Translation: Damrosch, Melas, and Buthelezi, *Princeton Sourcebook in Comparative Literature*, 24.

[50] For a more positive discussion of Scott's character Fenella, and what she reveals about the prehistory of the figure of Mignon, see Terence Cave, *Mignon's Afterlives: Crossing Cultures from Goethe to the Twenty-First Century* (Oxford: Oxford University Press, 2011), 128–34.

[51] Damrosch, Melas, and Buthelezi, *Princeton Sourcebook in Comparative Literature*, 25.

[52] In Jane K. Brown's discussion of the reworking of David Gamut in the *Novelle* the effect is only one way: Gamut responding to the Native American mourning. Jane K. Brown, "The Tyranny of the Ideal: The Dialectics of Art in Goethe's 'Novelle,'" *Studies in Romanticism* 19, no. 2 (1980): 217–31, here 229–30.

[53] Damrosch, Melas, and Buthelezi, *Princeton Sourcebook in Comparative Literature*, 20.

[54] Goethe, *Conversations of German Refugees*, 294.

[55] On the future-oriented aspect of world literature, as it is conceived by Goethe, see Martin Puchner, "Goethe, Marx, Ibsen and the Creation of World Literature," *Ibsen Studies* 13, no. 1 (2013): 28–46, here 28.

[56] Benedict de Spinoza, *Ethics Proved in Geometrical Order*, ed. Matthew Kisner, trans. Michael Silverthorne and Matthew Kisner (Cambridge: Cambridge University Press, 2018), 78. See also Eckart Förster, "Goethe's Spinozism" in *Spinoza and German Idealism*, ed. Eckart Förster and Yitzhak Y. Melamed (Cambridge: Cambridge University Press, 2012), 85–99.

[57] Naomi Rokotnitz, "'Too Far Gone in Disgust': Mirror Neurons and the Manipulation of Embodied Responses in the Libertine," *Configurations* 16, no. 3 (2008): 399–426.

[58] Paul Bloom, *Against Empathy: The Case for Rational Compassion* (London: Penguin, 2016).

[59] Morgan, "Embodied Cognition and the Project of the Bildungsroman," 353.

[60] Goethe, *Conversations of German Refugees*, 296.

[61] Goethe, *Conversations of German Refugees*, 294.

3: *Weltdeutschtum*: On the Notion of a German World Community from Schiller to Thomas Mann

Tobias Boes

ONE OF THE MOST influential academic hypotheses regarding the relationship between Germany and the world is put forth in the introduction of Edward Said's *Orientalism* (1978). There, Said draws a distinction between nineteenth-century German scholarship of the Orient on the one hand, and French and British attitudes towards the region on the other. Whereas France and Britain pursued active imperial interests in the Middle East—playing a "great game" of sorts that culminated in the Sykes-Picot Agreement of 1916—Germany, lacking similar investments, took a much more abstract view of the region: "There was nothing in Germany to correspond to the Anglo-French presence in India, the Levant, North Africa. Moreover, the German Orient was almost exclusively a scholarly, or at least a classical, Orient: it was made the subject of lyrics, fantasies, and even novels, but it was never actual."[1]

Said's distinction was carefully delimited both temporally and geographically: he never meant it to apply outside of the nineteenth century or to areas other than the Middle East. But because *Orientalism* became the de facto founding text of postcolonial studies, and postcolonial studies, in turn, was for several decades the dominant humanistic paradigm for discussing relations between Europe and the rest of the world, the idea that Germany's interest in the world was primarily academic or belletristic rather than strategic or power-political took unexpected roots. Only over the last fifteen years or so have scholars begun a concerted pushback, focusing both on the destructive consequences of German colonialism (such as the brutal suppression of the Boxer uprising in 1900–1901, or the Herero and Nama genocides of 1904–1907), and on the inadequacies of Said's hypothesis itself.[2] These efforts have, in turn, led to more vigorous discussions of Germany's colonial past within the public sphere.[3]

This chapter is inspired by such corrective measures, but nevertheless departs in a different direction. For, as it turns out, the thesis that Germans relate to the world in a fundamentally different way than the

Western European powers (i.e., through cultural rather than military means) is by no means original to Said. It can be found in many canonical German literary and academic texts from the period between 1800 and 1945 as well. And while it was indeed frequently employed to whitewash imperialist agendas and chauvinistic forms of cultural nationalism, it also opened the door to a much more progressive and imaginative conception of Germany's place in the world at large.

In 1945, Thomas Mann, nominally addressing himself to an American audience at the Library of Congress but actually speaking to his compatriots in defeated Germany, referred to this imaginative conception as *Weltdeutschtum* (world Germanism).[4] Reduced to the simplest possible terms, *Weltdeutschtum* for Mann referred to a form of national identity that is detached from any territorial basis and defined instead through the free flow of ideas in a global cultural system. It was a provocative claim in 1945, at a time when Germany seemed culturally reduced to a state of mere vassalage to the Allied Powers. And it is a claim that has lost nothing of its provocative force even seventy years later, amidst a global order defined by neoliberal economic exchange rather than by Cold War power politics.

Schiller and "German Greatness"

As Dieter Borchmeyer has pointed out, the starting point for the conceptual lineage that eventually leads to Mann and the notion of *Weltdeutschtum* lies within Weimar classicism, and specifically with Friedrich Schiller's fragmentary poem "Deutsche Größe" (German Greatness) which is frequently, but not universally, dated to 1801.[5] The chronology matters, for February 9, 1801 was the day on which France and the Holy Roman Empire signed the Treaty of Lunéville, which put an end to the War of the Second Coalition and compelled the empire to cede all of its territories west of the Rhine (inhabited by almost four million people, or roughly one-seventh of its entire population) to the French. Whether or not "Deutsche Größe" was written in 1801 or, as some bibliographers believe, in 1797, is thus also a question about whether Schiller was trying to rally a spiritual nation amidst times of political and territorial humiliation.[6]

The most frequently quoted lines from Schiller's poem read as follows:

> Das ist nicht des Deutschen Größe
> Obzusiegen mit dem Schwert,
> In das Geisterreich zu dringen
> Vorurteile zu besiegen
> Männlich mit dem Wahn zu kriegen

Das ist seines Eifers wert.

[It is not German greatness
to conquer with the sword.
To penetrate the realm of spirit,
to vanquish prejudices,
to battle valiantly with delusions
is worthy of the German's zeal.]

After a few lines in praise of the Reformation, Schiller continues:

Deutschlands Majestät und Ehre
Ruhet nicht auf dem Haupt seiner Fürsten.
Stürzte auch in Kriegesflammen
Deutschlands Kaiserreich zusammen,
Deutsche Größe bleibt bestehen.

[Germany's majesty and honor
do not rest on the heads of its princes.
Even if Germany's empire
should collapse amidst the flames of war,
German greatness will remain.]

This claim to a spiritual greatness that triumphs over mere political majesty is then explicitly contrasted with the supposed British attitude, for which cultural glory is always only a side effect of material gain, and specifically of imperial spoliation:

Mag der Brite die Gebeine
Alter Kunst, die edeln Steine
Und ein ganzes Herkulan
Gierig nach dem Kostbarn greifen
Und auf seiner Insel häufen
Was ein Schiff nur laden kann.
----
zum Leben
Nimmer werden sie leben, immer fremd und
verbannt bleiben, sie werden nie auferstehn.[7]

The Briton may greedily grasp
the bones of old art, noble gems,
and a whole Herculaneum,
heaping on his island
whatever treasures a ship may carry.

To life

Never will they live again, always remain
strange and banished; they will never rise again.

In a fateful coincidence, Schiller's fragment was not rediscovered until 1871, the founding year of the Second German Empire. It was quickly appropriated as a touchstone of chauvinistic nationalist rhetoric, and for a few decades exerted an outsized and deforming influence on the public reception of the poet. The bestselling author Emil Palleske, for example, completely rewrote the preface to his popular book *Schillers Leben und Werke* (Schiller's Life and Works) in 1879 in order to make the fragment the central focus, and the public commemorations on the centenary of the poet's death in 1905 were dominated by discussions of "Deutsche Größe" as well.[8]

Two characteristics of Schiller's fragment (and of the tradition that it spawned) are especially worth emphasizing in the present context. The first is that it draws a clear division between Germany as a cultural entity and Germany as a political construct, reserving the titular "greatness" for the former. "Abgesondert von / dem politischen hat der Deutsche sich / einen eigenen Werth gegründet" (Separate from politics / we Germans have created / a different kind of value), Schiller proclaims at a different part of the poem. The second is that culture is here conceived as a noumenal, rather than empirical, quality. German greatness, in other words, is demonstrated not through concrete manifestations of formal or technical excellence, but rather by claims upon such spiritual values as "Würde" (dignity) or "sittliche Größe" (moral accomplishment).

For Schiller, German greatness is still quite overtly tied to the history and the language of a specific people and a specific region. Only in central Europe can "deutscher Geschmack" (German taste) prosper, for only here has the population remained free of the corrupting tyranny of large cities (Schiller explicitly names Paris and London) and of courtly life. Nevertheless, Schiller's equation of culture with the realm of the noumenal creates the at least theoretical possibility that German greatness might arise *anywhere* and be produced by *anyone*, regardless of ancestry, biological makeup or, indeed, even language.

Empire, Nation, and the Concept of "German Freedom"

The notion of German *character* as an abstract, spiritual value was also pursued by a number of Schiller's contemporaries, for example by the poet Novalis in the essay *Die Christenheit oder Europa* (Christiandom or Europe, 1799). Nobody, however, went further in this regard than Johann Gottlieb Fichte in his *Reden an die deutsche Nation* (Addresses to the German Nation, 1807). Fichte, too, distinguishes between spiritual and political dimensions of German identity, or between what he calls (employing a conceptual division that has since become commonplace but was then still unsettled) the "nation" and the "state." And he clearly favors the former over the latter, arguing that the state should act foremost as a "Pflanzschule" (nursery) to the nation—that is, as a pedagogical institution in which the *Bildung* (self-formation) of the nation towards ever greater freedom might be actualized.[9] For Fichte, furthermore, freedom is a fundamentally German quality, a somewhat surprising judgment given that it was uttered less than twenty years after the French Revolution. He defends his verdict in terms very similar to those used by Schiller, when he appeals first to the Reformation, which freed religion from a hierarchical church, and second to contemporary Idealist philosophy, which was discovering the true sources of wisdom within the confines of the mind rather than in the Bible.[10] For Fichte, clearly, *Deutsche Freiheit* (German freedom) is what Isaiah Berlin would have called a "positive" rather than "negative" liberty: not primarily a freedom *from* oppression or interference, but rather a freedom *towards* self-realization.[11] At the same time—and this is where the real difference between Fichte's philosophy and Jacobinism lies—it is a fundamentally spiritual, rather than political, quality: *Deutsche Freiheit* is entirely compatible with monarchical governance, as long as the monarchy does not deprive the individuals of any room for self-cultivation.

It is precisely amidst the chauvinist rhetoric of *Addresses to the German Nation* that we find Fichte make the surprising assertion that any person anywhere in the world who devotes himself to the causes of freedom and progress belongs to the German "lineage," regardless of actual nationality: "Was an Geistigkeit, und Freiheit dieser Geistigkeit glaubt, und die ewige Fortbildung dieser Geistigkeit durch Freiheit will, das, wo es auch geboren sei, und in welcher Sprache es rede, ist unsers Geschlechts, es gehört uns an und es wird sich zu uns tun" (Those who believe in spirituality and in the freedom of this spirituality, who desire the eternal progress of this spirituality through freedom—wherever they were born and whichever language they speak—are of our race, they belong to us and they will join with us).[12] In uttering these words, Fichte not only shows his debt to the universalist spirit of the eighteenth-century Enlightenment but also makes a claim to a communal affiliation that fits only uneasily into our contemporary conceptual binary of nationalism and cosmopolitanism.

Nationalism, in most accounts, refers to a form of belonging to which one accedes through nativity rather than voluntarism: through ancestry, place of birth, mother tongue, and the like. By contrast, cosmopolitanism normally refers to a form of belonging that is voluntarily chosen and sustainable only by means of conditioning processes. In other words, cosmopolitans place great emphasis on markers of identity that are consciously acquired, such as specific tastes in dress, food, etc., while they deemphasize markers of nativity, such as complexion or native dialect. Hence also the frequently voiced complaint that nationalism is wholesome and organic, while cosmopolitanism is artificial and mechanic. Fichte's claim, however, combines features from both poles of this conceptual binary. It defines the German nation as an organic community, characterized by its formative struggle towards constantly increasing freedom. Yet this same community is also global in scope and may be joined through voluntary action.

The opposition that we find in both Schiller and Fichte between a valorized realm of culture on the one hand, and of politics on the other, would resurface at later points in the nineteenth century. So did their attempt to expand the reach of German culture beyond the confines of existing state structures. Dieter Borchmeyer refers in this context to the infamous closing lines of Richard Wagner's 1868 opera *Die Meistersinger von Nürnberg* (The Mastersingers of Nuremberg).[13] Sung first by the character of Hans Sachs, and then repeated by the people, these lines read:

> Ehrt eure deutschen Meister,
> dann bannt ihr gute Geister!
> Und gebt ihr ihrem Wirken Gunst,
> zerging' in Dunst
> das heil'ge röm'sche Reich,
> uns bliebe gleich die heil'ge deutsche Kunst!
>
> [Honour your German Masters,
> Then you will conjure up good spirits!
> And if you favour their endeavours,
> even if the Holy Roman Empire
> should dissolve in mist,
> for us there would yet remain holy German Art!][14]

Culture here is quite literally spiritualized when the Mastersingers, the archetypally German producers of "heil'ge Kunst" (holy art), are compared to benevolent jinns. By contrast, the political structures of the Holy Roman Empire are equated with mere "Dunst" (mist): a metaphor not only of immateriality but also of inconsequentiality.

According to Borchmeyer, these concluding lines can only be fully understood if we remember that the action of *Die Meistersinger von Nürnberg* takes place during the reign of Maximilian I, who governed as Holy Roman Emperor from 1508 to 1519. In light of this information, Sachs's vague exhortations about the possible dissolution of the empire may be read as a reference not just to 1806, when it actually *did* come to an end, but also to the reign of Charles V, who succeeded Maximilian as emperor. For in nineteenth-century German nationalist rhetoric, Charles

V was frequently denigrated as a "Spanish" ruler, during whose reign the empire supposedly lost much of its original central European character and became, in a sense, a foreign political entity. Borchmeyer quotes Johann Gottfried Herder's bitter remark that: "Zuerst kam spanisches Ceremoniell zu uns, bald schrieben die Fürsten, Prinzen, Generale italienisch, bis seit dem Glorreichen Dreißigjährigen Kriege nach und nach fast das ganze Reich an Höfen und in den oberen Ständen eine Provinz des französischen Geschmacks ward. Hinweg war jetzt in diesen Ständen der deutsche Charakter!" (First came the arrival of Spanish pomp and circumstance, then the noblemen, princes, and generals started writing in Italian, and after the glorious Thirty Years' War, the courts and the upper classes virtually throughout the entire empire became an outpost of French tastes. German character had been eradicated among these classes!)[15]

Implicit in Herder's assumption that the upper classes "virtually throughout the entire empire" began to lose their "German character" with the ascent of Charles V to the throne, however, is the premise that such "German character" at one point stretched far beyond the boundaries of its central European home. Viewed from this perspective, then, Fichte's idea of a form of belonging that might transcend the binary opposition of nationalism and cosmopolitanism becomes recognizable as a conceptual descendent not so much of eighteenth-century universalist thought, but rather of a distinctively imperial mode of self-understanding.

Friedrich Meinecke and the Cosmopolitan Foundations of the German National State

The paradoxes that result from Germany's birth as a nation out of the ashes of the transnational Holy Roman Empire play an important role also in the thought of Friedrich Meinecke, who in 1907 published the first edition of his *Weltbürgertum und Nationalstaat* (Cosmopolitanism and the Nation-State). Meinecke was at that point of his life a conservative nationalist and admirer of Bismarck, although after the First World War he would alter his stance and become a liberal democrat (he kept adding to *Weltbürgertum und Nationalstaat* throughout these years, and later editions thus have a palimpsest-like quality). *Weltbürgertum und Nationalstaat* is, first and foremost, an attempt to rationalize the nation-state as the most logical and practical form of the modern political community; as such, it treats all claims towards cosmopolitan universalism, whether they be based in human rights, class solidarity, or religion, with great suspicion. At the same time, however, Meinecke recognizes that the historical processes that gave birth to the German nation over the course of the nineteenth century are everywhere shot through with cosmopolitan influences. To become strong, so he acknowledges, the German state needs to acknowledge this legacy without thereby succumbing to the lure of universalist norms.

Towards the beginning of his study, Meinecke explains:

> Die eigentümliche Konstellation in Deutschland war die, daß die einzigen brauchbaren Grundlagen zu einem modernen Nationalstaate nicht auf dem Boden der deutschen Nation, sondern auf dem Boden des preußischen Einzelstaates lagen, daß dieser aber die geistigen Kräfte, die er zu seiner Nationalisierung brauchte, nicht aus sich alleine schöpfen konnte, sondern aus dem weiten Bereiche der deutschen Kulturnation mit entnehmen musste.

> [The peculiar situation in Germany was that the only usable foundations for a modern national state were not available in the German nation but in the Prussian state. However, this state alone could not supply the intellectual forces that it needed for its nationalization but had to take them from the wide spectrum of the German cultural nation.][16]

At the most literal level, this passage simply acknowledges that the various Prussian administrative reforms of the nineteenth century (the so-called Stein-Hardenberg reforms), which prepared the ground for a unified German nation-state, could not have taken place without the active support of thinkers whose cultural roots were quite different from those of the East Elbian Junker class. Karl Freiherr von Stein himself, for example, hailed from the Rhenish Palatinate. Meinecke draws much more radical conclusions from his analysis, however, arguing:

> Denn da die deutsche Nationalkultur einen ausgesprochen universalen Zug hatte, so stand es nun so, daß der preußische Staat, als er sich durch die Kräfte dieser Kultur auffrischte, auch ihren übernationalen, universalen Elementen Einlaß gewährte—eine Nationalisierung also durch zum teil übernationale, universale Mittel, ein Fortschritt der Staatsbildung durch Rezeption von zum Teil höchst unpolitischen Ideen.

> [Since the German national culture had taken on a clearly universalistic character, the Prussian state also admitted these supra-national, universalistic elements when it used the impulses of this culture to renew itself. Thus, what occurred was a nationalization through partially supra-national, universalistic means, an advance in the formation of the state through the reception of ideas that were, to some extent, highly unpolitical.][17]

For Meinecke, as for many thinkers following him, the historical ground zero of the modern nation-state was the French First Republic, which succeeded in defending itself against the efforts of the First and Second Coalition by wedding a strong appeal to nationalist sentiments to a messianic cosmopolitan ideology. Admirable as this fusion may have been, however, the universalist fervor that animated it eventually collapsed into Napoleonic imperialism. The creation of a German state in the wake of the wars of liberation needs to be seen as a reaction to this development: the Prussian administrative reforms, and eventually the drive towards national unification, were first and foremost a panicked response to revolutionary universalism. The irony, however, is that this process of unification itself depended on universalist remnants of Enlightenment philosophy. The Stein-Hardenberg reforms, for example, were intimately informed by the Humboldtian notion of *Bildung*, which is universalist in scope because it holds that all organic entities strive to actualize their inborn potential. Meinecke, somewhat mean-spiritedly, attacks this infiltration of Enlightenment thought as "das Werk einer Ideologie, welche die egoistischen Grundkräfte der Politik verkannte und die europäischen Gemeinsamkeiten überschätzte" (An ideology that failed to recognize the egoism of politics and overestimated the similarities of European nations).[18]

Weltbürgertum und Nationalstaat is far more than a conservative nationalist diatribe, however. Meinecke recognizes that the conservative hardliners within the Prussian state unwittingly embraced different forms of cosmopolitan universalism in their attempts to combat liberalism and the legacy of the Enlightenment. The ostensibly Christian values of the various member states that comprised the Holy Alliance, as well as the pan-European ambitions of thinkers like Metternich, were the two most important such forms. Meinecke accuses these hardliners of having condemned Germany to the "Neutralisierung der deutschen Nationalkraft durch den deutschen Bund und die ihn freundlich-gönnerhaft umstehenden europäischen Großmächte" (Neutralization of German national strength through the German Confederation and the great European powers that surrounded it in a friendly and patronizing manner).[19]

Weltbürgertum und Nationalstaat can ultimately be read as an apologia for Bismarck, the man who in Meinecke's eyes finally rid German politics of lingering cosmopolitan delusions and focused his attention on the "egoism in politics" that we now call *realpolitik*. What makes it so valuable in the present context, however, is that it presents an empirically precise case study about how national character might be conditioned by universalist elements. It also presents this process of conditioning as a two-way street, showing that "the world" (in the guise of such entities as Napoleon or the Holy Alliance) influenced "Germanness" just as much as "Germanness" would eventually influence the world (in its export of Humboldtian thinking to America, for example).

The Lexical Invention of *Weltdeutschtum*

In a 1921 article that has since been published as a kind of afterword to subsequent printings of *Weltbürgertum und Nationalstaat*, Meinecke sought to apply his analysis of fourteen years earlier to the contemporary situation in the young Weimar Republic. One of the biggest dangers confronting the new state, so he claimed, was the temptation of provincial particularism; Germans, he feared, might withdraw their emotional allegiance from the Republic and focus it only on local institutions. But the ability to accommodate the foreign—even if "foreign" in this context referred only to elements from another German state—had always made the country great.

Meinecke's subtleties were out of step with their time. The period around the First World War is the period also when the term *Weltdeutschtum* enters the German language, as an admittedly rare but nevertheless semantically stable term. We find it again and again in various articles published in conservative journals of the period, such as *Die Grenzboten* (The Border Herald) or *Die schöne Literatur* (Fine Writing). These articles invoke Schiller, Fichte, Humboldt, but do so without dialectical subtlety and with crude propagandistic intentions. *Weltdeutschtum* here describes the outcome of Germany's supposedly predestined mission to export its culture to the world—with violent force if necessary. A 1915 review article in *Die schöne Literatur* entitled "Weltkriegsdichtung" (Poetry of the World War), for example, invokes Fichte's claim, "Wenn das deutsche Volk versinkt, so versinkt die ganze Menschheit ohne Hoffnung einer einstigen Wiederherstellung" (If the German people should perish, all of humanity will perish without the hope of a future restitution"). It pairs this statement with a quote from the poet Otto Ernst Hesse: "Der Sieger [des Weltkrieges] wird der Weltgeist, das Weltdeutschtum sein" (The victor [of the First World War] will be the world spirit, will be *Weltdeutschtum*).[20]

The patriotic fervor of the time also infected more sophisticated minds, such as that of the liberal historian Veit Valentin, who in the preface to his book *Deutschlands Außenpolitik von Bismarcks Abgang bis zum Ende des Weltkrieges* (German Foreign Policy from Bismarck's Resignation through the End of the World War, 1921) asserts:

> Als der Weltkrieg begann, durfte und mußte unsere Generation hoffen, daß er die letzte Erfüllung brächte, daß Volkserlebnis und Führergenie sich jetzt endlich begegneten zur Vollendung grandioser Selbstbehauptung; daß das neue Weltdeutschtum als Offenbarung eines durch die größten geschichtlichen Werte verfeinerten Patriotismus die Sicherung zu werden vermöchte eines neuen Weltgleichgewichtes, einer neuen Weltharmonie.[21]

[When the world war began, our generation was given reason to hope that it would bring the final fulfillment, that the experience of the people and the genius of our leaders would finally merge to conclude the process of our self-assertion, and that the new *Weltdeutschtum* would assure a novel global balance by revealing a patriotism refined by the noblest historical principles.]

One might be forgiven for thinking that such musty reflections on the supposedly redemptive mission of German national culture would mark the absolute nadir of the literature on *Weltdeutschtum*, but one would be wrong. By the early 1930s, Nazi and proto-Nazi journals such as *Volk und Rasse* (Volk and Race) or *Das innere Reich* (The Inner Reich) had appropriated the term to designate a racialized understanding of German culture that ought to be aggressively spread beyond the borders of the Third Reich, especially in the east. Following the seizure of power, the term also figured repeatedly in the various publication of the Deutsches Ausland-Institut (German Institute for Foreign Cultural Affairs), a Nazi institute charged with maintaining contact between the regime and various German cultural organizations in foreign countries.[22]

It is all the more noteworthy, then, that Thomas Mann, in his 1945 lecture at the Library of Congress on "Germany and the Germans," chose the term *Weltdeutschtum* to designate an explicitly antinationalist attitude towards German culture. Examining Goethe's attitudes during the wars of liberation (a topic that he had already treated in fictional form in his 1939 novel *Lotte in Weimar*), Mann reflected on the "Vereinsamung dieses Großen, der jede Weite und Größe bejahte: das Übernationale, das Weltdeutschtum, die Weltliteratur" (loneliness of this great man, who approved everything of a broad and generous nature, the super-national, world Germanism, world literature).[23] When he spoke these words, Mann stood at the height of his American fame as what one American newspaper called "Hitler's most intimate enemy."[24] His direct appropriation of what had by then become a Nazi code word can therefore be understood as a salvo in a long-standing rhetorical battle with Nazism.

"Germany and the Germans" recapitulates many of the arguments concerning *Weltdeutschtum* that were already summarized previously in this chapter. Mann, too, presumes that German national character is characterized by a "ursprünglichen Universalismus und Kosmopolitismus . . . die als seelisches Zubehör ihres alten übernationalen Reiches, des Heiligen Römischen Reiches Deutscher Nation, zu verstehen sein mag" (fundamental universalism and cosmopolitanism . . . which may be regarded as a spiritual accessory of [an] ancient supernational realm, the Holy Roman Empire).[25] This "foundational universalism," however, was dialectically inverted (or, as Mann sardonically puts it, turned into "Kosmopolitismus in der Nachtmütze" [cosmopolitanism in a nightcap]) when the German people developed a philosophical conception of liberty that was quite different from that of the Western nations.[26] Mann does not evoke Fichte by name in his lecture. But he is clearly at least partially thinking of texts like the *Addresses to the German Nation* when he contrasts the French notion of liberty as a pan-European resistance to aristocratic enslavement with a German conception of the term as "völkisch und anti-Europäisch" (racial and anti-European) defined exclusively through the focus on spiritual rather than political liberty.[27] The connection is made especially clear because like Fichte (and, for that matter, Schiller), Mann too focuses heavily on Luther and the Protestant reformation as intellectual forerunners to "German freedom."

Fichte, as we have seen, ultimately arrived at the conclusion that anybody who believed in the superiority of spiritual values over political ones might rightfully be called "German," and thereby gave a universalist cast to German cultural identity. Mann, surveying the scene with the benefit of 140 years of accumulated historical experience, is less sanguine. For him, Bismarck and the Second German Empire are the logical outcome of a national culture that sought freedom exclusively in the spiritual domain. The universalism of this culture is grounded only in its imperial aspirations, its unshakable belief that its mission is to rule the world by advancing the German spirit. By contrast, *Weltdeutschtum* in the sense in which Thomas Mann uses the term, refers to a form of cultural cosmopolitanism that sees spiritual values not as completely independent from politics, but rather related to them in productive tension.

From *Weltdeutschtum* to Universal Humanism

We can arrive at a better understanding of what Thomas Mann may have meant by looking at the only other occasion on which he publicly used the term *Weltdeutschtum*, a radio address to liberated Germany on December 30, 1945. Reflecting on the arguments of those Germans who—like the novelist Frank Thiess—accused Mann of having abandoned his country during its time of greatest need, he responded:

> Das Exil ist etwas ganz anderes geworden, als es in früheren Zeiten war. Es ist kein Wartezustand, den man auf Heimkehr abstellt, sondern spielt schon auf eine Auflösung der Nation an und auf die Vereinheitlichung der Welt. Alles Nationale ist längst Provinz geworden. . . . Man gönne mir mein *Weltdeutschtum*, das mir in der Seele schon natürlich, als ich noch zu Hause war.[28]

> [Exile has become something very different from what it used to be. It is no longer a condition of waiting that ends upon a return home, but rather prefigures the dissolution of the nation and the unification of the world. Everything national has become merely provincial. . . . Do not begrudge me my world Germanism, which was already a part of my soul when I was still at home.]

Several things are noteworthy about these sentences. First, Mann's equation of *Weltdeutschtum* with a condition of exile stands in stark contrast to the Nazi use of the term to designate a racialized international community, and indeed also with Meinecke's attempts to see the fusion of national and cosmopolitan ideas as a precondition for state formation. Just as he had already done in "Deutschland und die Deutschen," Mann furthermore links *Weltdeutschtum* to Goethe's conception of *Weltliteratur* (world literature)—or at least he does if one assumes that the sentence "everything national has become merely provincial" is a veiled allusion to Goethe's statement that "Nationalliteratur will jetzt nicht viel sagen, die Epoche der Weltliteratur ist an der Zeit" (national literature is now a rather unmeaning term; the epoch of world literature is at hand).[29] *Weltdeutschtum* is thus a cultural characteristic, but not in the noumenal sense articulated by Schiller and Fichte. Instead, German character connects with the world through the concrete logic of economic exchange that Goethe first described in his conversations with Eckermann.

Indeed, Mann's time in America was a period in which he rediscovered both himself and his audience as a result of his life in exile. The Nazis had banned his books; their totalitarian terror had also put an effective end to German political society in any meaningful sense of the word. Mann thus found weighing upon him the burden of the historical condition rhapsodized by German thinkers throughout the nineteenth century—namely, that of upholding German culture at a time when the German state had perished. And what he discovered was that his career as a writer could be sustained only because Americans were willing to buy his books, circulate them, and thereby keep German culture alive. In a letter to his US publisher Alfred A. Knopf, he begrudgingly admitted that "the American public in recent years has stepped into the place that the German public once occupied for me, now that politics—and what politics at that!—have separated me from it."[30]

Weltdeutschtum, for Thomas Mann, was therefore a form of German identity that is produced, sustained, and adjudicated at geographical remove from the German national homeland. In this sense, the term resembles the contemporary critical keyword of "transnationalism," which the anthropologist Arjun Appadurai usefully defined as a form of communitarianism that "retains a special ideological link to a putative place of origin but is otherwise a thoroughly diasporic collectivity."[31] Whereas the "transnation" remains conceptually subordinate to the "nation," *Weltdeutschtum* hints at a universalism that does not accrue to the later term. German culture, so Mann believed, was of more than just incidental significance to the Americans who now kept it alive. The universal admixtures that defined it were instead of crucial relevance to US self-understanding in the fight against fascism, which Mann always conceived of as a struggle of universal humanism against nihilistic particularism, not just as a fight between one country and another. In a 1941 essay that was first published in English translation as "Germany's Guilt and Mission," Mann did not shy away from arguing "die Welt braucht Deutschland" (the world needs Germany)—not, however, because there was anything inherently superior to the German people, but rather because German history, more than that of any other nation, provided a blueprint for how a merely particular experience could come to stand in for a universally human one.[32] In his last great political speech of 1955, the "Essay on Schiller," Mann would again advance this idea within the context of a revisionist exegesis of the poem "German Greatness."

From our contemporary perspective, the idea that there would be a messianic kernel buried within any national cultural tradition, much less the German one with all its accumulated historical sins, may seem rather difficult to swallow. Nevertheless, at the present moment, when resurgent nationalisms are once again positioning themselves in opposition to cosmopolitan ideals, the example of Thomas Mann may again serve a practical purpose. Early in 2017, the German federal government purchased Mann's former American house in Pacific Palisades for roughly $13 million and renovated it to serve as a space for "transatlantic dialog." The ambition, clearly, is to harness Mann and his public proclamations about Germany for a specific form of cultural diplomacy, a specific image of "Germany in the world." Perhaps this is possible because, stripped to its essence, the idea of *Weltdeutschtum* as it was articulated by Mann was built upon a simple, and rather appealing, premise: that we should learn about other cultures not just out of a desire to do justice to the various forms of diversity that characterize the modern experience (the logic of multiculturalism), nor even because such knowledge can convey quantifiable economic benefits (the logic of globalization). Instead, we should care about other cultures because only in such care and attention do we become truly human.

Notes

Uncredited translations are my own.

[1] Edward Said, *Orientalism* (New York: Pantheon Books, 1978), 19.

[2] On the latter, see, for example, Todd Kontje, *German Orientalisms* (Ann Arbor: University of Michigan Press, 2004); Andrea Polaschegg, *Der andere Orientalismus* (Berlin: Walter de Gruyter, 2005); and Suzanne L. Marchand, *German Orientalism in the Age of Empire: Religion, Race, and Scholarship* (New York: Cambridge University Press, 2009).

[3] See, for instance, the organization Berlin Postkolonial, which advocates for a more critical engagement with the many sites of colonial memory culture in the German capital. http://www.berlin-postkolonial.de.

[4] Thomas Mann, "Deutschland und die Deutschen," in *Gesammelte Werke in Dreizehn Bänden*, vol. 13, ed. Peter de Mendelssohn (Frankfurt am Main: S. Fischer, 1974), 1138. The English lecture script is reprinted in Thomas Mann, "Germany and the Germans," in *Thomas Mann's Addresses, Delivered at the Library of Congress, 1942–1949* (Washington, DC: Library of Congress, 1963), 57.

[5] Dieter Borchmeyer, *Weimarer Klassik: Portrait einer Epoche* (Weinheim: Beltz Athenäum, 1994), 57–59.

[6] This bibliographical debate came to a head during the latter days of the Wilhelmine Empire, with the side arguing for 1801 led by the first director of the Goethe-Schiller Archive, Bernhard Suphan, and the side arguing for 1797 led by the Jena professor Albert Leitzmann. In truth, both camps may be correct; it is far from certain that the various fragments comprising the poem were all written at the same time.

[7] Friedrich Schiller, *Deutsche Grösse*, in *Sämtliche Werke in Zehn Bänden. Berliner Ausgabe*, vol. 1, *Gedichte*, ed. Jochen Golz (Berlin: Aufbau Verlag, 1980), 558–60. Just as the chronology of the fragments is unclear, so is the order in which they are meant to be placed. The so-called national edition of Schiller's works, for example, puts the passage about Britain before the other two fragments.

[8] For a detailed reception history of the poem, see Christian Grawe, "Schillers Gedichtentwurf 'Deutsche Größe': Ein Nationalhymnus im Höchsten Stil?" *Jahrbuch der deutschen Schillergesellschaft* 36 (1992): 167–96.

[9] Johann Gottlieb Fichte, *Reden an die deutsche Nation* (Hamburg: Felix Meiner, 1978), 177. English translation in Johann Gottlieb Fichte, *Addresses to the German Nation* (Cambridge: Cambridge University Press, 2008), 143.

[10] Fichte, *Reden an die deutsche Nation*, 100. English translation in *Addresses to the German Nation*, 80.

[11] On the conceptual history of the term "German freedom," see Hans Jörg Schmidt, *Die deutsche Freiheit: Geschichte eines kollektiven semantischen Sonderbewusstseins* (Frankfurt am Main: Humanities Online, 2010); Fichte is discussed on 33–35. For Berlin's distinction between negative and positive liberty, see his "Two Concepts of Liberty," in Isaiah Berlin, *Liberty*, ed. Henry Hardy (Oxford: Oxford University Press, 2002), 166–217.

[12] Fichte, *Reden an die deutsche Nation*, 122. English translation in *Addresses to the German Nation*, 97.

[13] Dieter Borchmeyer, *Weimarer Klassik*, 57. The interpretation is developed at greater length in Dieter Borchmeyer, *Was ist Deutsch? Die Suche einer Nation nach sich selbst* (Berlin: Rowohlt Verlag, 2017), 764–65.

[14] Richard Wagner, *Die Meistersinger von Nürnberg*, in *Dichtungen und Schriften: Jubiläumsausgabe in zehn Bänden*, vol. 4, ed. Dieter Borchmeyer (Frankfurt am Main: Insel Verlag, 1983), 212. English translation quoted from http://www.rwagner.net/libretti/meisters/e-meisters-a3s5.html.

[15] Quoted in Borchmeyer, *Was ist Deutsch?*, 764–65. The quotation is drawn from Johann Gottfried Herder, *Sämmtliche Werke*, vol. 18, ed. Bernhard Suphan (Berlin: Weidmann, 1883), 161–62.

[16] Friedrich Meinecke, *Weltbürgertum und Nationalstaat: Studien zur Genesis des deutschen Nationalstaates* (Munich: R. Oldenbourg, 1962), 39. This edition is essentially a reprint of the seventh edition of 1928; it contains passages that aren't present in the first edition of 1907. English translation in Friedrich Meinecke, *Cosmopolitanism and the National State*, trans. Robert B. Kimber (Princeton, NJ: Princeton University Press, 1970), 33.

[17] Meinecke, *Weltbürgertum und Nationalstaat*, 39. English translation in Meinecke, *Cosmopolitanism and the National State*, 33.

[18] Meinecke, *Weltbürgertum und Nationalstaat*, 162. English translation in Meinecke, *Cosmopolitanism and the National State*, 135.

[19] Meinecke, *Weltbürgertum und Nationalstaat*, 181. English translation in Meinecke, *Cosmopolitanism and the National State*, 151.

[20] Erich Jaeger, "Weltkriegsdichtung," *Die schöne Literatur* 15, no. 1 (1915): 7.

[21] Veit Valentin, *Deutschlands Außenpolitik von Bismarcks Abgang bis zum Ende des Weltkrieges* (Berlin: Deutsche Verlagsgesellschaft für Politik und Geschichte, 1921), ix.

[22] See Arthur L. Smith Jr., *The Deutschtum of Nazi Germany and the United States* (The Hague: Martinus Nijhoff, 1965), 33, 43.

[23] Mann, "Deutschland und die Deutschen," 1138. English translation in Mann, "Germany and the Germans," 57.

[24] Paul V. C. Whitney, "Distinguished Exile Speaks Here Tonight," *The Deseret News*, March 21, 1938, 1, 9.

[25] Mann, "Deutschland und die Deutschen," 1141. English translation in Mann, "Germany and the Germans," 60.

[26] Mann, "Deutschland und die Deutschen, 1129. English translation in Mann, "Germany and the Germans, 49.

[27] Mann, "Deutschland und die Deutschen," 1137–38. English translation in Mann, "Germany and the Germans," 57.

[28] Thomas Mann, "Deutsche Hörer! Drei Rundfunkansprachen," in *Gesammelte Werke in dreizehn Bänden*, vol. 13, 747. Emphasis in the original.

[29] Johann Peter Eckermann, *Gespräche mit Goethe in den letzten Jahren seines Lebens* (Munich: Beck, 1984), 198. English translation in Wolfgang von Goethe, *Conversations with Eckermann (1823–1832)*, trans. John Oxenford (San Francisco: North Point, 1984), 132.

[30] Unpublished 1939 letter to Alfred A. Knopf preserved in the William A. Koshland Files, box 5, folder 3, Harry Ransom Center, University of Texas at Austin.

[31] Arjun Appadurai, *Modernity at Large: Cultural Dimensions of Globalization* (Minneapolis: University of Minnesota Press, 1996), 172.

[32] Thomas Mann, "[Deutschland]," in *Gesammelte Werke in dreizehn Bänden*, vol. 12, ed. Peter de Mendelssohn (Frankfurt am Main: S. Fischer, 1979), 909. English translation published as Thomas Mann, "Germany's Guilt and Mission," *Decision* (July 1941): 13.

4: Nineteenth-Century German Travelers to Wales: Text, Translation, and the Manipulation of Identity

Carol Tully

THE ROLE OF THE GERMAN intellectual in shaping the thought and culture of nineteenth-century Europe has long been acknowledged, with significant influence evident from Scandinavia to the Mediterranean.[1] The cultural interface between the German-speaking lands and Great Britain was particularly rich, with key thinkers on either side of the North Sea—Goethe and Heine, Scott and Carlyle, to name but a few—engaged in a productive dynamic of mutual influence and often quite competitive comparison. As part of this exchange, in addition to the many literary works and cultural studies produced over the century, a number of writers penned lengthy and detailed travel accounts that brought the world—both near and far—to the reading circles of the emergent "Germany." Celebrated figures like the Humboldt brothers, Georg Forster, and Ida von Hahn-Hahn produced hugely influential works that served to reshape the German understanding of the world from the periphery of Europe to the Far East, their views absorbed by a readership struggling to place the German-speaking lands in the global context driven by the colonial expansionism of their near European neighbors, with its concomitant mix of orientalist appreciation and exoticized, often threatening, otherness. As well as these household names, there was also a large group of now largely forgotten scholars and travelers whose work was equally crucial in broadening the horizons of readers across the German-speaking lands. Given the keen interest in all matters "English," it is hardly surprising that the nineteenth century saw a steady stream of German travelers to the British Isles. They came in search of knowledge ranging from an understanding of the London theater scene, to the development of landscape gardens and country houses, to the expanding industrial power of the British Empire. This was the image of Great Britain already known to the German reading public, and each traveler added his or, occasionally, her input to the prevailing appreciative tone—often termed "Anglomania"—of the early-to-mid-century.[2]

What happened when these German travelers found themselves off the beaten track? There was, after all, more to the British Isles than Covent Garden theaters or Edinburgh's New Town. As the road and then the rail networks gradually improved, itineraries became more varied, taking travelers to less familiar places. It is in this context that a number made their way, intentionally or otherwise, to Wales, where they found themselves confronted with an unexpectedly foreign culture. The resultant travelogues are significant for their engagement with both the anticipated hegemonic culture (England) and an often unknown and unexpected minority culture (Wales). A selection of these texts will be discussed in this chapter: Christian August Gottlieb Goede, *England, Wales, Irland und Schottland: Erinnerungen an Natur und Kunst aus einer Reise in den Jahren 1802 und 1803* (England, Wales, Ireland, and Scotland: Recollections from a Journey in 1802 and 1803, 1804–5), Samuel Heinrich Spiker, *Reise durch England, Wales und Schottland im Jahre 1816* (Journey through England, Wales, and Scotland in 1816, 1818), Hermann von Pückler-Muskau, *Briefe eines Verstorbenen: Ein fragmentarisches Tagebuch aus England, Wales, Irland und Frankreich; geschrieben in den Jahren 1828 und 1829* (Letters of a Dead Man: A Fragmentary Journal from England, Wales, and Ireland; written in 1828 and 1829, 1830), Johann Georg Kohl, *Reisen in England und Wales* (Travels in England and Wales, 1844), Julius Rodenberg, *Ein Herbst in Wales: Land und Leute, Märchen und Lieder* (An Autumn in Wales: Land and People, Folktales and Songs, 1858), and Hugo Schuchardt, "Keltische Briefe" (Celtic Letters, 1875).[3] These texts highlight the chronological development of both the reading of Wales as an exotic, peripheral nation and the emerging sense of German selfhood that is evident in the travelers' self-stylization and positioning of their travel narratives as the century progresses. This complex set of encounters in what Pratt has termed the "contact zone" acquires another level of intricacy when the travelogues themselves are translated for a British readership.[4] The issues of identity formation (or, rather, manipulation) and textual traffic emerging from this tripartite relationship will be explored in this chapter.

Focusing first of all on the issue of identity, it is useful to consider to what extent these travel writers conceived of themselves explicitly as Germans abroad. It is perhaps obvious that the main objective of their work was to inform their peers. Johann Georg Kohl identifies this as an explicit driver in the foreword to *Reisen in England und Wales*:

> Es leben beständig viele Tausende von Menschen in unserem Vaterlande, welche nie dazu gelangen, die verschiedenen in oder außer ihnen liegenden Hindernisse zu besteigen, welche sich ihnen bei einer Reise jenseits des Canals, der das schöne, großbritannische Inselreich von dem europäischen Continente trennt, entgegenstellen, die aber,

am traulichen Herde der Heimath weilend, doch gern einmal wenigstens ihre Gedanken in solche schöne und interessante Länder auf Reisen schicken.[5]

[There are always many thousands of people living in our country who never manage to overcome the various personal or external obstacles that prevent them from making a trip across the channel that separates the beautiful British Isles from the European continent, who nevertheless still wish, while sitting in the comfort of their homes, to allow their minds at least to journey to such beautiful and interesting lands.]

These armchair travelers are one of three groups of potential readers with whom Kohl seeks to engage, the others being "die reiselustige Jugend" (the enthusiastic traveling youth) and "die ebenfalls zahlreichen gereisten Männer" (the equally numerous well-traveled gentlemen) who have not had the opportunity to record their travels for public consumption.[6] In engaging with these groups, Kohl's ambition is to share his experiences and further develop the knowledge of a group of like-minded German readers. The destinations chosen by German travelers—be they actual or armchair—reflected areas of key scholarly interest during the course of the nineteenth century. In the case of some, the traveler might already be aware of the culture he or she was about to encounter. Spain in the early part of the century is a prime example. Its language, culture, and history were a key focus of several Romantic thinkers such as Tieck and the Schlegel brothers. Although they never traveled there, their knowledge gleaned instead from the university libraries of Göttingen and Berlin, they and others produced translations and literary and historical studies that became seminal in the development of Hispanism in the German-speaking lands. Much was also reported in the press of the ongoing political divisions in Spain following the defeat of Napoleon in 1815. Consequently, when contemporary travelers reported on their experiences there, they were often encountering and discussing a culture, aspects of which were already quite well known, albeit vicariously, to themselves and their readers.

In other cases, however, travel to an unfamiliar destination was very much a voyage of social, cultural, and geographical discovery to an unknown contact zone. This need not be on the other side of the world. Ironically, given its close proximity to England, this was so with the German discovery of Wales. In this case, writers were very much dealing with a hidden nation. Although the travelers discussed here were mostly deliberate in their intentions to visit Wales, the responses of many others were complicated by the fact that travelers were often there simply because they were visiting England or on their way to Ireland, stumbling upon Wales almost by accident. Even those who traveled explicitly to visit Wales were often caught off balance by what they found. This created an unusual dynamic whereby responses to the expected or familiar destination (England) were destabilized by the unexpected, essentially exotic (Wales)—an essentially colonized nation with a different language—and it is not until the later century, partly as a result of the knowledge gained through the increasing number of travelogues, partly because of the development of Celtic studies at German and Austrian universities, which saw the emergence of what became known as "Keltomanie" (Celtomania), that they arrive prepared for what they were about to encounter. This preparation fosters a confidence in the textual self-representation of these later travelers as writers approaching their subject—Wales—with the authoritative security of their status as educated Germans.

Underpinned by the heuristic ethos set out in Kohl's foreword, it is possible to see a development in the self-perception and stylization of travelers as explicitly German as the century progresses. This parallels the gradual consolidation and growing confidence of the German-speaking states over time as the notion of "German national identity," which is both cultural and political, takes hold. Perhaps unsurprisingly then, travelers at the beginning of the century seem less self-conscious as traveling Germans, their interests allied more with individual political or professional interest than with cultural comparisons or notions of "national identity." These diverse interests are then reflected in their responses to Wales. For example, Christian August Gottlieb Goede, author of the first travelogue of the nineteenth century, *England, Wales, Irland und Schottland*, positions himself more as a stranger traveling in a strange land, presenting "England" as an example of a new mercantile utopia that fosters individual freedom, a vision that is then undermined by his experience of the English neglect of Wales, both politically and culturally. Samuel Heinrich Spiker, recording his travels in *Reise durch England, Wales und Schottland im Jahre 1816*, is keen to highlight his status as librarian to the King of Prussia and interim resident of London, but pays little attention to matters of identity beyond the paratext. His reading of Wales is framed by his interest in engineering and, in particular, the work of Thomas Telford, presenting Wales as a peripheral nation in dire need of modernization. Another traveler, Hermann von Pückler-Muskau, recording his journey in his *Briefe eines Verstorbenen*, styles himself more as an aristocrat than a German, focusing and reflecting on himself and his status rather than his experiences as a German abroad, perceiving Wales as both a stage setting for his own adventures and an inspiration for his interests as landscape gardener.

By the mid-century, however, writers such as Kohl are more explicit in their self-positioning as German travelers. There is a sense that writers feel they are contributing to a specifically German view of the world, to share with their peers in the way Kohl describes. In this regard, Julius

Rodenberg is perhaps the most self-conscious in traveling as a German abroad. Born into a Jewish family in the village of Rodenberg in Hessen in 1831, he gained a formidable reputation as the editor of the influential cultural magazine *Deutsche Rundschau* (German Review), which he founded in 1874. This role saw him occupy a position of influence at the heart of German intellectual life until his death in 1914. In his twenties he traveled extensively in Europe and produced a number of travelogues, including *Ein Herbst in Wales*. The text employs two distinct approaches: Rodenberg's often elaborate memoirs and information on the culture and history of Wales. This dual focus is conveyed through two pairs of related themes that are woven through the narrative. The first is that of national identity, emphasizing, on the one hand, the tense cultural relations between Wales and England, and, on the other, the impact of travel on Rodenberg's own German identity. The second pairing has its focus on the Romantic, with an emphasis both on Wales as a Romantic nation and on Rodenberg as an explicitly German Romantic traveler. Thus the text is driven by both the desire to understand and present a foreign culture and a high degree of self-reflection and stylization. Self and other therefore interact self-referentially in a symbiotic relationship of mutual affirmation: Rodenberg able to confirm and consolidate his status as a Romantic, German traveler, and Wales occupying center stage for the first time in German travel writing.

Echoing Goede's narrative in the early century, much of Rodenberg's critique of the situation in Wales is targeted at English misgovernment, and in particular the impact this is having on Welsh culture and identity. This provides a point of comparison for the author's own experience as a German abroad. Just as Welsh identity is threatened by English colonial interference, so Rodenberg's carefully crafted sense of self as a German is threatened by the potentially destabilizing effect of travel. It is worth noting at this juncture that his surname was originally Levy, but he changed it in 1854, choosing the name of the place he was born and for which he felt an enormous affinity. His visit to Wales took place two years after this, and on the very first page of his narrative, Rodenberg clearly defines his identity as a German and explicitly outlines his sense of affinity with his homeland. That affinity is then put to the test as a result of the experience of travel. The inclusion of his own verses enables Rodenberg to reflect on the emotions provoked by travel, as it distances him from home emotionally as well as physically. He then exploits this distance in order to reinforce his identity as a German and also validate his native culture by emphasizing his role as an outsider so as to take a comparative stance when exploring various aspects of Wales and Welsh culture. Writing during his stay in Bangor, he describes the challenges he is experiencing:

Mehrere Wochen waren so vergangen, und um mich und in mir hatte sich Manches verändert. Die Bäume waren dunkelbraun geworden, alles Feld stand in Stoppeln, über's Meer fegte schon dann und wann ein rauher Wind hinein. Und mich drängte es nun wieder, nach allen Mabinogis und Bardengesängen und Pennillion zu meiner "Trosteinsamkeit" zu greifen, nach dieser köstlichen Sammlung deutscher Lieder, die ich von der Schule her auf jeder Fahrt in der Nähe oder Ferne stets bei mir führte. Hier sollte ich ihren Segen recht verspuren.[7]

[Many weeks passed in this way and many things had changed around and in me. The trees had turned dark brown, all the fields were stubble, a raw wind blew from time to time across the sea. And I was driven once more, despite all the Mabinogion and bardic songs and Pennillion, to take up my "lonely solace," the precious collection of German songs that I had taken with me on every trip, be it near or far, since my schooldays. Here I truly felt its blessing.]

Reconnecting with the culture of his homeland, inculcated from his school days, enables Rodenberg to stabilize his sense of self, fending off the insecurities brought on by the experience of travel. This recalibration is driven from within—"mich drängte es nun wieder"—and results, upon reading of the *Lieder*, in a sense of calm. Reading these texts not only revitalizes his sense of self as a German but also highlights German cultural superiority, evinced here in its purest Romantic form, the *Volkslied* (folk song):

Ja, es geht Nichts über das deutsche Lied! Das "Lied" hat kein ander Volk, als das deutsche. Die englischen "songs," die französichen "chansons"—wie gemacht die einen, wie kühl die andren gegen das Herzblut, das in unsren Liedern quilt! Bist doch ein prächtig Volk, du deutsches—und mit Thränen in den Augen, mit Lächeln, mit Jubeln fühlen wir uns als deine Kinder, die ohne dich nicht leben mögen noch können. Denn als treue Gefährten gibst du uns auf die Reise deine Lieder mit, daß sie uns erinnern an die schöne Zeit, wo wir sie mit Freunden zusammen gesungen; daß sie uns gemahnen, in Lust und Leid deutsch und dem Vaterlande treu zu bleiben und daß sie uns, wie ein süßer Trost, in die Seele singen: "Haltet aus! wandert! wartet!—wenn Ihr heimkehrt, findet Ihr Alles wieder, was Ihr da draußen vermißt habt; die deutsche Liebe! die deutsche Treue! den deutschen Gott!"[8]

[Indeed, there is nothing better than the German *Lied*! No other people has anything like it. The English "songs," the French "chansons"—how artificial the former, how cold the latter when compared to the lifeblood that flows through our *Lieder*! You are a great people, you German race—and with tears in our eyes, with smiles, with cries of joy we consider ourselves to be your children who would not want or be able to live on without you. For you give us your songs as true travel companions who remind us of the beautiful time when we sang them together with friends; who remind us, through joy and suffering, to remain true to our people and our land; and who sing to our souls in sweet solace: "Endure! Wander! Wait!—when you return home, you will find everything that you missed abroad; German love! German loyalty! German God!"]

This effusive outburst could hardly be more patriotic, or, indeed, melodramatic. The message is clear: no matter where the German intellectual travels, he will find solace and strength in his own culture, and that culture will always surpass that of the newly discovered land, however well-disposed one might be towards it. Rodenberg finds confirmation that he is part of a greater national movement when he spots the words of the German *Volkslied*, "Heil dem Manne, der den grünen Hain" (Hail the man, who the green grove) scrawled on the walls of a grotto near Capel Curig. The presence of this graffiti demonstrates to both Rodenberg and his reader that he is not alone in feeling his German identity in this far-flung corner of Europe and that he is not the first to revert to the *Lieder* of his native land to find solace. This enthusiasm for the folk culture of Germany also extends to high literary culture. Rodenberg's text is peppered with references to the German canon—Goethe, Novalis, Lessing—and his own poetry contains numerous allusions to famous works. This is combined with lengthy and heartfelt expressions of love for his native country. Indeed, he opens his narrative with a reflection on *Heimat* (homeland) that sets the tone for the rest of the text:

> Ich war drei Tage in Liverpool und befand mich im Kreiße lieber Verwandten wol und munter. Verwandte im fremden Lande zu finden, ist immer doppelt angenehm. Wenn man die Heimat eben verlaßen hat, ist das Herz noch weich, und wie jeden unangenehmen Eindruck einer ungewohnten Umgebung empfindet man auch den Blick und das Wort der Liebe, die ja überall dieselbe bleibt, unendlich tiefer. Und so, nach der Seite des Gemüthes, die der Deutsche stets am Schwersten überwindet, zufrieden gestellt, nimmt man allmälig auch an Allem, was uns bisher fremd war, gern seinen Antheil; man hat seine Freude daran wie an einem schönen Geisteswerk, das aus seiner Sprache in die unsre übersetzt worden ist.[9]

> [I had been in Liverpool for three days and was happy in the company of dear relatives. It is doubly pleasant to find relatives in a strange land. When one has recently left one's homeland, then the heart is still tender, and just as one is struck by every uncomfortable impression in unfamiliar surroundings, so one is taken all the more

by the kind look and loving word that remain constant wherever one might be. And so, settled from the point of view of the emotions, which the German always finds hardest to overcome, one gradually takes part gladly in everything that was previously unfamiliar; one finds joy in this just as one would in a beautiful piece of writing that has been translated from the original into our own language.]

The sense of *Heimweh* (homesickness) expressed here is identified as a particularly German characteristic, suggesting that the German, above all other nationalities, has a bond with his homeland like no other. This love of country extends to the works of other cultures, which are appreciated as they are drawn into the German cultural sphere through translation. This affinity with compatriots and the shared absorption of the foreign becomes a theme in the text. Still in Liverpool awaiting passage to north Wales, he finds himself in the company of a young German woman:

> Ich stand allein neben einer jungen Dame, die sich gern mit mir unterhielt, weil sie eine Deutsche war und seit langer Zeit zuerst wieder mit einem Deutschen zu reden Gelegenheit hatte. Ich für meinen Theil freute mich, Jemanden zu haben, der, wie ich selber, Alles, was uns umgab, als etwas Fremdes empfand.[10]

> [I stood alone next to a young lady, who was happy to speak with me, for she was German and had not had the opportunity to speak with a German for a long time. I was happy for my part to have someone who shared with me the sensation that everything around was foreign.]

The contrast here between the familiarity of conversation with a fellow German and the shared experience of new strange surroundings is stark, the one enabling a full appreciation of the other. Later in the text, Rodenberg comes across a group of young men singing a German student song by Dolbadarn Castle at the foot of Snowdon. Hoping to have found fellow Germans, Rodenberg is disappointed to find they are instead young Englishmen. Nevertheless, he finds another example of German intellectual standing:

> Obgleich ich dem Accent anhörte, daß ich zu voreilig gehofft hatte, Landsleute zu finden, so war mir doch der Zufall sehr angenehm, der mir einen jungen Mann zuführte, welcher—wie er mir sagte—in München gewesen war, um Liebig zu hören, und dann auch einen Sommer in Heidelberg sehr glücklich verlebt hatte.[11]

> [Although I could tell from the accent that I had been premature in my hope of finding compatriots, it was nevertheless most pleasing to meet by coincidence a young man who—so he told me—had been

in Munich to hear Liebig, and who had spent a pleasant summer in Heidelberg.]

The reference to the scientist Justus von Liebig and the university town of Heidelberg help validate Rodenberg's native culture in a similar vein to his effusive praise of the *Lied*, this time, however, supporting German significance with third party, foreign, indeed English, views. A final confirmation of the extent and value of German culture comes when Rodenberg and his new English friends wander past a group of ladies out walking. The result is pure transcultural irony:

> Wir zogen ihnen mit Gesang vorbei. Wahrscheinlich hielten sie's für walisischen Volksgesang, den sie holten alle ihre Notizbücher heraus und schrieben mit sichtbarem Eifer. Was wir sangen war in der That aber ein deutsches Studenten Lied. Auch der Stockengländer sang dießmal mit; wir hatten ihm eine Longfellow'sche Übersetzung von unsrem Liede gegeben.[12]

> [We walked past them, singing. They probably assumed it was Welsh folk song because they took out their notebooks and wrote in them with great energy. What we were singing was in fact a German student song. Even the archetypal Englishman sang along this time; we have given him Longfellow's translation of our song.]

What Rodenberg presents is a clash of contact zones: English ladies believing a German song to be Welsh; an Englishman singing a translation of that song by an American author. This complex network of interactions and perceptions provides affirmation of the value of German culture on a global stage and, in so doing, justification for Rodenberg's own emotional responses as a German abroad, proud of his nation's literary and cultural achievements, themselves heightened by positive comparison with new discoveries and experiences.

Rodenberg's work, with its emphasis on the customs and culture of Wales, makes a sentimental contribution to the developing Celtomania that was an emerging feature of scholarship in Europe and in Germany, France, and Great Britain, in particular through the work of writers such as Ferdinand Walter and Matthew Arnold.[13] Contributing more directly to this was Hugo Schuchardt, the eminent Hispanist, Celticist, and fluent Welsh speaker. Schuchardt was very much an example of the educated German abroad and made much of his status as a Welsh-speaking German scholar when recording his visit to Wales in 1875:

> So werde ich den überall als Deutscher der Kymrisch versteht, aber nicht Englisch, herumgeführt und gezeigt; und das Letztere, das *dim Seisneg* [no English]! wird mir fast zum grösseren Verdienst gerechnet als das Erstere.[14]

[And so I am taken around and presented everywhere as the German who understands Welsh, but no English; and the latter, the *dim Seisneg* [no English]! is almost seen as a greater accolade than the former.]

Playing on the antagonism between the Welsh and their hegemonic neighbors, Schuchardt places himself in collusion with the former to the exclusion of the latter in a manner that other German travelers of the period are unable to do. He adds to this accolade by writing articles for the Welsh press—where he involves himself in critical debates on Welsh rhetoric—and finds himself the center of attention at the Pwllheli *Eisteddfod*:[15]

Da hörte ich auf einmal aus Clwydfardds Mund meinen Namen und die Aufforderung an mich in den Kreis zu treten. Ich leistete Folge, lies seine Beleuchtung meiner Verdienste über mich ergehen und empfing den Grad eines Ofydd. Man band mir eine grüne Schleife um den Arm (Weiss ist die Farbe der Druiden, blau der Barden), ich stellte mich auf den Stein, sagte: "Ich danke vielmals," und wurde vom Volke begrüsst. Das Pseudonym welches man mir gab, war *Celtydd o'r Almaen* (Keltist aus Deutschland).[16]

[Then I suddenly heard Clwydfardd mention my name and was called into the circle. I did so, listened with pleasure to his explanation of my achievements, and received the accolade of Ofydd. A green ribbon was tied around my arm (white is the druidic color, blue the bardic), I stood on the rock, said "Thank you very much," and was greeted by the people. The pseudonym I was given was Celtydd o'r Almean (Celticist from Germany).]

His commentary demonstrates his detailed knowledge of Welsh and, indeed, the *Eisteddfod* revival underway at the time. This allows him once more to emphasize his own identity as a German but also to incorporate himself into the culture he is visiting. That said, he is not averse to making comments that present his native culture as superior to the Welsh. He notes the following, writing from Bala towards the end of his trip:

Dünne Bäumchen ohne schattige Kronen, dünnes Bier ohne schäumende Blume, rauchende Herren, strickende Damen, Mandolinata und vaterländische Potpourris—die Vereinigung aller dieser Dinge gewährt ohne Zweifel einen bescheidenen Genuss. Und sagen zu müssen dass ich mich danach mehr als einmal während meines vierwöchentlichen Aufenthalts zu Caernarfon gesehnt habe! Den Mangel öffentlicher Alltagsvergnügungen, an die wir Deutschen nun einmal gewöhnt sind, konnte ich trotz aller Liebenswürdigkeit der Eingeborenen nicht ganz verschmerzen.[17]

[Thin trees without shady crowns, weak beer with no head, smoking men, knitting women, mandolin music and patriotic potpourri—the combination of all these things doubtless provokes a modest pleasure. And the need to admit that I longed for this more than once during my four weeks in Caernarfon! I could not bear the lack of the usual public entertainment, which we Germans are now used to, no matter how lovely the locals were.]

This conflicted yet honest appraisal of his Welsh experience is typical of his unsentimental approach that, although not entirely devoid of some of the *Selbstinszenierung* found in Pückler-Muskau and Rodenberg, is a characteristic of Schuchardt's writing throughout. Significant in his case, however, is the fact that he is, by his own account and that of others, acknowledged and revered as a scholar. This marks the pinnacle in a trajectory found in the texts discussed here. Goede's critical musings, Kohl's amateur scholarly self-perception, Rodenberg's Romantic pseudo-philology, and, finally, Schuchardt's obvious erudition all contribute to a sense of German scholarly authority aimed at educating and informing a reading public in the emerging "German" context.

Turning to the reading of these works in the context of the cultures they describe, it is evident that this German scholarly authority is both the rationale for translation of many texts into English (as a set of views worth reading) as well as the cause of substantial ambivalence. That ambivalence is born of a need to secure English superiority in what becomes a struggle for cultural dominance played out in the paratextual material and editorial decision-making processes behind the translated versions of these German travel texts. Translations and reviews of these narratives are revealing, both in the context of the esteem in which the authors were held but also the way in which their views are then repurposed to serve an English nationalist agenda. There is a development over time. For the first half of the century, the German view is accorded high status, albeit often with some caveats relating to the cultural differences apparent in their approach. This continues a trend that had already begun in the eighteenth century. The role of the German intellectual as an arbiter of taste and cultural mediator was already emerging and is reflected in the attention paid to German-language travel narratives in other cultures. Citing the work of Yasmine Marcil on reviews of travel writing in the French periodical press from 1750 to 1789, for example, Alison Martin and Susan Pickford note that "reviews of German travel narratives increase dramatically over the period, from 4 in the period 1750 to 1759 to 47 for 1780–1789, reflecting Germany's growing cultural significance over the latter half of the eighteenth century." They note also the fact that reviews of English travelogues diminish by a third over the period of Marcil's study, "being displaced in large part by German."[18]

This interest in German opinion can be seen to increase further as the German lands emerge as an economic and cultural powerhouse over the course of the following century, with reports on German politics, reviews of German books, and translations of German literature featuring prominently in the burgeoning periodical press across the globe. Despite this, however, as the century progresses and the struggle for cultural superiority heightens, the characterization of the German scholar shifts to become more critical. This results in the German view of Great Britain as both respected for its authority and erudition and undermined through its exploitation and manipulation. This becomes particularly clear in the treatment of Wales, where the reception of travel narratives through translation is at times highly selective, demonstrating the elision suffered by the Celtic nation at the time. For example, two of the texts discussed here that are specifically dedicated to describing Wales—those by Rodenberg and Schuchardt—were not translated in the nineteenth century. Rodenberg's later Irish narrative, *Die Insel der Heiligen* (The Island of the Saints, 1860) was translated into English almost immediately, but the opening chapter describing his brief return to Wales on the way to Ireland is omitted, and it was not until 1985 that *Ein Herbst in Wales* appeared in English translation. Schuchardt's text remains untranslated.[19]

As I have argued elsewhere, the reception in this context of Goede's travelogue is particularly telling.[20] The first translation, published anonymously in 1807, presents Goede as erudite observer who, "upon his return to Germany ... communicated his observations to his countrymen in five volumes; from which the editor has extracted such parts as he conceived would be most interesting to an Englishman, who wishes to know the opinion of foreigners respecting his nation."[21] In so doing, the translator provides what is effectively a summary of the main content that tones down Goede's criticism of the English and hugely abridges the section on Wales, thus effectively reshaping the text to meet the expectations of an English readership. Such was the interest in Goede's work that a second translation by Thomas Horne emerged a year later in 1808, with a revised edition appearing later in 1821. This second English translation sees Goede's work realigned to present a view of England that places the nation and its people in a favorable light far exceeding that presented in the original, while omitting the section on Wales altogether. Setting the tone for the early part of the century, appreciation of the German view is ambivalent. Horne notes the cultural differences that have impacted on his translation, signaling in so doing an acknowledgement of the German scholarly reputation for depth:

> In the following work, though occasionally adapted (as some may perhaps suppose by too liberal an accommodation) to the circumstances of the country in whose language it now appears, the reader

will not fail to discover, it is feared, more than enough to ascertain its native soil. This, indeed, forms the Editor's best apology for having here and there lopped the heavy luxuriance of the version, that it still retains so much of Germany. With less reverence for the principle of accurate translation, he would have made more considerable retrenchments . . . but this would have to publish not Goede but himself.

Despite these clear reservations expressed in relation to the content and literary style of the original, Horne nevertheless ends by according the text the authority: "The object in publishing this work, is not to give currency to the virulence, or permanence to the squabbles of party; but to shew Englishmen in what estimation they are held by foreigners, and to teach them to know, and to value their blessings."[22]

It is for this reason, I have argued, that the section on Wales is omitted from Horne's translation, as it contained overt criticism of the English government's handling of the Welsh situation in relation to social conditions, education, and law, which saw areas of Wales lag behind what was understood to be the burgeoning economy of England. Goede's text is, then, simultaneously critiqued for its heavy scholarly tone, valued for its authoritative presentation of English values, and undermined by an editing process that divests it of its original balance. However, other texts with a more straightforward appeal emerge intact from the translation process. Spiker's *Reise durch England, Wales und Schottland* was translated two years after publication as *Travels through England, Wales and Scotland in the year 1816 by Dr S. H. Spiker, Librarian to his Majesty the King of Prussia, dedicated to the Friends of England*. Here the intentions of the author in appreciating the English way are made explicit:

> He wishes to become accurately acquainted with our literary and scientific institutions; our charitable and economical establishments; our mechanical inventions; the efforts of our arts, manufactures, and commerce; and in short to obtain a knowledge of the true spirit of the system, on which the public and private greatness of Britain is founded. On these subjects he expresses himself with the candour and simplicity of a man anxious for improvement of his own countrymen, and far above the influence of petty national prejudices or of any feelings of personal vanity.[23]

The clear inference here is that this learned German—librarian to the King of Prussia, no less—is nevertheless able to learn from "the public and private greatness of Britain" in a way that will improve his own nation, which is clearly placed in a subordinate position. Tellingly, in this case, the text, with its appreciation of Telford (working for the English government) as a civilizing force in Wales, is translated in full, thus placing England in a dually positive light, improving Welsh infrastructure (and thus civilizing a barbaric peripheral nation) and setting an example for the German-speaking lands.

The authority of Spiker's office, with its royal credentials, carries a great deal of weight in all of this, and it is notable that the status of the author in Sarah Austin's 1832 translation of Pückler-Muskau's *Briefe eines Verstorbenen* is equally foregrounded, with his position as a "German prince" used in lieu of his actual name. Despite focusing on his status in this way, the opening remarks nevertheless present a typically ambivalent view of the German mind:

> Opinions have been retained throughout, without the least attempt at change or colouring. That on some important subjects they are not those of the mass of Englishmen, will, it is presumed, astonish no reflecting man. They bear strong marks of that *individuality* which characterizes modes of thinking in Germany, where men are no more accustomed to claim the right of thinking for others than to renounce that of thinking for themselves. This characteristic of the German mind stands in strong contrast to the sectarian division of opinion in England. The sentiments of the author are therefore to be regarded simply as his own, and not as a sample of those of any sect or class in Germany; still less are they proposed for adoption or imitation here. The opinion he pronounces on French and German philosophy is, for example, by no means in accordance with the popular sentiment of his country.[24]

This ambivalence aside, Austin gives over the majority of her "Translator's Preface" to a review of Pückler-Muskau's text by Goethe, an overwhelmingly positive appraisal that undoubtedly lends the author's work even greater status by association with the acknowledged colossus of German literature. Interestingly, Austin's translation includes the entire description of Wales, which contains some of Pückler-Muskau's most outrageous adventures, including sipping champagne on the summit of Snowdon. As with the original, it seems the translator's intention is to foreground the personality of the author rather than the places he visits.

The more ambivalent approach of the early century later gives way to more overtly critical interpretations of German intellectual authority. Thomas Roscoe's 1845 translation of Kohl's *Reisen*, which appeared as the first number in the *Western Family Library*—a cheaply priced series aimed at a broad audience—provoked a less reverent view of the German traveler. In a review in *Tait's Edinburgh Magazine*, the tone was critical: "Kohl is the James Grant of all Europe; the 'Random Recollector' of all lands. His travels, if sufficiently superficial, are generally entertaining; and these in England will to many, nay, even to the mass of English readers, be informing."[25] The condemnation inherent in the epithet "Random

Recollector" is here at least tempered by an acknowledgement that the text might interest the masses for whom it is intended—clearly, an English readership—but the sense that the content remains superficial is clear. While this is leveled at the work of one individual, more general criticism is emerging by the time Schuchardt publishes his "Keltische Briefe," as the status of the German scholar has shifted once more. As noted, Schuchardt's text itself was never translated but it did receive attention in the British press, something which the author himself highlights in the notes to his collection of essays:

> Meine "Keltischen Briefe" fanden im Lande des Humors eine Kritik deren letzte Worte ich wegen der darin den deutschen Gelehrten gegebenen Direktive mittheilen muss: *How romantic a German professor can be if he is inspired like Prof. Sch.! However, instead of describing continually the unendurable sermons, or the Sunday schools, where he was surprised to find that the Welsh know the Bible better than the German professors, or even the pair of dark eyes of a girl at Bala, which the professor found it worth while to follow into the church (where, again, the sermon and the prayers were unsupportable), Prof. Sch. would have done better to read books and copy manuscripts, as a learned German should.* (*The Athenaeum*, 6. Juli 1878).[26]

> [My "Celtic Letters" were subject to a critical review in the land of humor, the final words of which I must share, given the directive aimed at German scholars: . . .]

There is in this comment a clear pre-echo of the tone adopted in depictions of Germans in British writing in the late century, Jerome K Jerome's *Three Men on the Bummel* (1900) being perhaps the most famous example. Again, Schuchardt's text provides the pinnacle point in the trajectory, this time in relation to the reception of German travel writing, underpinned by the reputation of German scholarship in the nineteenth century. The ambivalent but mostly respectful tone of the early century gradually gives way as English translators edit texts to present England in a positive light in order to provide readers with what they want: a positive, confident view of their own nation. This tendency is evident also in reviews of the period that adopt an increasingly critical stance towards German narratives on the British Isles. This essentially sees these two hegemonic cultures surface in direct competition for superiority, while Wales—the peripheral nation—disappears from view once more as the German discovery of the Celtic nation is ironically erased from the British reception of their texts.

The German encounter with both the center and periphery of Great Britain can, then, be seen simultaneously to provoke a response to the land visited and also, increasingly, to reflect on the traveler's own identity as a

German. The intercultural dialogue underpinning this encounter of traveler and the nation traveled to is then further developed through the translation of these texts into English, not only as examples for a British reader of how the German eye/I traveled to the British Isles, but also of how mostly English-based translators and publishers dealt with the German reading of Wales as a peripheral and, effectively, colonized nation. This complex matrix of reception and counter-reception centers on the expression and manipulation of identity: Germans reflecting on themselves and on the relationship between England and Wales, and English translators receiving the German view of England and, where it suited, of Wales. As this chapter has shown, the process reinforces the inherent hierarchy of center/periphery, the hegemonic nations jostling for authoritative dominance at the expense of the minoritized nation, Wales, the reception of which becomes a background against which to play out a heightened sense of German identity on the one hand, while on the other serving as the means to exert English superiority through the exploitation of the German worldview to validate a very British, or rather English, sense of self, through both appreciation and derogation of German scholarly authority. These texts are, then, examples of both an assertion and a critique of German influence on the world stage at a time when an emergent German nation-state found itself in direct competition for economic and colonial power with a British imperial force that had both the benefit of longevity and scope. The defense of the peripheral other of its greatest adversary, England, was an unusual but nevertheless resonant tactic in the quest to bolster the emerging global significance that Germany was beginning to enjoy.

Notes

Uncredited translations are my own.

[1] This chapter is one of the outputs from the Arts and Humanities Research Council-funded project *European Travellers to Wales, 1750–2010*. The author would like to acknowledge the generous funding provided by the AHRC.

[2] See Ian Buruma, *Anglomania: A European Love Affair* (London: Atlantic, 2010).

[3] Christian August Gottlieb Goede, *England, Wales, Irland und Schottland: Erinnerungen an Natur und Kunst aus einer Reise in den Jahren 1802 und 1803*, 5 vols. (Dresden: Arnold, 1804–5); Samuel Heinrich Spiker, *Reise durch England, Wales und Schottland im Jahre 1816*, 2 vols. (Leipzig: Göschen, 1818); Hermann von Pückler-Muskau, *Briefe eines Verstorbenen: Ein fragmentarisches Tagebuch aus England, Wales, Irland und Frankreich; geschrieben in den Jahren 1828 und 1829*, 2 vols. (Stuttgart: Hallberger, 1830); Johann Georg Kohl, *Reisen in England und Wales*, 2 vols. (Dresden: Arnold, 1844); Julius Rodenberg, *Ein Herbst in Wales: Land und Leute, Märchen und Lieder* (Hannover: Rümpler, 1858); Hugo Schuchardt, "Keltische Briefe" (1875), in *Romanisches und Keltisches: Gesammelte Aufsätze* (Strassburg: Trübner, 1886), 317–438.

[4] Mary Louise Pratt, *Imperial Eyes: Travel Writing and Transculturation*, 2nd ed. (New York: Routledge, 2008), 8.

[5] Kohl, *Reisen*, iii.

[6] Kohl, *Reisen*, iv.

[7] Rodenberg, *Ein Herbst in Wales*, 243.

[8] Rodenberg, *Ein Herbst in Wales*, 243–44.

[9] Rodenberg, *Ein Herbst in Wales*, 1.

[10] Rodenberg, *Ein Herbst in Wales*, 8.

[11] Rodenberg, *Ein Herbst in Wales*, 281.

[12] Rodenberg, *Ein Herbst in Wales*, 290.

[13] See Ferdinand Walter, *Das alte Wales* (Bonn: Marcus, 1859); and Matthew Arnold, *On the Study of Celtic Literature* (London: Smith, Elder and Co., 1867).

[14] Schuchardt, "Keltische Briefe," 326.

[15] The *Eisteddfod* is a Welsh cultural festival held at both local and national levels as a celebration of Welsh-language culture. The central event is the crowning of the bards.

[16] Schuchardt, "Keltische Briefe," 338.

[17] Schuchardt, "Keltische Briefe," 347.

[18] Alison E. Martin and Susan Pickford, eds., "Introduction," in *Travel Narratives in Translation, 1750–1830: Nationalism, Ideology, Gender* (New York: Routledge, 2012), 1–24, here 5.

[19] Julius Rodenberg, *An Autumn in Wales (1856): Country and People, Tales and Songs*, trans. William Linnard (Cowbridge, UK: D. Brown and Sons, 1985).

[20] See Carol Tully, "'Pride in their port, defiance in their eye': English Translations of German Travel Writing on the British Isles in the Early Nineteenth Century," *InTRAlinea Special Issue: Translating 18th and 19th Century European Travel Writing* (2013), www.intralinea.org/specials/article/1964. Accessed November 25, 2019.

[21] Christian August Gottlieb Goede, *The Stranger in England; or Travels in Great Britain*, 3 vols. (London: Matthews and Leigh, 1807), vii–viii.

[22] Christian August Gottlieb Goede, *Memorials of Nature and Art Collected on a Journey in Great Britain during the years 1802 and 1803*, trans. Thomas Horne, 3 vols. (London: Mawman, 1808), n.p.

[23] *Travels through England, Wales and Scotland in the year 1816 by Dr S. H. Spiker, Librarian to his Majesty the King of Prussia, dedicated to the Friends of England*, 2 vols. (London: Lackington, Hughes, Harding, Mavor, and Jones, 1820), x.

[24] Hermann Pückler-Muskau, *Tour in England, Ireland and France in the years 1828 & 1829; with remarks on the manners and customs of the inhabitants, and anecdotes of distinguished public characters; in a series of letters by a German prince*, trans. Sarah Austin, 2 vols. (London: Effingham Wilson, 1832), vi–vii.

[25] *Tait's Edinburgh Magazine*, July 1845, 472.

[26] Schuchardt, "Keltische Briefe," 437–38.

5: "Weltliteratur aus der Uckermark": Regionalism and Transnationalism in Saša Stanišić's *Vor dem Fest*

Frauke Matthes

The "Migrant" Writer, German "Provincialism," and the World

THE QUESTION OF WHERE German is in the world is a particularly intriguing one when taking a closer look at German-language writing by authors whose mother tongue is not German and who came to Germany as migrants. Their entry into the German literary canon in the past twenty years or so also sheds a revealing light on the transformations German literature has undergone, and the challenges these pose, due to the global migratory flows of the late twentieth- and early twenty-first centuries and the transnationalism that, partly as a result of this migration, has simultaneously triggered redefinitions as well as redrawings of national and cultural borders as the world becomes increasingly accessible. In the context of this chapter, transnationalism is tied to "our own moment, marked by the escalation of migration and the amplification of technological, financial, and commercial interdependence between nations."[1] It is precisely this interdependence—the reciprocity between as well as among nations and, on a smaller scale, regions, based on the movements of people and goods, but also of ideas and cultures—that is significant for my understanding of transnationalism here.

Contrary to this idea of transnationalism based on reciprocity, German-language "migrant" writers have often been regarded as a positive, if somewhat one-way, contribution to German literature that spices up the German literary scene, enriches the German language, and opens German up to the world in a way that nonminority writers are perceived to be less likely to do.[2] Despite the clear recognition that migrant writers contribute to *German* literature rather than to a category of their own, which marks a shift between the 1980s and its *Gastarbeiterliteratur* (guest-worker literature) and the present day with prize-winning novels such as Melinda Nadj Abonji's *Tauben fliegen auf* (*Fly Away, Pigeon*),[3] winner of the German Book Prize in 2010, they still teeter on the brink of being "ghettoize[d],"[4] of not being read for the literary value of their works but for their "exotic" biographies that supposedly highlight the worldliness of German literature.

Saša Stanišić is a particularly interesting writer in this context. Born in 1978 in Višegrad, Bosnia, Stanišić fled to Germany with his family shortly after the outbreak of the Bosnian War (1992–95). He came to literary prominence in 2005 when he won the Kelag Audience Award at the Ingeborg Bachmann Prize competition for his story "Was wir im Keller spielen" (What We Play in the Cellar), which fed into his highly successful 2006 novel *Wie der Soldat das Grammofon repariert* (*How the Soldier Repairs the Gramophone*).[5] Stanišić won various prizes for his debut, including the now-discontinued Adelbert von Chamisso Prize of the Robert Bosch Foundation in 2008.[6] He also published various shorter pieces and essays and wrote a play. In 2014 Stanišić could build on his earlier novelistic success with one of the most acclaimed novels of recent years: *Vor dem Fest* (*Before the Feast*, 2014).[7] Enthusiastically celebrated as "Weltliteratur aus der Uckermark" (world literature from the Uckermark),[8] it was the winner of the Leipzig Book Fair Prize in 2014. Stanišić is widely perceived as a representative of the "eastern turn" or "Eastern European turn" in German literature,[9] one of a number of writers of Eastern European origin whose literary production seems since the early 2000s to have surpassed that of writers with Turkish roots, who belong to the largest minority group in Germany. Despite the wide acclaim and success of the works by, for example, Terézia Mora, another winner of the German Book Prize (2013), or Marica Bodrožić, the assumption lingers that there is something special about (former) migrant writers such as Stanišić. As recently as 2015 Rebecca Braun mentions him as part of a group of "exciting writers" who seem to have the privilege over what I call in this context "native German" authors when it comes to "bringing the wider world to German culture in both the themes and the style of their writing. However, none of them looks very credibly set to take German culture out into the world in the near future. . . . There is nothing germane to the knowingly 'edgy' or outsider position that will automatically make such writers into world authors."[10] The rationale for such an argument is certainly not far-fetched: someone who has fled or left a country, settled in a new country, and decided to write in a language other than their native language has probably appealing stories to share with a wide readership and is likely to bring fresh perspectives into play on, for instance, questions of Germanness, the appropriation of German literary traditions, or, on a meta level, the dynamics of the literary market.[11] Yet the focus on writers' biographies, which singles them out as being somewhat different from their "native German" peers, and the expectations that (former) migrant writers make creative use of their "outsider position," expectations that are based on their linguistic and cultural background alone, is rather unhelpful when considering German literature's position in the world. In this context, Stanišić's *Vor dem Fest* is a thought-provoking example of how a writer can defy those expectations with his work and offer engaging literary insights into German's position in a wider transnational context.

My introductory remarks leave us with the following question: What happens if a writer from a non-German background, faced with the critics' and readers' predominant expectation to "bring the wider world to German culture,"[12] writes a novel set in a village in the Uckermark region in Brandenburg close to the German-Polish border? Stanišić is in good company here, as *Vor dem Fest* can be read as part of a noticeable revival in an interest in regional identities in German literature. Writers as diverse as Feridun Zaimoglu, with his novel *Ruß* (Soot, 2011), set in Duisburg among former miners, and Juli Zeh, with her novel *Unterleuten* (2016), which translates as "Among People" but is the name of the village in the East German region of Brandenburg, where the novel is set, are only two examples of the various authors who zoom in on a specific place or region in their texts while being conscious of Germany's wider transnational context.[13] Despite running the danger of singling (former) migrant writers out again, I would like to point out that writers who were once quickly pigeonholed in the "migrant writer" category, such as Zaimoglu, have, for a number of years now, moved away from migrant stories and focused on "native German" characters. One can read this shift in their subject matter as these writers' deliberate "Germanization" of their work and partly also of themselves, or, as I would like to suggest in this chapter, as a timely complication of the construction of German's position in the world.[14]

In a recent article in the weekly newspaper *Die Zeit*, the literary critic Ursula März interprets the rediscovery of regionality in some German-language writing as a return to *Heimat*, or home, in the genre of the "village novel," and places biographical, cultural, or gender nomadism, of which she sees Stanišić a representative, at opposing ends of the current zeitgeist that concerns the identity of human beings.[15] I cannot entirely agree with this binary in literary production between what we could perhaps term more broadly the "regional" and the "transnational." As I will show with my reading of Stanišić's form of the village novel, it is exactly that regionalism that shapes his aesthetically engaging narrative and that, somewhat paradoxically, enables the author to explore the interaction between the regional and the transnational that has shaped "Germanness" as it is in the world today. The fact that Stanišić started his career as a migrant writer makes his play with the complexity of this interaction in his work even more intriguing. As I will demonstrate, Stanišić offers his readers access to a "new German-language world literature," a phrase that is, unfortunately, often used rather uncritically to signal that German literature has become more transnational in recent years, as I outlined in my opening paragraphs.

However, such "new" world literatures (in the plural) as the one just outlined are not inherently wider reaching, a fact that somewhat echoes Braun's assessment of writers of non-German descent who do not "take German culture out into the world," as one would perhaps expect of those with a diverse cultural and linguistic background at their creative disposal.[16] "New" world literatures are, according to Caroline Levine and B. Venkat Mani, marked by "contemporariness," which "creates the impression that they are ephemeral; their multifaceted, purportedly chaotic ambition is often measured against the timeless value ascribed to representative works of a national or a linguistic canon assembled under the rubric 'world literature.'"[17] *Vor dem Fest* is, in many ways, a novel of its time: as our world becomes increasingly accessible, as borders shift, and as migration very manifestly influences people's lives, a return to the regional can offer a more tangible understanding of the transnational movements that have shaped people's histories as well as presents. However, a concern with the novel's timelessness or national or linguistic canonicity becomes irrelevant if we consider *Vor dem Fest* as a comment on the shaping both of Germanness as explored within the novel and of German literature on a meta level by the interaction between the specific and the transnational. My reading of *Vor dem Fest* will offer an impulse for thinking about Stanišić's creative contribution to a long-lasting redirection of German Literature towards "a" world literature.

In the following I will therefore demonstrate how in *Vor dem Fest*, seemingly paradoxically, there is a "reimagining" of the supposedly narrow-minded regional as a concept that does not stand in opposition to the "cosmopolitan" transnational but is a lived experience shaped by turbulent histories and migratory movements across continents and by what Stanišić's villagers refer to as "old stories" and the way they have been passed on and archived, or silenced and forgotten. As Emily Jeremiah has rightly pointed out, "Local/global encounters are key factors in the construction of contemporary identities and cultures, where global and local stand in a relationship of 'mutual interconnection and interdependence.'"[18] I agree with Jeremiah's assessment of constructions of contemporary identities beyond unhelpful binaries. However, "regionalism" and "transnationalism," rather than the "local" and the "global," are more suitable terms for my analysis of *Vor dem Fest*, as they refer to lived spaces, rather than somewhat abstract ideas, and put significant emphasis on reciprocal relationships not only between but also among those spaces and their inhabitants, an idea with which I opened my chapter. Furthermore, these terms imply that borders, their overcoming, shifting, but also redefining, are key aspects in the repositioning of the (former) migrant writer and his work. Thus it is exactly Stanišić's questioning of fixed binaries within discourses of regionality and transnationality that contributes to German literature's moving away from what the German-Jewish writer Maxim Biller criticized as "provincialism," from which only writers with non-German cultural and linguistic roots can save German literature by continuing to write "wilde, ehrliche, bis ins Mark ethnische und authentische Texte" (wild, honest, and ethnic and authentic texts to the core).[19] With *Vor dem Fest* Stanišić pursues a literary avenue that stands in opposition to Biller's clear distinction between the regional as inherently German and thus provincial—that is, somewhat boring—and the transnational as something that is represented by non-German migrants and thus is by definition exciting. Stanišić's exploration of constructions of regional identities in a transnational context can thus help readers and critics to reassess German literature's position in the world.

Regionalism and Transnationalism in *Vor dem Fest*

Vor dem Fest portrays the people of the village Fürstenfelde in the Uckermark in the night preceding the eponymous feast, the traditional *Annenfest* (Anna Feast). Different narrative voices allow a long list of characters—villagers with strong roots in Fürstenfelde and those who have migrated there, historical figures, and visitors—to interweave their personal stories with an array of historical occurrences, regional legends (which have actively been passed on, silenced, or archived), and lies to form a network of narratives within the limited space of the village. These stylistically rather distinct narratives create a rhythm that may have little to do with the stories told within the rhythm of the metropolitan centers that readers know from world literary texts such as those by John Dos Passos or Alfred Döblin. However, the language, or rather languages, that Stanišić lends to his characters and the stories they tell or allegorically represent, and the various historical flashbacks that reach back to as far as the 1600s, enables those stories to function as "a magnifying glass of the world":[20] the reader experiences Fürstenfelde as a specific place, but its history and stories have implications well beyond the Uckermark, as they implicitly comment on the village's position and transformations in a transnational and transhistorical context.

Stanišić's aesthetic strategy, which creates the rhythm of the stories, is particularly effective due to the linguistic peculiarities with which Stanišić peppers his novel.[21] Most noticeably the overall structure of *Vor dem Fest* consists of various types of repetitions: anaphora, above all the phrase "Wir sind . . ." ("We are . . .") followed by an adjective indicating the emotional state of the "wir," which opens several of the chapters and sets the tone for the story that is about to be told; formulas such as "So eine Nacht ist das" ("It's that kind of night"); lists of statements, questions, or information; and recurring motifs, such as the name "Anna," variations of which are the first names of several of the female characters and a vixen who is looking for eggs for her young. The "wir" of the narrative voice, which dominates many of the chapters, is a particularly noteworthy choice, as it makes the reader aware of some of the novel's central themes. Not only is the "wir" Stanišić's narrative trick "to let the village speak as a person,"[22] but it also triggers several crucial questions: Who exactly is this "wir"—the villagers, the narrators, or even the readers; who does it, as a community, include and exclude; and how does it influence the rhythm of the narrated stories and lives of the village? This "wir" has an inherent power as a creative force because it lets the multiple, diverse voices speak in the novel by zooming in on specific characters, only to let go of them in the middle of their stories, which will be picked up again later; however, it is also caring and "protects" the villagers by preferring to hide delicate details rather than exposing the villagers concerned.[23] Together the novel's various voices form a choir, even if they are mediated via the "wir" or an omniscient narrator: they "sing" together, respond to one another, and are sometimes in conflict with one another. This technique brings the musicality of *Vor dem Fest* to the fore. It not only allows Stanišić, in Nicola Steiner's words, to create a "precise, poetic" language and "accurate" images, but it also gives the reader a multifacetted, nuanced, and even democratic access to the world of the village.[24]

Above all, Stanišić's aesthetic strategy, which does not present readers with a linear narrative but lets them dip in and out of the various lives narrated, enables the writer to, in his own words, "write along," that is, to experiment with, "what is possible."[25] In contrast to a large number of contemporary novels, *Vor dem Fest* does not require a realistic narrative.[26] Quite the contrary: it is perhaps this aesthetic strategy, the twisting of and playing with "what is possible" and "the real," that enables the (former) migrant writer Stanišić to tell supposedly "German stories" of, as I will demonstrate, memory and the past, of the archiving or silencing and hence forgetting of "old stories," and of flight and migration that occupy the villagers' minds in the night before the feast. I read this as Stanišić's poetic critique of the significance of such stories in the construction of regional and, by extension, national identity, but also as his way of revealing the novel's central stories as, to borrow Gayatri Chakravorty Spivak's terms, "singular, universalizable, but never universal" stories[27] that can relate to other contexts and whose relevance reach far beyond their specificity.

It is not surprising therefore that the novel opens with the *Fährmann* (ferryman), whose death the villagers mourn. His presence, or rather absence, reveals details about the location of Fürstenfelde by the "wild" lakes, which not only separate the village from the rest of the region but are also the source of many myths and legends, the village's historical beginnings, and, above all, its people, whose roots can be traced back to "jene Siedler, die sich vor hunderten von Jahren als erste an unseren Seen niederließen" (*VdF*, 95; "the settlers who first came to live beside our lakes, hundreds of years ago" [*BtF*, 95]). The ferryman does not have a name; instead, as an allegorical figure, he comes across as the people's rescuer who protects them and as a collector of some of the stories that make up what Nicola Steiner calls the "score" of *Vor dem Fest*.[28] The reader learns:

> Wer in der ersten Zeit zu der neuen Siedlung wollte, den setzte der Fährmann über den See. Tüchtig nahm er sich der Menschen und Waren an und verlangte von manchem Ortsfremden statt Talern Geschichten zum Lohn, und die gab er im Dorfkrug an seine Fürstenfelder weiter. (*VdF*, 95)

> [At first, when people wanted to get to the new settlement, the ferryman rowed them across the lake. He capably took them and their belongings on board, and instead of money he often asked strangers to the place for stories as his fee, passing the stories on to the locals at the village inn.] (*BtF*, 95)

The reception and circulation of those stories is not far removed from David Damrosch's perception of world literature as "a mode of circulation and of reading" "beyond their culture of origin," while acknowledging the market forces that underlie such processes of reception.[29] Damrosch's notion of "translation" as another key aspect in the circulation of literary works takes on a particularly intriguing meaning when considering the ferryman as the villagers' "translator" of the stories that he was given as remuneration.[30] The ferryman thus plays a key role in the novel's questioning of the "authenticity" of stories, but also of those who tell them, who pass them on, and who listen to them—that is, those who compose the village, the regional.

However, the ferryman is much more than the wheel that sets the stories in motion: he is also in charge of stories in the form of memories, as their creator and their guardian. For instance, the artist Frau Kranz, trying to capture the village in a painting in the night before the feast, "plagte ein beinahe körperliches Verlangen nach alten Geschichten. Es kommt von dem Ort, dem Fährhaus, kommt von der Nacht" (*VdF*, 101; "Frau Kranz is plagued by an almost physical desire for old stories. It comes of this place, the boathouse of the ferry, it comes of the night" [*BtF*, 102]). The ferryman's role in the narrative also highlights Stanišić's distinctive approach to notions of memory and the past, "a hotly contested territory" in the reunified Germany, and, what Anne Fuchs and Mary Cosgrove have termed "memory contests," that is, "highly dynamic public engagements with the past that are triggered by an event that is perceived as a massive disturbance of a community's self-understanding."[31] Here Stanišić portrays memory as a physical experience, but it is, above all, *Geschichten* (stories), not *Geschichte* (history), for which the villagers are craving and which they trust: "Wir vertrauen den alten Geschichten" (*VdF*, 53; "We trust the old stories" [*BtF*, 54]). These "old stories," which, having crossed many borders, the village bounds included, and having been conveyed by the ferryman, are flexible and adaptable, are more significant than official history. They make up the cultural memory of the village. However, the ferryman is dead, as the reader learns in the novel's first few lines, and with him "ein guter Erzähler" (*VdF*, 12; someone who "was good at telling stories" [*BtF*, 11]), which destabilizes village life and also sheds new light on the village archive.

The trust in stories, rather than history, can perhaps best be explained by the villagers' limited access to their official history: this aspect of their past and memory is centralized in the village archive (*Archivarium*), located in cellar of the *Haus der Heimat* (Homeland House), often simply referred to as *die Heimat*, which, according to Dora Osborne, functions as "the principal institution of cultural memory in Fürstenfelde."[32] Its administrator, a villager with the telling name Johanna Schwermuth ("Schwermut" being the German word for "melancholy"), "weiß Sachen," and "wer an uns historisch interessiert ist, der spricht mit Frau Schwermuth" (*VdF*, 124; "knows things, and anyone who takes a historical interest in us had better talk to Frau Schwermuth" [*BtF*, 124]).

It is perhaps no coincidence that this village archive is one of the recurrent settings in the novel. Here Stanišić's novel responds to a "recent turn to the archive in thinking about memory" in literature and culture.[33] However, significantly, the archive is guarded by Frau Schwermuth, who acts as a mediator, similarly to the ferryman, between, in her case, historical, "archivable" facts and the villagers: not only does she control the villagers' knowledge of their past but she also impacts their historical consciousness and their identity as Fürstenfelder and as Germans by occasionally putting on exhibitions with a selection of old documents and paraphernalia upstairs in the *Haus der Heimat* but also by forging facts and retelling stories. Only the *Geschichtsverein* (History Society) knows what details of the village's, and, implicitly, German history have been archived; the general public does not have access to the neatly organized folders hidden in the nearly inaccessible cellar. This control of the village's archive may remind us of Jacques Derrida's discussion of the meaning of "archive" in his seminal essay "Archive Fever." Coming from the Greek *arkheion*, the "archive" was "initially a house, . . . the residence of the superior magistrates, the *archons*, . . . where official documents are filed." As the "document's guardians" the *archons* "do not only ensure [their] physical security, [but also] have the power to interpret the archives."[34] However, although the "wir" is curious about what might be hidden in the cellar that clearly should not come to light and, above all, about who broke into the archive during the night before the feast, it tells the reader: "Historische Genauigkeit interessiert uns nicht" (*VdF*, 125; "We don't take an interest in historical accuracy" [*BtF*, 125]); it does not appear to be concerned with the archontic power that Frau Schwermuth and the History Society have over the selection of and access to the archived material. Perhaps the archive's limited accessibility and unreliability goes hand-in-hand with their lack of interest in history.

Stanišić has pointed out that "Verheimlichen" (concealing) is also a "Form des Erzählens" (form of narrating).[35] The village archive, and the villagers' different attitudes towards it, is certainly a comment on the villagers' relationship with their (hidden) past and raises questions about the authenticity and reliability of historical facts. But Stanišić presents his readers with historical interludes, whose frequency increases as the novel progresses. Although these interludes also tell stories rather than give facts, I read them as one of the novel's counternarratives to the gradual Verschwinden "disappearance" of those historical stories that are hidden in the archive from people's memory, and thus, no less significantly, of the people whose stories these are.[36]

If we agree with Aleida Assmann that "the archive is not simply connected to memory, it *constitutes* it, specifically what she and Jan Assmann have influentially termed cultural memory," then a look into Stanišić's portrayal of an alternative way of archiving and sharing stories, history, and memory that is accessible and not controlled by an authority is particularly revealing.[37] It is, namely, through the painter Ana Kranz that Stanišić shows how stories and memory relate not only to the German but also the European, a transnational past.[38] With Frau Kranz he particularly explores stories of flight and migration whose impact on regional German identities has often been downplayed to preserve ideas of authenticity. Frau Kranz, who, by contrast to Frau Schwermuth of the *Haus der Heimat*, stores an archive of her own paintings in her attic, chronicles village life in her work, but as a newspaper article on the occasion of her ninetieth birthday celebrates her:

> *Ana Kranz sieht sich nicht als Heimatmalerin. Verbunden zu sein mit einem Land und einer Kultur ist ihr nicht geheuer. Ihre Gemälde zeigen aber eine Heimat—unsere Uckermark. Sie zeigen unsere Erinnerungen, auch solche, von denen wir erst durch das Bild erfahren, dass wir sie haben.* (*VdF*, 288, italics in original)

> [*Ana Kranz does not see herself as a painter of local scenes. She doesn't like to be linked with a particular countryside and its culture. However, her paintings do show local scenes—the countryside of our Uckermark. They show our memories, even those that we first know we have only through our image of them.* (*BtF*, 286–87, italics in original)]

Frau Kranz's skepticism towards "belonging" can be traced back to her background as a *Vertriebene* (expellee) from Eastern Europe, a migrant to the Uckermark after the Second World War;[39] she is, perhaps not coincidentally considering Stanišić's background, a "Donauschwäbin" ("Danube Swabian") or "Jugoslawiendeutsche" ("Yugoslavian German") (*VdF*, 55; *BtF*, 56) who, "so jung ganz Europa . . . durchquer[te] in den Wirren des Krieges" (*VdF*, 54; "young as [she was] then, [was] going here and there all over Europe in the confusion of wartime" [*BtF*, 55]), as the journalist interviewing Frau Kranz for his article points out. Opposing the journalist who, not unlike some literary critics with whom I opened my essay, insists on her biographical difference or otherness,[40] Frau Kranz unsentimentally points out that this is a "Zufall der Geburt" (*VdF*, 55; "an accident of birth" [*BtF*, 56]), which is at the core of her skepticism towards geographical and cultural roots. For this woman, who lived through the history of almost one century, migration is nothing "exotic" and is not the sole definer of her identity. On the contrary, she does not, in Sara Ahmed's words, celebrate migration "as a transgressive and liberating departure from living-as-usual in which identity (the subject as and at home) is rendered impossible."[41] She is "eine Frau, die das Elend und den Wandel und den Elend bringenden Wandel erlebt hat, . . . die Bosheit, den Hass, den Neid, die Passivität, den Ehrgeiz, den Wahn—dieses miese, schöne, scheinheilige, lebensrettende, erfundene Europa—. . ." (*VdF*, 86–87; "a woman who has known misery and change and change that brings misery, . . . malice, hatred, envy, passivity, ambition, delusion—our lousy, lovely, hypocritical, live-saving [*sic*] reinvented Europe—. . ." [*BtF*, 88]). It is therefore not contradictory or paradoxical that she paints or, not unlike the ferryman, creates one form of the regional, "*eine* Heimat" (italics added), and its associated memory. This specific *Heimat* is as constructed, historical, and invented, as the transnational Europe that she has experienced in her life. Her paintings are therefore also her way of questioning assumptions of the narrow-mindedness of the specifically regional and the open-mindedness of a transnational Europe.

This ties in with Stanišić's exploration of the impact of migration as a transnational phenomenon on places and its people via his character. Here a migrant painter, if one with German ethnic roots, and, on a meta level, a "migrant" writer, who was previously praised for the way he wrote about migration, an experience that only seemed to concern ideas of "Germanness" tangentially, can emphasize how Germany, or German regions, have been shaped by such transnational movements. Thus the way the journalist describes Frau Kranz in the article quoted above can be read as "a poetological description of the novel."[42] Leaning on Ahmed's notion of "stranger fetishism," I would also like to suggest that Frau Kranz, the former migrant and "stranger,"[43] also serves as a mediator of key questions concerning "the other"—namely, who really is the stranger, the other;

how do we recognize them; and how can they belong?[44] Ahmed points out that "with the transnational movements of bodies, objects and capital, . . . the stranger has come close to home."[45] As my reading of selected characters of *Vor dem Fest* has shown, boundaries—between the stranger, or migrant, and the "native," between story and history, between the regional and the transnational—shift and become permeable in Stanišić's novel. This leaves us with the question: How can we differentiate clearly between the regional and the transnational when, as Stanišić wonders, "external powers are stronger than the individual"?[46] Or, as the "wir" asks: "Wer schreibt die alten Geschichten?" (*VdF*, 222; "Who writes the old stories?" [*BtF*, 222]).

Through his interest in questions of memory and the past, the archiving or silencing, and hence forgetting, of old stories, and flight and migration, Stanišić does give a fictional account of Fürstenfelde as a specifically local place in the Uckermark, in Germany, and in Europe. However, the stories he tells in his novel are not restricted to this regional context, as Frau Kranz in particular makes clear. Their relevance reaches beyond the specific and are, to borrow Stuart Taberner's words with reference to nonminority writers, "localized narratives of a global phenomenon."[47] Stanišić may offer his readers a distinctive approach to these "German stories" in transnational contexts, yet he does not "give a foreign voice to local material," as Mads Rosendahl Thomsen says with reference to migrant and bicultural writers.[48] Instead I read Stanišić's focus on, and choice of, a specific local setting as a political statement. Fürstenfelde is not where the major political, social, and cultural decisions are made, but this is a place, like countless others, where Germany, and Europe, are made, where stories are told or forgotten, memory shared or silenced—that is, where German history as transnational history is created.[49] This is not to say that the specificity of Fürstenfelde is a side issue for Stanišić. Quite the contrary: as he said in an interview, despite a common assumption that villages are universal, the local is very distinct in *Vor dem Fest*, and his novel turned out to be an "Uckermärkischer Roman" (a novel of the Uckermark).[50] Yet it is precisely this specificity that paves the way for the perception of his work, rather than his public persona, as "transnational."

Conclusion

Despite a continued emphasis on Stanišić's background that sidelines him as an outside commentator on the German condition,[51] the success of *Vor dem Fest*, both on the literary market and in the German feuilleton, suggests that the author's work is now appreciated for its aesthetic strategies, the power of his narrative voices, and the convincing language that constitutes his stories rather than for the "exotic" value of his biography, which would previously have explained his "unique" storytelling or been used to market the book. Perhaps even more important, it also shows how a writer of a non-German background no longer needs to be an "other" who can only tell the story of his own migration in order to be noticed beyond the niche of migration literature; that story has been told and its writer is no longer singled out by special awards such as the Adelbert von Chamisso Prize, whose rationale was based on the assumption of a homogenous, "authentic" German culture.[52] In fact, the recent award to Stanišić of the 2019 German Book Prize for his significantly titled work *Herkunft* (Origins, 2019) shows how "non-native" forms of Germanness have stopped being exotic accessories, not only on the German book market but also, perhaps more important, in a world where national and nationalist movements are on the rise.[53] Thus with the characters, voices, and stories Stanišić created in *Vor dem Fest* five years before receiving the nation's most prestigious literary prize, one of whose intentions is "to draw attention outside our national borders to authors writing in German,"[54] the writer already points to ethical and political questions inherent in the discussion of "German in the world" when teasing out a (former) migrant writer's position within this discourse. His voice can now unquestioningly be part of the construction and negotiation of specifically German regional identities with histories, stories, and memory—that is, a past—that he would not have been allowed to own previously. His novel signals—to borrow Francesca Orsini's words— "the importance of location" for and in his writing.[55] Thus in *Vor dem Fest* Stanišić may reappropriate ideas of "difference" and "otherness" to rethink the regional as well as Germanness in a transnational context. Yet with his novel he can also, on a meta level, comment on the conditions of German literary production by addressing the "painful unevenness" and,[56] in Mariano Siskind's words, "the asymmetric interaction of hegemonic and subaltern cultural and economic forces that determine the unequal making of the globe"[57] as he may have experienced them as a migrant writer.[58] The question would also be whether he would be known more widely, transnationally, if he were not writing in German but in Bosnian, and whether I would discuss his work in the context of "world literature" then.

Considering the ethical and political implications of the subject matter and setting, and the aesthetic strategies Stanišić uses to convey them in *Vor dem Fest*, I suggest that Stanišić takes on a central role in the redefinitions of German (literature) in the world by exposing the transnational in the regional. Challenging binaries such as migrant versus native, history versus story, and inclusion versus exclusion of people, facts, and cultural memory, and negotiating the tensions between those seemingly opposing concepts,[59] both within his novel and in what can be referred to as his poetological agenda, Stanišić demonstrates convincingly that the seeming paradox of "Weltliteratur aus der Uckermarck," with which I opened my analysis of *Vor dem Fest*, captures the essence of his work well. In this sense, *Vor dem Fest* also echoes B. Venkat Mani's take on world literature. Mani writes that "world literature as I imagine it is not a choice between . . . binaries. It is in fact the productive tension between . . . binaries that gives world literature its many contested meanings, which in fact are in turn historically constructed, culturally located, and politically charged."[60] Ursula März's binary "village novel" versus nomadism is therefore an inappropriate approach to Stanišić's novel. Thus the journalist who interviews Frau Kranz brings the doubt regarding the "local" as clear-cut entity to the point by pondering: "Lokal, was heißt das schon—Uckermark . . ." (*VdF*, 92, ellipsis in original; "Depends on what you mean by local—the Uckermark . . ." [*BtF*, 93, ellipsis in original]).

For Spivak, commenting on comparative literature in North America, "it's a time to singularize rather than provincialize the European context of comp lit."[61] Stanišić's story "Fallensteller" (Trapper), published two years after *Vor dem Fest* in the collection of stories of the same title,[62] seems to be the German literary counterpart to Spivak's claim and a cunning answer to those critics who are either too concerned with his "migration background" when reviewing his work or lament the provincialism of German literature, his novel allegedly being an example of it. As a metatextual story, within the world of the story "Fallensteller" directly engages with the success of *Vor dem Fest* and its implications for the villagers in the context of the worldwide "refugee crisis" of 2015. It is also, I argue, an ironic comment on perceptions and portrayals of writers who have entered the literary arena as "others" and therefore do not fit within the conventional mainstream of literary criticism.

With "Fallensteller," Stanišić looks closely into the impact of strangers on a community that, despite such characters as Frau Kranz, sees itself largely unaffected by the transnational movements that have shaped contemporary identities. However, Stanišić sends the world to Fürstenwalde and again triggers a creatively intriguing questioning of clear boundaries between native and stranger, regional and transnational, and fact, or reality, and fiction. The village is confronted by: the "Jugo-Schriftsteller, . . . der mit dem Buch über uns" ("FS," 173; Yugo-writer, the one with the book about us), who attracts tourists, who wish to visit the model for the village in the book; refugees, with whom, according to the narrator, the village deals more successfully than "die Herrschaften in Berlin" (FS, 175; the ladies and gentlemen in Berlin); and wolves who are coming ever closer and are therefore perceived as a threat to the village. As a way of dealing with the fact that "wir werden weniger, die Tiere werden mehr" (FS, 171; our numbers are falling, those of the animals are rising), a nameless *Fallensteller* (trapper), sometimes also pejoratively referred to as "Rattenfänger" (FS, 183, 185; rat-catcher), appears and raises suspicion due to his unknown origins and his unusual methods of catching unwanted animals. Thus while the entry of those strangers into the village may stir up the villagers' rather monotonous lives and open them up to the world beyond the village bounds, the new arrivals bring hidden truths and unwelcome opinions to light and shatter purportedly robust self-perceptions. These dynamics may, of course, remind us of the entry of migrant writers into German literature who were perceived as exciting additions to the literary scene but who then also quickly highlighted the asymmetries in literary production.

Yet, in a smart poetological twist, Stanišić adds even further food for thought by exploring the villagers' fears of as well as fascination for those others who are suddenly present in their midst, alongside the burgeoning literary ambition of the workman Lada, Stanišić's alter ego of sorts, who is constantly taking notes on the villagers' actions and behaviors. He finally gains a prize for his text, a story that turns out to be, or at least shares the first few sentences with, "Fallensteller" (FS, 254–55). The laudation, quoted by the "wir," is a sharp comment on the reviewers and critics who have pigeonholed writers such as Stanišić for too long:

> Robert Lada Zieschke komponiert in seinem rasanten Milieustück eine Sinfonie der Provinz jenseits der großen Themen und abseits des Mainstreams. Die originelle Musikalität seiner Sprache sucht ihresgleichen in seiner Generation, was sicherlich damit zu tun hat, dass Zieschke ein Autor mit Provinzhintergrund ist ("FS," 250)

> [With his rapid milieu piece, Robert Lada Zieschke has composed a sinfonia of the provinces beyond the great themes and far from the mainstream. The original musicality of his language is unparalleled in his generation, which probably has something to do with the fact that Zieschke is an author with a provincial background.]

Apart from clear references to reviews of *Vor dem Fest*, the ascription of the literary qualities of Lada's work to the author's provincial background is an ironic mirroring of the reception and critique of Stanišić's first novel *Wie der Soldat das Grammofon repariert* as "migration literature." It also points to Stanišić's understanding of German in the world: exploring the interaction and tensions between the regional and the transnational brings the singular, universalizable aspect of German literature to the fore; it does not provincialize German literature but moves it towards "a" world literature.

At a time when the world comes to the provinces, when writers such as Stanišić have brought the world to German literature, perhaps Lada has managed to bring the provinces, the regional, to the world, and his creator Stanišić has added a thoughtful dimension to German literature's position in the world.

Notes

Uncredited translations are my own.

[1] Caroline Levine and B. Venkat Mani, "What Counts as World Literature?" *Modern Language Quarterly* 74, no. 2 (2013): 141–49, here 143–44.

[2] See Stuart Taberner, "Transnationalism in Contemporary German-Language Fiction by Nonminority Writers," *Seminar* 47, no. 5 (2011): 624–45, here 626.

[3] Melinda Nadj Abonji, *Tauben fliegen auf* (Munich: Deutscher Taschenbuchverlag, 2012 [2010]). English translation: *Fly Away, Pigeon*, trans. Tess Lewis (London: Seagull Books, 2014).

[4] See Taberner, "Transnationalisms," 625.

[5] Saša Stanišić, *Wie der Soldat das Grammofon repariert: Roman* (Munich: Luchterhand, 2006). English translation: *How the Soldier Repairs the Gramophone*, trans. Anthea Bell (London: Weidenfeld and Nicolson, 2008).

[6] The Adelbert von Chamisso Prize ran from 1985 until 2017, when the Robert Bosch Foundation considered the project to have been completed. See http://www.bosch-stiftung.de/de/projekt/adelbert-von-chamisso-preis-der-robert-bosch-stiftung (accessed February 19, 2018). However, as the Chamisso Prize/Hellerau, it has again been awarded to "authors with a migrant story" by a consortium of enterprises, associations, and cultural institutions in Dresden since 2018. See https://www.chamissopreishellerau.de/ (accessed February 20, 2020).

[7] Saša Stanišić, *Vor dem Fest: Roman* (Munich: Luchterhand, 2014); references will appear in the text as *VdF*, followed by page number. English translation: *Before the Feast*, trans. Anthea Bell (London: Pushkin Press, 2014); references will appear in the text as *BtF*, followed by page number.

[8] Review by Andreas Platthaus in *Frankfurter Allgemeine Zeitung*, quoted on the back cover of the hardcover edition.

[9] Brigid Haines, "The Eastern Turn in Contemporary German, Swiss and Austrian Literature," *Debatte* 16, no. 2 (2008): 135–49; Haines, "Introduction: The Eastern European Turn in Contemporary German-Language Literature," in *The Eastern European Turn in Contemporary German-Language Literature*, ed. Brigid Haines, Special Issue *German Life and Letters* 68, no. 2 (2015): 145–53. See also her article on *Wie der Soldat das Grammofon repariert*: "Saša Stanišić, *Wie der Soldat das Grammofon repariert*: Reinscribing Bosnia, or: Sad Things, Positively," in *Emerging German-Language Novelists of the Twenty-First Century*, ed. Lyn Marven and Stuart Taberner (Rochester, NY: Camden House, 2011), 104–18, esp. 106–7.

[10] Rebecca Braun, "Introduction: The Rise of the World Author from the Death of World Literature," in *World Authorship and German Literature*, ed. Rebecca Braun and Andrew Piper, Special Issue *Seminar* 51, no. 2 (2015): 81–99, here 89. Braun mainly refers to Feridun Zaimoglu in her argument here.

[11] Regarding the appropriation of German literary traditions, see Frauke Matthes, "'Ich bin ein Humanistenkopf': Feridun Zaimoglu, German Literature, and Worldness," in *World Authorship and German Literature*, ed. Rebecca Braun and Andrew Piper, Special Issue *Seminar* 51, no. 2 (2015): 173–90.

[12] Braun, "Introduction," 89.

[13] Feridun Zaimoglu, *Ruß: Roman* (Cologne: Kiepenheuer & Witsch, 2011). Juli Zeh, *Unterleuten: Roman* (Munich: Luchterhand, 2016).

[14] For a more detailed discussion of this phenomenon of "Germanization" with reference to Feridun Zaimoglu, see Matthes, "'Ich bin ein Humanistenkopf'," 173–90.

[15] Ursula März, "Heimatromane: Auf einmal Heimat," *Die Zeit*, no. 44 (2017), http://www.zeit.de/2017/44/heimatromane-dorf-renaissance-literatur (accessed February 9, 2018).

[16] Braun, "Introduction," 89.

[17] Levine and Mani, "What Counts as World Literature?," 144.

[18] Emily Jeremiah, *Nomadic Ethics in Contemporary Women's Writing in German: Strange Subjects* (Rochester, NY: Camden House, 2012), 12.

[19] See Maxim Biller, "Letzte Ausfahrt Uckermark," *Die Zeit*, no. 9, February 20, 2014, http://www.zeit.de/2014/09/deutsche-gegenwartsliteratur-maxim-biller (accessed June 22, 2016). Biller's title is a direct reference to Stanišić's novel. Ijoma Mangold wrote a critical response to Biller's idealization of the migrant writer in "Fremdling, erlöse uns!" *Die Zeit*, no. 10, February 27, 2014, http://www.zeit.de/2014/10/erwiderung-maxim-biller-deutsche-gegenwartsliteratur (accessed December 28, 2019).

[20] März, "Heimatromane."

[21] Compare "*Vor dem Fest* von Saša Stanišić: Nicola Steiner im Gespräch mit dem Autor," 52 Beste Bücher, Radio SRF, September 14, 2014, https://m.srf.ch/sendungen/52-beste-buecher/vor-dem-fest-von-sasa-stanisic (accessed March 14, 2018).

[22] "*Vor dem Fest* von Saša Stanišić."

[23] "*Vor dem Fest* von Saša Stanišić."

[24] "*Vor dem Fest* von Saša Stanišić."

[25] "*Vor dem Fest* von Saša Stanišić."

[26] See Heribert Tommek, "Formen des Realismus im Gegenwartsroman: Ein konzeptueller Bestimmungsversuch," in *Poetik des Gegenwartsromans*, Sonderband *Text + Kritik: Zeitschrift für Literatur*, ed. Nadine J. Schmidt and Kalina Kupczynska (Munich: Edition Text + Kritik, 2016), 75–87, here 75–78.

[27] Spivak, in David Damrosch and Gayatri Chakravorty Spivak, "Comparative Literature/World Literature: A Discussion with Gayatri Chakravorty Spivak and David Damrosch," *Comparative Literature Studies* 48, no. 2 (2011): 455–85, here 468.

[28] "*Vor dem Fest* von Saša Stanišić."

[29] David Damrosch, *What Is World Literature?* (Princeton, NJ: Princeton University Press, 2003), 5 and 4.

[30] Damrosch, *What Is World Literature?*, 281; Damrosch explains the role of translation in world literature in detail at 288–97.

[31] Anne Fuchs and Mary Cosgrove, "Introduction: Germany's Memory Contests and the Management of the Past," in *German Memory Contests: The Quest for Identity in Literature, Film, and Discourse since 1990*, ed. Anne Fuchs, Mary Cosgrove, and Georg Grote (Rochester, NY: Camden House, 2006), 1–21, here 2.

[32] Dora Osborne, "'Irgendwie wird es gehen': Trauma, Survival, and Creativity in Saša Stanišić's *Vor dem Fest*," *German Life and Letters* 72, no. 4 (2019): 469–83, here 477. See also 477–81 for an analysis of the *Haus der Heimat* and Frau Schwermuth's role as archivist.

[33] Dora Osborne, "Introduction," in *Edinburgh German Yearbook 9: Archive and Memory in German Literature and Visual Culture*, ed. Dora Osborne (Rochester, NY: Camden House, 2015), 1–19, here 2.

[34] Jacques Derrida, "Archive Fever: A Freudian Impression," trans. Eric Prenowitz, *Diacritics* 25, no. 2 (1995): 9–63, here 9–10.

[35] "*Vor dem Fest* von Saša Stanišić."

[36] "*Vor dem Fest* von Saša Stanišić."

[37] Osborne, "Introduction," 3. Osborne refers here to Aleida Assmann, *Der lange Schatten der Vergangenheit: Erinnerungskultur und Geschichtspolitik* (Munich: Beck, 2006), 57; emphasis in original.

[38] On Frau Kranz's reaction to her traumatic memory as a refugee through her art, see Osborne, "'Irgendwie wird es gehen,'" 474–77.

[39] Brent O. Peterson also views *Vertriebene* as migrants, emphasizing his argument that "migration narratives" in German literature have a much longer history than the Chamisso Prize and scholars of "migrant literature" assume. Peterson, "*Peter Schlemihl*, the Chamisso Prize, and the Much Longer History of German Migration Narratives," *German Studies Review* 41, no. 1 (2018): 81–98, here 97 and 82.

[40] See also Osborne, "'Irgendwie wird es gehen,'" 475.

[41] Sara Ahmed, *Strange Encounters: Embodied Others in Post-coloniality* (London: Routledge, 2000), 80.

[42] "*Vor dem Fest* von Saša Stanišić."

[43] Ahmed, *Strange Encounters*, 78.

[44] Ahmed, *Strange Encounters*, 21–37.

[45] Ahmed, *Strange Encounters*, 13.

[46] "*Vor dem Fest* von Saša Stanišić."

[47] Taberner, "Transnationalism," 626: "In the work of nonminority authors, therefore, a conventionally 'German' story of belated statehood, contested modernity, exceptionalism, genocide, and ambivalent postnationalism patterns their engagement with today's transnational epoch and enjoins them to produce localized narratives of a global phenomenon."

[48] Mads Rosendahl Thomsen, *Mapping World Literature: International Canonization and Transnational Literatures* (London: Continuum 2010 [2008]), 61.

[49] Osborne looks further into the construction of the village's collective memory in response to trauma in her article "'Irgendwie wird es gehen.'"

[50] "*Vor dem Fest* von Saša Stanišić."

[51] Tibor Fischer, "*Before the Feast* by Saša Stanišić—A Witty Balkan Take on the Reich," *The Guardian*, November 12, 2015, https://www.theguardian.com/books/2015/nov/12/before-the-feast-by-sasa-stanisic-review (accessed March 21, 2018). Fischer's review largely focuses on Stanišić's portrayal of the GDR, neo-Nazis, and their treatment of eastern Europeans.

[52] For a critical analysis of the rationale and history of the Chamisso Prize, see Peterson, "*Peter Schlemihl*."

[53] Saša Stanišić, *Herkunft* (Munich: Luchterhand, 2019).

[54] "About the Prize," Deutscher Buchpreis, https://www.deutscher-buchpreis.de/en/the-prize (accessed November 4, 2019).

[55] Francesca Orsini, "The Multilingual Local in World Literature," *Comparative Literature* 67, no. 4 (2015): 345–74, here 346.

[56] Levine and Mani, "What Counts as World Literature?," 142.

[57] Mariano Siskind, "The Globalization of the Novel and the Novelization of the Global: A Critique of World Literature," *Comparative Literature* 62, no. 4 (2010): 336–59, here 358.

[58] Compare, for example, Aamir R. Mufti, *Forget English!: Orientalisms and World Literatures* (Cambridge, MA: Harvard University Press, 2016), 10: "The ability to think 'the world' itself, whether in literary-critical thinking or other discourses and practices, is hardly distributed evenly across the world, even though its cultivation is an important task and a necessity, given those very asymmetries and inequalities."

[59] Stuart Taberner, "Introduction: Literary Fiction in the Berlin Republic," in *Contemporary German Fiction: Writing in the Berlin Republic*, ed. Stuart Taberner (Cambridge: Cambridge University Press, 2007), 1–20, here 18–19.

[60] B. Venkat Mani, *Recoding World Literature: Libraries, Print Culture, and Germany's Pact with Books* (New York: Fordham University Press, 2017), 33.

[61] Spivak, in Damrosch and Spivak, "Comparative Literature/World Literature," 473.

[62] Saša Stanišić, "Fallensteller," in *Fallensteller: Erzählungen* (Munich: Luchterhand, 2016), 169–255; references will appear in the text as FS, followed by page number.

6: Postcolonial Studies in International German Studies: Postcolonial Concerns in Contemporary German Literature

Dirk Göttsche

Forty years after the publication of Edward W. Said's study *Orientalism* (1978), widely seen as a catalyst for the rise of international postcolonial studies over the course of its first twenty years, postcolonial theory and postcolonial research are probably as well established in international German studies as they will ever be.[1] There is a regular stream of publications in history, literary and cultural studies, and also in the political and social sciences that advances the "postcolonial project" (to take Bhabha's term)[2] of critically "rereading and rewriting"[3] wider German involvement in European colonialism and imperialism, as well as the specific memory and critique of German, Austrian, and Swiss colonial history overseas and domestically, including its ambivalent legacies today that range from multifaceted cross-cultural exchange to the backlash of residual racism and resurgent nationalism. There are dedicated research centers, websites, and academic book series, and postcolonial research has its place in many of the leading international journals in German studies, while research on German, Austrian, and Swiss (post) colonial history and culture are beginning to feature in courses and journals dedicated to international, mostly Anglophone, postcolonial studies that tend to focus on British and French colonialism. The substantial edited volume *Postkoloniale Germanistik: Bestandsaufnahme, theoretische Perspektiven, Lektüren* (Postcolonial German Studies: Review, Critical Perspectives, Readings, 2014), and the comprehensive mapping of the field in the German-language *Handbuch Postkolonialismus und Literatur* (Handbook of Postcolonialism and Literature, 2017), which contextualizes German postcolonial studies in the wider field of comparative literature, other arts and humanities subjects, and comparative postcolonial studies, mark the establishment of postcolonial studies in German academia some twenty years after German studies began to embrace this new paradigm in the later 1990s.[4]

At the same time, the "postkoloniale Blick" (postcolonial gaze), as Paul Michael Lützeler calls it, pioneered by authors such as Uwe Timm, Hans Christoph Buch, and Hubert Fichte since the 1970s, has proliferated since the 1990s.[5] Critical engagement with the legacies of European colonialism, the critical memory of Germany's own imperial history, and the critique of Eurocentrism and the rejection of racism and othering have since become normalized in contemporary German literature. Indeed, seminal novels such as Uwe Timm's *Morenga* (1978), about Germany's genocidal colonial war of 1904–7 in South West Africa, or the Swiss writer Urs Widmer's *Im Kongo* (In the Congo, 1995), a postmodern critique of neocolonialism that is also a postcolonial rewriting of Joseph Conrad's *Heart of Darkness* (1899), anticipate the emergence of postcolonial research in academia, highlighting the significance of literary discourse in the advancement of postcolonial awareness in Germany, Austria, and Switzerland. Similarly, postcolonial inquiry into German, Austrian, and Swiss history since the 1990s and the rediscovery of colonialism in the wave of mostly historical and family novels about the theme published since the later 1990s go hand in hand,[6] while German postcolonial literature—African migrants writing in German and black German literature since the feminist anthology *Farbe bekennen: Afro-deutsche Frauen auf den Spuren ihrer Geschichte* (Professing Color: Afro-German Women on the Trail of Their History, 1986; in English as *Showing Our Colors: Afro-German Women Speak Out*, 1992), a founding document of the black German movement—pioneered inquiry into the history and legacy of German colonialism, and into the unknown history of the African diaspora in Germany, a decade before academic research embraced these concerns.[7]

This chapter will therefore combine a brief historical overview of postcolonial studies in German studies with an introductory outline of postcolonial concerns in contemporary German literature: the critique of colonial history and thought in historical and other novels, and in German postcolonial literature with an African connection. Closely aligned with the new interest in transculturalism in a world of migration, increased mobility, and global interaction across continuing imbalances in power and wealth, postcolonial discourse firmly places Germany, Austria, and Switzerland on the map of neglected or forgotten colonial legacies, of often violent socio-cultural transformations, and the cultural resonances of globalization that include new forms of cosmopolitanism but also resurgent nationalism and racism. In other words, postcolonial studies within German studies is one way of using history, literature, and culture to rethink the place of Germany, Austria, and Switzerland in the world both historically and today, including the domestic repercussions of such global links. This renewed widening of horizons since the 1990s builds on the globalizing thrust of Europe's colonial expansion in the nineteenth century, but it is of course marked by different forms of connectivity and exchange, of competition and conflict, that a number of strands in contemporary German literature, as well as postcolonial research in Germany and internationally, register and address.

Postcolonial Studies in German Studies—History and Trends

The rise of postcolonial studies in German studies since the 1990s is part of a wider shift from traditional literary studies to broader cultural studies that foster interdisciplinary research across the arts and humanities as well as history and the social and political sciences. The rise of gender studies, media studies, and memory studies are related developments, all of which are distinctly transnational and interdisciplinary in nature, redefining the way in which knowledge is organized and how research and teaching work at the university level.[8] Disciplines rooted in national frames of reference, such as German *Germanistik*, were more radically affected by this paradigm shift than international area studies and modern languages, such as UK and US German studies, which are in a sense interdisciplinary in themselves, incorporating the study of German history and politics, language and linguistics, alongside German literature and culture, and more recently film and media. Institutional context and disciplinary networking are vital for the dissemination of new research paradigms. It is therefore no coincidence that it was English and American studies that first embraced postcolonial theory in German academia, while US German studies scholars such as Paul Michael Lützeler, Susanne Zantop, and Russell Berman were the first to apply postcolonial theory to German literature and culture in the later 1990s.[9]

What, then, is postcolonial studies? Building on the Francophone anticolonial theory of the mid-twentieth century, such as Aimé Césaire, Albert Memmi, and Frantz Fanon,[10] and on Western critical theory, Anglophone postcolonial studies emerged in the late 1970s as a new cultural studies paradigm that implicates the former colonizers in the world of colonial legacies and challenges power structures both between and within the Global South and the Global North. Foundational works, such as Said's *Orientalism* (1978), Homi K. Bhabha's *The Location of Culture* (1994), and Gayatri Chakravorty Spivak's essay "Can the Subaltern Speak?" (1988) became the basis for the international proliferation of postcolonial studies across the arts and humanities, combining—as the seminal book *The Empire Writes Back* (1989) puts it—the critical "rereading" of "the European historical and fictional record" with the "rewriting" of colonial history.[11] Postcolonial critique aims to overcome the history and legacy of European colonialism and imperialism in social, economic, and political terms, but also in terms of culture and thought: continuing Eurocentricism, asymmetrical power structures and new instances of racism are the most obvious targets. Bhabha therefore speaks of "the postcolonial project" and its "empowering strategies of emancipation"[12] that give postcolonial studies a political edge also within literary studies. As a result, postcolonial methodology has been extended to areas not directly linked to European overseas colonialism and its domestic repercussions: for example, the "colonial gaze" deployed historically in the treatment of German-speaking Europe's internal "others," such as "gypsies" and Jews,[13] the postcolonial reading of the literature of the Turkish-German migration,[14] or the postcolonial rereading of Habsburg history in central and southeastern Europe.[15]

As postcolonial research has developed beyond its initial theoretical framework and expanded in scope, it has extended well beyond the politics of overseas imperialism—showing, for example, how a country such as Switzerland, which never had colonies of its own, was nevertheless fully implicated in the colonial system and discourse.[16] At the same time, critical debate has pointed out the limitations of an approach that is often still focused primarily on European colonial history overseas and its continuing legacies in North-South relations at the expense of other and earlier forms of colonialism. As critics—often from within the field—have pointed out, the ongoing need to secure the relevance and reach of postcolonial studies in a world that is moving beyond the immediate aftermath of the decolonization era includes, to give just three examples, the need to also consider other empires and their legacies (for example, the Ottoman Empire or China), South-South relations (such as across the Indian Ocean), or, conversely, the complex conditions of intra-European colonialism (for example, the superimposed legacies of German, Polish, and Russian/Soviet colonial involvement in the Baltics).[17] Calls to consider properly Germany's history of colonial settlement and politics in central and eastern Europe (from early modern times through to Hitler's *Lebensraum*, or "living space" politics)[18] and attempts to reconstruct previously unacknowledged "African, Asian, and Oceanic Experiences" of German colonial rule[19] are as important for the vitality of the field in German studies as the continued search for the domestic and overseas "traces" of German colonial history along the lines of historical *Spurensuche* (retracing/search for traces), which is arguably the most successful and popular format of postcolonial inquiry in the German context.

Indeed, in historiography the paradigm of historical *Spurensuche* marks the transition from earlier research into German colonialism[20]— work that continues to be as relevant today as earlier research into exoticism, orientalism, and other cultural phenomena is for postcolonial literary studies—to conceptually postcolonial research produced since the 1990s. This retracing of Germany's forgotten colonial history often happens at a regional level—for example, in cities such as Hamburg, Berlin, Cologne, or Freiburg.[21] Political activism promoting the renaming of German streets that recall the colonial era is a particularly visible aspect of the proliferation of postcolonial debate and memory in wider German society.[22]

A wealth of publications indicates that in German historiography, postcolonial research has been well established since about 2000, reassessing Germany's colonial history both overseas and domestically, both in terms of addressing previous blind spots (such as the defining role of pre-existing African infrastructure for colonial conquest, or the agency of those supposedly colonized) and radically deconstructing older narratives steeped in colonial or post-imperial ideology (for example, the myth of the "loyal Askari" soldier in East Africa).[23] Historiography and cultural studies have also begun to map out the long road of sociopolitical, biographical, and discursive continuities and discontinuities between the end of Germany's colonial empire in World War I (or the Versailles treaty of 1919) and the emergence of postcolonial discourse during the 1990s. Superseding earlier assessment, both literary and historical research has shown that there was never a German "postcolonial amnesia" after the definite end of colonial aspirations in World War II:[24] anti-imperialism was part of the German Democratic Republic's politics of memory after 1945, while in the Federal Republic the long shadow of pro-colonial post-imperial discourse (following on from the colonial revisionism of the Weimar Republic aimed at restoring Germany's lost colonies)[25] on the one hand, and anti-colonial discourse reinvigorated by the defeat of National Socialism on the other, along with keen interest in the struggles of decolonization in the Global South, kept the colonial theme alive until anticolonial critique moved center stage in the context of the 1968 student movement and left-liberal intellectuals' "discovery" of the Third World as a global context of domestic politics. Anti-imperialism of the 1960s and 1970s is also the springboard for the social and political sciences in Germany embracing postcolonial theory in the 2000s for the critical reassessment of regimes of migration and exploitation along with a critique of Western concepts of modernity and (cultural) identity.[26]

German *Germanistik* followed the example of Anglo-American German studies with a few years' delay[27]—a fact explained at least in part by the prior existence of a competing paradigm that addresses some of the same questions: the German tradition of cross-cultural literary studies, notably *Interkulturelle Germanistik* (intercultural *Germanistik*), established (also since the 1970s) by Alois Wierlacher and others as a cultural studies-based reinvention of *Deutsch als Fremdsprache* (German as a foreign language), and more recently *Interkulturelle Literaturwissenschaft* (intercultural literary studies), which, unlike postcolonial studies within *Germanistik*, is also supported by dedicated professorial chairs.[28] In terms of the politics of theory and competition for staff and funding resources there is, therefore, at times rivalry between German cross-cultural and postcolonial literary studies, but there is also evidence that German studies makes its most original contributions to international postcolonial literary studies when combining the benefits of both, as reflected in the works of scholars such as Herbert Uerlings, Alexander Honold, or Axel Dunker, or indeed the research that emerged from the network "Postkoloniale Studien in der Germanistik" (Postcolonial Studies in *Germanistik*, 2008–2011) funded by the Deutsche Forschungsgemeinschaft (German Research Council, DFG).[29] While the anglophone tradition tends to emphasize the political edge of postcolonial research, the German blending of postcolonial and cross-cultural literary studies often highlights the specific "postcolonial potential," as Uerlings puts it, of literature as a form of art.[30] Literature was of course involved in endorsing and even promoting colonialism—the colonial novel between the 1890s and 1945 is the most obvious case in point—but it also has a prominent role in staging, critiquing, and deconstructing colonial discourse and thought both historically and today.

Adopting Said's methodology of "contrapuntal reading,"[31] the critical postcolonial rereading of the literary canon, such as in Dunker's *Kontrapunktische Lektüren* (Contrapuntal Readings, 2008),[32] has proved to be the most established form of German postcolonial literary research, covering a rich range of authors and work from the eighteenth century to modernism and triggering literary rediscoveries and reappreciations that feed into debates about the German literary canon.[33] Prominent examples include the discussion about the balance of colonialist othering and anticolonialism in Heinrich von Kleist's novella *Die Verlobung in St. Domingo* (The Betrothal in Santo Domingo, 1811),[34] the discussion about the "worldly provincialism" of late nineteenth-century German Realism,[35] the reassessment of Wilhelm Raabe as an author who engages extensively and critically with Germany's growing colonial fascinations in the later nineteenth century, or the postcolonial rereading of modernist classics such as Franz Kafka's *In der Strafkolonie* (In the Penal Colony, 1914) or Alfred Döblin's *Amazonas* trilogy (Amazon trilogy, 1937/38).[36] Other studies, such as Stefan Hermes's monograph about engagement with Germany's colonial war in South West Africa in German literature from 1904 to 2004,[37] focus on specific colonial themes, including inquiry into the rise of German colonial interest and discourse during the nineteenth century.[38] Anglo-American German studies have a significant role in advancing such postcolonial research, both historical and literary, as do African and Indian scholars who, supported by journals such as *Acta Germanica: German Studies in Africa*, *Weltengarten*, and *Mont Cameroun*, developed their own postcolonial approaches.[39] Finally, there is extensive research into colonial culture within Germany, Austria, and Switzerland in publications that look at the cultural resonance of key events in colonial history,[40] at the popular institution of the *Völkerschauen* (culture shows),[41] the trade and advertising of *Kolonialwaren* (colonial goods),[42] the colonial imagination involved in children's toys and young adult fiction,[43] the history of the colonial gaze in visual culture, and the prominent role of the colonial theme in early twentieth-century cinema or, via popular reenactments of the now exotic colonial past, on German television today.[44]

Similar to some of the more popular historical novels about the colonial period discussed below, television features and documentary dramas reminding Germany of her previously neglected colonial history are a particularly ambivalent instance of the normalization of postcolonial historical awareness, since their attempts to visualize the past often go along with the reinstatement of colonial myths and narratives. Nevertheless, they are part of a significant shift in German discourse about colonial history, as a brief comparison of two symbolic dates shows: first, the centenary in 1984 of the so-called Congo conference in Berlin, at which the European imperial powers settled their competing claims in Africa, sparking the "scramble for Africa" at the end of the nineteenth century and Germany's own imperial adventure; and second, the centenary in 2004 of Germany's genocidal colonial war against the Herero and Nama in South West Africa, which gave the colonial theme unprecedented public resonance and acted as a catalyst for the inclusion of colonial history in post-unification Germany's culture of memory. Although only twenty years apart, these two centenaries mark a step-change in Germany's own postcolonial history. The centenary of 1984 had nothing like the public resonance of the 2004 centenary, also because of the way in which the latter, including the memory of genocide, linked the colonial theme to Germany's dominant memory discourse about National Socialism and the Holocaust. This helped to overcome the misconception that the colonial past was irrelevant for contemporary Germany. In 1984 colonial history was on the one hand still very much a left-wing minority concern steeped in post-1960s anti-imperialism and the political controversies of the period, for example about the use of developmental aid and the tenacity of neocolonialism. At the other end of the political spectrum those once involved in German imperialism and the colonialist revisionism of the Weimar period also raised their voices one last time, for example through the Traditionsverband deutscher Schutz- und Überseetruppen (the association fostering the memory and tradition of German colonial troops overseas).[45] The memory discourse of 1984 was thus very much still a post-imperial one, marked by a radical divide between the Left and the Right.

The memory discourse of 2004 was entirely different, moving from post-imperialism to postcolonial discourse supported by the multicultural transformation of German society and new global frames of reference.

Generational change meant that there were no post-imperial voices left to defend Germany's colonial involvement, nor was there any of the political heat seen in the anti-imperialist publications of the 1980s. Critics suggested that there was a need for Germany finally to take responsibility for her colonial history, but there was equally a shared critical assessment of Germany's colonial involvement overseas. Despite the growing historical distance, German society has since taken greater interest in the colonial past and the everyday experience of colonialism by both the colonizers and the colonized. Such historical curiosity may at times slip into nostalgia and uncritical re-enactment, but the literary evidence along with historical publications, ambitious media productions, the local tracing of colonial history, and debates about the renaming of German streets or the reassignment of monuments all demonstrate that postcolonial awareness and memory have to an extent been "normalized."[46] Critical acknowledgement of Germany's involvement in colonialism and imperialism has become the norm in political discourse and cultural production, but this does not mean that postcolonial awareness has been embraced by all, nor does it preclude the persistence of elements of colonial discourse, such as racist stereotyping and exoticist projection in some popular fiction, politics, and media.

This fragile normalization of the "postcolonial gaze" is also reflected in the wave of historical novels and family novels produced since the mid-1990s that all engage in the memory of German colonialism, mostly in Africa, but also in the Pacific and in China. The writers' "postcolonial gaze" and academic research now effectively work hand in hand, also in the use of archival sources. This indicates the broader cultural context for new alliances between postcolonial studies and memory studies (as suggested by Michael Rothberg's *Multidirectional Memory*, 2009),[47] postcolonial studies and gender studies, or comparative postcolonial studies. There is little point in discussing the supposed specificity of German colonial history and German postcolonialism—the early end of Germany's colonial empire, the lack of significant postcolonial immigration, the limited global status of the German language, the primacy of National Socialism and the Holocaust in Germany's politics of memory—without taking due account of the distinct but interrelated colonial histories of the other European countries.

Postcolonial Concerns in Contemporary German Literature I: Historical Novels, Family Novels, Metafiction, and Crime Fiction

Postcolonial memory and critique in contemporary German literature since the 1990s builds on the long history of literary anticolonialism, which challenged colonial and post-imperial discourse and politics all along, providing a counter-voice to texts supporting colonial fantasies and ambitions. Precursors during the postwar decades include, among others, fictions questioning colonialist accounts of Germany's genocidal war in South West Africa of 1904–1907. Ferdinand May's *Sturm über Südwest-Afrika: Eine Erzählung aus den Tagen des Hereroaufstandes* (Storm over South West Africa: A Story from the Days of the Herero Uprising, 1962) and Dietmar Beetz's *Flucht vom Waterberg* (Escape from the Waterberg, 1989) represent East Germany's anti-imperialist politics of memory in using African perspectives to criticize German imperialism and capitalism, casting the Herero and Nama uprising as anticipation of the liberation wars of the 1950s and 1960s. In West Germany, Alfred Andersch's short story *Weltreise auf deutsche Art* (Journey Around the World the German Way, 1949/58) and Uwe Timm's historical novel *Morenga* (1978), whose mixture of documentary montage, a fictional anticolonial *Bildungsroman*, and historical vignettes in the style of magical realism created a postcolonial classic, focused instead on the experience of ordinary Germans deployed in the war, since, as Timm put it, for a German author to portray the African experience would create an "Einfühlungsästhetik" (aesthetics of empathy) that was tantamount to renewed colonial appropriation and "ein kolonialer Akt" (a colonial act).[48] As a result, the question of whether and how to portray the perspective and agency of the colonized has become a major concern in more recent German literature revisiting colonial history. East and West German authors were united, however, in suggesting historical resonances between the colonial past and the postcolonial present, and in linking the critical memory of Germany's imperialism to the dominant memory theme of National Socialism and the Holocaust along the lines established by Hannah Arendt's influential study on *The Origins of Totalitarianism* (1951). This interlinking of memory themes continues to be a leitmotif in contemporary literature on this topic, including in black German writing.[49]

The transition from postwar anticolonialism to contemporary postcolonial discourse during the 1990s is marked by a steep rise in the number of novels on the colonial theme (with a first peak around the 2004 centenary of the Herero and Nama war in 1904) and by discursive shifts as the sharp contrasts between "North" and "South," colonial perpetrators and colonized victims, oppression and liberation give way to more flexible narratives resonating with the new experiences of globalization and with the multicultural diversification of German, Austrian, and Swiss society since the 1980s. There are clearly synergies in the 1990s and early 2000s between the "postcolonial gaze," growing intercultural interest, and the "Afrika-Boom" (Africa boom) that critics noted in popular German fiction at the time.[50] The considerable number of Swiss authors involved (Alex Capus, Urs Widmer, Lukas Hartmann, Christian Kracht, and others) warns against linking this rediscovery of colonialism in German literature too closely to the effects of German unification and the debate about modern Germany's political place in the world. At the same time, postcolonial discourse in literature clearly benefited from the "memory boom" that has marked not just German but European culture and discourse since the 1980s.[51]

The majority of literary texts in the field are either historical novels, ranging from adventure stories via intercultural *Bildungsromane* (novels of individual development and growth) through to self-reflexive metafiction, or they use the new format of the transgenerational family novel, reinvented as a memory genre that enables the author to bridge the gap between the colonial past and the postcolonial present so as to underline the significance of that past for the present. Archival sources, intertextual references, heteroglossia, polyperspectivism, and ironic or grotesque style are often used to deconstruct the colonial discourse of the world represented. Germany's colonial involvement in today's Namibia and Tanzania are clearly the most popular themes, while there are hardly any novels to date about German colonial rule in Cameroon and Togo. The notable exception is Thomas von Steinaecker's *Schutzgebiet* (Protectorate, 2009), set in a fictionalized Togo and uniquely exploring the synergies between colonialism and technological modernity. More recently authors have also revisited German colonial involvement in the Pacific, while Germany's foothold in China (Qingdao/Tsingtau) has yet to be covered. Andreas von Klewitz's *Kegilé oder die seltsame Reise des Kammerdieners Jeremias Grobschmied von Brandenburg nach Afrika* (Kegilé, or the Strange Journey of Valet J. G. from Brandenburg to Africa, 2016) is probably the only novel to date recalling the often forgotten participation of German principalities in the early modern phase of Europe's colonial expansion, in this case Brandenburg/Prussia's colony Groß Friedrichsburg on the coast of today's Ghana.

This brief overview can only present a small selection from the large and growing corpus of novels and shorter narratives produced since the 1990s.[52] The prominence of the colonial war in South West Africa, which is today seen as a genocide, and the continued presence of a German settler minority in today's Namibia, gives novels about this theme a political edge that is absent, for example, in most novels about East Africa, where German colonial rule committed similar atrocities that, however, have not registered in Germany's collective memory.[53] Pertinent examples of postcolonial engagement with Namibia include the historical novel *Die schweigenden Feuer: Roman der Herero* (Silent Fires: A Novel of the Herero, 1994) by the Namibian-German author Giselher W. Hoffmann, who uses a fictional Herero with the telling name Himeezembi (I won't forget) to chronicle the history of his people from 1861 through to the aftermath of the anticolonial uprising in 1905.[54] Andrea Paluch and Robert Habeck's

Der Schrei der Hyänen (The Cry of the Hyenas, 2004) exploits the transgenerational family novel's ability to bridge past and present through the genetic conceit that the liaison of a German settler's daughter with the Herero chief Assa Riarua only transpires two generations later when scandalized white West German parents surprisingly have a black daughter. The novel spans a full five generations from 1899 to the eve of Namibia's independence in 1989, only to end by symbolically closing the chapter of Germany's colonial history. This is just the kind of attitude attacked by Christof Hamann in his novel *Fester* (2003) through the ironic critique of German tourism in today's Namibia. A more critical, metafictional use of the family novel, combined with a literary version of historical *Spurensuche*, is to be found in Stephan Wackwitz's *Ein unsichtbares Land: Familienroman* (An Invisible Country: A Family Novel, 2003, in English as *An Invisible Country*, 2005), a novel that situates the grandfather's work as a nationalist pastor and colonial revisionist in 1930s Namibia within the much wider framework of an essayistic critique of German cultural history since early modern times, including cross-references between colonialism, the Holocaust, and 1960s racism. By contrast, Bernhard Jaumann adapts crime fiction and the political thriller for a postcolonial critique in his remarkable trilogy *Die Stunde des Schakals* (The Hour of the Jackal, 2010), *Steinland* (Stoneland, 2012), and *Der lange Schatten* (The Long Shadow, 2015), all concerned with the conflicted politics of memory in today's multiethnic Namibia and in Germany to show how the colonial past continues to cast its long shadow into the present.[55]

The lack of a similar political focus in novels concerned with German rule in East Africa, combined with fascination with the ethnic, cultural, and religious diversity of the region, often leads to uneasy tensions between a critical postcolonial perspective and persistent exoticism, and between the decentering of Eurocentric narratives and the return to colonial myths. However, unlike in earlier texts, contemporary novels, in particular from the popular end of the spectrum, now tend to foreground female heroism, as the women protagonists experience colonial space as liberation from the confines of the Wilhelmine Reich, and the preponderance of characters who are critical of the colonial regime often leaves the reader wondering how the colonial system was ever able to work. Titles such as Monika Czernin's *"Jenes herrliche Gefühl der Freiheit": Frieda von Bülow und die Sehnsucht nach Afrika* ("That Wonderful Feeling of Freedom": Frieda von Bülow and the Yearning for Africa, 2008), a biographical novel about the founding figure of Germany's colonial novel, are indicative of the recycling of exoticist clichés, while novels such as Rolf Ackermann's *Die weiße Jägerin* (The White Huntress, 2005) and Ray Müller's *Ein Traum von Afrika* (A Dream of Africa, 2007) reinstate settler myths and verge on retrospective vindications of colonial involvement.

Zanzibar has emerged as one of the most popular East African locations thanks to a history that allows for the blending of African exoticism with orientalism, while also speaking to contemporary interest in transcultural experience—notably as seen in the life of Emily Ruete, Princess Salme of Oman and Zanzibar, who married a merchant from Hamburg and later published the story of her life in *Memoiren einer arabischen Prinzessin* (Memoirs of an Arabian Princes, 1886, in English as *An Arabian Princess between Two Worlds*, 1993). Lukas Hartmann's biographical novel *Abschied von Sansibar* (Farewell to Zanzibar, 2013) uses a transcultural memoryscape to map out the challenges of colonial globalization from non-European perspectives, while Hans Christoph Buch's *Sansibar Blues oder Wie ich Livingstone fand* (Zanzibar Blues, or How I Found Livingstone, 2008) is one of the most ambitious examples of postcolonial metafiction. Rewriting sections from Ruete's memoirs and from the German translation of the Swahili memoir of the prominent Zanzibari slave dealer and ivory trader Hamed bin Muhammed, better known as Tippu Tip, and combining these postcolonial rewritings within a framework travel narrative set in the present, an appendix with historical sources, and the fictional story of an East German diplomat, the illegitimate son of Germany's last governor of Togo and later the husband of the last Sultan of Zanzibar's daughter, Buch retraces the history of Zanzibar and its African hinterland, and of German involvement there, from the 1850s through to the present.

Buch's metafictional use of Ruete's and bin Muhammed's memoirs tries to give a voice to the colonized in a poetics of transcultural memory, while irony and humor aim to point out "the fact that the colonial past continues to have an effect on the present and how it does so."[56] In his bestseller *Der Weltensammler* (The Collector of Worlds, 2006, in English with the same title in 2008), the Bulgarian-born Ilija Trojanow similarly translates Said's postcolonial method of "contrapuntal reading" into a transcultural poetics of "contrapuntal writing"[57] by supplementing his retelling of the British explorer and officer Richard Burton's trips to India, Arabia, and East Africa with (fictional) indigenous counter-narratives, all polyphonous in themselves, which represent Indian, Arabic, and African perceptions of Europe's colonial expansion as well as the agency of the colonial "others." The European rather than specifically German reach of this postcolonial poetics is echoed in the Swiss writer Alex Capus's very different reconstruction of an episode in British-German imperial rivalry that feeds into World War I in East Africa: his historical novel *Eine Frage der Zeit* (A Question of Time, 2007, in English as *A Matter of Time*, 2009) tells the story of the German steamer *Graf Götzen*, which the imperial navy had built in Papenburg, dismantled and shipped to the eastern shore of Lake Tanganyika to secure Germany's supremacy in central Africa, while the British sent two gun boats from London via

Cape Town and the Belgian Congo to the lake's western shore to counter the German threat. Ending in an anticlimax of nonachievement on both sides, Capus's thoughtful novel deconstructs imperial ambitions and narratives and explores how and why ordinary Germans and Britons came to be involved in the colonial project in the first place. Historical critique thus combines with social and psychological concerns.

Another prominent Swiss author, Christian Kracht, produced the most widely noted historical novel about German involvement in the Pacific, *Imperium* (2012), whose title already indicates the ambition to portray the imperial period on the eve of World War I as a whole, although the specific subject is the life of German countercultural dropout August Engelhardt, who tried to establish a life-reformist "order of the sun" revolving around the coconut on the Pacific island of Kabakon. Linking the cultural history of colonialism with the history of countercultures, Kracht's ironic pastiche of colonial discourse includes oblique references to key events and figures at the time, ranging from Thomas Mann to Hermann Hesse to Adolf Hitler. In an earlier novel, the grotesque dystopian *Ich werde hier sein im Sonnenschein und im Schatten* (I Will Be Here in the Sunshine and in the Shade, 2008), an exercise in alternative history, Kracht also implicates Switzerland in the violent legacy of European colonial expansion into Africa. The earliest and probably most influential novel to critique Swiss involvement in (neo) colonialism, however, is Urs Widmer's *Im Kongo* (In the Congo, 1996, in English with the same title in 2015), whose emphatic critique of racism, commercial exploitation, and historical violence conceives of Africa and Europe as equal parts of *one* world, while also putting the postcolonial fascination with cultural hybridity in ironic perspective. Widmer again links the themes of colonialism and National Socialism, as does the Austrian writer Max Blaeulich in his *Menschenfresser* trilogy (Cannibals trilogy, 2005–8), which combines Austrian explorations in Uganda and colonial "race science" with the deployment of African colonial troops in World War I, and the demise of the Habsburg Empire with the emergence of National Socialism in Austria, in a violent and grotesque narrative that puts Austria center stage in its radically dystopian critique of European imperialism and racism.[58]

These Swiss and Austrian examples underline the fact that postcolonial memory in contemporary German literature is not confined to the overseas, nor specifically to German, colonialism; it includes the rediscovery of forgotten colonial history *within* Germany, Austria, and Switzerland, as well as a wider critique of European colonial activities. Many of the novels mentioned above include sections devoted to the domestic backgrounds and repercussions of colonial involvement, and to elements of colonial culture such as the culture shows or encounters with Africans in domestic space. Recurrent themes in the literary engagement with European colonialism more widely include the exploration of Africa, the role of the missionaries, and (more rarely) colonial trade. Two of the most ambitious novels in the field, Thomas Stangl's *Der einzige Ort* (The One and Only Place, 2004) and Christof Hamann's *Usambara* (2007), develop complex multistranded postmodern narratives to deconstruct the myth of colonial exploration. Stangl's novel retraces the "discoveries" of the legendary city of Timbuktu by Alexander Gordon Laing and René-Auguste Caillé, contrasting their different but equally colonialist approaches with African sources and the deeper cultural history of the myth of Timbuktu since antiquity. Hamann uses the format of the transgenerational family novel and the concept of "postmemory" to interlink the lives of a late nineteenth-century gardener who claims to have assisted Hans Meyer in his famous climb of Mount Kilimanjaro in 1888/89, while his grandson fails to retrace his steps in a "Kilimandscharo Benefit Run" portrayed as a travesty of neocolonial tourism and the global charity industry today.[59]

By contrast, novels focused on the ambivalent role of the Christian missionaries as both pioneers of colonial penetration and internal critics of the colonial system tend to combine postcolonial critique with representations of transcultural experience and intercultural dialogue that decenters colonialist perceptions. Successful examples include Hermann Schulz's East African novel *Auf dem Strom* (On the River, 1998), Jens Johannes Kramer's West African novel *Die Stadt unter den Steinen* (The City below the Rocks, 2000), and Sibylle Knauss's *Die Missionarin* (The Female Missionary, 1997), set in the Pacific. Economic ambitions and their political resonances, as well as competition between European and local trading networks, are explored, for example, in Kramer's second West African novel, *Das Delta* (The Estuary, 2010), about the beginnings of British involvement in Nigeria, and in Ilona Maria Hilliges's East African cycle *Sterne über Afrika* (Stars above Africa, 2007) and *Ein Kind Afrikas* (A Child of Africa, 2009), which combine a thriller from the world of tropical medicine and the pharmaceutical industry with a vision of African-German partnership in development. Clearly contemporary twenty-first-century concerns are reflected here in in the literary engagement with colonial globalization.

Postcolonial Concerns in Contemporary German Literature II: African Migrants' Writing, Black German Literature, Remembering the African Diaspora

This overview would be incomplete without considering the pioneering role of black Germans and Africans writing in German in advancing postcolonial discourse in contemporary German literature. These are the most prominent strands in the small field of German postcolonial literature in the sense of a literature whose authors have a biographical link to those regions formerly colonized by Europe or to the global African diaspora resulting from the slave trade. The transnational frames of personal and cultural reference in such postcolonial literature help to unsettle entrenched national notions about literature and cultural identity; they interrelate German literature with other cultures and international diasporic networks, contributing significantly to the "worlding" of German literature and its share in the ultimately global postcolonial project. During the 1980s African migrants and Afro-German women helped to shape the "postcolonial gaze" in German literature by promoting inquiry into Germany's neglected colonial history, the unknown history of the African diaspora in Germany, and the "postmemory" of colonialism in African immigrants whose parents and grandparents had either still experienced German colonial rule or were part of oral memory cultures in countries such as Togo and Cameroon, where Germany's more distant colonial rule is often part of a politics of memory targeting more recent French colonialism. As both strands of German postcolonial literature with an African reference expanded and diversified with generational change since the 1990s, critical engagement with Germany's colonial period and its legacies today continues to be a leitmotif in the politics of memory of Afro-German and African migrants' writing.

Probably the earliest examples of German postcolonial literature critically remembering German colonialism are Dualla Misipo's autobiographical novel *Der Junge aus Duala: Ein Regierungsschüler erzählt* (The Boy from Douala: A Government-Sponsored Student Tells His Story: ms. c. 1960, print 1973), which reflects the identity conflicts of a young member of the Cameroonian elite, sent to Germany for education on the eve of World War I, who takes a clear stand against racism and apartheid, and the documentary play *Ach Kamerun! Unsere alte deutsche Kolonie...* (Oh, Cameroon! Our Old German Colony; ms. 1970, print 2005) by the political scientist and Douala prince Kum'a Ndumbe III. This play uses comical and grotesque language to recall the German colonization of his country and the failure of anticolonial resistance, while also remembering the Douala rebel Rudolf Duala Manga Bell as a prominent precursor of post-1945 liberation movements. Staying with Cameroon, the memory of German colonial times inspires a father to send his son to study in the GDR in Daniel Mepin's novel *Die Weissagung der Ahnen* (The Ancestors' Prophecy, 1997), whose tragic modeling of African diasporic identity— the protagonist commits suicide after German unification—is redeemed by magical realism, as the epilogue gives him a second lease on life as a successful writer and politician in independent Cameroon. The character of the father serves to promote critical memory of Germany's imperialism but also the postcolonial idea of cultural advancement through hybridization as the father advises his son "ihre [the Germans'] Weisheit mit unserer [zu] verschmelzen" (to blend German wisdom with ours).[60] The artist El Loko from Togo uses a similar combination of tragic (anticolonial) identity discourse and postcolonial memory in his autobiographical narrative *Der Blues in mir* (The Blues Inside Myself, 1986), as it is the legacy of German colonialism that motivates the first-person narrator's study of art in Germany, where he finds his identity as an African artist blending elements from both cultures, but then, forced to return to Togo in 1979, is left stranded, unsure where to go: "Aber wohin?" (But where to?).[61] The story places memory discourses center stage, as the narrator first portrays his native village—in childhood perspective and highly poetic language—as though it had been a precolonial African idyll, a paradise from which he was expelled by the French colonial school system, only to return to the setting later and reread it—now in critical postcolonial perspective—as a world deeply influenced by German colonial rule, in which the narrator's own family had a significant stake as they embraced colonial modernization as an opportunity for social advancement.

More recent German autobiographies by African migrants addressing German colonialism—such as Lucia Engombe's *Kind Nr. 95: Meine deutsch-afrikanische Odyssee* (Child no. 95: My German-African Odyssey, 2004) and Stefanie-Lahya Aukongo's *Kalungas Kind: Wie die DDR mein Leben rettete* (Kalunga's Child: How the GDR Saved My Life, 2009), both by Ovambo authors sent to the GDR for education by Namibia's liberation movement SWAPO during the 1970/80s—no longer have a generational link to the colonial past and take a more traditional historical approach to recalling Germany's involvement in Namibia. A remarkable memoir combining personal memory of (Portuguese) colonialism, life in the GDR, and the political struggle against resurgent racism and xenophobia in post-unification Germany is Ibraimo Alberto's assertive account of African migration in *Ich wollte leben wie die Götter: Was in Deutschland aus meinen afrikanischen Träumen wurde* (I Wanted to Live Like the Gods: What Became of My African Dreams in Germany, 2014).[62] In this exceptional case the late end of Portuguese rule in Mozambique still allows for direct memory of colonial conditions; for all other Africans writing in German this period has now passed into history, even though its legacies continue to make an impact. In all these cases "worlding" German autobiography through lives marked by (post) colonial migration is linked to political activism against lingering racism, claiming for members of the African diaspora their equal place in German society.

In the parallel strand of black German literature, the seminal volume *Farbe bekennen: Afro-deutsche Frauen auf den Spuren ihrer Geschichte*—note again the metaphor of *Spurensuche*, in this case retracing colonial and diasporic history—and the poetry of co-author May Ayim set the scene for a tradition of Afro-German writing and activism that continues right through to today.[63] Critical memory of German colonialism is a leitmotif in this tradition, as seen, for example, in the essayistic works of Noah Sow (*Deutschland Schwarz Weiß: Der alltägliche Rassismus*; Germany Black and White: Everyday Racism, 2008) and ManuEla Ritz (*Die Farbe meiner Haut: Die Antirassismustrainerin erzählt*; The Color of My Skin: The Antiracism Coach Tells Her Story, 2009), or in Michael Götting's small novel *Contrapunctus* (2015) about Afro-Germans' lives today, which continues to draw on the imaginary of the slave trade and the "Black Atlantic."[64] Such postcolonial literature is of course a small field in the German case and one that stands very much in the shadow of other minority literatures (such as the much larger corpus of Turkish-German writing), but it reflects the multicultural transformation of German society as a vital context for the rise of postcolonial discourse and awareness.

In pioneering inquiry into the previously unchartered history of the African diaspora in Germany, Austria, and Switzerland, Afro-German writing of the 1980/90s also opened the door to this area of postcolonial concern in contemporary German literature, which authors from all three countries have since explored in more detail, often with an element of regional *Spurensuche*. Relevant sources include Dieter Kühn's metafictional novel *Beethoven und der schwarze Geiger* (Beethoven and the Black Violinist, 1990), about George August Polgreen Bridgetower, the black violinist of Polish-German and Afro-Caribbean descent to whom Beethoven originally dedicated his Violin Sonata No. 9 in A Major, Op. 47 ("Kreutzer"), and Johann Glötzner's historical novel *Der Mohr: Leben, Liebe und Lehren des ersten afrikanischen Doctors der Weltweisheit Anton Wilhelm Amo* (The Moor: Life, Loves, and Teachings of the First African Doctor of World Wisdom, Anton Wilhelm Amo, 2003), about the eighteenth-century "moor" slave whom Duke Anton Ulrich of Braunschweig-Wolfenbüttel sent to study at university so that he became a professor of philosophy at Halle and Jena before returning to his native Ghana. Regionalist examples include Christa Langer-Löw's *Antonio Congo: Sein Weg von Afrika über Brasilien nach Hamburg und ins Weserbergland: Roman auf der Grundlage einer historisch wahren Geschichte* (Antonio Congo: His Journey from Africa via Brazil to Hamburg and to the Weser Mountains: A Novel Based on a True Story from History, 2009), whose title speaks for itself, and the Swiss author Lukas Hartmann's historical novel *Die Mohrin* (The Female Moor, 1995), about a liberated Caribbean slave and her son in eighteenth-century Switzerland. Hartmann uses the child's perspective to give a moving account of African diasporic experience in a predominantly racist Europe while also implicating Switzerland in European colonialism. Varigated African diasporic experience in nineteenth- and twentieth-century history, including the persecution of Africans and black Germans during the Nazi period, is addressed, for example, in two biographies based on academic research: Gorch Pieken and Cornelia Kruse's *Preußischer Liebesglück: Eine deutsche Familie aus Afrika* (Loving Happiness in Prussia: A German Family from Africa, 2007), which retraces three generations of Afro-Germans from 1843 through to the present, the descendants of a "moor" given to Prince Albrecht of Prussia by the Viceroy of Egypt, and Marianne Bechhaus-Gerst's *Treu bis in den Tod: Von Deutsch-Ostafrika nach Sachsenhausen—eine Lebensgeschichte* (Loyal unto Death: From German East Africa to Sachsenhausen—a Life, 2007) about the difficulties faced by a former Askari child soldier from German East Africa who was looking for a better life in Weimar Germany and ended up in a concentration camp. Harald Gerunde's biographical novel of his Afro-German wife, Bärbel Kampmann, *Eine von uns: Als Schwarze in Deutschland geboren* (One of Us: Born Black in Germany, 2000), takes such postcolonial inquiry into African diasporic history through to the postwar generation of black Germans typically born to African American fathers and their white German partners in West Germany after 1945.

Conclusion

These examples from a rich range of different literary strands show how postcolonial discourse in contemporary German literature continues to flourish well beyond its initial peak in the early-to-mid-2000s. Authors use a full range of genres—from autobiography, biography, and historical novels to transgenerational family novels; from popular formats, such as crime fiction and the thriller, to advanced metafiction—to remember and critique the place of Germany, Austria, and Switzerland in European colonialism and its continuing legacies in the present, both overseas and at home. Indeed, authors are highly inventive in finding new ways of interlinking the past and the present, and domestic and overseas spaces, and their mutual entanglement. While postcolonial literature by black Germans and African writers tends to be more outspoken in its political interventions, historical and other novels on the theme, often working hand in hand with postcolonial scholarship, are no less powerful in their postcolonial critique of the impacts of globalization, migration, and the multicultural diversification of societies in a world of increased mobility as well as continuing imbalances in power and wealth. The "postcolonial project" in German literature is certainly not finished, not in terms of critically retracing and rereading the ramifications of colonial history, nor in terms of the postcolonial critique of contemporary German society and its global resonances. Contemporary German literature thus offers postcolonial literary studies internationally ample food for thought.

Similarly, postcolonial studies, although now established in UK and US academia for some thirty years and in German studies for more than fifteen years, continues to produce innovative research that transforms our understanding of Germany, Austria, and Switzerland's place in the world—and its cultural resonances—both historically and today. At the same time, postcolonial studies have to widen their range and rethink their methodology to stay relevant in the face of new national and international challenges in an increasingly interconnected world marked by new forms of violence, exclusion, and competition for resources. Postcolonial research is well placed to address a range of social and cultural concerns in a universe of continued asymmetries in power and wealth, new forms of cosmopolitanism, but also resurgent nationalism and parochialism. This potential is unlikely to be realized, however, if research questions and methodology are restrained by the anglophone classics of postcolonial theory from thirty years ago. German postcolonial studies make their own original contribution to international and interdisciplinary research by researching distinct colonial histories, interlinking postcolonial memory with other memory discourses, and engaging in dialogue with intercultural studies, with its particular interest in the aesthetics and ethics of literary discourse. This helps redefine the field and take it beyond its Anglo- and Francocentric beginnings for a fuller and more differentiated understanding of European (post) colonial history and its continued relevance today.

Notes

[1] Edward W. Said, *Orientalism* (London: Routledge & Kegan Paul, 1978).

[2] Homi K. Bhabha, *The Location of Culture* (London: Routledge 1994), 171.

[3] Bill Ashcroft, Gareth Griffiths, and Helen Tiffin, *The Empire Writes Back: Theory and Practice in Post-Colonial Literatures*, 2nd ed. (London: Routledge, 2002), 221.

[4] Gabriele Dürbeck and Axel Dunker, eds., *Postkoloniale Germanistik: Bestandsaufnahme, theoretische Perspektiven, Lektüren* (Bielefeld: Aisthesis 2014). Dirk Göttsche, Axel Dunker, and Gabriele Dürbeck, eds., *Handbuch Postkolonialismus und Literatur* (Stuttgart: Metzler, 2017); see in particular Gabriele Dürbeck, "Deutsche und internationale Germanistik," 38–53, and "Institutionen und Webseiten," 440–45.

[5] Paul Michael Lützeler, ed., *Der postkoloniale Blick: Deutsche Schriftsteller berichten aus der Dritten Welt* (Frankfurt am Main: Suhrkamp, 1997).

[6] See Dirk Göttsche, *Remembering Africa: The Rediscovery of Colonialism in Contemporary German Literature* (Rochester, NY: Camden House, 2013).

[7] *Farbe bekennen: Afro-deutsche Frauen auf den Spuren ihrer Geschichte*, ed. May Ayim, Dagmar Schultz, and Katherine Oguntoye (Berlin: Orlanda Frauenverlag, 1986). *Showing Our Colors: Afro-German Women Speak Out*, ed. May Opitz, Katharina Oguntoye, and Dagmar Schultz, trans. Anne V. Adams (Amherst: University of Massachusetts Press, 1992).

[8] See the relevant articles in Göttsche, Dunker, and Dürbeck, *Handbuch Postkolonialismus und Literatur*, 101–26.

[9] Paul Michael Lützeler, ed., *Schriftsteller und Dritte Welt: Studien zum postkolonialen Blick* (Tübingen: Stauffenburg, 1998); Susanne Zantop, *Colonial Fantasies: Conquest, Family, and Nation in Precolonial Germany, 1770–1870* (Durham, NC: Duke University Press, 1997); and Russell Berman, *Enlightenment· and Empire: Colonial Discourse in German Culture* (Lincoln: University of Nebraska Press, 1998).

[10] See Charles Forsdick and David Murphy, eds., *Postcolonial Thought in the French-Speaking World* (Liverpool: Liverpool University Press, 2009). For a general introduction, see Neil Lazarus, ed., *The Cambridge Companion to Postcolonial Literary Studies* (Cambridge: Cambridge University Press, 2004).

[11] Ashcroft, Griffiths, and Tiffin, *The Empire Writes Back*, 221.

[12] Bhabha, *The Location of Culture*, 171.

[13] See Iulia-Karin Patrut, "Conceptualizing German Colonialisms within Europe," in *(Post-)Colonialism across Europe: Transcultural History and National Memory*, ed. Dirk Göttsche and Axel Dunker (Bielefeld: Aisthesis 2014), 279–304.

[14] See Hansjörg Bay, "Migrationsliteratur (Gegenwartsliteratur III)," in Göttsche, Dunker, and Dürbeck, *Handbuch Postkolonialismus und Literatur*, 323–32, for a discussion of the potential and limitations of postcolonial readings of literatures of migration.

[15] See, for example, Johannes Feichtinger, Ursula Prutsch, and Moritz Csáky, eds., *Habsburg postcolonial: Machtstrukturen und kollektives Gedächtnis* (Innsbruck: Studien-Verlag, 2003).

[16] See Patricia Purtschert, Barbara Lüth, and Francesca Falk, eds., *Die postkoloniale Schweiz: Formen und Folgen eines Kolonialismus ohne Kolonien* (Bielefeld: transcript, 2012).

[17] See, with a mind to German postcolonial concerns, for example, Russell A. Berman, "Colonialism, and No End: The Other Continuity Theses," in *German Colonialism: Race, the Holocaust, and Postwar Germany*, ed. Volker Langbehn and Mohammad Salama (New York: Columbia University Press, 2011), 164–89; Monika Albrecht, "German Multiculturalism and Postcolonialism in Comparative Perspective: Prolegomenon for the Framework for a Postcolonial Germany," in Göttsche and Dunker, *(Post-)Colonialism across Europe*, 33–56; Epp Annus, "Layers of Colonial Rule in the Baltics: Nation-Building, the Soviet Rule and the Affectivity of a Nation," in Göttsche and Dunker, *(Post-)Colonialism across Europe*, 359–84; and Dirk Göttsche, "Afrasian Prisms of Postcolonial Memory: German Colonialism in East Africa and the Indian Ocean Universe in Contemporary Anglophone and German Literature," in *Postcolonialism Cross-Examined: Multidirectional Perspectives on Imperial and Colonial Pasts and the Neocolonial Present*, ed. Monika Albrecht (London: Routledge, 2020), 217–39.

[18] See, for example, various chapters in Langbehn and Salama, *German Colonialism*.

[19] Nina Berman, Klaus Mühlhahn, and Patrice Nganang, eds., *German Colonialism Revisited: African, Asian, and Oceanic Experiences* (Ann Arbor: University of Michigan Press, 2014).

[20] For example, Horst Gründer, *Geschichte der deutschen Kolonien* (Paderborn: Schöningh, 1985), and more recent editions.

[21] See Heiko Möhle, ed., *Branntwein, Bibeln und Bananen: Der deutsche Kolonialismus in Afrika—Eine Spurensuche* [in Hamburg, D.G.] (Hamburg: Verlag Libertäre Assoziation, 1999); Ulrich van der Heyden and Joachim Zeller, eds., *Kolonialmetropole Berlin: Eine Spurensuche* (Berlin: Berlin-Edition, 2002); Marianne Bechhaus-Gerst and Anne-Kathrin Horstmann, eds., *Köln und der deutsche Kolonialismus: Eine Spurensuche* (Cologne: Böhlau, 2013); for Freiburg, see the website http://www.freiburg-postkolonial.de/, accessed November 30, 2017. For other cities, see relevant chapters in Ulrich van der Heyden and Joachim Zeller, eds., *Kolonialismus hierzulande: Eine Spurensuche in Deutschland* (Erfurt: Sutton, 2007).

[22] See, for example, Christian Kopp and Marius Krohn, "Blues in Schwarz-Weiß: Berlins Black Community im Widerstand gegen kolonialrassistische Straßennamen," in *Black Berlin: Die deutsche Metropole und ihre afrikanische Diaspora in Geschichte und Gegenwart*, ed. Omar Diallo and Joachim Zeller (Berlin: Metropol 2013), 219–31.

[23] See Andreas Eckert, "Geschichtswissenschaften," in Göttsche, Dunker, and Dürbeck, *Handbuch Postkolonialismus und Literatur*, 78–83; Bradley Naranch and Geoff Eley, eds., *German Colonialism in a Global Age* (Durham, NC: Duke University Press, 2014).

[24] See Monika Albrecht, *"Europa ist nicht die Welt": (Post)Kolonialismus in Literatur und Geschichte der westdeutschen Nachkriegszeit* (Bielefeld: Aisthesis, 2008); Britta Schilling, *Postcolonial Germany: Memories of Empire in a Decolonized Nation* (Oxford: Oxford University Press, 2014).

[25] See Florian Krobb and Elaine Martin, eds., *Weimar Colonialism: Discourses and Legacies of Post-Imperialism in Germany after 1918* (Bielefeld: Aisthesis, 2014).

[26] See Julia Reuter and Paula-Irene Villa, eds., *Postkoloniale Soziologie: Empirische Befunde, theoretische Anschlüsse, politische Interventionen* (Bielefeld: transcript, 2010); Adam Ziai, ed., *Postkoloniale Politikwissenschaft: Theoretische und empirische Zugänge* (Bielefeld: transcript, 2016).

[27] For a fuller outline see Gabriele Dürbeck, "Postkoloniale Studien in der Germanistik: Gegenstände, Positionen, Perspektiven," in Dürbeck and Dunker, *Postkoloniale Germanistik*, 19–70; Dürbeck, "Deutsche und internationale Germanistik," in Göttsche, Dunker, and Dürbeck, *Handbuch Postkolonialismus und Literatur*, 38–53.

[28] See Dirk Göttsche, "Postkolonialismus als Herausforderung und Chance germanistischer Literaturwissenschaft," in *Grenzen der Germanistik: Rephilologisierung oder Erweiterung?*, ed. Walter Erhart (Stuttgart: Metzler, 2004), 558–76.

[29] See Dürbeck and Dunker, *Postkoloniale Germanistik*, which summarizes key results of the network's research.

[30] Herbert Uerlings, *"Ich bin von niedriger Rasse": (Post-) Kolonialismus und Geschlechterdifferenz in der deutschen Literatur* (Cologne: Böhlau, 2006), 15.

[31] Edward W. Said, *Culture and Imperialism* (London: Vintage, 1994), 78.

[32] Axel Dunker, *Kontrapunktische Lektüren: Koloniale Strukturen in der deutschsprachigen Literatur des 19. Jahrhunderts* (Munich: Fink, 2008).

[33] See Herbert Uerlings and Iulia-Karin Patrut, eds., *Postkolonialismus und Kanon* (Bielefeld: Aisthesis, 2012).

[34] See Hansjörg Bay, "Postkolonialismus," in *Kleist-Handbuch: Leben—Werk—Wirkung*, ed. Ingo Breuer (Stuttgart: Metzler, 2009), 400–402.

[35] Patrick Ramponi, "Orte des Globalen: Zur Poetik der Globalisierung in der Literatur des deutschsprachigen Realismus (Freytag, Raabe, Fontane)," in *Poetische Ordnungen: Zur Erzählprosa des deutschen Realismus*, ed. Ulrich Kittstein and Stefani Kugler (Würzburg: Königshausen & Neumann, 2007), 17–53 (20), with reference to H. Glenn Penny and Matti Bunzl, eds., *Worldly Provincialism: German Anthropology in the Age of Empire* (Ann Arbor: University of Michigan Press, 2003); Roland Berbig and Dirk Göttsche, eds., *Metropole, Provinz und Welt: Raum und Mobilität in der Literatur des Realismus* (Berlin: de Gruyter, 2013).

[36] See Axel Dunker, "18. und 19. Jahrhundert," in Göttsche, Dunker, and Dürbeck, *Handbuch Postkolonialismus und Literatur*, 244–59; Oliver Simons, "Moderne," in Göttsche, Dunker, and Dürbeck, *Handbuch Postkolonialismus und Literatur*, 268–74; Dirk Göttsche and Florian Krobb, eds., *Wilhelm Raabe: Global Themes—International Perspectives* (London: Legenda, 2009).

[37] Stefan Hermes, *'Fahrten nach Südwest': Die Kolonialkriege gegen die Herero und Nama in der deutschen Literatur (1904–2004)* (Würzburg: Königshausen & Neumann, 2009).

[38] See, for example, Florian Krobb, *Vorkoloniale Afrika-Penetrationen: Diskursive Vorstöße ins "Herz des großen Continents" in der deutschen Reiseliteratur (ca. 1850–1890)* (Frankfurt am Main: Peter Lang, 2017).

[39] See Dürbeck, "Deutsche und internationale Germanistik," 45–47.

[40] See, for example, Alexander Honold and Oliver Simons, eds., *Kolonialismus als Kultur: Literatur, Medien, Wissenschaft in der deutschen Gründerzeit des Fremden* (Tübingen: Francke, 2002); Alexander Honold and Klaus R. Scherpe, eds., *Mit Deutschland um die Welt: Eine Kulturgeschichte des Fremden in der Kolonialzeit* (Stuttgart: Metzler, 2004).

[41] See, for example, Eric Ames, *Carl Hagenbeck's Empire of Entertainments* (Seattle: University of Washington Press, 2008); Rea Brändle, *Wildfremd, hautnah: Zürcher Völkerschauen und ihre Schauplätze 1835–1964* (Zurich: Rotpunktverlag, 2013).

[42] See, for example, David Ciarlo, *Advertising Empire: Race and Visual Culture in Imperial Germany* (Cambridge, MA: Harvard University Press, 2011).

[43] See, for example, Jeff Bowersox, *Raising Germans in the Age of Empire: Youth and Colonial Culture, 1871–1914* (Oxford: Oxford University Press, 2013).

[44] See, for example, Wolfgang Struck, *Die Eroberung der Phantasie: Kolonialismus, Literatur und Film zwischen deutschem Kaiserreich und Weimarer Republik* (Göttingen: V&R unipress, 2010); Joachim Zeller, *Weiße Blicke—Schwarze Körper: Afrikaner im Spiegel westlicher Alltagskultur; Bilder aus der Sammlung Peter Weiss* (Erfurt: Sutton, 2010).

[45] See Göttsche, *Remembering Africa*, 59–62, for further details.

[46] On normalization, see Jürgen Link, *Versuch über den Normalismus: Wie Normalität produziert wird*, 4th ed. (Göttingen: Vandenhoeck & Ruprecht, 2006).

[47] Michael Rothberg, *Multidirectional Memory: Remembering the Holocaust in the Age of Decolonization* (Stanford, CA: Stanford University Press, 2009).

[48] Christof Hamann and Uwe Timm, "'Einfühlungsästhetik wäre ein kolonialer Akt': Ein Gespräch," *Sprache im technischen Zeitalter* 168 (2003): 450–62 (452).

[49] See, for example, Dirk Göttsche, "Colonialism and National Socialism: Intersecting Memory Discourses in Post-War and Contemporary German Literature," *Gegenwartsliteratur: A German Studies Yearbook* 9 (2010): 217–42; Langbehn and Salama, *German Colonialism*; Sara Lennox, ed., *Remapping Black Germany: New Perspectives on Afro-German History, Politics, and Culture* (Amherst: University of Massachusetts Press, 2016).

[50] For example, Jürgen Zimmerer, "Review of *Das Afrika Lexikon*," *Literaturen*, June 2002, 92.

[51] See, for example, Jay Winter, "The Generation of Memory: Reflections on the 'Memory Boom' in Contemporary Historical Studies," *Bulletin of the German Historical Institute* 27 (2012): 69–92.

[52] For a fuller account, see Göttsche, *Remembering Africa*; and my chapters 56–59 in Göttsche, Dunker, and Dürbeck, *Handbuch Postkolonialismus und Literatur*, 275–322.

[53] See, for example, Winfried Speitkamp, *Deutsche Kolonialgeschichte* (Stuttgart: Reclam, 2005), 173–87; Sebastian Conrad, *Deutsche Kolonialgeschichte* (Munich: Beck, 2008), 116–24.

[54] Giselher W. Hoffmann, *Die schweigenden Feuer: Roman der Herero* (Wuppertal: Peter Hammer, 1994), 443.

[55] See Dirk Göttsche, "'Die Schatten der Vergangenheit': Kolonialzeit und Geschichtspolitik in Bernhard Jaumanns Namibia-Krimis," in *Literatur als Interdiskurs: Realismus und Nominalismus, Interkulturalität und Intermedialität von der Moderne bis zur Gegenwart. Eine Festschrift für Rolf Parr zum 60. Geburtstag*, ed. Thomas Ernst and Georg Mein (Munich & Paderborn: Fink, 2016), 497–510.

[56] Hans Christoph Buch, *Sansibar Blues oder Wie ich Livingstone fand: Roman* (Frankfurt am Main: Eichborn, 2008), 224 (my translation).

[57] Jana Domdey, "Intertextuelles *Afrikanissimo*: Postkoloniale Erzählverfahren im Ostafrika-Kapitel von Ilija Trojanows *Der Weltensammler* (2006)," *Acta Germanica: German Studies in Africa* 37 (2009): 45–65 (53).

[58] See, for example, Matthias N. Lorenz, *Distant Kinship—Entfernte Verwandtschaft: Joseph Conrad's "Heart of Darkness" in der deutschen Literatur von Kafka bis Kracht* (Stuttgart: Metzler, 2017), 365–89, 472–82.

[59] Marianne Hirsch, *The Generation of Postmemory: Writing and Visual Culture after the Holocaust* (New York: Columbia University Press, 2012). Christof Hamann, *Usambara: Roman* (Göttingen: Steidl, 2007), 13. See also Laura Beck, *Kolonialgeschichte(n) neu schreiben: Postkoloniales Rewriting in Christof Hamanns "Usambara"* (Marburg: Tectum, 2011).

[60] Daniel Mepin, *Die Weissagung der Ahnen: Roman. Kamerun* (Bad Honnef: Hörlemann, 1997), 76.

[61] El Loko, *Der Blues in mir: Eine autobiographische Erzählung* (Oberhausen: Graphium Press, 1986), 98.

[62] See Dirk Göttsche, "Schreiben gegen Rassismus und Ressentiment: Selbstbehauptungsstrategien in neuerer Literatur von afrikanischen Migranten und Schwarzen Deutschen," *Der neue Weltengarten: Jahrbuch für Literatur und Interkulturalität* (2017/18): 281–300.

[63] See Lennox, *Remapping Black Germany*; Natascha A. Kelly, *Afrokultur: "der raum zwischen gestern und morgen"* (Münster: Unrast, 2016); Dirk Göttsche, "Deutsche Literatur afrikanischer Diaspora und die Frage postkolonialer Kanonrevision," in Uerlings and Patrut, *Postkolonialismus und Kanon*, 327–60.

[64] Paul Gilroy, *The Black Atlantic: Modernity and Double Consciousness* (Cambridge, MA: Harvard University Press, 1993).

Part II

German in World Locales

Introduction to Part II: German in World Locales

James Hodkinson and Benedict Schofield

THUS FAR, THIS VOLUME has primarily explored the ways in which German-language literature, and the disciplinary and canonical approaches that are often used to structure it, have nevertheless addressed notions of "worldliness," whether that be in the ways in which German-language culture has contributed to world literature; in the ways it has been shaped by voices and cultures from around the globe; or in the ways in which postcolonial and transnational approaches have fruitfully destabilized any notions of "center" and "periphery," or indeed of "nation"—that "deterritorialization" of German studies as a discipline outlined in the introduction to this book. Part 1 has thus explored what we argue is ultimately a productive tension between the local and the worldly, and the ways in which the traditional boundaries we use to delineate and describe our discipline are, in fact, already inherently permeable. Without ignoring the continued dominance of the nation and the canon, and the patterns of exclusion these undoubtedly still create, the preceding chapters have attempted to showcase this more "intrinsic" mobility of German-language culture across a range of regional, national, and transnational contexts.

Yet German studies is mobile in other ways. After all, it is not just texts and authors that cross boundaries and are shaped by wordily influences: the discipline itself is co-constructed across global locations, and we as its scholars are equally part of this global mobility through our careers across institutions, continents, and disciplines. In this second part, then, we seek to innovatively map this wider mobility by looking at the shape and scope of German studies across a range of diverse cultural and geographic contexts, and the agility of German studies in those contexts, even at a time of perceived disciplinary crisis.

Part 2 opens with Carlotta von Maltzan's chapter on German studies in a South African context. Picking up directly from Dirk Göttsche's closing chapter in Part 1 on the development of a postcolonial German studies, von Maltzan explores how German studies has the "the dubious status of claiming the longest [disciplinary] history on the African continent" because of its roots in the colonization of the Cape and the early "paracolonial presence" of Germany through its settlements and missionary work. Her chapter traces the development of the discipline out of this context, before turning to the post-apartheid era: a period that had a profound impact on the size and shape of German studies, with new policies implemented that sought to remove the inequalities of apartheid by fostering university access and multilingualism. As von Maltzan articulates, though, such ideals are "still far removed from being fully realized," leading her to explore how one can continue to articulate the value of German studies in a context where the majority have "neither true access to [South Africa's] wealth or to the quality education that it offers, despite the new democratic dispensation introduced in 1994."

Crucially, von Maltzan's chapter helps us see how the questions raised by this volume cannot be answered solely with reference to either a North American or UK German studies context and the specific teaching and research agendas of those regions, and that in considering how German studies is configured elsewhere, we can enrich our understanding of the continued value of studying German in all its forms. This notion is echoed in the other two contributions to Part 2 by Kate Rigby and Sai Bhatawadekar: chapters that expand our focus even further beyond the European German-speaking countries to a range of locations across Australia and the Asia-Pacific, the United States and Hawai'i, and India.

These chapters build a case for recharting the global flow and impact of German studies—and for rethinking the way in which we as scholars shape and are impacted by that global flow. Rigby traces her intellectual journey from German studies, through comparative literature, and into the environmental humanities, and its parallel in a career that has crossed the United Kingdom, Germany, and Australia. As she powerfully demonstrates, this move across continents and disciplines—indeed, seemingly "beyond" the world of German studies entirely—is, in fact, less of a "defection" from one subject to another and more "a tale of elective affinities" between them, which, she argues, reveals how German studies is continually enriched by interdisciplinary crossings and, in turn, can contribute to the genuinely global issues addressed by the environmental humanities. Bhatawadekar similarly reflects on the inherent connectivity between her different disciplinary lives: what she terms a "spectrum of German-Indian interaction" that lies behind her approach to a "cross-cultural German studies" and continues to influence her role as a professor of Hindi/Urdu and Indo-Pacific Languages and Literatures at the University of Hawai'i. Whether developing new language pedagogy in Hindi or researching into theater and film studies and philosophy, Bhatawadekar explores how it is her "training in German studies that has positively sculpted [her] current avatar," at the same time as she articulates an approach to a transnational form of study that moves beyond a "strictly comparative" mode of analysis and is rooted instead in the "creative complexity" of a more mobile and multifaceted form of cross-cultural research.

Common to all the contributions in Part 2 is thus a sense of the transformative potential of German studies when considered transnationally, and of the significance of our own *Bildungsreisen* (journeys of education). The chapters reveal how we can still articulate the significance of a common focus on German studies, even as that subject increasingly—and fruitfully—positions itself as productively transient and culturally hybrid.

7: German in a South African Context: From Colony to Decolonization

Carlotta von Maltzan

IN 2017, THE BESTSELLING AUTHOR of espionage and thriller novels John le Carré gave a speech at an award ceremony for German teachers at the German Embassy in London entitled "Why We Should Learn German." He recalled his early career as a German teacher and his love for the language, still trying to explain to himself "why it was love at first sound." He fondly remembered his first teacher, Mr. King, who despite the anti-German propaganda during World War II, inspired his "little class with the beauty of the language, and of its literature and culture." Le Carré then also explained why he learned and taught the language:

> The decision to learn a foreign language is to me an act of friendship. It is indeed a holding out of the hand. It's not just a route to negotiation. It's also to get to know you better, to draw closer to you and your culture, your social manners and your way of thinking. And the decision to teach a foreign language is an act of commitment, generosity and mediation.[1]

John le Carré echoes my personal enthusiasm for German and the reasons why I chose to teach the subject in South Africa at a time when foreign languages seem to have lost their appeal at tertiary institutions—small as it was in the past.

Moreover, in South Africa, German as a subject at tertiary institutions has the dubious status of claiming the longest history on the African continent because of its inextricable link to the colonization of the Cape, and thus to colonialism as practiced first by the Netherlands, then by the British Empire, and finally as practiced in the apartheid era. The end of the latter era is marked by two significant turning points that changed the political and social landscape in Southern Africa. First, the former German colony South West Africa became independent Namibia in 1990. It had been mandated by the League of Nations to the Union of South Africa in 1915 and was regarded as a fifth province by the Republic of South Africa despite the abolishment of the mandate by the United Nations in 1966. Second, in 1994 the African National Congress (ANC) won a landslide victory in the first democratic elections ever held in South Africa. Only in the 1980s, when it could no longer be denied how unstable the apartheid system was, did academics involved in teaching German at universities start reflecting on the state of the subject and its future.

The first part of this chapter will critically examine the beginnings of German studies in South Africa, providing a brief overview of the German paracolonial presence through German settlements and missionary work in Southern Africa and outlining the evolution of German as a subject, first at schools and later at universities, focusing on how German studies was conceptualized until the end of apartheid. The second part of this chapter interrogates the changes German studies underwent in post-apartheid South Africa, arguing that new political dispensations and educational policies within the country, rather than the effects of globalization that also influenced how some universities conceptualized themselves in the last decade, drove these changes. The chapter will conclude by looking at the role of German studies beyond the academy to highlight how a play by a German author was adapted as social and political commentary at a crucial historical moment, thereby participating in the prevailing public discourse.

German Studies—Its Roots and Evolution until 1994

Acting on behalf of the Vereenigde Oost-Indische Compagnie (VOC, or Dutch East India Company), Jan van Riebeeck landed in the Cape in 1652 with three ships and with Germans as part of his crew. He proceeded to build the Fort de Goede Hoep (Fort of Good Hope)—the first European settlement, which later developed into Cape Town. Germans subsequently constituted the largest immigrant group during the reign of the VOC, which lasted until the Cape Colony was formally ceded to Britain in 1814. Although the British Parliament decided to abolish slavery in 1834, the descendants of slaves who had been "imported" from Asia, Madagascar, and the African continent under Dutch rule were only nominally freed. Already in 1809 pass laws were introduced that forced African laborers to leave their workplace only with the express permission of their employers, a law that was later extended to the freed slaves.[2] Furthermore, the Cape Masters and Servants Ordinance of 1841 decreed that imprisonment or severe corporal punishment could be meted out on the labor force, whereas an employer could be taken only to a civil court in case of disagreements. Both these measures enforced by law underscore the asymmetrical power relations between employers and employees at the time. Added to racialized control of labor was the segregation of living places. These measures were refined throughout the nineteenth and early twentieth centuries, and furthermore paved the way to strict, formal segregation and controls over the movement of labor that was legislated in the apartheid system. This law proved such an effective means to control workers that it remained in force until 1974.

According to Hildemarie Grünewald, those Germans who arrived in the Cape Colony assimilated quickly: they learned to speak Dutch, the only official language permitted by the VOC, and either married into Dutch communities or took wives from the local population.[3] Because of this process of assimilation, and since under Dutch rule no formal schooling had been established, German-language teaching did not play a significant role initially. In 1825, the British introduced formal schooling that was open to everyone, with English as both the official language and the medium of teaching. It is therefore unsurprising that the teaching of German within an institutional framework can be traced only as far back as 1830, despite the much earlier arrival of Germans.[4] These and other measures (like taxation and freeing of the slaves) by the British regime were resented by many inhabitants of Dutch descent in the colony and they decided to leave, starting a migration from 1835 onward that became known as the Great Trek and led to the founding of several Boer republics further north in the Transvaal and the Orange Free State, and east in Natal. In these regions, as well as in the Eastern Cape, the first German settlements were founded from the mid-nineteenth century onward. In 1848, 189 immigrants from Oldenburg, including a teacher, founded what is now known as New Germany, close to Durban, thereby paving the way for the establishment of German as a school subject.

From 1853 to 1867 five groups consisting of missionaries as well as so-called colonists were sent out to Natal by the Hermannsburg Mission Society, where they founded mission stations in New Hannover, Wartburg, Lüneburg, and, most important, Hermannsburg. Founded in 1849 by Ludwig (Louis) Harms, the Hermannsburg Mission Society, which had sent out missionaries to the colony of Natal to preach to and convert the "heathens" in the Zulu kingdom bordering on their settlements, firmly adhered to Lutheran confessionalism in the spirit of post-revolutionary revivalism. This orientation is manifested in the emblem of the first German school established in Southern Africa, the Deutsche Schule zu Hermannsburg, founded in 1856: it depicts an oak branch with leaves, acorns, and the words "treu und fest" (loyal and steadfast). Similarly, the Lutheran Berlin Mission Society, the Rhenish Mission Society, and the Moravian Church, together with various German immigrant groups, started numerous settlements in the second half of the nineteenth century, particularly in the Eastern Cape, building their own churches and schools. As a result, German became the dominating language in these areas (*GDK*, 71). In areas such as Hermannsburg, German is still spoken today by descendants of early settlers who still support the school and the church. Becoming farmers or traders and later choosing other professions as well, they mainly kept to their own community. Due to Hermannsburg's remote location in the hinterland as well as lack of contact with their country of origin, inhabitants were isolated politically and socially from developments in Germany while strictly upholding Lutheran traditions well into the 1980s, throughout conforming to the regime of the day in South Africa, thereby also largely supporting apartheid.

German immigrants across the country played a key role in shaping the development of German as a subject both at schools and universities. The earliest instance of German as a school subject can be traced to 1832 (*DGS*, 1609). Schooling under the VOC had been left up to the Dutch Reformed Church until the late eighteenth century, when the government took over the provision of schooling. Resisting the enforced anglicization of schools under British rule, the descendants of Dutch settlers, who now referred to themselves as Boers, opened many private schools. Given its linguistic affinity to Dutch, the intermarriage between German and Dutch settlers from early on, and the anti-British hegemonic stance by the Boers, German easily established itself in these schools. German was examined for the first time in 1860 after it had been recognized formally by the Public Examination Board two years earlier. It took another two decades before German was also offered as an optional subject by state-supported schools in the Cape.

In the late nineteenth century, several German schools were founded. Built on grounds purchased by the Lutheran St. Martini congregation in 1875, the Deutsche Internationale Schule Kapstadt (German International School of Cape Town), as it is known today, dates back to 1883. After the discovery of gold in the Transvaal, gold mining prospectors and their families arrived, leading to the founding of Johannesburg in 1886—among whom were many Germans. By 1897 the German community had grown to 4,000 persons and had opened its own school in Hillbrow on a property donated by Paul Kruger, the former president of the South African Republic. In Pretoria, about 100 kilometers away, a German school was opened in 1899 despite the outbreak of the Anglo-Boer War in October that year and the subsequent internment of many German families. At his death in 1897, the farmer Friedrich Klinkenberg bequeathed 10,000 pounds sterling (the capital from which the Deutsche Schule Pretoria still profits today), enabling the founding and upkeep of a Lutheran congregational school.

The first universities in South Africa were established in 1918 after the adoption of the University Act in 1916 by the then Union of South Africa Parliament. Nevertheless, their origins can be traced back much earlier. The University of Cape Town (UCT), South Africa's oldest university, was founded in 1829 as the South African College, a high school for boys where mathematics and classical languages were taught in both

English and Dutch. In 1830 German was introduced by Leopold Marquard, an assistant in the Dutch department who originated from Germany but had been sent to the Cape by the Rotterdam Mission Society in 1815 (*DGS*, 1610). South Africa's second oldest university, Stellenbosch University, emerged from the Victoria College. German was offered at both UCT and Stellenbosch from their inception, as the general curriculum and examination system at both universities was modeled on and influenced by both German and British views on university education. Furthermore, German was considered as part of an educational outlook (*Bildungskonzept*) developed by German universities in the nineteenth century. German professors at these and other universities were responsible for examining the subject at the senior certificate level in each province, which was administered by the Joint Matriculation Board (JMB), also founded in 1918. The JMB regulated admission to universities until the 1970s. Until then the study of German was generally considered as part of an overall well-rounded education (*Bildung*) within a bachelor of arts degree, particularly by white speakers of Afrikaans who felt a particular affinity to the German-speaking countries because many could trace their roots back to them.

The practice of racial segregation could be found in one form or another from the beginning of colonization of the Cape. These were intensified under the system of apartheid implemented after the National Party came to power in 1948. Apartheid fundamentally influenced how education was conceptualized at schools and universities. Thus the Bantu Education Act (No. 47) of 1953 stated that education should be organized along racially defined categories, which meant that whites, blacks, coloureds, and "Indians" had to be taught separately at schools and at universities. Except for the Cape, where German was offered at some schools for coloureds, it was otherwise offered mostly as an optional subject only at schools for whites and followed a grammar-oriented curriculum where canonical literary texts were read mainly with a view to improve language competency. Although German was offered at all white universities from the beginning, it was also introduced at university colleges founded around 1960 that were open only to "other" South Africans, such as the University of Durban-Westville (for Indians), the University of the Western Cape (for coloureds), and the University of the North and the University of Zululand (for blacks). These institutions achieved full university status in 1969.

Until the 1970s curricula for German, which could be studied as part of a three-year bachelor's degree, were similarly structured at all universities, emphasizing literary studies and modeled on offerings at German universities, as professors had either trained there or immigrated from Germany or Austria. This meant that *ab initio* students of German had first to acquire the language in a one-year intensive language course before they were admitted to the regular undergraduate program taught exclusively in German. The first year of study covered literary and cultural history; during the second year, nineteenth-century literature was offered along with an introduction to the history of the language and teaching of Middle High German; and the third year dealt with medieval literature, classicism (*Klassik*), and twentieth-century literature. Throughout the undergraduate degree additional language courses were offered for non-mother-tongue speakers as well. The fourth year of studies consisted of a one-year honor's degree in which electives were offered in accordance with the research specializations of staff in the various German departments. The honor's degree coursework formed the first part of the postgraduate program, followed by coursework for an MA and a PhD.

The structure of German studies programs across the country started changing from the mid-1970s onward, mainly because of generational changes as new professors, again mostly from Germany or who had completed their PhDs there, were appointed.[5] Influenced by debates following the 1968 student movement and by the increasing importance of *Interkulturelle Germanistik* (intercultural German studies) as propagated by Alois Wierlacher, it was no longer considered desirable to maintain German programs that did not align to recent developments in the discipline in Germany and were inappropriate for South African students, especially after the Soweto student uprising in 1976. First, the study of Middle High German was completely removed from the curricula of German programs at universities in favor of highlighting literary movements and texts from the Enlightenment onward. Second, offers were diversified, both in terms of structure and content. Previously only students who had taken German at school or had learned it in a special course were admitted to the first year of study. Taking account of insights gained from the new field of *Deutsch als Fremdsprache* (DaF, or German as a foreign language) at German universities, it was decided that students now could study German *ab initio* in their first year of study. Thereby a parallel system—a DaF stream that gradually included literary components, and a literary stream—was created for achieving the bachelor degree. Third, new teaching and research directions were explored, on the one hand taking account of foreign-language learning requirements in the DaF stream—for example, through the introduction of language laboratories—and through the development of a South African language textbook *Deutsch ZA*, developed at the University of the Western Cape under the leadership of Silvia Skorge. On the other hand, taking account of insights gained through *Interkulturelle Germanistik* (intercultural German studies) as developed in German-speaking countries, intercultural approaches to teaching literature were introduced at some universities, thereby increasingly acknowledging the South African teaching context, while literary theory was included in the curriculum by other universities following curriculum developments at tertiary institutions in Europe and the United States after 1968.

In 1965 the Südafrikanischer Germanistenverband (SAGV, or South African Association for German Studies) was founded, then renamed the Germanistenverband im südlichen Afrika (Association for German Studies in Southern Africa) after South West Africa, now Namibia, became independent in 1990.[6] Besides organizing biannual conferences, the SAGV also publishes two journals—namely, *Acta Germanica* (commencing in 1966), an accredited journal, and *Deutschunterricht in Südafrika* (DUSA, Teaching German in South Africa), devoted to reflecting foreign-language teaching both at universities and schools.[7] Current debates relating to the discipline as well as methodologies and teaching approaches were reflected in both journals since the mid-1970s. However, the state and relevance of German within the South African sociopolitical context, let alone how the discipline could be reflected in the curricula at universities, was never seriously questioned. This changed only in the 1980s when the growing unrest in the country and student protests at universities could no longer be ignored.

Social instability and apartheid's crisis of legitimacy culminated in the declaration of a state of emergency in 1985. There were several critical reflections on the relation of German studies to this crisis, which incidentally also coincided with the beginnings of the supposed crisis in the humanities, albeit for different reasons. Jürgen Lieskounig challenged the teaching of "Landeskunde" (regional and cultural studies) in South Africa, arguing that language textbooks conceptualized in Germany—many of them highlighting consumerism through, for example, chapters on living (Wohnen, Häuser, environments) or shopping—were often inappropriate in a country plagued by inequalities.[8] Jan Christoph Meister and Gudrun Oberprieler scrutinized the subject itself, calling for a critical reassessment of teaching goals and necessary curricula changes at both school and tertiary levels.[9] Gunther Pakendorf responded to the crisis by asking whether the subject could be transformed into a people's *Germanistik*.[10] Could German, its language and literature, be relevant when the majority of people were disempowered? In the event that this should change, should the subject reinvent itself along the lines of its "usability" on the job market, and what could this mean in terms of maintaining the integrity of the subject if one were to pursue this approach? In contrast, Peter Horn anticipated the death of the subject itself.[11] Although Horn's deliberations were formulated as a satirical and provocative wake-up call to colleagues in German studies, he had a point. In the coming years all German departments at universities ceased to exist as independent units. They were amalgamated with other foreign-language departments, such as French, Italian, Portuguese, or even Chinese, into larger departments or schools. These were usually called either "European studies" or "Modern Foreign Languages" or "Foreign Language and Literature studies," and the like.

German Studies in Post-Apartheid South Africa

Three factors influenced the development of German studies at the tertiary level following the ANC's landslide victory in the 1994 elections and the implementation of the new constitution in 1996. First, the National Education Policy Act (No. 27 of 1996), which led to the passing of the language in education policy a year later. Second, the introduction of a new countrywide school curriculum in 2005. Third, universities were restructured between 2001 and 2004.

The value and meaning assigned to languages changed significantly in post-apartheid South Africa, as evidenced in the language in education policy, which laid the basis for the decision to develop a new language policy in the country. The policy acknowledged that about twenty-five languages were used by mother-tongue speakers in South Africa.[12] However, only two of them—namely, Afrikaans and English—had been used as official languages and as mediums of instruction at schools and universities in the past, thereby assuring their dominance in public life. Multiple languages are used and spoken in most African countries, and multilingualism is thus the norm. After gaining independence, most African countries decided to choose two official languages, an indigenous language and the former colonial language. However, South Africa's 1996 constitution assigned eleven languages the status of an official language. This meant that 99 percent of all mother-tongue speakers' languages are official languages. Besides the nine indigenous languages and the two colonial languages, Afrikaans and English, chapter 1, §6 of the constitution also mentions languages spoken by the descendants of laborers "imported" by the colonial powers (Tamil, Hindi, and others) and Portuguese, German, and Greek still spoken by the descendants of immigrants to the country. As Ingrid Laurien points out, that could mean that in principle any language spoken in South Africa could attain the status of an official South African language.[13] However, by now, English has become the *lingua franca*, while the other ten remaining official languages are supported to a much lesser extent by the state. The other languages mentioned in the constitution, among them German, do not receive any state support at all. The effect of the South African language policy was not the implementation of all eleven official languages at an equal level but rather the recognition of a multidimensional multilingualism, as propagated by the motto "One nation, many languages" by the Pan African Language Board (PanSALB) constituted in 1999.[14]

To this day, the question of which language should be used in tuition at educational institutions, and the right of choice of language of tuition, remains a contentious social and educational issue. As must be recalled in this context, the student uprising in Soweto in 1976 started as a protest action against the introduction of Afrikaans as a medium of tuition at schools in townships. Historically, first Dutch (and since 1921 Afrikaans) or English were the dominant languages, thereby privileging the white minority. While the Bantu Education Act of 1953 provided a limited status to indigenous African languages, in that pupils could be taught in their mother tongue at the primary level, this also proved disadvantageous because of a lack of available teaching material in those languages, thereby further disadvantaging the education of these pupils. The new curriculum introduced in 2005 countrywide took account of this historical legacy in that it sought to encourage multilingualism by first promoting the mother tongue of pupils and only then other languages and cultures. In that way pupils (or their parents) were supposedly given the opportunity to make informed choices regarding which other languages they wanted to acquire.

From a practical point of view this policy was difficult to realize. English has become the dominant language in public discourse, in politics, and in the judicial system; thus it has status as the language of power if one wants to achieve professional and financial success.[15] The unequal social status of indigenous languages persists. Despite these drawbacks in the implementation of educational policies, it is noteworthy that South African educational policies do not emphasize difference but rather mutual respect and tolerance between diverse cultural groups. As such, culture is conceptualized as a dynamic process that sees education as a dialogical exchange of value systems, as reiterated by Kader Asmal, a former minister of education: "Values cannot be simply asserted. They must be placed on the table, debated, negotiated, synthesized, modified, earned. And this process, this dialogue, is in itself a value—a South African value—to be cherished."[16]

Negotiating value systems and achieving their recognition by all parties concerned therefore means that educational policies will be successful inasmuch as transcultural competencies are included in the educational process. This ideal is still far from being fully realized and indeed has proved to be problematic. Education and culture are imbedded in a much larger process of social transformation where the gap between the rich and the poor is widening, and access to equal education for all is denied by the demographic spread of a population that has not significantly changed since the end of apartheid. At the same time, a black middle and elite class has emerged. But most of the poor and unemployed remain black and discontented. This has become evident through increasing social unrest and protests against the lack of service delivery, and the continuing xenophobic attacks against migrants from other African countries, which reached a first peak between May and July 2008 with a renewed outbreak of violence against African "foreigners" in 2019.

Against this background it is unsurprising that European languages such as Portuguese, German, French, Italian, and Greek—classified in the constitution as languages of (privileged) minority groups and not seen as foreign languages—have been marginalized and some even excluded at schools despite the credo of fostering multilingualism. Current education policy requires every pupil to learn two official languages, one of which can be the mother tongue. Although in principle it is possible to choose a third language, the school curriculum is structured so tightly that learning a third language would seriously disadvantage the learner in achieving matriculation exemption and thereby fulfilling university entry requirements. While in 1982 there were still 32,000 learners of German countrywide, taught by 511 teachers, the number decreased to 8,406 learners and about 80 teachers by 2008.[17] Due to a lack of financial support by the Ministry of Education, most government schools were forced to drop foreign languages, including German, from their subjects on offer. An exception to this trend are private schools and some government schools where Afrikaans is used as a medium of instruction, most of them located in the Western Cape. Possibly this can be explained because of the traditional affinity of Afrikaans and Afrikaners to Germans and their language. Because of these changes, the intake of students at universities who had learned German at school sank steadily after the introduction of the new school curriculum in 2005.

The third factor influencing the development of German studies and other foreign languages at the tertiary level was the restructuring of higher institutions of learning between 2001 and 2004.[18] This sought to undo the inequalities created by the Extension of Universities Act of 1959 during the apartheid era, where universities were organized along racial lines and thus instituted discriminatory criteria, as outlined above. Through mergers and new groupings, the restructuring also led in some cases to the renaming of universities, and three types of universities were created. The traditional universities, altogether eleven in number, which had been recognized as such previously, remained largely intact. They are viewed as offering theoretically orientated degrees. The second group consists of so-called universities of technology, which were formerly called "technical training colleges," of which there had been six. Three more have been created, making the total nine universities that are focused on vocationally oriented education. The six comprehensive universities make up the third group, offering a combination of academic and vocational diplomas and degrees. German is now offered by eight of the twenty-six universities thus created, all eight of which belong to the traditional universities.

German was directly affected by the restructuring of tertiary institutions. German was discontinued at seven universities because of declining student numbers or because staff resigned and no replacement could be found, as was the case with the University of Zululand in 2017. There has been a drastic downsizing of lecturing staff for German at all universities. In 1994 altogether fifteen universities offered German, with fifty-six permanent lecturing positions, of which eight were designated for full professors (*Lehrstuhl*) teaching around twelve hundred students. By 2008 the numbers of permanent positions had declined to twenty-four, and two German sections were closed.[19] By 2018 the number of permanent positions had shrunk to eighteen and five more German sections had closed. Between 1994 and 2008 the number of students of German remained stable at around twelve hundred, but in 2016 that number shrunk to just below one thousand.[20] Despite the closure of German at some universities, the relative stability of student numbers between 1994 and 2016 was the result of rising student numbers at some universities. Reasons for this trend can be found in the fact that overall student numbers increased at all universities since 1994, including those for German studies. Furthermore, some universities, such as Stellenbosch University, have a language requirement (thus making up a fourth of the overall number of students of German in the country), and developing bilateral partnerships with German universities provide an attractive option for students to spend one semester overseas. The German Academic Exchange Service (DAAD) became active in South Africa only after the end of apartheid in 1994 by opening an Information Centre at the University of the Witwatersrand, supporting both Stellenbosch University and the University of Cape Town with a DAAD lectureship and a language assistant. Nevertheless, German is facing a crisis because of serious understaffing at most universities, where sometimes only one or two permanent staff members have to carry the entire teaching load. They are unable to renew subject content, redesign or adjust curricula, or develop new teaching approaches beyond offering a combination of face-to-face teaching and blended learning.

In contrast to 1994, programs in German studies at those universities that still offer the subject are much more diverse today.[21] Some German sections adjusted to ensuing changes by developing common teaching programs with other universities. Others established research cooperations and partnerships or developed modules that are relevant within the region, the university, the faculty, or the respective unit, thereby also sometimes switching to English as a medium of instruction (*DAU*, 107–14). How German studies in South Africa will eventually develop or change will not, however, lie solely in the hands of its academic teachers and promoters. It will also depend on the ways in which German studies situates itself contextually and on the development of higher education in general, since South African universities are in a state of crisis that has become apparent since 2015.[22]

In the past, stability and a definitive view of the role of education may have been self-evident preconditions for academic work in Western contexts. Universities and their educational mandates have come under the sway of neoliberalism and are increasingly dependent on the market economy, as evidenced by financial and administrative remodeling and educational goals. Globalization has effected change in university environments, requiring a comprehensive networking of universities, faculties, and disciplines. The digital age has changed both teaching and research, third-stream funding is supposed to fill increasing shortfalls, initiatives on "excellence" deepen competitiveness and rivalry, and teaching and research have become marketing tools. Higher education in South Africa is not exempt from this process either, except that student protests starting in 2015 brought home the crisis that higher education is facing.

In a joint statement issued after a consultative meeting in August 2016, Minister of Higher Education and Training Dr. Blade Nzimande, Universities South Africa (USAf), and the University Council Chairs Forum (UCCF) declared that South African universities had been chronically underfunded over the past two decades; historically disadvantaged institutions during the apartheid era were particularly negatively affected. To compensate for this systemic underfunding, student fees were increased disproportionally, "to the point that they are now unaffordable to many who are offered places in the various institutions."[23]

Towards the end of 2015, virtually every South African university campus was rocked by student protests. The catalyst was the "Rhodes must fall" student-led protest movement at the University of Cape Town, which originally centered on the removal of the statue of the British colonialist Cecil John Rhodes from the main campus of the university.[24] The campaign soon included calls for widespread transformation of the university, including decolonizing the curriculum and raising issues around the low number of senior black academic staff.[25] In other words, the movement called for an Africanization of the university. Soon the demands broadened to include "fees must fall," which led to countrywide protests at nearly all South African universities. Lectures were disrupted and examinations and tests were postponed. When the higher-education sector threatened to collapse, President Jacob Zuma announced that fees for 2016 would not be increased. While this measure averted the acute crisis, it did not address it. The statement of August 12, 2016 reads: "The three parties recognised the importance of the universities to enable economic growth, to address the prevailing structural poverty and deep socioeconomic inequality. The universities enable social mobility for many from poverty-stricken backgrounds, and in doing so create the potential for transformative socially inclusive ripple effects across society."[26] Vice chancellors and UCCF chairs made it clear that a minimum increase of 8 percent for 2017 would be unavoidable in order to ensure quality education and financial sustainability; otherwise at least seventeen of the twenty-six South African universities would be subject to serious financial difficulties. Given this precarious situation and despite all attempts to find solutions, underfunding of institutions of higher education threatens to become a permanent feature. Further cuts in teaching and research are thus foreseeable.

Against this background of fundamental changes at universities in South Africa, German studies has to ask itself how it will assess its future prospects. So far it could sustain itself and even expand at some universities. Nowadays, however, not only German and other languages but the humanities per se find themselves in dire straits, as Sander Gilman has argued with reference to the state of education in the United States, which is defined by an ethos of pragmatism.[27] No one is interested in which competencies are conveyed by the humanities. What counts for students is only this: What job will I get after having completed my education? The question thus arises as to the competencies we stand to lose if the humanities and (foreign) languages are sidelined. Will it be enough to address the crisis by critically reviewing and restructuring the curriculum? Probably it will not suffice merely to offer language tuition and approach the mediation of literature and culture from an intercultural perspective. As has already been implemented by some universities, German could cooperate with cognate disciplines. It remains to be seen, however, whether cross-disciplinary offerings in English, which have become the *lingua franca* at all South African universities, will prove viable.

The Relevance of German Literature in a Postcolonial Context

It is sometimes difficult to find the validity of one's work in a South African environment, teaching the literature of a colonial language such as German, while also keeping in mind the mixed colonial legacy of Germans in Southern Africa. Germany laid claim to South West Africa as a colony from 1884 to 1914, a process brilliantly explored by Uwe Timm in his novel *Morenga* (1978), which focuses on the Herero genocide. This novel is presented and often part of a course I regularly offer on "Writing Africa." Germans also were responsible for much of the missionary work through various mission societies, which was a mixed blessing. Their attempts to alphabetize the "natives" often paved the way for domination by the colonizers,[28] while German immigrant communities participated in the progressive racialization of South African society right from the start when the Cape became a colony soon after Jan van Riebeeck landed there in the seventeenth century. Yet the fact that major literary works and plays by German authors serve at critical moments to highlight social tensions within South African society is perhaps not surprising, given that Germany has its own very mixed past with major social upheavals and the burden of two world wars—let alone the Holocaust—for which they are held responsible. While these connections between German and South African social changes cannot be explored here in any detail, this chapter will end nevertheless by pointing to one instance where a play was used to explore current affairs and thereby participate in public discourse.

The play is Peter Weiss's *Die Verfolgung und Ermordung Jean Paul Marats dargestellt durch die Schauspielgruppe des Hospizes zu Charenton unter Anleitung des Herrn de Sade* (The Persecution and Assassination of Jean-Paul Marat as Performed by the Inmates of the Asylum of Charenton under the Direction of the Marquis de Sade, 1963), usually shortened to *Marat/Sade*, which was performed in the University of Cape Town's own Baxter theater in February and March 2017. Weiss wrote the play to address social and political conditions in West Germany vis-à-vis East Germany, at the time querying whether true revolution comes from changing society or changing oneself. The themes of the play, such as revolution, class difference, madness, and the abuses of power, all resonate with the current South African context, and more specifically with the "Rhodes must fall" campaign started by students at the very university where the play was performed. Jaco Bower wrote in the program notes on his own role as the director of the play:

> To be honest, I find it difficult to talk about revolution, Fees Must Fall, Rhodes Must Fall and the current political climate today from a personal perspective; and I'm asking myself why, maybe because I am white and privileged. Here I find myself in an authoritative position as director making this work in this country at this moment and I seriously question myself, my position, my authority. There is a Sadean aspect to being in this position, guiding, manipulating, provoking actors, and although I might not have a personal history regarding revolution as such, I can connect to it emotionally.[29]

Bower's comments resonate with how I see myself as an academic and teacher of German in South Africa, specifically as a scholar who teaches in the highly privileged context of Stellenbosch University, surrounded by mountains and vineyards, which is why Stellenbosch is such a sought-after tourist attraction, especially in the German speaking countries. Stellenbosch is the least transformed university in the country, where both white students and staff are still in the majority because for black, coloured, and Indian students and staff the cost of living in this environment is either prohibitive or else to be avoided as the hegemonic cradle of apartheid minds. My position is privileged compared with the majority of people in this country, who have very limited access to its wealth or to quality education, despite the new democratic dispensation introduced in 1994. The same contradiction faced me when I lived here under the apartheid regime, all the time working towards and hoping for change.

But despite my privileged position, as a teacher (through my courses) and as a scholar (through my publications), I have something meaningful to contribute to this country. To quote John le Carré again: "to teach a foreign language is an act of commitment . . . and mediation." Our students come from both privileged and very disadvantaged communities with a high incident of poverty, unemployment, gang cultures, and (gender-based) violence. Our society's ongoing economic, social, and racial schisms are reflected in the lecture halls. The student protests of 2015—an echo of the Soweto student uprising in 1976—and the call for decolonization of the universities and the curriculum brought this home. Therefore, some of my courses raise critical contemporary issues through literature. When discussing literary texts, I challenge students to think differently, and through such discussion to reconsider how they see themselves and others. An example of these are recent novels on the plight of (African) refugees in Europe with obvious parallels to xenophobia and gender-based violence in South Africa.[30] This means to also query identity politics and the meaning of decolonization.[31] I do this because I have a responsibility as an educator to reflect on my own privilege as well as the contradictions confronting students. As a scholar, I explore and analyze writing Africa in German literature, Africa's colonial history, as well as German literature's postcolonial engagement with the African continent, and I thereby contribute to the broader social and academic discourse in South Africa.

Notes

[1] John le Carré, "Why We Should Learn German," *The Guardian*, July 2, 2017, https://www.theguardian.com/education/2017/jul/02/why-we-should-learn-german-john-le-carre (accessed December 10, 2018).

[2] See Christoph Marx, *Geschichte Afrikas von 1800 bis zur Gegenwart* (Paderborn: Ferdinand Schöningh, 2004), 44.

[3] Hildemarie Grünewald, *Die Geschichte der Deutschen am Kap*, 2d ed. (Cape Town: Ulrich Naumann Verlag 1993), 14. Hereafter cited as (*GDK*, page numbers).

[4] See Rainer Kußler, "Deutschunterricht und Germanistikstudium in Südafrika," in *Deutsch als Fremdsprache: Ein internationales Handbuch*, vol. 2, ed. Gerhard Helbig, Lutz Götze, Gert Henrici, and Hans-Jürgen Krumm (Berlin: De Gruyter, 2001), 1609–19, here 1609. Hereafter cited as (*DGS*, page numbers).

[5] See Rolf Annas, "Zur Frage der Zugehörigkeit. 150 Jahre deutsche Sprache und Kultur am Kap," *Acta Germanica* 43 (2015): 78–89.

[6] For the history of the SAGV, see Gunther Pakendorf, "Zur Geschichte des Germanistenverbands im Südlichen Afrika (SAGV) im sozialpolitischen Kontext," *Acta Germanica* 44 (2016): 82–104.

[7] For a complete overview of publications in *Acta Germanica*, see Michael Eckardt, "Gesamtinhaltsverzeichnis der Jahrgänge 1 bis 43 (1966–2015)," *Acta Germanica* 44 (2016): 50–77. For the changes the journal DUSA underwent, see

Marianne Zappen-Thomson and Julia Augart, "Vom DUSA zum eDUSA. Zu Geschichte und Wandel einer Zeitschrift des SAGV," *Acta Germanica* 44 (2016): 78–81.

[8] Jürgen Lieskounig, "Zur Problematik des 'Landeskunde'-Unterrichts in einem Land wie Südafrika," *InfoDaF* 14, no. 1 (1987): 55–60.

[9] Jan Christoph Meister and Gudrun Oberprieler, "Vom Nutzen und Nachteil der Germanistik für die Bildung des Menschen: Zur Notwendigkeit einer kritischen Reflexion von Selbstverständnis und Funktion der Schul- und Hochschulgermanistik im heutigen Südafrika," *Deutschunterricht in Südafrika* 18, no. 2 (1987): 1–4.

[10] Gunther Pakendorf, "People's Germanistik?" *Acta Germanica*, Supplement 1 (1990): 11–25.

[11] Peter Horn, "Nekrolog auf eine Germanistik für Nekrophile oder die Germanisten sterben aus," *Acta Germanica* 21 (1992): 263–72.

[12] Cf. Anne-Marie Beukes, "The First Ten Years of Democracy: Language Policy in South Africa," paper read at the World Congress on Linguistic Diversity, Sustainability and Peace, Barcelona, 20–23 May 2004, http://www.barcelona2004.org/www.barcelona2004.org/esp/banco_del_conocimiento/docs/O_35_EN_BEUKES.pdf (retrieved August 30, 2017).

[13] Ingrid Laurien, "Das Fach Deutsch an Universitäten im 'Neuen Südafrika'— eine Laborsituation für Europa?" *Info DaF* 33, no. 5 (2006): 438–45, here 440.

[14] See Carlotta von Maltzan, "Sprachenpolitik und die Rolle der Fremdsprachen (Deutsch) in Südafrika," *Stellenbosch Papers in Linguistics PLUS* 38 (2009): 204–13.

[15] See Francesca Balladon, "The Challenge of Diversity: The National Curriculum Statement and Foreign Languages," *Journal for Language Teaching* 40, no. 2 (2006): 42–66.

[16] Kader Asmal, "Pride versus Arrogance," in *Spirit of the Nation: Reflections on South Africa's Educational Ethos*, ed. Kader Asmal and Wilmot James (Claremont: Human Sciences Research Council and the Department of Education, 2002), 2–10, here 4.

[17] See Rudolf Rode, "Deutsch an südafrikanischen Schulen: Eine Bestandsaufnahme," *eDUSA* 3, no. 2 (2008): 26–29.

[18] See *The Restructuring of South African Higher Education: Rocky Roads from Policy Formulation to Institutional Mergers, 2001–2004*, ed. Theresa Barnes, Narend Baijnath, and Kalawathie Sattar (Pretoria: Unisa Press, 2009).

[19] See Carlotta von Maltzan, "Deutsch in Südafrika," in Helbig, Götze, Henrici, and Krumm, *Deutsch als Fremd- und Zweitsprache*, 1805–8.

[20] For details, see the statistics compiled by Rolf Annas, "Deutsch an Universitäten im südlichen Afrika. Zur Entwicklung des Fachs seit 2003," *Acta Germanica* 44 (2016): 105–18, here 116–17. Hereafter cited as (*DAU*, page numbers).

[21] Currently German is still offered by the University of the Witwatersrand, Johannesburg (Wits), the University of Pretoria (UP), Northwest University (NWU), the University of the Free State (UFS), Rhodes University (RU), Stellenbosch

University (SU), the University of the Western Cape (UWC), and the University of Cape Town (UCT).

[22] The following outline is based on my editorial in the fiftieth anniversary edition of *Acta Germanica*. See Carlotta von Maltzan, "Editorial on the 50th Anniversary," *Acta Germanica* 44 (2016): 14–17.

[23] USAf statement on the outcome of the consultative meeting between the Minister of Higher Education and Training, Dr. B. E. Nzimande, and the Boards of USAf and UCCF, August 12, 2016, http://www.universitiessa.ac.za/statement-outcome-joint-meeting-between-dr-blade-nzimande-and-usaf-and-uccf-boards (retrieved August 19, 2017).

[24] See Camalita Naiker, "From Marikana to #feesmustfall: The Praxis of Popular Politics in South Africa," *Urbanisation* 1, no. 1 (2016): 53–61.

[25] For the ensuing debate on the student protests and their demand to decolonize curricula at universities, see Lesley le Grange, "Decolonising the University Curriculum," *South African Journal of Higher Education* 30, no. 2 (2016): 1–12, http://dx.doi.org/10.20853/30-2-709 (retrieved August 2, 2017).

[26] See USAf statement on the outcome of the consultative meeting, August 12, 2016.

[27] Sander Gilman, "Why Study Ancient and Defunct Languages Such as German?" *Acta Germanica* 44 (2016): 25–26.

[28] See Gunther Pakendorf, "Deutsche Afrika-Missionare zwischen Oralität und Schriftkultur," in *Oralität und moderne Schriftkultur*, ed. Leo Kreutzer, David Simo, and Hans-Peter Klemme (Hannover: Revonnah Verlag, 2008), 210–22.

[29] Jaco Bower, "Director's note," in "Cape Town: Programme by the Baxter Theatre Centre on the Occasion of the Performance of Peter Weiss's Play *The Persecution and Assassination of Jean-Paul Marat as Performed by the Inmates of the Asylum of Charenton under the Direction of the Marquis de Sade*" (2017).

[30] For recent German novels on refugees in Europe, see Maxi Obexer, *Wenn gefährliche Hunde lachen* (Vienna: Folio Verlag, 2011); Merle Kröger, *Havarie* (Hamburg: Argument Verlag, 2015); Jenny Erpenbeck, *Gehen, ging, gegangen* (Munich: Knaus, 2015); Abbas Khider, *Ohrfeige* (Munich: Hanser, 2016); and Julya Rabinowich, *Dazwischen: Ich* (Munich: Hanser, 2016), to name but a few.

[31] See Carlotta von Maltzan, "Deutsch im Kontext der südafrikanischen Bildungspolitik und der Ruf nach Dekolonisierung," *Jahrbuch für Internationale Germanistik* 1 (2018): 99–110. See also the introductory chapter by Jonathan D. Jansen, "Making Sense of Decolonisation in Universities," in *Decolonisation in Universities: The Politics of Knowledge*, ed. Jonathan D. Jansen (Johannesburg: Wits University Press, 2019), 1–12. There he observes that "student protests starting in 2015 added a new term to the lexicon of South African universities—decolonisation" (1). This led Jansen to edit a book in which various chapters explore, among other things, questions such as: Where does the press for decolonisation come from—intellectually, socially, culturally, and politically? How does it relate to concepts such as "Africanisation" or "indigenous education" or "postcolonial education"?

8: From German Studies to Environmental Humanities (and Back Again): A Journey across Continents and Disciplines

Kate Rigby

IN HIS 2014 OVERVIEW of German environmental literary studies in the *Oxford Handbook of Ecocriticism*, the British Germanist and pioneering ecocritic Axel Goodbody notes that in the early years of the second decade of the new millennium, literary ecocriticism still remained relatively invisible in the German-speaking world, despite the comparative strength of environmental concern in Germany, Austria, and Switzerland. The German region has long been a leader in ecological science, politics, and philosophy, as well as a significant contributor to recent and current research in environmental history, theology, ethics, and aesthetics. Until recently, however, *Germanistik* (continental germanophone German studies) has been peculiarly resistant to ecocriticism. In part, Goodbody suggests, this could be related to the prominence of ecology and environmental thought in other fields. But he also observes that the core concerns of the kind of environmental literary studies that took off in the English-speaking world in the 1990s, foregrounding nature conservation, celebrating affective relations with place, and often deploying apocalyptic rhetoric, could have "seemed to skeptical academics [specifically, Germanists] a potentially dangerous throwback to Romantic and turn-of-the-century forms of antimodernism" and irrationalism.[1] Where ecocriticism had nonetheless found a small niche in the German academy was in English studies, or *Anglistik*, departments, primarily through the work of Americanists. The development of ecocritical *Germanistik*, meanwhile, was being undertaken by a geographically widely dispersed, and generally institutionally isolated, band of German studies scholars working outside germanophone territory. In addition to Goodbody and Colin Riordan in England, these included Jost Hermand, Heather Sullivan, Bernhard Malkmus, and Sabine Wilke in the United States, Serenella Iovino in Italy, and Nevzat Kaya in Turkey.

I also feature in this lineup of ecocritical scholars, and this chapter charts my own journey, at once intellectual and geographical, from Australian German studies into the inter- and transdisciplinary field of the environmental humanities as it emerged in Australia in the late 1990s and began to be institutionalized in Britain in the 2010s. This is, in part, a story of straying, testimony to my own inability to stay on the straight and narrow demarcated by disciplinary (and other) boundaries. But it also bears witness to the vibrant intellectual milieu in which I came of age as a Germanist in Melbourne in the 1980s: one that was enlivened by the experiences and perspectives of many largely Central and Eastern European migrants, and that proved highly conducive to interdisciplinary adventuring. Undertaken, in large part, in the company of migrants, my own transcontinental and transdisciplinary journey has also been something of an odyssey: having set out for foreign parts as a non-German Germanist, my encounter with the environmental humanities prompted me to turn back and explore my own (vexed) heritage as a nonindigenous Australian; and having moved well away from my home discipline, I now find myself drawn back there in a growing company of ecocritical Germanists, among whom there are now also several German scholars. Not unlike the protagonist of Novalis's *Heinrich von Ofterdingen* (Henry of Ofterdingen), I too, it seems, have been "always going home" (*immer nach Hause*).[2]

Setting Forth: The Lure of German

Having elected to study German at secondary school, my appreciation of the language and dawning interest in the German region received positive reinforcement during a month spent with my father, the Sovietologist T. H. Rigby, at a German-language school in Innsbruck in my mid-teens. The language classes were not particularly memorable, though lolling around listening to pop music amidst the wildflowers on gentle Alpine meadows with fellow students of my own age, as crisp spring edged towards sultry summer, certainly was. So too were the first glimpses this sojourn afforded me of the ghastliness of mid-twentieth-century German history. Our host was an émigré from what had been East Prussia, a monumental and mischievously playful woman, who dwarfed her sprightly Tirolean husband. Every day for lunch she served us fabulous soups, some of which she had learned to cook from an apparently very agreeable Russian soldier stationed with her family immediately after the Second World War. Yet one weekend we were visited by her equally monumental and deeply troubled (indeed alcoholic) niece from East Germany, whose mother had been one of the many thousands, possibly even millions, of German women raped by members of the victorious Red Army: crimes that were acknowledged at the time but became unspeakable in the

Soviet-aligned German Democratic Republic, leaving the children born of these rapes scarred by a double stigma.

Back home in Canberra for year eleven, following a year at school in England, it was not so much my German classes as the twentieth-century history course that fomented my desire to pursue German at university. To be precise, it was our marvelous history teacher, a daughter of Polish Jewish émigrés. To be even more precise, it was the fury with which she turned upon the girls giggling in the back row during our class on the Holocaust, yelling something along the lines of: "You think this is funny, do you? Well most of my family died in Auschwitz . . ." In the awkward silence that ensued I sensed a sudden rending of the fabric of the comfortable middle-class world of white Australian suburbia in which I had been raised by the upsurge of an alien and dreadful reality: the coming into presence, here and now, of an unthinkably appalling past that was still relatively recent.

I had a similar sensation a couple of decades later when confronted with the Australian Human Rights Commission's report "Bringing Them Home" (1997), which revealed that "mixed race" children were still being stolen from their Aboriginal mothers and adopted into suitably "white" families when I was growing up Australia's federal capital, where this genocidal policy was framed: a city, whose very name, Canberra, *Ngambra*, thought to mean "meeting place," bore oblique witness to those First Nations, including Ngunnawal, Ngarigo and Wiradjuri, whose crafting of, and displacement from, what British settlers dubbed the "Limestone Plains," were still largely veiled during my school years. Subsequently, my work in German studies would be ghosted by my growing awareness of the terrible damage both to Indigenous peoples and to the ecology of their well-tended country wrought by colonization in Australia. For this, too, could be seen as a manifestation of the violent propensities of a civilization that prided itself on its enlightened outlook, which had suddenly become apparent to me in that memorable history class.

German (and Other) Studies "Down Under"

Following a gap year, I entered the University of Melbourne to study history and languages in the late 1970s. The Australian education system is modeled on the Scottish rather than the English variant, allowing for a greater range and number of subjects to be taken at both upper secondary and undergraduate university level. Having gained the equivalent of British "A" levels in English, Asian studies, human biology, history, and German, I continued with the latter two at university, but also added beginner's Russian to the mix. This was motived partly because I had always loved hearing it spoken at home and had relished my brief visit to the Soviet Union in my impressionable teens, but also because I was intrigued by Germany's geopolitical position between East and West and wanted to learn more about the Eastern side of the equation.

Melbourne's Germanic studies department was lavishly well staffed in those days, compared with later, leaner years, and I reveled in the range of optional module electives that supplemented the language and culture cores, with the latter providing a systematic, if rather conventional, overview of the literary, cultural, and sociopolitical history of the German-speaking world from the Middle Ages to the present. I chose courses on topics such as musical settings of Romantic poetry, German proverbs, and Norse mythology. The one that proved most compelling, though, was taught by a brilliant lecturer, Hans Pott, who was one of the many postwar German émigrés who staffed the department. Entailing close readings of Nietzsche's use of natural imagery, this elective informed my subsequent forays into ecophilosophy. Many years later, Zarathustra's call to "sei der Erde treu" (be true to the earth) inspired the title of the inaugural conference of the Australia-New Zealand Association for the Study of Literature and Environment, which I cohosted as founding president, in collaboration with a bevy of brilliant PhD students, at Monash University in 2005. My fourth-year honor's dissertation was supervised by another outstanding teacher, Hein Hesse, also a postwar German migrant. Somewhat pompously entitled "Zum Phänomen der Autorität und deren Aufhebung in vier Erzählungen Franz Kafkas" (On the Phenomenon of Authority and Its Suspension in Four Stories by Franz Kafka), the dissertation was heavily indebted to Yale deconstructionism, the "authority" in question being narratorial as well as familial, social, and political. This approach owed little to my Germanic studies course, which was largely innocent of theory, and much to the intellectual ferment then taking place under the leadership of Yale graduate Howard Felperin in the English department.

My thus-far incidental induction into the heady realm of poststructuralist ponderings was continued in a more formal guise over the course of a concertedly hedonistic and personally formative year at the University of Freiburg, courtesy of a DAAD postgraduate scholarship. In addition to mulling over more Nietzsche, getting a taste of Heideggerian philosophy of language, and immersing myself in eighteenth-century drama through the lens of the sociology of literature, this afforded the opportunity to study with the charismatic Friedrich Kittler during his Foucauldian phase. Taking Foucault back home with me to my alma mater, I went on to write a vast (and regrettably unpublished) fifty-thousand-word New Historicist master's dissertation on Heinrich von Kleist's *Der Prinz von Homburg* (*The Prince of Homburg*) under the quizzical but tolerant supervision of the eminent Novalis and Kleist scholar Gerhard Schulz.[3]

Meanwhile, a range of other theoretical perspectives were now being aired in the lively debates and discussions that continued in the English department, as well as those that were getting underway in the newly founded Ashworth Centre for Social Theory. Among the guest lecturers whom I recall from this time were Gayatri Spivak, J. Hillis Miller, and Terry Eagleton in English, and Jean Baudrillard and Anthony Giddens in social theory. Among my coevals, ecological considerations were now beginning to be brought into these conversations. Recognizing the critical importance of bridging disciplinary divides to address complex socioecological challenges, my partner Robert Hartley (whose family had migrated to Australia from England as "ten-pound Poms," beneficiaries of the Australian government's assisted passage migration scheme), transformed the 1988 annual English postgraduate conference into a richly multidisciplinary gathering of students from Melbourne and other metropolitan universities working across a wide range of fields, including medicine and physics, as well as the humanities and social sciences.

My own paper, "Realism and Reification: The Place of the Female Body in the Interplay of Tragedy and Enlightenment," published in the postgraduate journal *Antithesis*, along with other contributions to this conference, bore witness to my defection from Melbourne to Monash University to pursue a PhD in German and comparative literature with the post-Marxist critical theorist and British émigré David Roberts (on the recommendation of one of his previous supervisees, Rita Felski, who subsequently took a post at the University of Virginia and became general editor of *New Literary History*).[4] If my straying into the wilds of poststructuralism had been viewed askance by my lecturers in Germanic studies at Melbourne, relocating to German studies at Monash was seen as positively traitorous. Both were regarded as among the best German departments in the country, and each was fortunate to have a number of Central and Eastern European émigrés on their staff, including their then chairs: Schulz had begun his career in the GDR, while Leslie Bodi, who became the Foundation Professor of German at Monash in 1962, had fled to Australia from Hungary in the wake of the suppressed uprising in 1956.[5] Unfortunately, their relations were not particularly cordial, doubtless adding to the predictable element of rivalry between these two very different departments (which now enjoy a fruitfully collaborative relationship, as evidenced not least in their coproduced Yearbook of German Literary and Cultural Studies, *Limbus*, launched in 2008).

The intellectual jewel in the crown of the Monash arts faculty in the 1980s and 1990s was the Centre for General and Comparative Literature (i.e., Allgemeine and vergleichende Literaturwissenschaft). Germanists had played a key role in its establishment in 1977, in the company of colleagues from French, Russian, Classics, and English. When I joined

Monash, the Centre was teaching a boutique undergraduate program (to which I was recruited as first-year tutor), attracting many fine PhD students, and hosting a lively staff and postgraduate research seminar series (among the guest speakers were Fredric Jameson, Geoffrey Hartmann, and Jacques Derrida). Later renamed the Centre for Comparative Literature and Cultural Studies, this was not only a place where critical theories from elsewhere were debated, it was also a site where influential new approaches were generated and tested, with Kevin Hart, Elizabeth Grosz, and Claire Colebrook counting among its most renowned professors. As recalled by Andrew Milner, a leading scholar in utopian studies (with whom I came to collaborate closely for many years), during the 1980s the Centre "was engaged in an attempt at something very like a Jamesonian 'cognitive map' of postmodernity," as evidenced in its first published volume, *Postmodern Conditions*.[6]

Through David Roberts, I discovered a theoretical perspective that resonated with my socioecological concerns far more readily than had the francophone theories so eagerly embraced in many English departments at this time: namely, Adorno and Horkheimer's critique of the domination of nature, both "inner" and "outer," in its complex entanglement with sundry forms of social domination (notably, classist, sexist, and racist).[7] David was a close associate of the Hungarian refugee intellectuals Agnes Heller and Férenc Feher, with whom he cofounded one of Melbourne's two major Marxist journals, *Thesis Eleven* (the other being *Arena*). Agnes and Féri had been students of Georg Lukács, and one of my first academic articles, published in *Thesis Eleven* in 1989, was a discussion of Lukács's then little-known early work on the history and theory of drama.[8] After Adorno and Horkheimer's *Dialektik der Aufklärung*, this formed the second of the three main theoretical strands of my doctoral thesis, subsequently published under the title of *Transgressions of the Feminine: Tragedy, Enlightenment and the Figure of Woman in Classical German Drama* (1996), the other being feminist theory, principally anglophone, and inclining towards the kind of nonessentialist critical ecofeminism exemplified by the work of the Australian ecophilosopher Val Plumwood.[9]

Feminist "Dialectics of Enlightenment"

Shortly after submitting my thesis, I was appointed to a lectureship in German studies at Monash, which also entailed teaching in the General and Comparative Literature program. I was soon concocting new research plans in the emerging field of "ecological aesthetics," on which I had published an article and a translation in a special issue of *Thesis Eleven* in 1992.[10] First up, though, was a volume on German feminist theory, commissioned by Melbourne University Press for their Interpretations series, which provided introductions to current theories and critical practices in the humanities and social sciences. My contribution to this book, coauthored with my colleague Silke Beinssen-Hesse, was supported by an Alexander von Humboldt Fellowship that took me to Paderborn to work under the generous mentorship of Gisela Ecker, recently appointed to West Germany's first chair of women's studies.[11]

One of the things that puzzled me when I embarked upon this project was the lack of a German equivalent to the French and English coinages *écoféminisme*, ecofeminism. Once I got reading, though, I soon discovered why: one of the hallmarks of German second-wave feminist thought, at least up until the early 1990s, was the widespread recognition that the rationalist project of the mastery of nature, and the consequent industrial despoliation of the Earth, was historically interlinked with the patriarchal domination of women (and other "others"). In this context, there was no reason to attach the prefix "eco-" to any particular strand of feminism (one that remained relatively minor, and widely misconstrued as biologically essentialist, in the English-speaking world), because the proposal that women's emancipation inevitably entailed rethinking modern human relations with the natural world was so widely accepted among feminists in the German-speaking world. A key factor here, as Sigrid Weigel explained to me in a phone interview, was the influence of the early Frankfurt School on the generation of feminists who came of age in the late 1960s (especially, in the West, in the context of the student movement).[12] In their analysis, though, Adorno and Horkheimer's critique of instrumental reason left women, with nature, in the position of the imaginary "other" of the Enlightenment, rather than recognizing women (and other "others") as historical agents of emancipatory change, potentially operating out of a changed concept of freedom—that is, not *from*, but *with*, the natural world. This pessimistic view was countered by German-speaking feminists such as Christine Kulke, Elvira Scheich, Brigitte Weißhaupt, and Maria Mies (who collaborated with the influential Indian ecofeminist Vandana Shiva), for whom, as for ecofeminists elsewhere, women's emancipation was part of a bio-inclusive project of collective socioecological flourishing.[13]

As we explain in the Preface, the title of our book has a double referent:

> German feminist thinking has been articulated in the shadow not only of the internationally dominant francophone and anglophone variants of feminist knowledge, but also of Germany's fascist past. Indeed, the felt necessity of confronting this past has contributed to what is in our view one of the strengths of German feminist theory, namely its characteristically historical and sociological perspective and concomitant stress on the importance of understanding

the origins of one's ideas and taking responsibility for their political implications.[14]

Recognizing also that many German women were complicit with the persecution of Jews (among others) during the Third Reich also contributed to an early awareness of differences among women in relation to other forms of oppression, such as was only brought home to white middle-class American feminists by the objections of women of color to their homogenizing view of women's perspectives and interests.[15] Having been persuaded that German voices had something valuably distinctive to offer international feminist debates and discussions, I regret that we did not follow up with an edited anthology of theoretical texts in translation. Since much of the excellent work that we discuss remains unavailable to anglophone readers, our book has itself remained very much in the shadows.

Towards the Environmental Humanities

For my part, our failure to supplement and promote *Out of the Shadows* was due to my impatience to get on with a new project: one that would take me back to the Goethezeit, where I spent most of my time for my doctorate, but now in an explicitly ecocritical and ecophilosophical perspective. On the track that I now took, one that would eventually lead into the wide-open field of environmental humanities, I found myself among a host of new companions, some of whom were valued guides. One of the first of those was the ecophilosopher Freya Mathews. Internationally regarded as one of the keenest minds in the realm of "radical ecology," Freya generously initiated an "Ecophilosophy in the Pub" discussion group in a grungily hip corner of Melbourne in the mid-1990s, the first nine months of which provided a systematic introduction to anglophone environmental philosophy and ethics. Freya's intention was to build a bridge between the deliberations of academic ecophilosophers and the passions of environmental activists, and when the discussion group began to run out of steam after a few years, this project was taken forward in the new guise of our journal *PAN* (*Philosophy Activism Nature*), coedited by Freya, myself, and Sharron Pfueller, a microbiologist and environmental health specialist in environmental science at Monash. Publishing refereed articles, short prose pieces, and poetry exploring the "philosophical, psychological and mythological underpinnings of ecological thought and practice," *PAN* was "dedicated to voicing connections between people and place, especially, but not exclusively in Australia," and sought to "conjoin the re-hallowing of earth being(s) with the fostering of human well-being."[16] In this, *PAN* took inspiration from a series of outdoor symposia initiated by researchers in social ecology at the University of Western Sydney concerned with exploring how nonindigenous

Australians might develop a deeper sense of place in ways that respected the infinitely longer history of Indigenous place-making, acknowledging the violence of colonization and seeking pathways of decolonization in partnership with First Nations Australians. This project came to the fore in our second issue, *Coming into Country*, whereby "country" was intended in the Aboriginal sense to refer neither to nation nor countryside, but to a collective dwelling place co-constituted by diverse human and nonhuman agencies, understood as "a living entity with a yesterday, today and tomorrow, with consciousness, action and will toward life," as the environmental anthropologist Deborah Bird Rose explains in Freya's editorial introduction.[17] To "come into country," then, was to encounter an Indigenous praxis of relating to, and becoming with, place that undercut the "dualised concept of nature that prevails in the modern west"; as such, it was also to enter into "new metaphysical terrain."[18] Together with Spinozan and Taoist thought, this understanding of "country" contributed to Freya's later articulation of a scientifically informed "contemporary panpsychism" and associated praxis of "ontopoetics":[19] a variant of "new materialism" that I have since brought to bear in a rereading of Novalis's *Heinrich von Ofterdingen* and *Lehrlinge zu Sais* (*The Apprentices at Sais*).[20]

Among my other guides at this time were Debbie Rose and the historian of science Libby Robin, who in 2001 jointly convened the first meeting of the National Working Group for the Ecological Humanities at the Centre for Resource and Environmental Studies at the Australian National University. This multidisciplinary gathering, which met again the following year, formed one of the first shoots to spring up around the world in the now-flourishing field that has become known under the American coinage of "environmental humanities."[21] In addition to producing a "Manifesto for the Ecological Humanities," we negotiated a regular "Ecological Humanities Corner" in the open-access journal *Australian Humanities Review*, a forerunner to the *Environmental Humanities* journal (now published by Duke), cofounded by Debbie and one of her erstwhile PhD students, Thom Van Dooren, in 2012.[22]

Having been drawn into this new intellectual milieu, I was led to reflect anew on my prior formation in German studies. This was one of those moments in which, venturing into unfamiliar territory, I found myself simultaneously "coming home." As a Germanist, I was able to contribute to these discussions a keen awareness of how "green" sentiments had been historically, and could be once more, recruited to far-right political agendas; but I could also warn against the danger of relying on cultural critique and aesthetic practice alone to avert catastrophe. In my contribution to a 2009 special issue of the Ecological Humanities Corner on "Writing in the Anthropocene," I recalled Adorno's gloomy analysis in his essay on the prospects for "poetry after Auschwitz"

("Cultural Criticism and Society," 1951) of how the "reification of the mind" engenders a situation in which "even the most extreme consciousness of doom threatens to degenerate into idle chatter." Moreover, just as, "in George Steiner's words, the Shoah confronted humanists with the devastating realisation that 'a man can read Goethe or Rilke in the evening . . . and go to his day's work at Auschwitz in the morning,'" so too, I argued, "ecocritics must acknowledge that a woman might well read Wordsworth or Thoreau in the evening (well, in the unlikely event that she has any time for reading at all), and go to her day's work for Exxon-Mobil in the morning."[23]

This was not to say, however, that literature, and other forms of creative practice, might not have a role to play in fostering more ecologically oriented ways of seeing, feeling, and thinking. Indeed, my other contribution to the ecohumanities push in Australia was as an environmental literary scholar, having discovered at the inaugural conference of the UK Association for the Study of Literature and Environment (held at Bath Spa University College in 1998) that I was one of a growing band of ecocritics around the world. Among those I met at this conference was my fellow ecocritical Germanist Axel Goodbody from the University of Bath, whose proto-ecocritical monograph on the Romantic trope of *Natursprache* ("natural language" / "language of nature") and its reception in modern lyric poetry I had already encountered in researching a new project on German and English philosophies and poetics of nature and place.[24] Published in 2004, *Topographies of the Sacred* also manifested my budding interest in religion and ecology, and I have recently returned to Axel's work on *Natursprache* in an ecotheologically and biosemiotically inflected discussion of language, nature, and religion in the age of Goethe. Axel became the founding president of the European Association for the Study of Literature, Culture and Environment, and together we coedited a volume dedicated to enriching ecocritical theory through engagement with European philosophy.[25] In addition to Axel's and Heather Sullivan's contributions that bring new theoretical approaches to bear on the analysis of German literature, this anthology includes essays on several German-speaking thinkers, including the German Estonian forefather of biosemiotics Jakob von Uexküll, Walter Benjamin, Martin Heidegger, Wolfgang Iser, Hubert Zapf, and Niklas Luhmann. My own contribution focuses on Gernot Böhme's phenomenologically inflected critical theory of ecological aesthetics, which draws on Hermann Schmitz's philosophy of corporeality (*Leibphilosophie*) to rehabilitate aesthetics, as originally proposed by A. G. Baumgarten, as a theory of sensuous experience. Together with the work of his brother, Hartmut, Gernot's *Für eine ökologische Naturästhetik* (Towards an Ecological Aesthetics of Nature, 1989) had comprised one of the main theoretical strands in my analysis of Romantic-era poetics and philosophies of nature and place in *Topographies of the Sacred*.[26] Here, though, I engage his ecological aesthetics in reading a work of nineteenth-century Australian poetry. As such, this essay bears witness to the swerve that my research had taken in the first decade of the new millennium: namely, towards a concerted engagement with the fraught history, and postcolonial prospects, of settler Australian place-making, viewed in the horizon of a perilously changing climate.

At the heart of this project was an ambitious project to produce a deep history of the Canberra region, from its geological formation to its vexed human present and future socioecological outlook. This undertaking got off to a modest start with a research fellowship at the Australian National University's Humanities Research Centre in 2003. While I was there, I found myself in the midst of the kind of calamity that is becoming more frequent in southeastern Australia (and elsewhere) as the planet warms: the firestorm that swept down upon Australia's federal capital from the forested mountains beyond the city on January 18, 2003, burning to within a few kilometers of Parliament House, destroying over five hundred homes and badly damaging many more. Despite another brief stint in Canberra in 2008 at the National Museum of Australia's Historical Research Centre, the big Canberra project remains unfinished (although I have published a few articles arising from it).[27] Instead, I brought my ever more pressing concerns about climate change—especially in relation to human entanglement, both moral and material, with nonhuman others, in disaster preparedness, mitigation, and recovery—back to my intellectual home territory of comparative literature in my exploration of "environmental histories, narratives, and ethics for perilous times," as I put it in the subtitle of *Dancing with Disaster*.[28]

By the time this monograph made its way into the world in 2015, I had begun to despair of the prospects for comparative literature (not to mention those for Earth's biosphere in the face of escalating extinctions and rising greenhouse gas emissions). I therefore determined to focus my next book exclusively on English-language literature. As befits my advancing years, another major driver for this project is grumpiness: specifically, in relation to the proliferation of reductive critiques of Romanticism, including among those ecocritics who have consigned Romanticism scholarship to an alleged "first wave" of environmental literary studies.[29] Pushing back against this tendency, I delineate within English Romantic verse a number of ecopoetic arts of resistance to what Plumwood termed the "logic of colonisation," as well as tracing some of the ways in which these arts have been taken up in modern and contemporary poetry from North America and Australia, and beyond the page, in practices of socioecological transformation.[30] It was with a view to advancing this project that I took up a Marie Curie Co-Host Fellowship at the Freiburg Institute of Advanced Studies in 2015. And it was while I was working there that I accepted a newly created Chair of Environmental Humanities at

Bath Spa University: delightfully, the very place where I first discovered that I was an "ecocritic"; regrettably, however, at a small new university that lacks a school of languages.

Back to German (in the World)

This seemed to seal my reluctant departure from German studies and comparative literature. Yet when I was emptying my commodious study at Monash, I nonetheless packed up virtually my entire German collection to be shipped to the United Kingdom. This was not purely nostalgic. Ironically, just as I was bidding farewell to German studies, *Germanistik* was beginning to embrace ecocriticism in a big way. From having been very much on the margins of my home discipline, I suddenly found myself flooded with requests to speak at German symposia and conferences, contribute articles and book chapters, review manuscripts, and write endorsements for a rash of publications in ecocritical *Germanistik*.[31] After all this straying from the disciplinary straight and narrow, perhaps I am coming home to German studies after all (as indeed I have been repeatedly along the way).

In tracing my own intellectual journey, I hope to have shown how German studies has been enriched by the perspectives of Germanists outside the German-speaking European fold (albeit many of them postwar émigrés from Europe), as well as indicating what the environmental humanities stands to gain from the perspectives of Germanists. In addition, and crucially, I want to conclude with a *pläydoyer* for German, not only in the world, but answerable to its more-than-human denizens; that is, for a transnational and transdisciplinary *Germanistik* that is mindful of the exigencies of the geohistorical hour: one dubbed the "Anthropocene" (not unproblematically, since this terms veils salient differences in responsibility and vulnerability), in which the activities of industrial and industrializing societies are transforming the planet in largely deleterious ways that will be legible in the geological record in future millennia. This record will provide grim evidence of a period of massive biodiversity loss, rapid planetary warming, an efflorescence of novel entities (such as cement, steel, and plastic . . . plastic . . . plastic), and disruptions to phosphorus and nitrogen cycles. Perhaps, too, it will bear the trace of practices of care, compassion, and restorative ecojustice. For while the German studies in which I was schooled took shape in the shadow of the Shoah, and in the wake of two hundred years of colonial violence in Australia, we now find ourselves all (to significantly varying degrees) complicit with, and imperiled by, an unfolding ecocide of global proportions.

Notes

[1] Axel Goodbody, "German Ecocriticism: An Overview," in *Oxford Handbook of Ecocriticism*, ed. Greg Garrard (Oxford: Oxford University Press, 2014), 548.

[2] Novalis, *Heinrich von Ofterdingen*, ed. Paul Kluckhohn (Stuttgart: Port Verlag, n.d.), 199.

[3] Kate Rigby (under the name of C. E. R. Hartley), "*Der Prinz von Homburg*: Übertretung und Entstellung," unpublished MA thesis (Department of Germanic Studies, University of Melbourne, 1986).

[4] Kate Rigby (under the name of Cate Hartley), "Realism and Reification: The Place of the Female Body in the Interplay of Tragedy and Enlightenment," *Antithesis* 2, no. 2 (1988/89): 53–59.

[5] Leslie Bodi, "A Short Memoir," in *Passagen: 50 Jahre Germanistik an der Monash Universität*, ed. Franz-Josef Deiters, Axel Fliethmann, and Christiane Weller (St. Ingbert: Röhrig, 2010), 13–20.

[6] Andrew Milner, "Professing Comparative Literature," in *Die Lektüre der Welt / Worlds of Reading: Festschrift for Walter Veit*, ed. Helmut Heinze and Christiane Weller (Frankfurt: Lang, 2004), 151–58; and *Postmodern Conditions*, ed. Andrew Milner, Philip Thomson, and Chris Worth (Melbourne: Centre for General and Comparative Literature, Monash University, 1988).

[7] Theodor Adorno and Max Horkheimer, *Dialektik der Aufklärung: Philosophische Fragmente* (circulated unpublished, 1944) (Frankfurt am Main: Suhrkamp, 1981 [1947]).

[8] Kate Rigby (under the name of Kate Hartley), "Georg Lukács and the Disintegration of Dramatic Form: The Tragedy of Modernity," *Thesis Eleven* 24 (1989): 112–31; Georg Lukács, *Entwicklungsgeschichte des modernen Dramas* (1911), trans. D. Zálan, in Lukács, *Werke*, ed. F. Benseler, vol. 15 (Neuwied: Luchterhand, 1981).

[9] Val Plumwood, "Women, Humanity and Nature," *Radical Philosophy* 48 (1988): 16–24. See also Val Plumwood, *Feminism and the Mastery of Nature* (London: Routledge, 1993).

[10] Kate Rigby, "Beyond the Frame: Art, Ecology and the Aesthetics of Nature," *Thesis Eleven* 32 (1992): 114–28; Martin Seel, "An Aesthetic Theory of Nature," trans. Kate Rigby, *Thesis Eleven* 32 (1992): 76–89.

[11] Silke Beinssen-Hesse and Kate Rigby, *Out of the Shadows: Contemporary German Feminism* (Carlton: Melbourne University Press, 1996).

[12] See Sigrid Weigel, "Body and Image Space: Problems and Representations of a Female Dialectic of Enlightenment," in *Discourse and Difference: Poststructuralism, Feminism and the Moment of History*, ed. Andrew Milner and Chris Worth (Melbourne: Centre for General and Comparative Literature, Monash University, 1990), 107–26.

[13] Beinssen-Hesse and Rigby, *Out of the Shadows*, 1–17.

[14] Beinssen-Hesse and Rigby, *Out of the Shadows*, viii.

[15] See, for example, Angela Davis, *Women, Race and Class* (New York: Random House, 1981).

[16] *PAN* 1 (2000), front matter.

[17] Deborah Bird Rose, quoted in Freya Mathews, "Editorial," *PAN* 2 (2002): 3.

[18] Mathews, "Editorial," 4.

[19] Freya Mathews, *For Love of Matter: A Contemporary Panpsychism* (New York: State University of New York Press, 2003); Freya Mathews, *Reinhabiting Reality: Towards a Recovery of Culture* (Sydney: UNSW Press, 2005); and Freya Mathews, ed., *PAN* 6, Special issue on ontopoetics (2009).

[20] Kate Rigby, "'Mines Aren't Really Like That': German Romantic Undergrounds Revisited," in *German Ecocriticism in the Anthropocene*, ed. Heather Sullivan and Caroline Schaumann (New York: Palgrave MacMillan, 2017), 111–28.

[21] David Nye et al., *The Emergence of the Environmental Humanities*, background paper for the Swedish Foundation of Strategic Environmental Research, 2013, 9–10, https://www.mistra.org/wp-content/uploads/2018/01/Mistra_Environmental_Humanities_May2013.pdf.

[22] Rose and Robin wrote a widely cited introduction to the first "Corner" in 2004: Deborah Bird Rose and Libby Robin, "The Ecological Humanities in Action: An Invitation," *Australian Humanities Review* 31, no. 2 (2004). See Kate Rigby, "Weaving the Environmental Humanities: Australian Strands, Configurations, and Provocations," *Green Letters: Studies in Ecocriticism* 23, no. 1, Special issue on the Environmental Humanities, ed. Graham Huggan (2019): 5–18, for a longer account of the Australian ecological humanities.

[23] Theodore W. Adorno, "Cultural Criticism and Society," in *Prisms*, trans. Samuel and Shierry Weber (Cambridge, MA: MIT Press, 1981), 34. Kate Rigby, "Writing in the Anthropocene: Idle Chatter or Ecoprophetic Witness?" *Australian Humanities Review* 47 (November 2009): n.p.

[24] Axel Goodbody, *Natursprache: Ein Dichtungstheoretisches Konzept der Romantik und seine Aufnahme in der modernen Lyrik* (Neumunster: Kurt Wachholtz, 1984).

[25] Axel Goodbody and Kate Rigby, eds., *Ecocritical Theory: New European Approaches* (Charlottesville: University of Virginia Press, 2011).

[26] See, for example, Hartmut Böhme, *Natur und Subjekt* (Frankfurt: Suhrkamp, 1988), an important work of German ecocriticism *avant la lettre*.

[27] See, for example, Kate Rigby, "(Not) by Design: Utopian Moments in the Creation of Canberra," in *Imagining the Future: Utopia and Dystopia*, Special Issue of *Arena Journal*, New Series, No. 25/26, ed. A. Milner, M. Ryan, and R. Savage (2006): 155–77; and Kate Rigby, "Learning to Live on the Limestone Plains," in *Canberra Red: Stories from the Bush Capital*, ed. David Headon and Andrew McKenzie (Sydney: Allen and Unwin, 2014), 1–28.

[28] Kate Rigby, *Dancing with Disaster: Histories, Narratives, and Ethics for Perilous Times* (Charlottesville: University of Virginia Press, 2015).

[29] I contributed to a critical discussion of the wave theory of ecocriticism in Hannes Bergthaller, Rob Emmett, Adeline Johns-Putra, Agnes Kneitz, Susanna

Lidström, Shane McCorristine, Dana Phillips, Isabel Pérez Ramos, Kate Rigby, and Libby Robin, "Mapping Common Ground: Ecocriticism, Environmental History, and the Environmental Humanities," *Environmental Humanities* 5 (2014): 261–71.

[30] Plumwood, *Feminism and the Mastery of Nature*. Kate Rigby, *Reclaiming Romanticism: Towards an Ecopoetics of Decolonization* (London: Bloomsbury Academic, 2020).

[31] Among those to which I have contributed are: Kate Rigby, "Art, Nature, and the Poesie of Plants in the *Goethe-Zeit*: A Biosemiotic Perspective," *Goethe Yearbook* 22, no. 1, Special section edited by Luke Fischer and Dalia Nassar (2015): 23–24); Kate Rigby, "Of Mice and Men and Surging Seas: Discerning Distributed Agency in Storm's *Der Schimmelreiter*," *New German Critique* 128, Special issue edited by Heather Sullivan and Bernhard Malkmus (2016): 153–76; Kate Rigby, "Earth's Poesy: Romantic Poetics, Natural Philosophy, and Biosemiotics," in *Handbook of Ecocriticism and Cultural Ecology*, ed. Hubert Zapf (Berlin: De Gruyter, 2016), 45–46; Kate Rigby, "Language, Nature, and Religion in the *Goethezeit*," in *Ecological Thought in German Literature and Culture*, ed. Gabriele Duerbeck, Urte Stobbe, Hubert Zapf, and Evi Zemanek (Lanham, MD: Lexington Books, 2017), 31–42; and Rigby, "'Mines Aren't Really Like That.'"

9: A Philo-Selfie Approach to German-Indian Studies

Sai Bhatawadekar

Figure 9.1. Poster for the 2014 conference "Asia and the Pacific in German Culture." Photo by the author.

Introduction

IN 2014, I CO-ORGANIZED a conference at the University of Hawai'i titled "Asia and the Pacific in German Culture." Along with organizational responsibilities, I also helped design the poster and website for the conference. I clicked the photo that you see here and chose it as our logo. That's my mother and aunt under a tree on a beautiful beach in Hawai'i. There were aesthetic reasons for choosing this picture: it provided a nonspecific landscape and figures that could fit many regions of Asia and the Pacific, and the sky provided a subtle color scheme and enough negative space for the text. But more important, it represented for me a kind of reversal, a "decolonizing," if you will, of Caspar David Friedrich's 1818 painting *The Wanderer above the Sea of Fog*. Instead of a nineteenth-century white man standing on top of a mountain in Europe with active Wanderlust in his posture and feet overlooking a mysterious faraway landscape, I chose two brown women at sea level somewhere in the Asia-Pacific, sitting in a lotus position, contemplating the wanderings that brought them there. Caspar David Friedrich was the quintessential representative of Romanticism in the late eighteenth and early nineteenth centuries, when German intellectual *Wanderlust* fueled exploration in the East, particularly India. German Romantic thinkers established a literary, linguistic, and philosophical kinship with the East, yet exoticized it as the birthplace of ancient mystical wisdom. And now, here I am, born and raised in India, educated in the United States and Germany, and working in Hawai'i, where I find myself literally and philosophically between East-West currents that rise and flow within me in turbulent and pacific waves.

My reverse conference image was not meant as a counterattack on the colonial gaze; I did not mean that the Eastern perspective was somehow more down-to-earth (sea level) and hence superior to the high-and-mighty (mountaintop) *othering* Western perspective. To claim that would simply tilt the power to the other side rather than restoring a balance between them or showing a dynamic interplay, which was ultimately my goal in the "decolonizing" effort. My conference image was meant to be deeply self-reflexive, as my approach to cross-cultural German studies is inseparably intertwined with my personal journey. After all, in at least two respects I represent the *other* side of the nineteenth-century German thinkers who tried to understand India: first, I am an Indian who has been a student and scholar of German language, literature, film, art, and philosophy for years. And second, now as a professor of Hindi-Urdu, Bollywood film and dance, and Indian philosophy in the United States, I am responsible for representing Indian culture to a Western audience. I am also keenly aware that it is my training in German studies that has positively sculpted my current avatar: it was only after learning and teaching German in India and the United States for several years that I could single-handedly create innovative Hindi-Urdu programs. My master's work in German *Literaturverfilmung* (film adaptations of literary works) informed my research and teaching of Indian cinema and theater and helped me codirect a major theater production—a Bollywood adaptation of *A Midsummer Night's Dream*. And it was through my PhD on Hegel's and

Figure 9.2. Caspar David Friedrich's The Wanderer above the Sea of Fog *(1818). Wikimedia Commons. https://commons.wikimedia.org/wiki/File:Caspar_David_Friedrich_-_Wanderer_above_the_sea_of_fog.jpg.*

Schopenhauer's interpretation of Hinduism that I came to work on apophatic theology in the Upaniṣads.

In these respects, I must be conscientiously guided by the same concerns with which I evaluate German thinkers: I must wonder, for example, what cultural and intellectual "prejudices"—to speak in Gadamerian terms—filter my understanding of the German literary periods, film schools, or philosophies I chose. If I accuse German philosophers of selectively reading Eastern thought to fit their systems, am I guilty of the same top-down approach towards them? In comparative ventures, do I emphasize similarities between East and West, irreconcilable differences, or creative influence and interaction? What does that say about my ideological universalism, relativism, and identity flows? Do I feel confined and oppressed by the image the West has created of my tradition, or empowered as an Eastern interpreter of the West? Beyond the act of interpreting another culture, there is also the question of self-representation. I must be aware that in everything I do, from Bollywood dancing to writing essays such as this one, I not only portray but also perform my identity, often selectively so, to facilitate a functional understanding between East and West and even to attempt a creative fusion (for the lack of a better word). That takes at once assimilating and standing out, playing off of stereotypes that I subvert, and operating within the expectations of two systems and traditions, while challenging and transforming their core notions and mine. "Transforming" is the operative word here that can take me beyond the dichotomies of "interpretation," "performance," or even "dialogue." My German studies on three continents have transformed me, as I have transformed the discipline itself. I do not feel more or less Indian or German or American in my identity or value system; they merge and move me as the subject of constant cross-cultural "becoming."

I gave an "endnote address" at my Asia-Pacific-German conference, in which all this methodological introspection flowed forth in a stream of consciousness. I had, until then, followed our scholarly conventions: distancing myself from the subject matter, analytically parsing others' research, theorizing in abstract statements, churning the work of dead philosophers, and turning them in their graves. Since the endnote address, I have felt compelled to bring my living, breathing self into the mix as a matter of truly self-reflexive methodology and pedagogy, to penetrate the sound barrier of jargon, to experience how theories actually play out in our daily cross-cultural lives, and to be aware of how we shape our work and how it shapes us intellectually, artistically, ethically, and even emotionally. I have come to articulate this approach as my "Philo-Selfie," which I present to you here in three snapshots of my journey in language pedagogy, theater/film, and philosophy. I hope they give you glimpses into my pursuits through three decades, three continents, and many cross-currents of cultures and methodologies. Here is my Philo-Selfie, as we pan across the far reaches of German studies in personal, local, intercultural, and global play.

Language Pedagogy

"Why did you learn German?" is a question I still get asked after thirty years. "You know, I had studied Sanskrit in school and had heard that German was closely related to it. I wanted to explore that connection," is the answer I used to give in the hope of sounding intellectually purposeful. Yes, I had studied Sanskrit and I was good at languages, but the truth was that there was an old Indian lady within walking distance from my home in Mumbai who gave private lessons in German, and it seemed like the perfect use of long school holidays. From then on, German and my frightened commitment to adventure went hand in hand: I went to a cosmopolitan college outside my comfort zone because German was offered there; I chose German over economics for my BA because it meant leaving home and moving to another city, and continuing German for my MA and PhD meant moving to another country and traveling by plane for the first time in my life. It is crucial to note that I went to a school where Marathi was the language of instruction. We hardly spoke English in school, at home, or outside; English was trapped in a grammar-translation mode. For as long as I remember, I was riddled with self-doubt about expressing myself in English; I had even begun to write my dissertation in German. What is important here is that English was *not* the easy vehicle, not the primary facilitator of my Western ventures—German was. It was my pursuit of German that gave my English its global momentum.

German-language pedagogy three decades ago in India was akin to that of Sanskrit. On the first day of classes, we were asked to memorize the "der-die-das" table without much explanation. Sanskrit and Marathi, with their eight cases and declensions, made it easy for me; I had to simply align them with English or German for a comparative perspective. German was also taught, like Sanskrit, in a grammar-translation mode. It was hardly surprising then, that both languages were considered "high-scoring" subjects for state exams: once you memorized the structure and vocabulary, you were sure to boost your marks high enough to get into an engineering or medical college: dissect a sentence now, dissect a body later, so to speak. To be fair, though this grammar mode is outmoded now, I credit it for building a solid base for learning and teaching the eight languages I know. I am aware that this structure—declensions, conjugations, tenses—is an Indo-European, even a colonial, straightjacket; it was nevertheless very exciting and challenging when other languages did not fit in its structure. It created a foundation for comparative self-examination.

Although comparative or historical linguistics was never an explicit part of language pedagogy, it was certainly an impulse of our trilingual upbringing. It was interesting to discover that *pitru, pater, Vater, father* were the same word, or *vid, Veda, vidya, wit, vision,* and *wissen* were the same root with sound shifts. To a Devanagari user like me, the consistency of German spelling and pronunciation was comforting, much more so than English; indirect constructions like "mir gefällt es" (I like it, or rather, it pleases me) were familiar from Marathi and Hindi. Conversely, "der Fluss" (the river) as a masculine noun was an emotional adjustment from a winding, curvy, nourishing, feminine river in Indian languages. It made axiomatic sense that structural intricacies of a language are subliminally connected to one's *Weltanschauung*. Years later, that gave an entry point into the Sapir Whorf hypothesis, into Friedrich Schlegel's *Über die Sprache und Weisheit der Indier* (On the Language and Wisdom of the Indians, 1808), and Wilhelm von Humboldt's *Über die Verschiedenheit des menschlichen Sprachbaues und ihren Einfluß auf die geistige Entwicklung des Menschengeschlechts* (On the diversity of human language construction and its influence on the mental development of the human species, 1836).[1] For me as a language learner, there was no judgment attached to the language-worldview relation. However, the racial and hierarchical implications of that premise revealed themselves in world intellectual and political history.

In the early 1990s in college, we were still using *So Einfach*—a German textbook first printed in 1943 in England, or possibly even in 1900.[2] It came with illustrations of "Bergwandering" (hiking) boys in lederhosen and also with Fraktur (an old germanophone typeface), for which I was later thankful when I had to read old editions of Schopenhauer. From the grammar-translation-comparative method, there was a sudden shift to an immersive experience when I went to Max Müller Bhavan—the Goethe Institute's Indian branch. Back then, Max Müller and Goethe were the two names vaguely associated with German appreciation of India; the word on the street was that Müller had studied Hinduism thoroughly, and Goethe had danced with joy, holding on his head Kālidāsa's fifth-century play *Śākuntala*. It was a reverse romanticizing of the German Romantic exoticization of India, to reinforce the self-image of an Indian golden age. More on that later in this chapter; as for language acquisition, Max Müller Bhavan changed the game. In summer intensive courses, we would speak only German among ourselves in and outside of class. I recall instinctively cursing in German in a crowded bus full of Marathi speakers! In class, we debated issues like "Zusammenleben ohne Heirat" (unmarried cohabitation), which was a sensational, sensitive, even rebellious topic for our milieu. As a matter of language learning, we were examining ourselves through a cross-cultural lens, questioning our social and moral values, and negotiating tradition and modernity.

On the creative side, we were singing Schubert's and Goethe's "Heidenröslein" (Little Rose on the Meadow) and also performing Bollywood-inspired comedy skits in German. "Ich bin in Dich (Akkusativ) Verliebt" (I'm in Love with You [Accusative Case]) was one that stayed with me, with its silly song-and-dance melodrama full of language lessons. Writing, directing, and performing Bollywood spoofs would shape my most joyous and effective language pedagogy years later. In the meantime, in the mid-1990s, the communicative approach was in full bloom. In 1996, I moved to the United States, to The Ohio State University, where we were rigorously trained in communicative pedagogy, creating countless handouts and assessment rubrics. Our textbooks, like *Deutsch Na Klar!* or *Fokus Deutsch*, proved to be very helpful, as they contextually organized grammar and vocabulary under useful themes—daily routine, food, clothing, travel, etc.[3] By 2001, when I was given the enormous responsibility of single-handedly building a Hindi program, I realized that the Hindi textbooks available at the time were lacking in coherent design. With *Deutsch Na Klar!* by my side, I could create a Hindi curriculum from simple building blocks to complex structures, meaningfully contextualizing grammar under topics specifically catered to Hindi-language needs. Comparative linguistics had already helped analyze my language; the communicative approach arranged it pedagogically on a time-continuum. It was like stretching a musical composition out on a linear band of soundwaves, clearly setting the opening notes, the motifs, the refrain, the buildup, and yet ultimately having the musical experience as a whole in one's ears and vocal chords. *Deutsch Na Klar!* gave me the tools to linearly parse the music of my own language and to pedagogically compose opening grammatical notes and themes that would ensure a smooth progression to a more elegant fluency.

Where I surpassed *Deutsch Na Klar!* was its generic textbook form (which was its purpose after all), because in my program-building I could survey students' specific needs and motivations to learn Hindi—heritage, nonheritage, linguistic, cultural, scholarly, artistic, religious, etc. I could let my teaching materials adapt and evolve with each batch of students and weave Indian culture within the fabric of chapters: for example, the "family" chapter included debates on arranged marriage or patriarchal hierarchies; the chapter on yoga, paired with imperative instructions (for yoga poses), discussed religion, cultural appropriation, or mental health. I created a Bollywood poetry chapter around singular-plurals, obliques, and post-positions. Without rigorous German teacher training however, I could not have created a pedagogically sound and long-lasting Hindi program or trained others to become effective cross-cultural communicators.

This cross-pollination between German and Hindi was crucial, especially given the nationwide treatment of less commonly taught languages (LCTL). Often for an LCTL like Hindi, native speakers who have no language teaching experience are hired on contract, which leads to overwork, underpay, lack of guidance and quality, and the eventual withering away of language programs themselves. Thanks to my German training, the Hindi program at Ohio State thrived and led to South Asian majors, minors, and a solid tenure-track position. I owe my own hire and tenure at the University of Hawai'i as an associate professor of Hindi-Urdu to my degrees and training in German studies, as disciplinarily distant as they may seem. My wanderlust for German brought me home to Hindi.

Lest this narrative sound like self-celebratory swagger, let us tug at two methodological threads from the introduction. First, my self-other relationship with South Asian and German studies, reversing the Eurocentric sense of Asian *otherness*. German was my *other*, the pursuit of which trained me to understand my evolving self. And second, a methodological maturing from a purely comparative stance to an inspired, creative exchange between cultures: from separating similarities and differences, to adapting ideas to another context, to transforming the theory and practice of one's discipline itself. I moved on from the communicative approach to what I call a "creative project-process-and-performance-based learning." The most fun and effective of those projects were reminiscent of the "Ich bin in Dich (Akkusativ) Verliebt" skit from Max Müller Bhavan. In my Hindi class we wrote and recited Bollywood-inspired love poetry, and we cowrote, directed, performed, and made short films parodying world classics—from Kwik-e-Mart Apu's wedding in *The Simpsons*, to a happy-ending version of *Titanic*, to a secondhand spoof of a Hindi blockbuster based on *Romeo and Juliet*.[4] "Project based" is the newest approach that is transforming language teaching across the board, be it more commonly taught languages (like German) or less (like Hindi), heritage-oriented (like Samoan), or strategic (like Arabic). The project-based approach itself needs to catch up to my performance-based one—a more creative, joyous, humorous, aesthetic avatar that has far-reaching cross-cultural and psychological benefits.[5]

Theater and Film

Granted, my Hindi adaptations of world classics are over-the-top and ridiculously amateur by design, but parodies (Mel Brooks would tell you) should be grounded in the thorough study of the original. My spoofs were fueled by my work on film adaptations of German literature. For my MA I had analyzed many adaptations—Peter Handke and Wim Wenders's collaboration on *Die Angst des Tormanns beim Elfmeter* (The Goalie's Anxiety at the Penalty Kick, 1970), Kafka's *Der Prozess* (The Trial, 1925) and Orson Welles's stylized American version *The Trial* (1962), Kleist's *Marquise von O. . .* (The Marquise of O. . ., 1808) and its picturesque framing by Eric Rohmer (1976), Ingeborg Bachmann's

Malina (1971), and Werner Schroeter's haunting French-German film by the same name (1991).

To give a more pertinent example, I wrote a comparative paper on Heinrich Mann's *Professor Unrat* (Professor Garbage, a.k.a. Small Town Tyrant, 1905), Sternberg's *Der blaue Engel* (The Blue Angel, 1930), and its Indian (Marathi) adaptation *Pinjra* (The Cage, 1972)—a regional classic (though barely known in the West), directed by one of the most acclaimed filmmakers of India, V. Shantaram, who had been a pioneer since 1927.[6] It was only in the course of my German studies that *Der blaue Engel* triggered my childhood memory of *Pinjra*: both told a story of the humiliation of an idealistic schoolteacher who falls for a cabaret dancer. The plotline was too similar to be a coincidence, but in the popular reception of *Pinjra* one hardly knew of its German inspiration—a fact that needs to be set right for artistic credit and public education. The paper I wrote then was tediously comparative of the three works, explaining the changes in the story, the character development, and its cultural significance. But *Pinjra* and many such international adaptations of German works taught me that "loyalty to the original" is only the first piece of the puzzle; strictly comparative analyses only scratch the surface with one's bare fingernails. What needs to be unearthed is the creative complexity of cross-cultural synergy—from the electrifying discovery of ideas to the courage to experiment with one's own tradition. *Pinjra* transformed the German inspiration for its Indian context; it rooted the story in the social and moral soil of India and flourished it with the folk-dance traditions of Maharashtra. The film went on to hold an esteemed place in Indian cinema as a brilliant example of narrative and musical artistry.

Artistic inspiration has been a two-way street between India and Germany. The first example of this I knew was Goethe, who, along with Herder, the Schlegel brothers, Wilhelm von Humboldt, and others, was enthralled by Kālidāsa's fifth-century play *Śākuntala*.[7] Goethe wrote:

> Willst du die Blüte des frühen, die Früchte des späteren Jahres
> Willst du was reizt und entzückt, willst du was sättigt und nährt
> Willst du den Himmel, die Erde mit Einem Namen begreifen
> Nenn' ich Sakontala dich, und so ist alles gesagt.[8]
>
> [If you wish the blossom of the early, the fruit of the later years,
> if you wish what allures and excites, what satiates and nourishes,
> if you wish to grasp the heaven and earth with a single name,
> I name you Sakontala, and thus everything is said.]

Goethe's "Vorspiel auf dem Theater" (Prelude in the Theater) in *Faust I* was famously inspired by *Śākuntala's* prologue—a conversation between the director and actress discussing which play they should present to their audience.[9] It is less known that Schubert wrote an unfinished opera titled *Sakontala* (1820).[10] But it is even less known that such theatrical and musical appreciation has been mirrored in India; *Faust*, for example, has been translated and staged in numerous Indian languages, including in a 1976 Kathakali production.[11] Kathakali is an interesting example, because it is an Indian classical dance-drama form, rooted in Hindu mythology, with elaborate makeup and costumes, intricate gestures and expressions, and highly specific storytelling techniques that are cryptic and laborious even to Indian audiences.[12] If David John is correct in saying that *Faust* has become "an addition to the repertoire" and a "part of the Kathakali canon," then it is quite a cross-cultural feat indeed. Adrian Hsia and Philip Zarrilli remind us that adapting *Faust* and other Western plays into regional Indian productions was a nation-building exercise to vitalize and modernize age-old traditions and to gain greater global visibility and legitimacy.[13] Such experiments continue to happen worldwide today, with their online distribution virtually at our fingertips, as for example, Michel Lestréhan's Kathakali rendition of a classical aria from Charles Gounod's French opera *Faust*.[14] I leave it to the experts to judge the success of its multicultural hybridity, the "fusion" of dance, music, and theater, and the blending of tradition and modernity. The point here is that such experiments, whether hits or misses, bring far corners of time and space together into a warp. There is no doubt that they satisfy our lust to face, exoticize, or even internalize *other* cultures, and to feel both humbled and smugly elite in our expanded self-image. But in the process, such experiments also become vehicles of promotion and innovation of one tradition with another.

With *Śākuntala*, *Faust*, or *Der blaue Engel*, some other examples also deserve a mention here. Hermann Hesse's *Siddhartha* is an iconic and cultic example of German's vicarious spiritual journey through India. But Conrad Rook's American film adaptation (1972) with acclaimed Indian actors did not fare well in the popular or critical view. On the other hand, Thomas Mann's novella *Die vertauschten Köpfe: Eine indische Legende* (The Transposed Heads: an Indian Legend, 1940) was reclaimed by the renowned Indian writer Girish Karnad in his play *Hayavadana* (1971), which is a stunning masterpiece on the Indian regional, national, and world theater scene. Mann reformulated an eleventh-century Indian myth for his German readers, and Karnad reframed it within regional Indian folk drama to reveal caste, class, gender, and political disharmonies in postcolonial India.[15] Karnad and his contemporaries, well-versed in multilingual global theater, also blended Indian folk narrative techniques with Brecht's *Verfremdungseffekt* (alienation effect), which itself is said to be drawn from Asian theater. Starting in the early 1970s, unprecedented theatrical collaboration occurred between East Germany and India with Brecht at the center (of the *Caucasian Chalk Circle*, as it were!). The renowned directors Fritz Bennewitz and Vijaya Mehta worked together over two decades to bring Brecht to Marathi and Hindi theater, and Sanskrit plays to German audiences. These collaborations went beyond exotic appreciation or cultural commonalities; they brought about mutual aesthetic, political, and ideological change.[16] A few months ago, seventeen years after I compared *Der blaue Engel* with *Pinjra*, I wrote an article on Vijay Tendulkar, a contemporary of Karnad and Mehta.[17] My home in India was a few blocks from Tendulkar's house, and I grew up watching my parents act in his plays, so researching him was quite literally a coming home for me, but it also involved wandering back into German literature: in arguing for Tendulkar as a world literary figure, I discovered how he borrowed a spark from Dürrenmatt's *Die Panne* (A Dangerous Game, 1956) to set the Marathi stage ablaze with a violent critique of patriarchy, the likes of which Indian audiences had never seen before.

Tugging at the methodological threads again, German studies guided me back to my own tradition and its nuanced rediscovery. This process was at once analytically distant, emotionally close, and hence artistically innovative, much the same way that German literature led Indian playwrights to revolutionize their own artistic and sociopolitical practices. My comparative methodology had to evolve to appreciate this creative and transformative dynamic of German-Indian interaction, to experience its multilayered implications: from exoticized imitations to inspired works of art, from true grassroots education to ivory-tower elitism, from borrowed sparks that ignite revolutions, to collaborations that shape cultural diplomacy, hierarchies, kinship, and self-legitimization. Added to these are the politics of global circulation, canonization, and the sexy sale of "fusion" in today's world. I am conscientiously aware of these nuances as I venture into codirecting a Bollywood adaptation of *A Midsummer Night's Dream*, a large-scale mainstage production in Honolulu designed to educate and entertain.

Philosophy

From comparison to (con)fusion, I followed the cross-cultural breadcrumbs wherever they took me. In 2001, the same time that I juxtaposed *Der blaue Engel* with *Pinjra*, I stumbled upon Arthur Schopenhauer. It was his passionate embrace of Indian thought, enthusiastic and depressed at the same time (only Schopenhauer can pull off that combination), that made me curious about Indian philosophy. Schopenhauer, in his magnum opus *Die Welt als Wille und Vorstellung* (The World as Will and Representation, 1818), declared that fundamental tenets of his philosophy, along with Plato's and Kant's, were practically synonymous with Hindu and Buddhist thought.[18] Explaining Plato's allegory of the cave, Schopenhauer wrote, "Die selbe Wahrheit, wieder ganz anders dargestellt, ist auch eine Hauptlehre der Veden und Puranas, die Lehre von der Maja, worunter eben auch nichts Anderes verstanden wird, als was Kant die Erscheinung, im Gegensatze des Dinges an sich nennt . . ." (the same truth, presented again quite differently, is also a principal doctrine of the Vedas and Purāṇas, the doctrine of Māyā, by which too nothing else is to be understood than what Kant calls "appearance," as opposed to the thing in itself).[19] His incessant conceptual parallels with the Advaita Vedānta school of nonduality were backed by quite a team of Romantic comparatists—from William Jones to Anquetil Duperron, from Herder to Friedrich Schlegel. Schopenhauer claimed, in a nutshell, that his idea of *Vorstellung* (representation) was identical to the Indian veil of māyā; *Wille* could be illustrated using the mythical *Bildersprache* (imagery) of the divine brahman; and the act of *Verneinung des Willens* (Denial of the will) landed one somewhere close to Buddhist nirvana.

So far with language and theater, I was exploring Indian adaptations of German culture; now the equation was reversed in discovering German interpretations of Indian philosophy. I had to proceed conscientiously and fairly with my methodologies to grant the same creative impulse to the other side. First though, I dove into the comparative mode to examine Schopenhauer's conceptual parallels. I realized that the exciting similarities on the surface revealed deeper differences rooted in the history of each tradition, not just between Schopenhauer and Eastern philosophy but between Hinduism and Buddhism as well, which were often conflated. As I was arguing for those differences, I remember a distinct intellectual emotion—a triumphant self-esteem, if you will—for having rediscovered my own tradition and defended it vis-à-vis the mighty forces of Western misunderstanding. When I added G. W. F. Hegel to my research, this sense of self-defense got justifiably stronger: Hegel was, after all, the culmination of the Eurocentric *othering* line of thought—a progressive, teleological Hegelian line. He banished India to the primitive, childhood stages of human history, which the rational European had already overcome. Unlike Schopenhauer, Hegel declared Indian thought irreconcilably different from his own philosophy of *Geist* (Spirit). I cross-examined their respective comparative claims, trying to argue that Schopenhauer clearly missed crucial differences (miserable *Wille* vis-à-vis blissful *brahman*, for example), and Hegel possibly had more in common with Indian thought than he admitted (e.g., the idea of absolute consciousness manifesting itself as the world). Many scholars followed this comparative approach to determine the extent of East-West conceptual compatibility.[20] This is indeed a very challenging philosophical exercise, which leads to further questions, such as the comparative necessity of translating one system into the terminology of another. In the process, however, it was clear that Hegel's, Schopenhauer's, and our own comparative judgments necessarily required selective reading: there were both similarities and differences, and what we emphasized had to do with whichever zeal we fed—cultural universalism or relativism.

This opened a new window into the politics of representation. What kind of image of India had Hegel and Schopenhauer created with their self-other comparisons? Hegel fashioned a Eurocentric idea of India—primitive, prerational, feminine, lacking in sociopolitical sophistication, and having extravagant or empty religious concepts.[21] Schopenhauer, declaring a kinship with Indian wisdom, associated it with his own brand of pessimism.[22] What was in their Indian sources that led them to these evaluations? Conversely, what was in their philosophical agenda that distilled their interpretations? I meticulously examined their Indian material to see if they had selectively read, reformulated, or misunderstood it. But here too, I was compelled to reexamine the notion of "misunderstanding." Is objective understanding even possible? Do we not all come with our cultural sieves that strain and filter our interpretations? Then for Hegel and Schopenhauer too, the grooves of their European philosophical lineage must have led them to their readings. This, in a nutshell, was the Gadamer-Halbfass approach that provided a counterexplanation to Eurocentric image-making.[23] In my conscientious journey through German-Indian contact, I was thus advancing step by step through the methodological milestones—looking into comparative connections, analyzing forced stereotypes with a critical, postcolonial eye, and understanding our "prejudices" and "horizons" with an hermeneutic balance.[24]

By the time I completed my dissertation in 2007, I had brought these approaches in conversation together, showing Hegel's and Schopenhauer's comparisons with Indian thought, their hermeneutic quests that led them to impose a definition on "Hinduism" that streamlined its multidimensionality.[25] More important, I had discovered that Indian thought, even as they tried to fit it in their philosophies, had destabilized their tight systems, exposed the inconsistencies in their structures. Hegel gradually changed his opinion about the extent of the primitiveness of Indian concepts,[26] to the point that his anxiety was evident: he was afraid that Indian thought could threaten the progressive linearity of his world history from ancient to modern, east to west.[27] In Schopenhauer's case, the simultaneous parallels of his philosophy with Hinduism and Buddhism shook his system from absolute being to nothingness; he grappled with the philosophical conundrum of defining ultimate reality and then renouncing it.[28] Perhaps logical inconsistencies were the price to pay for it, but Indian philosophy influenced his system tremendously and actually helped him change the course of European philosophy itself: he could banish Hegel's *Reason* from the ultimate rule of human existence and shed light on the forces of instinct, will, survival, power, and renunciation that inspired subsequent thinkers and artists, from Nietzsche to Wagner and Darwin.[29] The trajectory of transformation did not stop there. Nineteenth-century

European interpretations of India percolated into Indian self-understanding, which was sold back to the West as India's new self-image in the time of rising national consciousness vis-à-vis the colonial powers. It was a two-way encounter between Germany and India, which could not be contained in examining the power and hermeneutics of the West alone. East and West both had agency to adapt, affect, and transform each other.

For the third and last time, we must tug at our methodological threads: German philosophers led me to read Indian religious texts, which were part of my upbringing more or less as ambient noise. We grew up chanting Sanskrit hymns with a vague, culturally enforced idea that ancient Indian texts contained the most profound wisdom. Prodding German interest in it pushed me to deconstruct that idea in the nuances of global dynamics. As I followed German philosophers' comparative methodology, I realized that conceptual comparisons in timeless limbos can only go so far. Concepts cannot be divorced from their histories, which include their transfigurations within their traditions as well as in cross-cultural contexts. My comparative approach thus extended with critical and hermeneutic analysis to a more reciprocal, dialogic interaction, to finally realize that we need a self-reflexive and creative approach to appreciate how intellectual history moves and how ideas shape and reshape from hand to hand, land to land, as if in a dance of cross-cultural contact improvisation.

Conclusion

We have laid out quite a spectrum of German-Indian interaction: first, my foreign-language acquisition and its comparative and creative impulses that benefited German, Hindi, and second-language studies; second, a transformative phase starting in the 1970s, where German literature was instrumental in revitalizing Indian theater and film aesthetics; and finally, nineteenth-century German philosophy, whose path was altered by Indian thought. The spectrum revealed that our self-other images and methodologies can be persistent but never static. They should be reexamined even at the cost of our long-held interpretive convictions. Self-revision through time towards nuanced self-awareness should be our academic and personal quest. To speak in Hegelian terms, in my journey, I, an unself-aware entity at the beginning, actualized myself in my research and methodologies, rethinking them through stages in time; and it is only through such concrete actualization that I arrived at self-knowledge as a dynamic *Subjekt* of cross-cultural "becoming." This was my journey to freedom in the Hegelian sense. Ironically, framing my claim to freedom this way, if I demonstrate my colonization in Hegelian structures, then more power to him! Yet it shows my self-awareness of acquired prejudices and horizons. If from within the Hegelian framework I demonstrate that in cross-cultural engagement, in methodologies, and in myself the East proves its agency to shape global intellectual history, then I have subverted Hegel from within.

In our methodologies, we oscillate between counterpositions until we come to a higher synthesis, which contains yet overcomes them: discovering similarities between cultures is balanced by acknowledging differences; uncovering hegemonies and power structures is balanced by understanding our hermeneutic situatedness. Eventually we grant that both parties—East/West, interpreter/interpreted—have actual, textual, and creative agency to challenge and change each other. As Mohanty says, the real step forward is to see that our interaction is "not simply necessary from a cross-cultural point of view, or from the viewpoint of understanding the 'Indian mind' (if there is such a thing)," (or European mind for that matter), "but that it is most urgently needed for increasing creativity and comprehensiveness in the philosophic endeavors of modern professional philosophers."[30] Slowly but surely, in our vocabulary the dichotomy inherent in words like "encounter" and "other side" is moving towards the dynamics of "dialogue" and "fusion." As Jay Garfield states, the variety of interpretive practices "facilitates the kind of cross-cultural dialogue that ultimately leads to greater self-understanding." Our common goal—our "homology of function"—"can then provide a fulcrum for understanding difference, for dialogue, and eventually, perhaps, for the fusion of horizons that can permit genuine collegiality and eventually the appreciation of those features of our own life invisible to us precisely because of their proximity."[31]

My endnote address at the Asia-Pacific in German Culture conference opened with Monty Python's famous comedy sketch, "Philosophers' Football," an exciting match between the superstars of Greek and German philosophy. When the match starts, rather than kicking the ball to the goal post, the philosophers all turn around, wander about by themselves, and with dramatic "thinking" gestures contemplate their big questions.[32] In addition to providing the comic relief of "something completely different," the sketch helped us wonder if in the game of academia we get into opposing teams (first to challenge each other but then perhaps just for the game), and then in isolation, strenuously and self-indulgently contemplate away what it all means. This chapter clearly shows such self-indulgence, quite personally so, but in my defense against my own accusation (and there's the isolation too!), I hope it is at least a self-reflexive indulgence. We are so trained to externalize our research and produce hagiographies of great minds or critical visions of eras past that we neglect ourselves in the present time. In my own case, in a profound yet tangible sense, I recognize at every step how my research shapes me. My methodologies at different stages reveal to me who I was, how I changed, and what I am becoming in my day-to-day cross-cultural life. Ever since I started my research, I have kicked the ball around: played happily on the comparative teams, protested my *other* image, genuinely understood the other side of the hermeneutic coin, and creatively fused forces that produce good art and self-reflection. It has explained my urge to find common ground to relate to people yet assert my cultural uniqueness, assimilate yet stand out; it has showed me the quests and values I live by—fairness, equality, giving credit where credit is due, understanding the complexity of a story, enriching each other's creativity; and it has sparked brilliant epiphanies but also exposed the power structures that evoke debilitating anxiety, guilt, suspicion, anger, aggression, disappointment, or submission, even in interpersonal interactions. My methodological explorations started at the turn of this century, and here I am finally acknowledging that I am becoming increasingly self-aware not just as a recipient but as an agent of cross-cultural dynamic change; and that I can identify how others have changed me, whose interpretive frameworks have become mine, but also how I am capable, even playing by the rules within the system, of unsettling it, transforming it.

I have been told that this piece has a rather celebratory tone. Rest assured, the tone is not a naïve but a hard-earned, purposeful stance, almost in protest of the cynicism, defensiveness, and aggression that pervades us. It is a positive, empowering reminder of our creative, collaborative journeys, through and despite the power-plays, angst, and ethical burdens of our cross-cultural interactions. It is interesting that I started my German-studies career with a football metaphor: my MA thesis analyzed Wim Wenders's film adaptation of Peter Handke's *Die Angst des Tormanns beim Elfmeter*, which was essentially about the interpreter, the receiver of signs, and his defensive nervousness about both his role and others' expectations of him. Now here I am again with football, Monty Python's this time, also in a context of interpretive interaction, but decidedly more self-aware as an agent, and genuinely but playfully self-analytical. Does that indicate my psychological and methodological evolution from anxiety to humor? May it be so.

Notes

Uncredited translations are my own.

[1] Friedrich von Schlegel, E. F. K. Koerner, *Über die Sprache und Weisheit der Indier: Ein Beitrag zur Begründung der Altertumskunde* (Amsterdam: Benjamins, 1977). Wilhelm von Humboldt, *Über die Verschiedenheit des menschlichen Sprachbaues und ihren Einfluss auf die geistige Entwickelung des Menschengeschlechts* (Berlin: Königliche Akademie der Wissenschaften, 1836).

[2] Magda Kelber, *So Einfach: An Elementary German Reader for Adult Students* (London: Georg C. Harrap & Co., 1943). If amazon.com is to be believed, the book came out as early as 1900: https://www.amazon.com/So-Einfach-Magda-Kelber/dp/B000VC8T5U.

[3] Robert Di Donato, Monica Clyde, and Jacqueline Vansant, *Deutsch Na Klar! An Introductory German Course* (Boston: McGraw Hill, 1999). Daniela Dosch Fritz, Stephen Newton, Lida Daves-Schneider, and Karl Schneider, *Fokus Deutsch Intermediate German* (Boston: McGraw Hill, 2000).

[4] "Bollywood Parody of Romeo and Juliet: A Project Prototype by Sai Bhatawadekar," June 30, 2016, http://nflrc.hawaii.edu/pebbles/prototype/doc/158/.

[5] "Task Designs for Creativity," February 18, 2015, https://www.youtube.com/watch?v=fH_RlZFlOmI.

[6] Sai Bhatawadekar, "Femme Fatale and Fallen Teacher: The Images of the 'Self' in *Der blaue Engel* (Germany) and *Pinjra* (India)," in *The Image of the Twentieth Century in Literature, Media, and Society*, ed. Steven Kaplan and Will Wright (Pueblo: Society for the Interdisciplinary Study of Social Imagery, University of Southern Colorado, 2000), 339–45.

[7] Georg Forster, *Sakontala, oder der Entscheidende Ring* (Frankfurt am Main: Bey August Hermann, 1803).

[8] In Walter Leifer, *India and the Germans: 500 Years of Indo-German Contacts* (Bombay: Shakuntala Publishing House, 1971), 80. Dorothy Figueira, *Translating the Orient: The Reception of Śākuntala in Nineteenth-Century Europe* (Albany: State University of New York Press, 1991), 12. Douglas McGetchin, *Indology, Indomania, and Orientalism: Ancient India's Rebirth in Modern Germany* (Madison, NJ: Fairleigh Dickinson University Press, 2009), 204.

[9] McGetchin, *Indology, Indomania, and Orientalism*, 58.

[10] For a sample, please see https://www.youtube.com/watch?v=gCUrM7Et-DI.

[11] David John, "Goethe's *Faust* in India: The Kathakali Adaptation," in *International Faust Studies: Adaptation, Reception, Translation*, ed. Lorna Fitzsimmons (London: Continuum: 2008), 161–76.

[12] For an example, see https://www.youtube.com/watch?v=49lTzt1cZgI.

[13] Adrian Hsia, "On the Reception of *Faust* in Asia," in Fitzsimmons, *International Faust Studies*, 154. Philip B. Zarrilli, *Kathakali Dance-Drama: Where Gods and Demons Come to Play* (London: Routledge, 2000), 178.

[14] Michel Lestréhan, "*L'air des bijoux* de Faust," https://vimeo.com/207827597.

[15] Anand Mahadevan, "Switching Heads and Cultures: Transformation of an Indian Myth by Thomas Mann and Girish Karnad," *Comparative Literature* 54, no. 1 (2002): 23–41. Dorothy Figueira, "Theories of Myth and Myths of Theory in Thomas Mann and Girish Karnad," in *Theatres in the Round: Multi-Ethnic, Indigenous, and Intertextual Dialogues in Drama* (New York: Peter Lang, 2011), 197–210.

[16] Joerg Esleben, Rolf Rohmer, and David G. John, *Fritz Bennewitz in India: Intercultural Theatre with Brecht and Shakespeare* (Toronto: University of Toronto Press, 2016), 15.

[17] Sai Bhatawadekar, "'And I Have the Same Restlessness Today': Vijay Tendulkar—A Connected Reading," in *A Companion to World Literature*, vol. 5b,

1920 to Early Twenty-First Century II, ed. Ken Seigneurie, et al. (Malden, MA: Wiley-Blackwell, 2020), https://doi.org/10.1002/9781118635193.ctwl0274.

[18] Arthur Schopenhauer, *Die Welt als Wille und Vorstellung*, 2 vols., in *Zürcher Ausgabe: Werke in Zehn Bänden*, ed. Arthur Hübscher and Angelika Hübscher (Zürich: Diogenes, 1977).

[19] Schopenhauer, *Die Welt als Wille und Vorstellung*, vol. 1, 516.

[20] For example, Richard White, "Schopenhauer and Indian Philosophy: On the Limits of Comparative Thought," *International Philosophical Quarterly* 50, no. 1 (2010): 57–76. Or Michael von Brück, "Trinitarian Theology: Hegelian vis-à-vis Advaitic," *Journal of Dharma* 8 (1983): 283–95.

[21] See the classics, such as Kamakshi Murti, *India: The Seductive and Seduced "Other" of German Orientalism* (Westport: Greenwood, 2001); Richard King, *Orientalism and Religion: Postcolonial Theory, India and "The Mystic East"* (London: Routledge, 1999); or Dorothy Matilda Figueira, *The Exotic: A Decadent Quest* (Albany: State University of New York Press, 1994).

[22] J. J. Gestering, *German Pessimism and Indian Philosophy: A Hermeneutic Reading* (Delhi: Ajanta, 1984).

[23] Wilhelm Halbfass, *India and Europe: An Essay in Understanding* (Albany: State University of New York Press, 1988).

[24] Bradley Herling, "Hermeneutical Consciousness or Critical Consciousness: Renegotiating Theories of the Germany-India Encounter," *The Comparatist* 34 (2010): 63–79.

[25] Sai Bhatawadekar, "Symptoms of Withdrawal: The Threefold Structure of Hegel's and Schopenhauer's Interpretation of Hindu Religion and Philosophy" (PhD dissertation, The Ohio State University, 2007).

[26] Robert Bernasconi, "With What Must the History of Philosophy Begin?: Hegel's Role in the Debate on the Place of India within the History of Philosophy," in *Hegel's History of Philosophy: New Interpretations*, ed. David Duquette (New York: State University of New York Press, 2003), 35–50.

[27] Bhatawadekar, "Symptoms of Withdrawal," 155–59. See also Sai Bhatawadekar, "Islam in Hegel's Triadic Philosophy of Religion," *Journal of World History* 25, nos. 2–3 (2014): 420. I am glad to see this point being taken up in recent times by Aakash Singh Rathore and Rimina Mohapatra, *Hegel's India: A Reinterpretation with Texts* (New Delhi: Oxford, 2017), 80. Or Nicholas Germana, *The Anxiety of Autonomy and the Aesthetics of German Orientalism* (Rochester, NY: Camden House, 2017).

[28] Bhatawadekar, "Symptoms of Withdrawal," 332.

[29] Christopher Ryan, *Schopenhauer's Philosophy of Religion: The Death of God and the Oriental Renaissance* (Leuven, Belgium: Peeters, 2010); Moira Nicholls, "The Influence of Eastern Thought on Schopenhauer's Doctrine of the Thing-in-Itself," in *The Cambridge Companion to Schopenhauer*, ed. Christopher Janaway (Cambridge: Cambridge University Press, 1999), 171–212; Douglas Berger, *"The Veil of Māyā": Schopenhauer's System and Early Indian Thought* (Binghamton, NY: Global Academic, 2004).

[30] J. N. Mohanty, "On Matilal's Understanding of Indian Philosophy," *Philosophy East & West* 42, no. 3 (1992): 397.

[31] Jay Garfield, *Empty Words: Buddhist Philosophy and Cross-Cultural Interpretation* (New York: Oxford University Press, 2002), 259.

[32] Monty Python, "Philosophers' Football," YouTube, n.d., https://www.youtube.com/watch?v=QXOKsJViHtY.

Part III

German Worlds beyond the Academy

Introduction to Part III: German Worlds beyond the Academy

James Hodkinson and Benedict Schofield

THE CONTRIBUTIONS IN THIS third part critically assess the importance and relevance of a German-language contribution to the world, where the world refers not merely to the geographical but to a plurality of cultural practices and forms of social transformation. Each explores how knowledge of German-language cultural products, ideas, and traditions has provoked and driven activity beyond the academy, and how this has impacted on the communities that come into contact with them. The chapters thus question what the world of art, culture, and society takes from German-language culture, exploring which language(s), which traditions, and which intellectual insights are required to undertake the work they do. In assessing these cultural and community contexts, these chapters also question what role, if any, academic work might have in supporting or articulating this cultural response to "Germanness"—and what academia might learn in turn from work undertaken in the cultural and community sectors.

In his opening chapter, James Hodkinson explores how processes of collaboration and co-creation have extended the reach of his research into two new worlds: first, "away from the physical space of campus and academic modes of discourse," and second, "transnationally, by making culturally remote (German and historical) material relevant to the contemporary UK context." Some of these materials indeed return us to a figure familiar from earlier parts of this book—namely, Goethe—with one of Hodkinson's most innovative examples of "impact" revolving around responses to the Hafez-Goethe monument in Weimar, inspired by Goethe's *West-östlicher Divan* (West-Eastern Divan, 1819) and his imagined encounter with the Persian poet Hafez of Shiraz. In looking at Goethe and others, Hodkinson's chapter thus demonstrates the "abiding value of German cultural products to make culturally specific contributions to contemporary debates." At the same time, however, he showcases different models of impact and knowledge exchange, such as public lectures, exhibitions, work with schools, and artistic collaborations with figures such as the Bangladeshi artist Mohammed Ali and the Iranian-born

Birmingham painter Mohsen Keiany. In exploring how we might "evaluate" these collaborations in quantitative and qualitative ways, Hodkinson ultimately argues that these collaborations and networks "beyond the world of the academy" reveal how "academics can equally benefit from engaging with nonacademic constituencies."

Hodkinson's chapter raises crucial questions about the nature of the networks of exchange and transfer that are constructed between the academy and the arts or community work, and about the tools that we have at our disposal as academics to map these networks of exchange. This question of mapping is also central to Benedict Schofield's chapter, which critically examines perceptions of Germany and Germanness in the world of theater and performance, exploring how this world both knowingly (and sometimes unknowingly) draws on and adapts German-language traditions. Through interviews with UK-based theater makers, Schofield attempts to "map" the way that German theater is seen from within the sector itself. He explores how UK-based theater makers from German backgrounds negotiate their German identity, and what this "Germanness" might facilitate in their work. Drawing on Bruno Latour's actor-network theory, he also examines the extent of the United Kingdom's openness, or "porosity," to Germany, exploring which elements of German practice transfer easily and which less so, and the different knowledge bases (linguistic, contextual, and political) that might be required to enable full engagement with German traditions. The United Kingdom, he reveals, "is remarkably porous to German theater, actively drawing on German practices, above all those of *Regietheater* (director's theater)," but this porosity does not result in direct acts of cultural transfer but rather in processes of cultural transformation: "a continual process of encounter, translation, and productive dislocation." This, intriguingly, reveals a vision of "Germany" in the United Kingdom that ultimately involves a relatively narrow exposure to Germany, which comes to be represented by just a handful of theaters and practitioners operating largely in just one city, Berlin.

In mapping these cultural exchanges and flows in theater, Schofield interrogates what knowledge bases are required to engage with German and the German-speaking countries. What, though, makes "German" visible, and what invisible? Emily Oliver and Uwe Schütte reflect directly on these questions of visibility and invisibility. Oliver looks at what initially appears to be a highly visible attempt to render influence through culture, in the form of the BBC German Service. Exploring the role of the service during the Second World War and especially in its immediate aftermath, Oliver outlines how "technology enabled Britain to cross into enemy territory via the airwaves, actually speaking to Germans in a language they understood, in a tone to which they would respond favorably, about topics that interested them." However, this also required highly nuanced levels of linguistic and cultural competence, that—as her innovative assessment of the letters received by the service from its German listeners demonstrate—was not always easy to achieve. In exploring which "bodies of knowledge and intellectual insights" the BBC's employees drew on to maintain its transnational broadcasting effort, Oliver argues that the BBC German Service's "development during the immediate postwar years serves as a case study for two nations' attempts to redefine their position in the world after a period of embittered conflict," a reminder of the role of German language and culture as tools of "soft power" in worlds beyond the academy.

In our final chapter, Uwe Schütte similarly explores the visible and more invisible impacts that can arise when German culture goes global, in his chapter on Kraftwerk and its influence both in the United Kingdom and on Afro-Germanic techno. Schütte argues that while in the United Kingdom Kraftwerk's "performance of Germanness was perceived as an ambivalent gesture that mixed the deeply engrained xenophobic clichés about Germany with an admiration for [their] musical achievements," in the United States the situation was quite different, where Kraftwerk had impact on African American artists and producers of techno and house music. In this context, for Schütte, "Kraftwerk was not so much Germans as exotic 'others'; the complete antithesis to the white rock'n'roll aesthetics that governed US mainstream music." Ultimately, for Schütte, "the patterns of musical transmission that were unknowingly started when Kraftwerk began to work on an electronic form of pop music led to one of the most remarkable transnational processes of cultural hybridization and exchange in the history of pop music."

As a whole, then, Part 3 demonstrates how the "worlding" of German culture goes hand in hand with an expansion of the concept of "Germanness" not only beyond neatly defined national boarders but beyond the academy: into the world of practice beyond theory or text. This daily engagement with German in the world of the arts and other communities is, we argue, of genuine impact—not just in the sense of the academy adding value to the nonacademic but in a fully synergetic manner that also forces us to reflect back on how we articulate the wider value of our own discipline as something that is intrinsically coproduced and codetermined by partnerships both within and beyond the academy.

10: Towards a Socially Engaged Academy: Islam in German History and Its Relevance for Nonacademic Publics

James Hodkinson

Conceiving Impact

SINCE 2007 I HAVE BEEN engaged in research into the representation of Islam and Muslims in German-speaking culture from the late Enlightenment to the early nineteenth century. Latterly I have also been working to make my material and themes, and my critical discussion of them, more relevant to nonacademic communities in the United Kingdom, despite my work's obvious anchoring in a historical and cultural context detached from that of contemporary Britain. This has taken the form of an ambitious public-facing project, which has run from 2015 to date. The project, which has trialed differing methods for making my work more widely accessible and beneficial to nonacademic audiences, has also been shaped by a series of wider political contexts within the United Kingdom and further afield. The first of these has been the growth in global Islamist terrorism and the rise of ISIS / the Islamic State, and wars in Iraq, Afghanistan, and Syria, as well as the resurgence of parochial nationalisms and populism within the political and media cultures of many Western democracies, often marked by Islamophobic rhetoric and treatments of Islam focused on its apparent "externality" and "otherness." In this context, any academic work that seeks to impact the public sphere and raise awareness of how political forces shape the ways in which one culture views and represents another might be felt to be of broad social value.

Yet my work has also coincided with key developments within British academia referenced in this volume's introduction: the rise of the "impact" agenda, by which academics and their departments were compelled not only to submit research for peer-reviewed assessment but also to engage in project work that developed ways of extending and measuring its benefit to the nonacademic world.[1] What is being termed in this volume as the natural "porosity" of the academy in its relationship to different sectors of society became, for a researcher working in my field and at this time, both a compulsion and an opportunity.

The project brought with it a number of requirements and challenges. In devising and executing an impact project in the United Kingdom, I needed to extend the reach of my work along two axes—effectively away from the physical space of campus and academic modes of discourse towards different publics and their communicative idioms, and transnationally, by making culturally remote (German and historical) material relevant to the contemporary UK context. The challenge in carrying my work away from its usual medium of academic language was to establish and maintain a meaningful connection between my materials, themes, and concepts and my broadening audiences. I had to determine, for instance, at what point those connections might become banal or tangential. Finally, there remained the dual challenges of winning the interest, the engagement, and, given the political landscape, the trust of those constituencies with whom I would be working and of maximizing the benefit to them by asking them to help shape and deliver the project.

This chapter offers a reconstruction of that project from conception to delivery. It charts, first, the themes of the research underpinning my work, it then reconstructs the project as it was conceived, as it evolved, and as it was delivered. In presenting the project in this way, I aim to offer more than chronological narrative and to highlight the emerging self-critical evaluations I undertook as I progressed, showing how it was only through self-critique that I would begin to succeed, in the project's last stages, in balancing my own voice as researcher with the voices of my collaborators. The very concept of "impact" seemed quite unilateral and to focus upon and even privilege the knowledge base and communicative methods of the researcher over those of his or her nonacademic interlocutors. It would be for me to show how researchers might begin to move to a more collaborative way of working, recognizing that academics can, equally, benefit from engaging with nonacademic constituencies and that the academy's "porosity" is thus a two-way phenomenon.

Underpinning Research: Beyond Representations of Islam in German Culture

My first publications could not be more distant from the social reality with which my work would seek to connect. My writing was largely literary in focus and grew out of my research in German Romanticism, specifically the representations of women and female creative agency in the works of Novalis (Friedrich von Hardenberg, 1772–1801). In Novalis I had identified both a poetics of "identity transformation" and a "polyphonic" model of communication, which were outlined in the poet's theoretical writing and informed his literary writing.[2] Of particular interest was the figure of Zulima, a female Muslim slave depicted in Novalis's unfinished novel *Heinrich von Ofterdingen* (Henry of Ofterdingen, 1801). The novel is set in an idealized version of medieval Germany, through which the eponymous German protagonist journeys in search of his destiny as a poet. Zulima is the Muslim captive of a band of veteran templars returning from the Crusades, and in her encounter with Heinrich she describes her homeland and its culture in great depth. The encounter has been read critically, with Zulima seen as a representation of an oriental *Exotin* (exotic woman), who merely serves to enrich the imagination and hone the poetic skills of a male, European protagonist who ultimately passes her by as he continues along his own journey.[3] In a spin-off essay generated by my doctoral research, I argued, however, that the encounter was more nuanced. Heinrich was attracted by Zulima's song, which was no outpouring of idealized oriental folk art, but marked the beginning of a narrative in which she inducted him into the poetry and culture of her homeland and, also, highlighted Islam's veneration of Jesus as a tenant of shared belief between two faiths, which complicated binary, mutually exclusive notions of interfaith relations.[4]

Zulima's position in the text is fleeting, even tenuous. Yet her episode did begin to challenge reductive images of Islam typical of so much European literature of the period and, crucially, raised the possibility of representing Muslim agency and a Muslim subject in European culture: Zulima arguably attains a degree of intellectual, if not political, agency and, crucially, serves to question the notion that European literature of the period was locked into practices of representing Islam as the "other" of Europe. In the texts I was reading, then, the relationship between Islam and the Christian West both evolved beyond a pairing of simple binary opposites, though also, on occasion, snapped back into that configuration, just as those texts seemingly both empowered and disempowered the voices of women.

Beyond Orientalism: Evolving Critical Tools

My work quickly led me to reconsider the key theoretical work in the field, Edward Said's *Orientalism* (1978). Said's concept of "orientalism" described the exercise of soft cultural power, which ran parallel to European hard colonialism of the eighteenth and nineteenth centuries in Africa and Asia, and resulted in largely uniform practices of reductive "othering" in the representation of non-European peoples and cultures within Western works of art, literature, scholarship, and thought—and the effective silencing or suppression of any notion of the "coauthorship" or "agency" of the culture represented. The sources I was examining both fitted with and also broke free from the classic model of orientalism. This ambivalence was reflected in existing scholarship dealing with German literary representations of the Orient, and a range of critics had already begun the process of rethinking the theoretical tools for analyzing German orientalism, suggesting, by and large, less unilaterally driven processes of representation producing less binary models of Occident and Orient.[5]

Ultimately, it was my work with the Indian Germanist Anil Bhatti that introduced me to the emerging conceptual development within cultural studies that would provide my project with its key framing concept—that of "similarity." Together with his coeditor Dorothee Kimmich, Bhatti defined "similarity" as a strategically fuzzy concept, which allowed for fluctuating and contextually contingent readings of intercultural encounters. Similarity did not, contended Bhatti and Kimmich, seek to collapse all notion of the mutual distinctiveness of cultures, but sought rather to reilluminate the commonalities that almost always accompany even the starkest of differences and, thus, usher in more nuanced and less binary thinking to scholarly discourse. Neither was "similarity," as a concept, trope, or representational technique, a necessarily progressive force: its radically contingent nature meant that it could just as aptly be used not only to describe a problematic pull towards banal comparison but also to underpin historical instances of forcibly imposed cultural and social norms.[6]

As I assembled the theoretical apparatus for my forthcoming book, it became clear that I also needed to approach historical representations of Islamic-German encounters as expositions of cultural similarity that could end up both diffusing dualisms of self and other while also highlighting threats to the notion of Islam's "cultural particularity." Indeed, the period I had chosen seemed, increasingly, to demand such a framework. The colonial power relations that so characterized French and British orientalism during the Age of Empire, while absent from the German context around 1800, increasingly came to exert an influence on how certain strains of germanophone writers, scholars, and commentators thought and represented Islam as the century neared its end, which made for a modulating set of ideological perspectives on the Islamic world across the period. However, as I worked through the long nineteenth century, I also noted that the material I uncovered shifted away from solely literary texts, and I began to chart the growth in germanophone travel writing from Muslim territories, the growth and diversification of the academic study of oriental languages at German-speaking universities, and the growth of German involvement in world politics and colonialism throughout. It quickly became clear that, across a century of time in which Germany and Austria went through great political, cultural, and social shifts, I would also be working on sources that were produced within radically differing genres, discourses, and media and that required me to develop an understanding of how my themes of interest were treated in those differing contexts.

Yet a fundamental issue remained. Those initial readings of Novalis and his Zulima had opened up deep critical questions around the position of the voices of the Muslim world within and in relation to Western discursive and representational practices. There was a prevalent danger, it seemed to me, that much of the critical discussion centering on orientalism still very much had its origins in the West's postcolonial thinking about itself. The time critics spent pulling apart Western fictions of the Oriental/Islamic worlds was, in itself, in danger of displacing the concerns, questions, perspectives, and voices of those cultures misrepresented. Gayatri Chakravorty Spivak's seminal question as to whether the subaltern could speak, be that within Western cultural production or in critical discourses, now weighed in heavily to my project.[7] Even those instances in my work focusing on German writing that attempted to relinquish its own cultural hegemonic position and include the voice of the other, however symbolically, would need to be reconsidered critically in light of this.

My own academic writing, it seemed, could become locked into a circular and unproductive discussion about German representations of Islam—one that ran the risk of excluding anew those very voices whose trace I was seeking in my sources. My approach, when it emerged, involved keeping Spivak's question close, reminding me of the ever-present danger that the way I worked potentially threatened the position of marginalized cultures and voices for whom they sought, ironically, to advocate. I concluded there was space to envision a more dialogical or even fluid and overlapping sense of cultural identity and to imagine how Western writing might, without losing itself, surrender its discursive autonomy to make space for Muslim voices. Yet how could I enact, reflect, or promote the ideals of cultural decentering and inclusivity at the project's heart, and do so in a way that genuinely engaged and empowered Muslim and BAME (Black, Asian, and minority ethnic) communities? The solution, when it came, required more than citing the ideas of Asian and African scholars in written debate, and more than setting up and fostering, as I had, an Occident-Orient Research Network, which drew together scholars from Europe, the Americas, Africa, and India to work and publish on these themes collaboratively between 2010 and 2013.[8] In fact, the solution would lie beyond the academy itself.

Para-Academic Engagement and Impact

My public engagement work began in earnest in fall 2015. I was awarded a grant by Warwick University's Impact Fund to run a program of public-engagement events entitled "Transnationalizing Faith: Rethinking UK Cross-Community Relations through Historical German-Islamic Encounters." The project included a sequence of public lectures at religious centers and interfaith groups around the United Kingdom and also involved the curation and management of a touring banner exhibition to similar locations and in schools and universities. The approach adopted in both lectures and exhibition was to present, in a form digestible to my various audiences, a set of contrasting representations of Islam, both in text and image, from across the period of my research. Set against a reconstruction of key developments in the history of German-speaking Europe circa 1750–1918, both the lectures and the written commentaries in the exhibition offered close readings of primary sources, showing how changes in germanophone concepts of "nation building," shifting political agendas, and the policies and funding of academic institutions all influenced and inflected how Islam and Muslims were written about and pictured within German culture, highlighting the values and functions that were ascribed to them.

Both the lectures and the exhibition gave me an opportunity to outline and apply key aspects of critical thinking for my audiences. On one level, this meant raising a general critical awareness that images of any culture are always the products of their era and environment and often express ideological bias. However, I was also able to show that, while Western critical thinking had traditionally identified the "othering" of Islam, the sources I was referring to demonstrated a less binary set of relations, with Islam also exhibiting forms of continuity and commonality with the Western cultures alongside which they were represented. Framing these tendencies in terms of my critical application of "similarity," I sought to show how the quality of similarity could serve both progressive and more sinister ideological ends across history and ought to figure in our critical thinking about media representations of Islam today.

In the lectures, for example, I referred to two contrasting figures from late-nineteenth-century academia: the better-known German-speaking Hungarian Jewish orientalist Ignaz Goldziher (1850–1921), and the lesser-known Prussian statesman and orientalist Carl Heinrich Becker (1876–1933). Goldziher, who counts as something of a poster boy for progressive contemporary Jewish studies, wrote tellingly in the diaries he kept during an early study visit to Cairo of how he had come to identify so closely with Islam that he had thought of himself, for a time, as a Muslim. Goldziher had been so impressed not only with the piety of his Egyptian peers but also with the fact that Islamic theology conducted its own rational debates without appealing to Western philosophical paradigms in so doing. Rather than convert, however, he saw himself as a conduit between the Muslim world and his own: in Islam he had discovered aspects of Judaism that had been lost to the more assimilated Jewish communities living in Christian Europe, and he took Egyptian Islam as a template for the renewal and enrichment of the scholarly discourses and public practices of European Judaism.[9]

Becker, conversely, was given a chair at the Hamburger Kolonial Institut (Hamburg Colonial Institute), a forerunner of today's Hamburg University, which provided aspirational German colonials with the cultural and intellectual tools needed to run the nascent German Empire. Becker's job was to teach *Islamkunde*, a discipline providing competence in a broad-based pallet of oriental languages, Islamic scriptural sources, law, and history, all to assist in the roll-out of German imperial power in Muslim Africa. In fact, his publication *Ist der Islam eine Gefahr für unsere Kolonien?* (Is Islam a Danger to Our Colonies?, 1909) contested that, while Islam was a traditional enemy of Christianity, it need not be an enemy of modern, secular civilizations per se and was perfectly compatible with such civilizations as it could embrace Enlightenment rationalism. Given that modern European empires were no longer wholly defined by Christianity but also by modern, secular, enlightened, and civilizing tendencies, so the potential Islamic threat of Becker's title could be neutralized if Islam were to be civilized and educated according to European models—to be made more compatible, that is, with the characteristics of modern Europe.[10] After my lectures, it was this point, in particular, that often drove audience discussions on the tensions that exist today between the social and legal frameworks of Western societies and the values, beliefs, and practices of Muslim minority communities living within them. It had been easy to present Becker as an imperialist, yet less comfortable discussions followed when Muslim audience members drew comparisons between his writing and the language and ideas attached to Muslims in much contemporary UK political and media discourse.

In evaluating the lectures, I used a blend of quantitative and qualitative methods to help me understand whom I had reached with my work and how it had added to their knowledge and thinking. Working with Professor Leslie Francis and Dr. Ursula McKenna of the Centre for Education Studies, Warwick University, I set up a series of questionnaires and distributed them at events, seeking to capture anonymized demographic data pertaining to the gender, age, faith, and level of education of all participants, and also asking participants to rate how strongly they agreed or disagreed with a series of statements on interfaith relations in contemporary Great Britain. These included such statements as, "I have positive feelings towards people of different faiths," and "I feel pessimistic about the future of interfaith relations," as well as other comments such as, "Media representations give fair coverage to harmony between faiths." Using a modified method developed by Leslie Frances in his work on cathedral visitors, the banks of statements were presented twice, both before and after the lecture, with the aim of tracking shifts in audience attitude that might have occurred as a result of the lecture and discussion. Comparing data from lectures held at three institutions—Coventry Cathedral, Guildford Cathedral, and St. Albans Abbey in Hertfordshire—we noted several changes in my audience's thinking and feeling after the lecture and public discussion. In all three locations, there was a decrease in people (8%, 12%, and 15%, respectively) reporting trust in the objectivity of coverage of faith communities in printed press and television news, and also a decrease (4%, 9%, and 8%) in optimism about the future of interfaith relations in the United Kingdom.[11] It seemed the elements of the presentation that critically assessed ideologically loaded historical images of Islam had most held the attention of the audiences and had thus been more impactful than those dealing more idealistically with cross-cultural dialogue or progressively nonbinary thinking. Moreover, the anonymized demographic data also showed most attendees to have been over thirty-eight years of age, university educated, and attached to a faith institution of one form or another. In addition to the fact that the data collected did not really test the longevity of any changes in thinking provoked by the event, my work was clearly engaging groups who were arguably conversant in the topics dealt with—and more work would need to be done to expand the range of those I was reaching, to expand the range of messages communicated, and to chart their effect on audiences over time.

The exhibition, entitled "Following Islam through German History and Its Implications for the UK Today," also sought to draw connections between historical sources and the contemporary Muslim experience. The exhibition was spread across eighteen collapsible and transportable banners, the first four of which highlighted universal themes of cultural "difference" and "similarity" and thus provided the rationale for considering Islam in German history in connection with contemporary Britain. The material included in the exhibition ranged from the Enlightenment, through Romanticism, into the Age of Empire, and included excerpts from literary works, images of architecture and painting, and analyses of the politicization of Islam in the visual and textual propaganda of Imperial Germany and the Austria-Hungarian Empire.

This format offered a great opportunity to present and commentate on visual sources. It made extensive reference, for example, to a fin-de-siècle Austrian children's story by Franz Ginzkey entitled *Hatschi-Bratschis Luftballon* (Hatschi Bratschi's Hot-Air Balloon, 1906), which tells the tale of a young Austrian boy, Fritz, who is abducted by a balloon-piloting Turkish magician and flown away to "Türkenland" (Land of the Turks). Luckily for Fritz, Hatschi-Bratschi is quite literally toppled from power as he falls down a well to his death, and Fritz is able not only to rescue the other children of the world imprisoned in the magician's oriental lair but also to break the "magic spell" he held over them (which can be read as "Islam"), making possible their reconciliation with Austrian Fritz and other Christian Europeans. The generations of illustrations that have accompanied the book's many editions present Hatschi-Bratschi variously as a malign, monstrous figure with a turban and sharp teeth, and also as a buffoon in elaborate oriental garb. Either way, he becomes the "other" that must be dispensed with, in order that the remaining Turks, who often end up as supplicant waiters serving the children food, can be presented as Europe's friends—images of which captured the attention and fueled the discussion of many younger visitors.[12]

The exhibition also marked a certain evolution in approach, as it sought to capture qualitative, narrative responses. As the banners stood in a variety of public spaces, often for as long as a week, we sought to record cumulative responses across the whole of this longer period, whether these were the shorter, free narrative comments written in the exhibition's guestbook or more extended prose responses to open-ended questions on purpose-made postcards, which asked what visitors had learned and in what ways, if any, their thinking had changed as a result of the exhibition. The exhibition had stood in the public thoroughfares, generally atriums, at three universities: Queen Mary and Westfield College, London; University College, Dublin; and Stockholm University; and has also spent a week in several UK schools—the independent St. Catherine's School, Bramley; John Hampden Grammar School, and the Roman Catholic Notre Dame High School in Sheffield (see figs. 10.1, 10.2, and 10.3).[13]

These contrasting venues generated a range of responses. The university environment produced contrasting responses, from the more critical voices that felt the material showed a "pro-Muslim bias," or the more traditional, scholarly voices that objected to the "selective" approach to sources, through to more enthusiastic responses that appreciated the "close readings" and the conceptual framework that sought to "move beyond simplistic binaries."[14] In the school environments we gathered responses both from pupils aged between twelve and eighteen and from groups that had been sent to view the exhibition as part of a lesson, as well as from the "passing trade" of pupils viewing it freely. A colleague at one school found that although the historical context and close analysis eluded younger pupils aged twelve to fifteen, she was still able to use visual representations of Christians and Muslims to mobilize discussions around the core topic of differences and similarities of faiths, which could be reinvested in classroom discussions on interfaith relations.[15] A particularly rich outcome came from a colleague at John Hampden Grammar who had noticed a close engagement with the exhibition by male Muslim students, and who testified in writing about how it had "fueled debate in the school around what had been a fraught and at times taboo subject."[16]

For all its achievements, this phase of the project had begun to reveal various limitations. First, the data captured represented a fleeting response to an event or stimulus, which did not track any impact the project had upon individuals or groups beyond a single moment or event. Second, in functioning as the curator of the exhibition and the lecturer, my own presence remained ironically in the foreground—I was a white,

Figure 10.1. The exhibition banners in production.
Photograph by James Hodkinson.

Figure 10.2. The exhibition at Gordon's School, UK.
Photograph by James Hodkinson.

Figure 10.3. The exhibition at the university of Stockholm. Photograph by James Hodkinson.

male academic at a prestigious UK university speaking to Muslims about representations of Islam. How could I in effect "decenter" my own position within the project and collaborate with and open the project to other voices from within the communities with which my work dealt—albeit through the medium of German history? Third, the audiences I was attracting, although diverse, tended to already see value in the core aims of rethinking the dialogue around static notions of cultural "otherness." How, if at all, could my project engage with and benefit more remote sections of my target communities—those who potentially saw little or no value and remained mistrustful of my project and its aims, and even of me?

Reaching into Schools: The Two Chairs Exchange

One of the most abiding and popular images I dealt with in my lectures and presented in the exhibition was that of the Hafez-Goethe Monument in Weimar, Germany. Inspired by Goethe's *Divan* and the imagined encounter he represents there with the fourteenth-century Persian poet Hafez of Shiraz, the monument consists of two huge stone chairs set to face each other atop a bronze plinth (see fig. 10.4). The chairs signify an encounter or dialogue between two poets and between two distinct cultures and faiths. A closer examination, however, shows both chairs to have been hewn from the same piece of granite, implying that, for all of their mutual distinctiveness, the chairs are connected through their common material—which might refer to the common biology underlying all human ethnicities and cultures, or to the shared Abrahamic heritage of Christianity and Islam. Through its formal and material execution the monument offered itself up as an ideal "meme" for conceiving two faiths and cultures as similar, as existing in nonbinary relationships, as different yet connected. The use of chairs, rather than more personalized statues,

Figure 10.4. The Hafis-Goethe Denkmal, Weimar (E. Thevis and F. Rabsch, 2001). Wikimedia Commons. Creative Commons Attribution ShareAlike 3.0 License. https://commons.wikimedia.org/wiki/File:Hafis-Goethe-Denkmal_in_Weimar.jpg.

also allows participation in the monument: viewers can actually sit on the chairs and swap positions. This, in turn, implies the interchangeability of cultural perspectives and hints, too, at what would later become another key thematic driver of my impact work—namely, the power of the arts to stimulate imaginative, empathetic thinking across perceived cultural boundaries. Crucially, it was this image that drew the eyes of audiences and remained memorable and would prove itself the ideal vehicle around which to construct a narrative for work with schools.

Although I presented myself as a Germanist, the most immediate appeal that my work seemed to have was not to modern linguists interested in multicultural Germany but to teachers of Religious studies. Working with two heads of Religious studies, one from St Catherine's, the other from the less privileged but culturally extremely diverse state school in Coventry, Lyng Hall, we conceived a way of using my work to enrich pupils' learning and enhance examination performance. One version of the General Certificate of Secondary Education (GCSE) school exam in Religious studies sat by sixteen-year-olds in the United Kingdom, provided by the Assessment and Qualifications Alliance (AQA) examinations board, was entitled "Christianity and Islam." Rather than teach the two faiths in isolation, this syllabus encouraged comparative reflection and writing from school pupils.[17] In this context, the image and core message of the Hafez-Goethe Monument, as I read it, became a useful model for expounding and making memorable the need to think in non-dualistic, non-mutually exclusive modes about Christian and Islamic doctrine—effectively a memorable guide to more differentiated thinking and writing about both faiths.

The sequence of lessons we produced involved a short account of the genesis of the monument in Weimar and the core message of the two chairs, and provision was made for reinforcing its relevance in different contexts throughout the lessons' delivery. The lessons, each lasting fifty minutes, treated themes from the syllabus such as "interfaith dialogue," "human rights," "conflict, peace and resolution," and "women's rights," and could be adapted to teachers' needs. Generally, though, we recommended tasking pupils with the collaborative planning of short essay responses to those themes that would illuminate, through reference to scripture and exegetic texts, the continuities and differences in what both faiths taught on those matters. The scheme of work was uploaded to my webpages at Warwick University, where it could be accessed by the public, and was advertised on social media accounts.[18] Since its launch in mid-December 2016, the project outline file alone has been viewed 8,219 times to date and downloaded 1,883 times from distinct UK-based IP addresses located off campus.[19] Perhaps more significant is the fact that the project generated a number of testimonials from teachers about the value of the materials in enhancing learning and writing; one from a colleague in Cardiff, South Wales, commented that his lessons based on the scheme had received particular commendation from the Welsh inspectorate of schools (ESTYN) during a school evaluation.[20]

The lessons were also taught in the Warwick University School of Education during March 2017. The teachers from St Catherine's and Lyng Hall each brought groups of pupils and ran lessons in parallel as part of a study day, and we also invited a group from North Leamington School—a nonselective comprehensive school from a relatively prosperous area. In practice we were able to mix the school groups and teach students from radically different regions and social backgrounds, and the implementation of the planned lessons ensured pair work between students from different schools and different faiths. As well as producing a portfolio of essay work, we also gained further testimony from students, who believed the experience of encountering and working with peers from different backgrounds had enriched their thinking and learning as much as the lesson content itself.

My work with schools actually reached beyond the classroom and primed a range of extracurricular activities for young people of school age. I developed a short pitch, which allowed me to visit and show to different groups an image of the monument's two chairs, presenting it as a response to Goethe's poetry and the relationship he imagined there with Hafez and the Islamic world. A creative response to these ideas, ran the thinking, need not require reference to or knowledge of Goethe, Germany, or Islam specifically, but could be driven by reflection on and responses to what the two chairs might imply about cross-cultural relationships generally.

Visiting Woking College in Surrey, I presented the ideas to an A-level fine art group. One pupil, of mixed Russian and English heritage, found the idea particularly relevant, as it fired her thoughts on how life with multiple cultural affiliations, effectively within and between two cultures, could be experienced as culturally enriching rather than as a struggle or an affliction.[21] This, in turn, inspired a cycle of print work in which photographs of friends and prominent celebrity faces were reproduced in symmetrical pairings or clusters and manipulated with printing techniques to show the same face in differing forms: the cycle was exhibited at the Lighthouse Gallery in Woking, Surrey, as part of a college exhibition in summer 2017 (see fig. 10.5). In the same year, at nearby St. Catherine's, the Pulse drama group responded with a piece of physical theater. Using two chairs quite literally as props, as a platform for dialogue, or as a staging ground for the integration of a refugee by a border official, the group scripted and choreographed a cycle of short vignettes using movement and dialogue to explore themes such as marital breakdown, cultural difference, and integration. The play was taken to the Edinburgh Fringe Festival, performed on three occasions to a small and in each case sold-out venue (see fig. 10.6).[22] Above and beyond the play's popularity with audiences, all of whom knew little or nothing of Goethe and Hafez, one teacher commented and wrote on the value of the underlying ideas: "The actors are trying to spin the ideas off in directions that interested and spoke to them, but the chairs as a prop, as an image, and as an underlying idea hold it all together."[23]

During the academic year 2017–18 the project also involved a creative-writing competition. Spending out on high-level advertising (both online and in the *London Review of Books*), we also invested in hiring three prominent judges, including the Cardiff-born Welsh-Iraqi poet Hanan Issa, the British-Somali poet (and current young persons' laureate for London) Momtaza Mehri, and the established poet, performer, and radio host Ian McMillan. Concerned to see if the project might also reengage with German in schools, we allowed bilingual entries. We received over 130 entries for this competition, around a third of them in German.[24] Working with anonymized entries, the judges chose an incredibly diverse set of winners from the four entry categories—a sixteen-year-old pupil from Northeast England whose short story about working through racial bullying, "Moongirl," was a unanimous choice. Other entries included

Figure 10.5. Original artwork by Jo Rotherham.

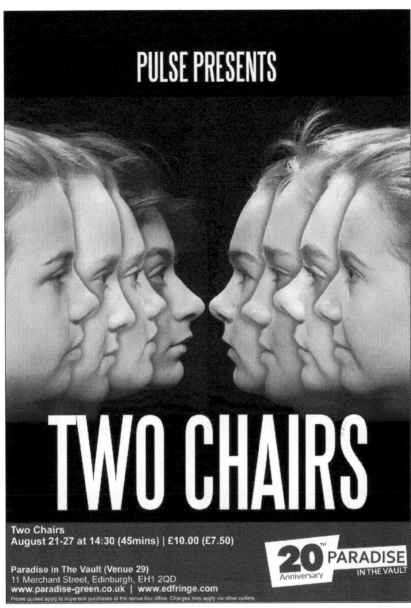

Figure 10.6. Poster advertising the Two Chairs *production, Edinburgh. Photographs by James Hodkinson.*

a poem by a retired teacher entitled "For the Boy in Damascus Who Leaned Out of a Car to Shake My Hand," which dealt with the experience of cultural and linguistic barriers during foreign travel, as well the precociously mature entry from an eight-year-old boy, imagining how the two stone chairs of the monument, although distinct, had erupted from the same earth.

The competition elicited a pool of entries that was diverse in terms of age, gender, and social and cultural backgrounds. It marked a completely open-ended opportunity for the public to respond to my research, which had moved away from the initial pitch to engage with captive audiences in school classrooms. Yet for all their motivation in entering, how diverse a group had our entrants been? The team of colleagues working with me in Warwick's Research Support Services had invested considerable time and money in making the competition visible and accessible in less-privileged local schools. As I continued to reflect critically it was obvious that, for all our relative success in engaging schools and communities through the arts, theater productions and writing competitions would naturally appeal to students already well established in mainstream education. If I were to engage with and make my research speak to young people, indeed to people of all ages, within some of Britain's more beleaguered Muslim communities, who were living through renewed political and social tensions on matters racial and religious, I would need not merely to extend my project to include those community voices but also coauthor the next phase with them. The project should not only speak to Muslim communities through their own cultural idioms but also bring genuine and measurable benefits to their experience of life in the United Kingdom in this decade.

Communities and the Coauthoring of Impact

Late in summer 2017 I was awarded the most substantial grant to date, which provided funding for me to work with minority communities and community arts groups and extend the reach of my research impact. Colleagues at my institution had brokered a meeting between myself and Abigail Shervington, a freelance consultant, project manager, and community liaison who brought with her a wealth of experience working in the arts and with diverse communities across the public sector. Our resulting working relationship would present a significant, though benevolent and highly productive, challenge to my mode of working and trigger the most constructive transformation to my project hitherto.

I was quickly introduced to the Soul City Arts collective, which had been founded by the award-winning British-Bangladeshi artist Mohammed Ali MBE and is based in Sparkbrook, Birmingham, and comanaged by a board of trustees representing different community groups in the area. Together with Abigail Shervington and executive producer Steven McLean, I introduced my work to Ali. He had begun life as an urban artist, specifically as a painter of graffiti murals, though he had increasingly diversified to work with different media, including sound, dance, spoken word, and had also developed a performative style of delivery that saw him creating art in front of large, live audiences in the United Kingdom and internationally. Amidst all of these developments, Ali has remained rooted in local communities, both his own in Birmingham and those he engages with as part of commissioned work. He is a passionate believer in channeling the stories of communities through his work and in practices of coproduction.[25] The point of collaboration settled upon the notion of imaginative empathy as a facilitator for crossing lines of cultural difference, as implied by the two chairs' monument and in the tradition of Goethe's *Divan*.

Working towards the idea of a large-scale outdoor art installation consisting of multimedia artworks and performative elements, we ran a series of pilot events with communities and schools designed to gather audio recordings and visual material to feed the project, which was to be created and curated by Ali. In addition to presenting original artworks as stimuli to our audiences, our approach involved allowing audiences to share their own personal experiences of our themes of choice and thus to help shape the language, images, and narratives that would populate the installation. The intention was also to create a working practice by which artists engaged closely with the testimonies of communities and then sought to represent those experiences in original artworks in which they exercised their own imagination but also incorporated the voices and testimonies of those communities. These works, according to our thinking, would be born of empathetic experiences and would thus champion the ideal of empathy in future audiences.

Using an existing format, we ran a "Hubb Debate" in Ali's engagement space in Sparkbrook (known as "the Hubb"). An open invitation was extended to members of diverse communities, who attended in numbers ranging from twenty to fifty, and who spent two hours in free dialogue on a matter of topical concern. The space was dimly lit and intimate, with participants sitting in a circle around a single light source, which atmosphere Ali described as "part confessional, part campfire."[26] After consulting with communities, Ali, in dialogue with Abigail Shervington, discerned a connection between local concerns regarding the rise of alt-right politics; the rise of populist, right-wing demagogues in politics and via social media; growing intercommunity violence; and our key theme of empathy. Was this, asked the title of our event, a new "age of hatred" and were we witnessing the "death of empathy"? The US award-winning spoken-word artist Buddy Wakefield, who was touring UK venues at the time, was engaged to respond creatively to the discussion. He wove his poetry in between the voices of the audience as they spoke and projected a range of visceral images of the 2017 Grenfell Tower fire in London and the Charlottesville car attack to provoke discussion. The debate ran for several hours and an audio recording was made. The divergence of views was fascinating. While empathy between individuals and cultures was seen as paramount to future coexistence in culturally plural communities, so too was the need to remain engaged in political and cultural activism and not shy away from confrontation: "conflict in one form or another might be necessary," said one participant, adding, "if you're pushed, you push back."[27] Building on the archive of voices from the Hubb Debate, the Soul City team went to high schools from the Coventry and Birmingham areas, where they presented the "two chairs" concept and facilitated discussions about empathy, or the lack thereof, in the lives and experiences of pupils. Again recordings were made and, with legal permission to use the students' voices in an anonymized form, the material flowed into the project's growing archive.

The final element of the project saw the involvement of the Iranian-born Birmingham painter Mohsen Keiany.[28] Having fought as a boy soldier in the Iran-Iraq War in the early 1980s, Keiany subsequently came to the United Kingdom and set himself up as an academic researcher and a painter. His prolific work showcases his Persian folk heritage and Islamic mysticism, though at the point he became engaged with my project he was working on a cycle of paintings titled *The Desensitized Artist*, funded in part by Arts Council England. The paintings drew on Keiany's experiences of war, his own experience of PTSD (post-traumatic stress disorder), and also thematized the rising violence he found in the wake of the apparent clash of civilizations and the rise of Islamic and far right terrorism. During ensuing discussions, I learned that Keiany originated from Shiraz, the home of the Persian poet Hafez, whom Goethe had chosen as his imaginary interlocutor in the poems of the *Divan*. We learned about each other's research interests, with me focusing on Goethe, Hafez, and the memorial in Weimar, and him speaking about how his most recent work drew on his personal experiences of religious indoctrination in 1980s Iran and his memories on the battlefield.

Our interests converged particularly on issues of intercultural dialogue and how it could redress the cultural or religious xenophobia often underlying a society and deliberately whipped up in wartime. Building on this synergy, funds from my grant were used to commission a painting by Keiany titled *Meeting Point*: atop a wasteland made up of the same disembodied mechanical parts that had made up the dehumanized bodies of those dragooned into religious conflict, two chairs are depicted, referencing the Weimar monument and implying the same open-ended invitation to a new form of relationship in the aftermath of horrendous conflict. The briefest of glances at Keiany's cycle of paintings could tell that he

Figure 10.7. Soon After, *painting by Mohsen Keiany.
Photograph by the artist.*

had already been influenced by German expressionism, though my discussions with him had impacted the thematic and emotional trajectory of the cycle, introducing the conviction that cross-cultural empathy needed to play a role in the cultivation of any successful, culturally plural future.

A final cluster of activities in which my work with Ali, Keiany, and Soul City came to fruition we called "Reimagining the Opposition: The Art of Empathy." It included a collaboration with Coventry Cathedral, where Keiany showed a number of his works inside St. Michael's House at the base of the Diocesan Reconciliation Ministry, his paintings replacing the house's usual art collection for a week. At the launch event a small but diverse audience was invited to follow a selection of his works—from those representing dehumanizing conflict and irreconcilable opposition, such as *Soon After*, through to the chairs of *Meeting Point* (see figs. 10.7 and 10.8)—before being ushered through to see a short film composed

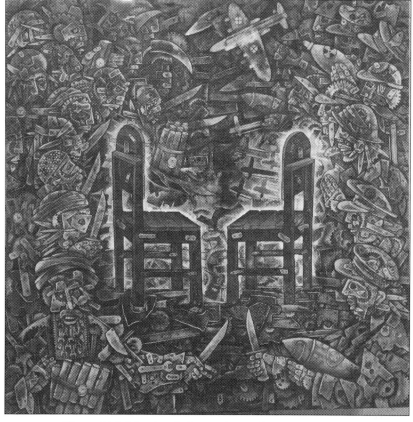

Figure 10.8. Meeting Point, *painting by Mohsen Keiany. Photograph by the artist.*

by Ali chronicling a range of testimonial material from our outreach program and interviews to date. This formed the basis of a public discussion in the "long table" format: the artists and organizers discussed their work, its themes and motivations, while seated at a table; the audience was seated in the round, though they were free to join the table, effectively "unseating" the initial discussants and adding their personal responses to the artwork and themes. Beyond this first event, a final showcase event saw an outwardly unappealing urban space (one floor of a city center, multistory parking lot) transformed into a multimedia viewing environment. Keiany's art was enlarged, printed to weather-proof vinyl, and installed upon scaffolds; the passing public was asked to look at the paintings and consider simply-worded slogans and ideas such as "opposition," "dehumanization," "representation," "voice," and "empathy," before being asked inside to view the full and final version of Ali's

Figure 10.9. From "Reimagining the Opposition: The Art of Empathy," an event at the Paradise Circus car park, Birmingham, UK, June 2019. Photograph by Mohammed Ali.

film. This film, which contained footage of the voices of those individuals, schools, and communities interviewed during the project's pilot phase, not only articulated and promoted empathetic artistic practices but also showed how the testimonies of those involved had effectively coauthored the narrative of the film. Indeed, support workers on site continued to conduct interviews and record and archive community voices responding to the film during and after the event (see fig. 10.9).

The "Reimagining the Opposition" installations and associated events sought not only to engage a wide and diverse nonacademic public but also to maintain a sense of ongoing impact over time. Both events culminated with the audience making voluntary pledges: they signed a huge sheet of paper with a short statement that they would introduce different forms of culturally empathetic behavior into their personal and professional relationships and would contact us over a period of several months to help us track this process. Among the project team this form of impact was thus referred to as a kind of ongoing ripple rather than a transient splash.

Conclusion

Over the course of four years the "Transnationalizing Faith" project has sought to reflect critically on how it has brought benefit to different nonacademic communities. Throughout, certain key messages have underpinned the work: the project has always derived particular value from revisiting the culture of this particular period of German history as it made visible how both the absence and advent of nationalist ideology and values can skew the representations of a culture originating outside that nation. The germanophone focus also provided a usefully "cool" topic that was distant enough from the fraught topic of Muslim / non-Muslim relations in the United Kingdom, though it remained relevant enough to speak to our audiences. This history was also used to question the more rigid concepts of "otherness" applied to representations of Islam in earlier postcolonial thinking and to find telling examples of Islam represented in terms of an ambivalent "similarity" to European culture. In turn, that insight was both reinvested in lively public discussions of how contemporary discourses set up problematic notions and also used, in the two chairs of the Weimar monument, to model nonoppositional and nonexclusive relationships between Islam and the West in order to stimulate critical and creative responses in education. This flexibility of the material I used testifies to the abiding value of German cultural products to make culturally specific contributions to contemporary debates when framed squarely within their century and culture of origin, though also to their ability to resonate in radically dehistoricized, deterritorialized, and linguistically shifted contexts. In this way, my project speaks directly to core concerns of this volume.

Impact work consists of articulating and evaluating how research has benefited different publics by showing how ideas and concepts have been transferred between groups and practitioners, and how they have, in turn, been passed on through new modes of engagement appropriate to their target audiences and changing beneficiaries, ultimately engaging those beneficiaries as collaborators and coauthors in the process. By the time my key research findings made their way from the printed page to the flickering projections of Mohammed Ali's light pen projected upon a whitewashed wall, their connectedness was often no longer recognizable. At the center of this chapter, though, lies the conviction that academics are not compromising the quality of their work by transforming how they use it in reaching beyond their own traditional constituencies. It would seem a necessity that, as we evaluate this new way of working, we do not merely apply markers of quality and excellence dictated by our traditional disciplines. Objections to the changing work practices implied by projects such as mine will remain. Yet if we work towards new notions of quality alluded to above, we see the genuine benefit and self-declared empowerment that diverse publics can derive from the work of the academy. This work testifies to a deeper sense of value and success that arguably transcends contemporary debates and offers a useful model of how society and the academy are inextricably bound up with each other.

Notes

[1] One of the key definitions of what "impact" is and how it is to be captured and presented in the UK context is laid out on the webpages of the Arts and Humanities Research Council (AHRC): https://ahrc.ukri.org/research/impact/. All webpages in this chapter were last accessed June 12, 2019.

[2] On this see James Hodkinson, *Women and Writing in the Works of Novalis: Transformation beyond Measure?* (Rochester, NY: Camden House, 2007), 134–67.

[3] See Kamakshi P. Murti's entry on the "Exotin" in *The Feminist Encyclopedia of German Literature*, ed. Friederike Ursula Eigler and Susanne Kord (Westport, CT: Greenwood, 1997), 133–35.

[4] See James Hodkinson, "Der Islam im Dichten und Denken der deutschen Romantik: Zwischen Kosmopolitismus und Orientalismus," in *Islam in der deutschen und türkischen Literatur*, ed. Michael Hofmann and Klaus von Stosch (Paderborn: Schöningh-Verlag, 2012), 61–80.

[5] See Todd Kontje, *German Orientalisms* (Ann Arbor: University of Michigan Press, 2004), 1–14. See also Andrea Polaschegg, *Der andere Orientalismus: Regeln deutsch-morgenländischer Imagination im 19. Jahrhundert* (Berlin: de Gruyter, 2004), 39–59.

[6] On the insidiously normative tendencies that can impact thinking about similarity, see *Ähnlichkeit: Ein kulturtheoretisches Paradigma*, ed. Anil Bhatti and Dorothee Kimmich (Konstanz: Konstanz University Press, 2015), 7–26.

[7] See Gayatri Chakravorty Spivak, "Can the Subaltern Speak?" in *Marxism and the Interpretation of Culture*, ed. Cary Nelson and Lawrence Grossberge (London: Macmillan, 1988), 271–313.

[8] See https://warwick.ac.uk/fac/arts/modernlanguages/academic/jameshodkinson/occident_orient_research_network/.

[9] See Ignaz Goldziher, *Tagebuch*, ed. Alexander Schreiber (Leiden: Brill, 1978), 58–60.

[10] Carl Heinrich Becker, *Ist der Islam eine Gefahr für unsere Kolonien?* (Berlin: Reimer, 1909), 39–41.

[11] Calculations were made by the author and colleagues from Research Support Services, Warwick University, based on samples of between thirty and fifty questionnaires gathered at lectures collected at Coventry Cathedral (May 2016), Guildford Cathedral (August 2016), and St. Albans Abbey (January 2017).

[12] Franz Ginzkey, *Hatschi Bratschis Luftballon* (Langenzersdorf: Trans-World Verlag, 2011).

[13] See the websites for St. Catherine's School: http://www.stcatherines.info/; John Hampden Grammar School: http://www.jhgs.bucks.sch.uk/; and Notre Dame High School: https://www.notredame-high.co.uk/.

[14] References are taken from the exhibition guestbook and diverse feedback postcards.

[15] Testimonial letter from Ms. Cecilia Scott, Head of Religious Studies, St Catherine's School, Bramley.

[16] Email from Mr. Daniel Lawrence, German teacher, John Hampden Grammar School, to the author, March 16, 2018.

[17] See https://www.aqa.org.uk/subjects/religious-studies/gcse/religious-studies-a-8062/subject-content/component-1-the-study-of-religions-beliefs,-teachings-and-practices.

[18] See https://warwick.ac.uk/fac/arts/modernlanguages/academic/jameshodkinson/twochairsexchange/.

[19] Data provided by Warwick University Sitebuilder 2.0 "Statistics" function. Figures accurate as of June 12, 2019. Individual lesson plans and other resource files were viewed and downloaded with similar frequency during this period, testifying to a significant take up in Religious studies departments of UK secondary schools.

[20] Email to the author from Mr. G. Williams, assistant head and teacher of Religious studies at Bishop of Llandaf Church in Wales School, Cardiff (https://www.bishopofllandaff.org/), June 24, 2018. Following an external inspection by education authorities, the "two chairs" material was judged "outstanding."

[21] Email from art student Jo Rotherham to the author, July 20, 2017, and short reflective coursework essay on the role of the "two chairs" idea in the conception and delivery of her project.

[22] Watch a filmed performance of the *Two Chairs* production at: https://livestream.com/accounts/7260962/events/7690704/videos/162116772?fbclid=IwAR0mnekyZH8WK-lr3yANk9ZkvJfD9P_42UG0RdYjCO7WYT31h5EFMrwPThY.

[23] Email from drama teacher Mrs. Sally Gallis to the author, November 24, 2016.

[24] See this news item: https://warwick.ac.uk/newsandevents/pressreleases/two_chairs_creative/.

[25] See the following journal publication reflecting on Ali's motivation and artistic practice: https://imagejournal.org/article/mosque-outside-mosque-aerosol-arabic-one-experience/.

[26] Email from Mohammed Ali to the author, August 2, 2017.

[27] See this link to the Hubb Debate event: https://www.iambirmingham.co.uk/2017/08/09/event-world-champion-poet-perform-birmingham-august/.

[28] See the artist's website: https://www.mohsenkeiany.com/.

11: Theater without Borders? Tracing the Transnational Value of German Theater beyond Germany: A UK Case Study

Benedict Schofield

IN JANUARY 2017, the British playwright David Hare found himself at the center of a debate about the state of UK theater. In an interview with Jeffrey Sweet, Hare expressed his concern over the extent to which British theatrical traditions were being eroded in the face of corrupting influences from abroad: "Now we're heading in Britain towards an over aestheticized European theater," he told Sweet, "and all that directorial stuff that we've managed to keep over on the continent is now coming over and beginning to infect our theater."[1] Hare's comments gained considerable attention in the British press, coinciding as they did with a wider debate about Britain's relationship with Europe, the result of the UK's 2016 referendum on its membership of the European Union. In particular, Hare's theatrically "Eurosceptic" tone stood in opposition to the predominantly pro-European stance of the UK's creative and cultural sector. The largest network of UK-based theater professionals, *UK Theatre*, published a briefing note in 2017 that voiced its members' concern that Brexit "may lead to a decline in the sector's ability to produce world class art," with one-third to half of theater staff in Britain being non-UK European citizens. This, combined with the potential loss of European funding and the end to freedom of movement, could, according to *UK Theatre*, potentially result in the UK "losing opportunities for cultural and artistic exchange."[2] In a direct response to Hare in the *Guardian*, theater critic Lyn Gardner similarly emphasized the politically peculiar timing of his comments, highlighting how, "with a hard Brexit on the horizon, the arts world is working hard to strengthen its ties with Europe," rather than withdrawing into an "insular" national culture that "feels threatened by other forms."[3]

Hare's interview not only appeared to demand a form of cultural secession for the United Kingdom; it was also voiced, problematically, in terms that chimed with wider anti-European rhetoric. Invoking the image of an island nation that has successfully defended its theatrical borders against foreign invasion, his comments echoed a form of conservative cultural nostalgia for the political tradition of splendid isolation. Similarly, his concept of a foreign "infection" uncomfortably mirrored the use of disease metaphors in more explicitly xenophobic political rhetoric, though this was surely not his intention. Nevertheless, Hare's comments presented a "great British [theater] tradition" that is under threat from Europe,[4] a tradition consisting of "'state of England' plays"[5] that reject the "high-falutin' unreality of academia" and are instead "the intelligent form for thinking people."[6]

In presenting state-of-the-nation dramas as "the pinnacle of political playmaking in Britain," Hare is (at best) upholding an outdated "model of theatre developed in the 1970s,"[7] one that has been already been displaced, as Dan Rebellato has argued, by a more recent cosmopolitan tradition in Britain of "writing the global."[8] At worst, Hare's comments reveal a form of cultural defensiveness and cultural essentialism that pitches a myth of a sensible and socially recognizable British theater against the supposed intellectualism of European theater, whose interest, Hare emphasizes, is above all on performance rather than text: "We've got all those people called theatre makers—God help us, what a word!—coming in and doing director's theatre where you camp up classic plays and you cut them and you prune them around."[9] Here Hare develops a short, sardonic definition of "European" theater: as lacking in fidelity and aesthetically radical. While it is easy to criticize both his broad-brush approach and derisive tone, it should be acknowledged that this characterization of European theater nevertheless builds on prevalent tropes within theater criticism. Aneta Mancewicz, for instance, has convincingly demonstrated how critics and practitioners often invoke core elements of a "radical" European theater, which include textual experimentation, provocative imagery, and self-reflexivity.[10] Indeed, such tropes can even be put to "productive" use by the theater; Alexa Huang has outlined, for example, how the perceived "exoticism" of Chinese theater has become "familiarly known" by international audiences, and is thus part of what shapes its cultural "value," for good or ill, as it circulates transnationally.[11] Even critics of Hare, like Gardner, are in fact less concerned with disputing his rather sweeping characterization of European theater, and instead focus on demonstrating the positive impact this radical European theater has had on UK practice.

Behind the broad term "Europe," though, Hare does appear to indicate one "national" tradition above any other: that of Germany, through his specific focus on "director's theater" (in German, *Regietheater*, or simply *Regie*).[12] As Marvin Carlson has noted, director's theater "became in the late twentieth century one of the most familiar critical terms in German theatrical discourse," developing into a form of theatrical shorthand for any dramaturgy that gives precedence to directorial vision over textual fidelity (exactly what Hare rallies against).[13] There is an awareness of Germany, then, in Hare's comments—a sort of German theatrical trace—formed of a palimpsest in which the word "Europe" comes to stand for a "radical theatrical aesthetic," behind which sits the concept of "director's theater," behind which (in turn) stand German practices of *Regie*.

The debate sparked by Hare's comments reveals two crucial aspects for any attempt to think about the way in which theater works across borders. First, it shows how the theater remains "deeply implicated in constructing the nation . . . explor[ing] national histories, behaviors, events and preoccupations"—a process, as Nadine Holdsworth has demonstrated, that is frequently a response "to moments of rupture, crisis or conflict" (in this case, Brexit).[14] Second, it demonstrates how this often requires processes of cultural essentialization and homogenization—seen more generously, cultural tropes—which can both underpin forms of cultural rejection (as in the case of Hare's dismissal of Europe), but which can also carry positive cultural values (as in the case of Gardner's espousal of Europe). For Hare's critics such as Gardner, he is simply unaware of the long-established porosity of British theater to Europe—a porosity that has only led to the "enrichment" of UK theater.[15]

This chapter is precisely interested in this porosity and process of transnational enrichment: a less obviously direct and more multidirectional mode of theatrical exchange than, for example, the more institutional mapping that has been undertaken by David Barnett.[16] Based on interviews I undertook with five current UK-based theater makers and reviewers, I outline three different features of UK-German theatrical exchange. First, I seek to identify what value is attached to German theater and, more broadly, "Germanness." How and where is UK theater porous to Germany; how do UK-based theater makers from German backgrounds negotiate their German identity; and what might this facilitate? Second, I explore the extent of the United Kingdom's porosity to Germany. Which elements of German practice transfer easily, and which less so? What knowledge (linguistic, contextual, political) is required to enable full engagement with German traditions? Finally, I consider which networks underpin and enable this Anglo-German theatrical exchange. Are there crucial gatekeepers or mediators that support this transnational flow? Is it possible to distinguish between a specifically German influence and something closer to the homogenized European aesthetic identified (and seemingly so feared) by Hare?

Methodology: Interviews, "Actors," Networks

The interviews analyzed in this chapter were held over the summer of 2018. Each lasted between sixty and ninety minutes and followed a semistructured format. This approach, regularly used in ethnographic research, involves the preparation of a set of questions that, however, are not posed in a "canonic interviewer / interviewee format."[17] On the contrary, the semistructured format encourages both "researcher [and participant] to divert from the questions and pursue topics that arise in the course of the talk," thus mimicking a more organic form of conversation.[18] Each interview began with a general discussion of the current and past projects of the interviewees, with the intention of encouraging them to approach the topic of Germany from the perspective of their own practice rather than as an abstract notion. The second half of each interview, however, did focus more specifically on German theater, including direct questions on the topic. Michael Agar calls such leading questions "baits," which interviewees can follow, but also contradict or even reject.[19] As Fiona Copland and Angela Creese note, such "baits" are crucial if a researcher's primary aim is to engage with the emic perspective of its subjects—in other words, to engage with "what the participants know in the way that they know it," as is the aim of this chapter.[20]

Following ethnographic practices, the interview subjects in this chapter were also chosen deliberately for their "explicit, tacit, professional or occupational knowledge,"[21] often referred to as their "elite" status.[22] My aim was thus to engage with a broad range of figures active in the UK theater industry—directors, artistic directors, actors, and reviewers—with a secondary aim of speaking to subjects from backgrounds not only in the United Kingdom and Germany but also elsewhere in the world. This resulted in interviews being held with: (1) Arne Pohlmeier, a Cameroonian-born German director who was educated in the United States, currently the co-artistic director of the company *Two Gents*, and who has produced theater in Cameroon, Germany, and the UK.[23] (2) Tonderai Munyevu, a Zimbabwean-born actor and the co-artistic director of *Two Gents*, who has acted in both the United Kingdom and Germany.[24] (3) Caroline Steinbeis, a German-born director, currently the co-artistic director of Sheffield Theatres, and former International Associate at the Royal Court, who has directed works in both the United Kingdom and Germany.[25] (4) Matt Steinberg, the Canadian-born and US-trained director, actor, and artistic director of the company *Outside Edge*.[26] (5) Andrew Dickson, a UK-born journalist, reviewer, and former theater editor for the *Guardian*.[27] Further details of the training, previous productions, and wider background of these participants can be found on their webpages.

Of course, such a deliberate selection of "elite" participants can result in data that shares certain "ideological and theoretical assumptions."[28] Despite this limitation, interviews with practitioners and critics can reveal insights that complement other methods in theater and performance studies (for instance, performance analysis), not least because they focus attention away from the cultural product (in other words, a specific production) and on to the individuals and networks that produce and enable theater. In his work on actor-network theory, Bruno Latour indeed encourages us to "follow the actor," an approach that Rebecca Braun has compellingly applied to literary networks.[29] For Latour, the term "actor" indicates an agent in a network; more specifically, it designates "not the source of an action but the moving target of a vast array of entities swarming toward it."[30] Latour further argues that "actors" are always "dislocated": that is to say, "borrowed, distributed, suggested, influenced, dominated, betrayed, [and] translated," and that they can be both human and "non-human."[31] The latter is not simply the "symbolic projection" of human activity onto something inanimate, but rather an acknowledgement that there are nonhuman elements that actively leave "trails" through a network.[32] This notion of the "actor" not as an origin but as a potential recipient is of great value for this chapter, given its focus on how UK-based theater makers are porous—in other words, receptive—to German theater. In "following the actor" to trace a transnational network between Germany and the United Kingdom, I thus aim to analyze how these "actors"—both the interviewees but also the "nonhuman" institutions and sites that they invoke—are influenced, appropriated, and transformed through their transnational circulation, assessing the extent to which German theater is received and made manifest in worlds beyond Germany.

"Misplaced Intrigue" and the Cultural "Value" of Germanness

In February 2017, a new production of Christopher Marlowe's *Edward II* (1593) opened at the Cambridge Arts Theatre, directed by Caroline Steinbeis. The *Cambridge Independent* previewed the show with an article bearing the headline "German Director Getting to Grips with King of England."[33] Steinbeis picked up on the article, posting an image on Twitter, quipping: "Quite a cliffhanger . . . Will this German get to grips with Edward II?"[34] Steinbeis's "Germanness" is deployed in several ways in the article and tweet. For the newspaper, it becomes a lure for the reader, playing on the potential oddity of a German director taking on several elements of the British establishment: first, a play about a member of the royal family; second, a work by a significant English dramatist; and third, and more indirectly, a production by a cultural institution, Cambridge University's Marlowe Society, known in the arts sector as a key springboard for the so-called Cambridge mafia that has dominated postwar British acting.[35] Steinbeis's response on Twitter satirizes both the approach of the newspaper and her own supposed role as the culturally "foreign"

German: mocking the question of whether a "German" can ever comprehend a play about British royalty, but, at the same time, acknowledging that her perceived cultural difference is something that can be commodified (both by the newspaper and herself) as a way to sell more tickets.

Looking back, Steinbeis notes how she was caught off-guard by this national labeling: "It was really odd, I was so surprised. . . . It's so funny, I think, what people choose to see."[36] For Steinbeis, the emphasis on her Germanness, which was also reflected in reviews that stressed the production's "almost Brechtian feel, . . . post-modern additions and . . . self-reflexivity,"[37] was particularly odd, since her design had been deliberately rooted in British traditions of vaudeville. However, "quite a few people really didn't spot that, despite the fact we had a Punch and Judy show, we had the giant crocodile, and a lot of the conventions" (Steinbeis). Instead, she discovered many perceived her *Edward II* as a deliberate provocation—as a deconstructive "punk" take on Marlowe, in opposition to the tradition of "the Marlowe Society [which] is usually corsets" (Steinbeis). Reflecting how "you could immediately feel the audience cooling," Steinbeis recalls a further peculiar effect: audiences believed she had made radical changes to Marlowe's words. Yet, aside from the opening lines, "everything else that happened was in the text. But people felt that we had made vast, vast changes. It was extraordinary to hear that." Such reactions demonstrate the extent to which audiences can read their own preconceptions into a production—here, a desire to seek radicalism—which in this case was potentially partially determined by the emphasis placed on Steinbeis's Germanness in the show's press and publicity. Indeed, in seeing "Brechtian" style and linguistic infidelity, audiences and reviewers responded to *Edward II* in ways that directly echo Hare's description of European director's theater as an art form that "camp[s] up classic plays" where "you cut them and you prune them."[38] Reflecting on this reception of her "German" radicalism, Steinbeis is ultimately stoic: "If [my Germanness] is what you believe my intrigue is, where the intrigue is in the production, then sure—but it felt oddly misplaced to me."

That Steinbeis's production was read in terms of her Germanness does indeed appear to be an example of misplaced intrigue. Nevertheless, it also demonstrates the extent to which an awareness of German theater and its dramaturgical vocabularies is present among UK critics and audiences. Indeed, for Andrew Dickson, the former theater editor at the *Guardian*, there is not only an "awareness" but a deliberate attempt to engage with and be receptive to German theater, which is profoundly shaping UK theater practice: "There is a very strong influence and I think it's really been strong in the last decade or so. . . . Suddenly Germany is everywhere, in terms of the influence on design, on staging, on directing practices . . . It's very conscious."[39] Matt Steinberg similarly stressed the recent nature of this phenomenon: "Since I moved to London in

2011 everyone has gone, like, German theater crazy. . . . The number of times one of my friends would say to me: 'Come see this thing I've directed; you know I've done this really "German" thing with it!'"[40] Recent productions mentioned as characteristic of this trend include two *Hamlets*—Ian Rickson's 2011 production at the Young Vic, designed by Jeremy Herbert, and Lyndsey Turner's 2015 production at the Barbican, designed by Es Devlin—as well as Joe Murphy's 2017 version of *Woyzeck* at the Old Vic, designed by Tom Scutt. This latter production made a visually striking use of sliding panels on an otherwise bare stage—a clear reference to both the updated historical context of the play (which had been reset in a 1981 Berlin) and to Woyzeck's social and psychological imprisonment. Yet for some reviewers, such as Lloyd Evans, the design was precisely an example of the tendency towards an overblown aesthetic in contemporary UK theater: "Tom Scutt's grandiose set could win the Turner Prize," Evans noted facetiously.[41]

For Dickson, the recent impact of Germany has been so significant that its "historical precedent" is indeed the Berliner Ensemble coming to the United Kingdom in 1956, a moment credited by theater historians such as John Willet as "chang[ing] the face of the English theatre."[42] According to Dickson, "it feels like we've had a second version of that moment . . . and that's really creating a dynamism, a revivification of what's happened in British theatre." The interviewees further agreed that the primary area for this receptiveness and dynamism was a desire to engage with the practices of director's theater; Steinbeis herself noted that "the British theater scene is fundamentally influenced aesthetically by *Regietheater.*" UK-based directors named as particularly symptomatic of this trend towards *Regie*, in addition to those noted above, included Joe Hill-Gibbins, Rufus Norris, and above all Katie Mitchell (a director who divides her time between the United Kingdom and Germany) and Ivo van Hove (a Belgian national who works around the world).

Given the widespread cultural influence of German theater identified by the interviewees, perhaps it is not so surprising that audiences and critics attempted to view Steinbeis's *Edward II* through the prism of her Germanness, however reductive this stance. Following Huang, their awareness of supposedly "German" theatrical tropes could precisely have become the "familiarly known" features then used to orientate themselves and to "understand" the production.[43] Here, following Latour, Steinbeis's position in a transnational network between the United Kingdom and Germany is precisely that of an "actor" who is "not the source of an action but the moving target of a vast array of entities swarming towards it," in this case, certain preconceptions of German theater, its forms and values, which result in the conflation of these preconceptions both with a director's nationality and with his or her work.[44] Indeed, Arne Pohlmeier, the other director of German nationality interviewed for this chapter, stressed how this conflation is something he has to work actively against: "There's so many levels on which I resist being German. Because it's the simplest 'go to,'" both for audiences and for himself.[45] Pohlmeier indeed acknowledges the potential value attached to his Germanness, which he could capitalize on to promote his career ("you know, I'm just thinking about the popularity that German theater is enjoying at the moment," he added), and yet ultimately "it would be misleading to say that I'm a German director."

For Pohlmeier there is a double "misplaced intrigue" in conflating his nationality with his work, since his aesthetic is not German, nor is his identity: "I was in Ethiopia before I can remember. I was in Cameroon for the first four and a half years of my life." These experiences led directly to the foundation of his production company *Two Gents* with Tonderai Munyevu; a company that, he argues, works beyond any specific national tradition and instead engages an intercultural mode that is "committed to this idea of diversity and working across cultures and creating a space where the previously oppressed or undermined are given a level playing field." Pohlmeier thus rejects the idea that he is a "German" director who does intercultural theater, and instead stresses his position as an intercultural director who happens to have a "German" heritage. Steinbeis also notes how calling herself a "German" director would be "lying to myself a little bit." She might have been born in Munich, but as far as her Germanness goes, she jokes: "Und basta damit Schluss!" (And that's really that!). Acknowledging that "there has to be a little glimmer [of Germanness], of course," like Pohlmeier, she stresses that "I don't think I draw consciously on it in my work; I think for me the work is about each project, individually, and thinking about the needs of the project." While acknowledging the wider value associated with German theater, both directors of German nationality thus resist the essentialization that comes with conflating their theater work with their nationality, and the peculiar misreadings of their work this can result in.

Nevertheless, Steinbeis and Pohlmeier also volunteered situations in which they have gained value from recourse to their Germanness. Steinbeis described a scenario from her rehearsal process, in which she plays with her German roots: "What does happen in the rehearsal room is the joke of the 'German choice,' and that's only if I want to encourage an actor to make a stronger choice." In this technique, Steinbeis plays with certain clichés attached to German theater. The "German choice" is, for her, the absurdly "radical" option, which, as a rehearsal technique, liberates the actor to experiment and find the "truth" within a scene (Steinbeis). For Steinbeis, this is helpful because actors frequently "have too good a taste to actually do what is natural, and so the 'German choice' joke is beautiful because it allows them to be freer than that, and it's the freedom of choice that makes ultimately for an electric moment on stage." She even relates this to an aural difference she can deploy: "perhaps it is my German accent that allows people to go with that, because it allows them to go outside themselves. And I think that's quite fun, but it's a very different way of using the idea of [Germanness]." Indeed, what is so fascinating about Steinbeis's highly self-aware deployment of her Germanness is that it is not as a synecdoche for radicalism at all but subverts and transforms the cliché of "radical" Germanness into a rehearsal tool. Her use here of national identity within her theater work is thus far removed from the more explicit model of the onstage "reflection and debate" of national questions as explored by Holdsworth.[46] Instead, the "German joke" is part of the "backstage labor" (as Christin Essin has termed it) that is vital for a production to come into being but is ultimately invisible on stage.[47] Essentially, Steinbeis's Germanness can be "performed" in rehearsal but is elided in the performance.

Pohlmeier also recalls a time when he deployed his Germanness, specifically during *Nangaboko!–Brigands!* (2014), an adaptation of Schiller's *Die Räuber* (The Robbers, 1781) in collaboration with Theaterzentrum OTHNI (Theater Center OTHNI) in Yaoundé. In this case, it was the combination of his German nationality and his childhood connections to Cameroon that enabled his access to cultural institutions, above all the Goethe Institut (Goethe Institute) and the German Embassy, which "made it possible for me to actually do a project in Cameroon, which I guess otherwise would have been quite difficult" (Pohlmeier). This more infrastructural iteration of "backstage" labor consists here of the director/producer's work of securing funding. Given Germany's colonial legacy, Pohlmeier was aware of the dangers of leveraging his Germanness in this manner, and was particularly anxious that he not be seen as "coming to Cameroon to show them how to do theater." Thus he states he focused on "developing partnerships with local theater directors" offstage, rather than the approach to intercultural theater identified by Dennis Kennedy, in which the interculturalism "takes place *onstage* through mixing of scenic or dramaturgical elements."[48] Without Pohlmeier's Germanness, the work might not have taken place, but the performance in turn required the elision of this Germanness to prevent the reinscription of colonial practice through the production.

For Steinbeis and Pohlmeier, there is a clear desire to deflect the "misplaced intrigue" that results in them being seen not as the origin of sovereign work but as "actors" (following Latour) on to which conceptions of "Germanness" are projected. The interviews reveal how "being German" does have offstage value—in rehearsal, or in securing connections—but is not the driving force for onstage practice. Yet it is precisely in this need to reject the label of "Germanness" that we can identify the extent to which the United Kingdom has become porous to German theater practice—a porosity that is widespread enough to involve not just the practitioners and critics interviewed here, for whom it seems strongly rooted, but also wider audiences. In this sense, Hare's attempt to defend British theater against European influences such as *Regietheater* seems particularly futile, for these influences appear very well engrained.

Aesthetics, Politics, and Partial Transfers, or a "Sort of" German *Regietheater*

While the interviewees for this chapter were unanimous in noting the porosity of UK theater to German influences—above all the influence of *Regietheater*—an equally striking feature of their comments was their sense of the limits that applied to this influence. In particular, several noted a derivative quality in attempts by UK theater makers to engage with *Regietheater*, which, far from producing innovative productions, results in the replication of banal dramaturgical formulae. Steinberg, for instance, jokingly outlined the tropes of a typical "German"-influenced production: one where the audience sits "in front of stark neon lights with someone dousing themselves with a blood pack and riding around naked." Pohlmeier and Munyevu noted similar "German" features, explaining how their own productions fall into the category of "political theater," but actively attempt to avoid the stereotypes associated with "German political [theater]."[49] "It's not going to be peeing on stage," quipped Pohlmeier; "there's not going to be nudity," laughed Munyevu. These responses are quite distinct from what Barnett has outlined as an older cliché of German theater, where "the charge of being overly heavy and leaden [was] a prejudice that German theater . . . often encountered."[50] Instead, the "surge of stage viscera—blood, mud and ketchup" is now the more dominant cliché of German theater practice that, as Matt Trueman has recently argued, has become a core German "echo in British designers' work."[51]

What is particularly striking about these clichés of *Regietheater* is that they are primarily visual or scenographic. Two different processes of cultural transfer appear to be at play here. On the one hand, Dickson identifies a trend in British productions to mimic German design practices but without the involvement of German practitioners: "There is, in my mind, your slightly off-the-peg, German-influenced classic, and the recipe would be very straightforward. . . . It's like it looks German, there's always some slightly whacky concept to it, and the staging is somehow taken apart or ripped up," Dickson referring here in part to productions by Hill-Gibbins. The name of Jan Pappelbaum was also repeatedly mentioned as a major influence for British designers: a figure best known in the United Kingdom for his collaborations with the German director Thomas

Ostermeier and the latter's restagings of Shakespeare and Ibsen that have regularly toured to London. This is a model of cultural "receptiveness," which results in an "interweaving performance culture" (to borrow Erika Fischer-Lichte's influential term) in which UK theater practitioners are "inspired . . . and appropriate elements and techniques [in this case from Germany] in their own productions."[52] On the other hand, Pohlmeier also acknowledges an increasing trend for German designers to work on UK-based productions, lending those shows "that caché of being a sort of German *Regietheater*." Trueman has also identified this development, particularly noting the recent work in the United Kingdom of the Swiss-born but Berlin-based designer Magda Willi.[53] Here the porosity of the UK scene revolves around a slightly different model, one rooted in the transnational movement of theater makers into the United Kingdom, which Mark Ravenhill has argued is central to intercultural theater practice because of its ability to promote "the exchange of ideas [between] theatre workers and . . . exposure to varying theatre practices."[54]

Several of the interviewees warned, however, that the United Kingdom's focus on the design of *Regietheater* comes at the expense of an understanding of its deeper dramaturgical methods. For Steinberg, for instance, the United Kingdom's understanding of *Regietheater* is almost uroboric: "We see this a lot in the industry: some people are making conscious design choices which make it appear as though they're doing 'German' theater. But when you ask them what makes German theater German theater, often they'll say things like, 'Well, the design. . . .'" What arises from the interviews is thus a sense that despite the pervasive influence of the aesthetics of *Regietheater*, British theater is resistant to other crucial features of *Regie*—above all the political impetus of its dramaturgy. In his work on *Regietheater*, Peter Boenisch notes the centrality of the "political act" for *Regie*. This political latency "marks the potential of *Regie* to stage dissensus [and is] the difference between 'mere directing' and *Regie*," and Boenisch further stresses that it is in "distorting the playtext" that *Regie*'s ability to stage dissensus is to be found.[55] Dickson also stressed how these textual-political questions at the heart of *Regie*— the question of "why are we doing this to a classic text?" (Dickson)—are rarely asked in the United Kingdom. "In Germany, that would be a really interesting, fraught, and difficult question," he continues, "but here, I think it's often like: 'Oh God, we've got to find a fresh way of doing Chekhov or Shakespeare.'" In many ways, it is this form of "derivative" *Regietheater* that Hare critiques and conflates with European theater in his comments noted at the start of this chapter.

This partial transfer of the aesthetics of *Regie*, but not the politics of that aesthetic, mirrors Latour's sense that when "following the actor" in tracing a transnational network we can uncover patterns of "dislocation," with elements "borrowed . . ., betrayed, [and] translated."[56]

Three factors in particular appear to drive this process of dislocation when it comes to *Regie*. The first is linguistic and concerns the knowledge that is required to "access" things in German. For Dickson, for example, it makes sense that the response to *Regie* by UK theater makers is primarily aesthetic, since without the German language, it is the visual that is more easily assimilated: "My hunch . . . is that most [UK directors] don't speak German and many of them have been watching these productions in German," and thus "at some level, what is being transmitted is probably the aesthetic in the design" rather than "all of those big questions in German theater on canonicity and what an active theater is." Steinberg concurs: "Many of us don't actually speak German well enough to fully pick up the subtleties."

The second factor is the question of audience. For Munyevu, German theater may be "very conceptual and sort of daring . . . but ultimately it . . . isn't very concerned about getting audiences, you know? Whereas . . . in the UK it has always been entirely commercial." Indeed, all the figures interviewed for this chapter raised this point: that the funding structures of German theater, with its extensive state subsidy, enables theatrical experimentation in a way impossible in the United Kingdom. Dickson recalls interviewing Nicholas Hytner when Hytner was artistic director of the National Theatre, and Hytner's "impatience, a degree of annoyance sometimes, with . . . 'mainstream' European theater, with its sometimes contempt for the audience, because financially you don't need to worry about it." As Dickson notes, "even with a heavily subsidized theater like the National Theatre, you really can't afford to disdain the audience." Of course, the idea that the radicalism of German theatrical "aesthetics flow[s] from this financial reality" (Dickson) is only partially true—Pohlmeier in particular noted that it also leads to much "deadly" theater (here echoing Peter Brook's influential terminology),[57] especially in regional theater—but the financial question remains an important site of differentiation between the two countries, and one that undoubtedly shapes the perception of German theatrical radicalism in the United Kingdom, as also outlined by Barnett.[58]

Even taking such issues into consideration, Steinbeis was still dubious whether Britain was quite ready for a director-driven model of theater. "I think that it still perhaps feels, amongst more mainstream theaters in the UK, [that] people still tend not to approve of, or want to use the platform of making a piece, in order to make a statement about the world that they are living in." A third factor for the primarily aesthetic appropriation of *Regietheater* in the United Kingdom is thus a deference towards textual and authorial intentionality: "I think that still there is a certain level of resentment towards the director, imposing (imposing is a strong word, but I think that's certainly how it is perceived) their vision on any material," notes Steinbeis. This is echoed by Barnett, who notes how "British theater is thus steeped in . . . the hallowed words of the playwright."[59] Taking her 2018 production of Caryl Churchill's *Love and Information* as an example, Steinbeis notes how the play is "an invitation to make something inherently political." However, a review in the *Guardian* "sort of implied that we had imposed meaning on to the play" (Steinbeis). Yet precisely this political interpretation is, for Steinbeis, "fully my prerogative as a director." Because of the United Kingdom's continued preference for text over performance (a feature Hare sees as positive in his comments), directors attempting anything else, especially anything political, are thus forced, in Steinbeis's view, to be "apologetic." For Dickson, this is a core difference in the two theatrical cultures: "We like political theater [in the UK] but we don't actually want to be activist [unlike in Germany]. That's interesting in terms of the kind of clash of cultures."

While British theater is porous to Germany, then—through the flow of practitioners across borders, the international touring of productions, and the cultural receptiveness of British practitioners to Germany—the extent of the cultural receptiveness and transfer is shaped, and dislocated, by a range of factors. These include linguistic understanding (or the lack thereof), infrastructural constraints (not least around audience and finance), and a different cultural-historical approach to the text-performance nexus, which, taken together, result in (to borrow Pohlmeier's phrase) only "a sort-of German" *Regietheater* in the United Kingdom.

"Institutionalized Apprenticeships" and Accessing German Networks

Despite the elements of partial transfer outlined in the preceding discussion, it is clear that the practitioners and critics interviewed for this chapter nevertheless see British understanding of German theater as a crucial feature of the current UK theatrical landscape. Indeed, exposure to German theater is repeatedly invoked by the interviewees as a form of necessary "apprenticeship." In the words of Dickson: "If you want to make your way as a young director in this country, you need to get out to Berlin and see what's going on there." Steinberg outlined his own experience of this, recounting how he was encouraged to visit Berlin by a colleague while based at Shakespeare's Globe Theatre in the summer of 2007: "And the first play that I saw there was at the Volksbühne . . . It blew my mind . . . I then saw stuff at the Schaubühne and . . . I walked away, and I just—I had never realized that theater could do that at that scale. . . . It was the most startling experience." Dickson further identifies a recent institutionalization of this "apprenticeship model" with a "really conscious effort" by figures such as David Lan, the artistic director of the Young Vic, to send young directors to "hang around the Volksbühne and the Schaubühne and everywhere else, and go out to the Theatertreffen (theater meeting festival) and really be exposed to this work in a way that British directors weren't [traditionally]."

Such comments raise, however, a crucial question: Which "Germany" is being accessed here? Already, the experiences of Steinberg and comments by Dickson reveal the significance of Berlin, and the theaters it contains, in shaping the United Kingdom's understanding of "German" theater. Seen from the perspective of Latour's network theory, these cities and theaters are the "nonhuman" actors within the network. In this case, the "actor" of Berlin plays a crucial role, indeed, to the extent that Berlin becomes a synecdoche for Germany. Various factors stand behind this. One is Berlin's status as a capital that "seems kind of cool following reunification" (Dickson). But two further elements, both identified in the previous section, further shape this conflation of Berlin with Germany—one linguistic, and one infrastructural/financial. Dickson notes, for instance, that "at some level, . . . Berlin has become so preeminent in theater and other cultural areas because it's the most internationalized city and a lot of people speak English there, so it's much, much easier." The ease of travel, and the lack of expense, are also cited as reasons for Berlin's dominance: "it's the same . . . as everything else, it's EasyJet, Ryanair flights . . . it's cheap, it's not expensive to hang around" (Dickson). Such infrastructural issues of cost and travel might initially appear far removed from the question of the porosity of the UK stage to Germany, but as scholars of transnational theater repeatedly point out, "internationalization in the theatre [is] the result of increasing human mobility and the opportunities for easy international communication that arose at the end of the twentieth- and the beginning of the twenty-first century."[60] Precisely these forms of movement enable transnational theater-making: infrastructures that are entirely "offstage," but without which the "onstage" interweaving of performance cultures (to use Fischer-Lichte's term again) would be impossible.

Germany is thus often conflated with Berlin. But within this, it is even possible to identify a narrower frame of reference, also visible in the interviewee's statements above. For Steinbeis, it is above all "productions from the Volksbühne and Schaubühne" that have shaped UK understanding of German theater practice, with Dickson similarly stressing that "often what we mean [are just] two theatrer in Berlin." Significantly, even within this nexus of two institutions, the interviewees were able to narrow their focus even further—above all, and repeatedly, to the figure of Thomas Ostermeier at the Schaubühne. Munyevu stressed the impact of "Ostermeier's brand," with Steinbeis describing him as the "most significant" figure. Dickson too stressed how he couldn't "think of another director who has been as influential really in terms of how the aesthetic [of Germany] has traveled . . . He's phenomenally important." What lies behind this impact of Ostermeier? In part, it is due to the Schaubühne pursuing an extraordinary internationalization agenda under Ostermeier's artistic directorship: "Mit uns kaufen sich die internationalen Festivals Berliner Identität . . . Wenn der Erfolg im Ausland nicht gewesen wäre, hätte ich mit der Schaubühne aufgehört" (With us, international festivals buy Berlin identity . . . If the foreign success had not happened, I would have called it quits with the Schaubühne), Ostermeier has noted.[61] Indeed, as Peter Boenisch has detailed, "no other German theatre company, and no other contemporary German theatre artist, is as present around the world today" as Ostermeier, with approximately 68,000 people seeing Schaubühne works outside of Berlin in the 2014/15 season.[62]

Yet, as Pohlmeier stresses, there is an irony to this dominance, since Ostermeier is "not perceived as being the preeminent example of *Regietheater* [within Germany]," or, as Steinberg states directly: "Ostermeier is the least German director in Germany." Indeed, Ostermeier himself has argued that he does not belong to "den avant-garden des internationalen Regietheaters" (the avant-gardists of international *Regietheater*), and has stressed how his reputation has bifurcated: "Ich weiß, dass ich [in Deutschland] . . . nicht mehr das *enfant terrible* bin . . . wie ich es einmal war, oder wie ich es im Ausland noch immer bin" (I know that [in Germany] I'm no longer the *enfant terrible*, as I once was, or as I still am abroad).[63] Ostermeier's reputation as "das Gesicht des modernen deutschen Theaters in der Welt" (the face of modern German theater in the world) and of *Regie* is thus largely one that exists outside of Germany, rooted in, and the result of, his transnational circulation.[64] Here, Ostermeier's role in the transnational network of German theater appears to be not just that of an "actor" but that of a "mediator," which, according to Latour, is precisely a figure that "transform[s], translate[s], distort[s], and modif[ies] the meaning or the elements they are supposed to carry," in this case leading to very different understandings of German avant-garde theater within and beyond Germany.[65]

While access to German theater is thus presented by the interviewees as a crucial form of apprenticeship for UK theater makers, it is one that reveals multiple levels of dislocation and distortion when we "follow the actors." Berlin stands in for Germany; the Volksbühne and Schaubühne stand in for Berlin; and, on one level, Ostermeier stands in for all of these as a central point of mediation. As Steinbeis notes: "The [German] frame of reference [for UK practitioners] is actually tiny. . . . [A] lot of people think they know the frame of reference, but I don't think that's actually true," for ultimately, the British understanding of Germany resides in just "a handful of productions."

Conclusion: Transnationalism, Translation, Dislocation

This chapter has considered the place and function of a German contribution to UK theater from the perspective of UK-based practitioners and critics. In "following these actors," it has sought to ascertain what UK-based theater understands and codes as "German," and the values attached to this, as well as what UK theater takes from the world of German theater and how this is accessed. In doing so, it has outlined a form of theatrical network between the two countries in which the United Kingdom is revealed to be remarkably porous to German theater, actively drawing on German practices, above all those of *Regietheater*. In contrast to Hare's isolationism, with which this chapter opened, the interviewees instead emphasized the extent to which there has been, in the words of Dickson, a "window of openness [to Germany] around British theater," which has transformed a UK theater that has "traditionally, I think, been pretty insular and inward looking, and disdainful, suspicious, of mainland European theater." Echoing a concern voiced by many of my interviewees, Dickson continued: "If Brexit happens, will that close down again? Does the drawbridge swing up and shut? . . . That's a tragedy if that happens."

Although the United Kingdom has been shown to be profoundly open to Germany, this chapter has also argued that this porosity does not result in direct acts of cultural transfer, but rather in processes of cultural transformation, strongly echoing Latour's stance that points of connection or mediation within a network are often places of dislocation, distortion, and translation. It has shown how the transnational network between the United Kingdom and Germany is enabled not just by an abstract flow of aesthetic practices, nor simply by exposure to Germany through touring productions, but through the physical movement of UK practitioners to Germany to gain exposure to different practices, akin to a form of international apprenticeship. This circulation of practitioners is, however, heavily skewed to produce a vision of "Germany" that is ultimately filtered through a specific city (Berlin), specific theaters (the Volksbühne and Schaubühne), and even a specific practitioner (Ostermeier).

Mapping these "actors" within the Anglo-German network has, in turn, helped identify three crucial moments of transformation: first, the primarily aesthetic appropriation of *Regietheater* by UK directors and the limited space for a more political dramaturgy in the United Kingdom; second, the ultimately relatively narrow exposure to German theater mapped by the interviewees, revolving around certain crucial mediators such as Berlin and Ostermeier; and third, the extent to which cultural awareness (and cultural stereotypes) of German practices are in circulation in the United Kingdom and can be projected onto directors and their productions, sometimes correctly, but equally often in acts of "misplaced intrigue." Taken together, the Anglo-German network traced by this chapter thus demonstrates how Hare's desire to prevent the "infection" of a British national theater by those of Germany and Europe can only be considered a chimera, since that British theater itself embodies multiple practices from multiple places, in what I have identified as a continual process of encounter, translation, and productive dislocation.

Notes

Uncredited translations are my own.

[1] David Hare, cited in Jeffrey Sweet, *What Playwrights Talk about When They Talk about Writing* (New Haven: Yale University Press, 2017), 69.

[2] "Confidential Briefing Note for UK Theatre Members," UK Theatre, accessed February 1, 2018, https://uktheatre.org/EasySiteWeb/GatewayLink.aspx?alId=51654.

[3] Lyn Gardner, "Why David Hare Is Wrong about the State of British Theatre," *The Guardian*, January 30, 2017, https://www.theguardian.com/stage/theatreblog/2017/jan/30/david-hare-state-of-british-theatre-europe.

[4] Hare, in Sweet, *Playwrights*, 59.

[5] Sweet, in Sweet, *Playwrights*, 68.

[6] Hare, in Sweet, *Playwrights*, 59.

[7] Dan Rebellato, "From the State of the Nation to Globalization: Shifting Political Agendas in Contemporary British Playwriting," in *A Concise Companion to Contemporary British and Irish Drama*, ed. Nadine Holdsworth (Oxford: Blackwell, 2007), 259, 245.

[8] Rebellato, "From the State of the Nation to Globalization," 255.

[9] Hare, in Sweet, *Playwrights*, 69.

[10] Aneta Mancewicz, *Intermedial Shakespeares on European Stages* (Basingstoke: Palgrave Macmillan, 2014), 8.

[11] Alexa Huang, *Chinese Shakespeares: Two Centuries of Cultural Exchange* (New York: Columbia University Press, 2009), 39.

[12] Hare, in Sweet, *Playwrights*, 69.

[13] Marvin Carlson, *Theatre Is More Beautiful Than War: German Stage Directing in the Late 20th Century* (Iowa: University of Iowa Press, 2009), 41.

[14] Nadine Holdsworth, *Theatre & Nation* (Basingstoke: Palgrave Macmillan, 2010), 6–7.

[15] Gardner, "Why David Hare Is Wrong."

[16] David Barnett, "'I've Been Told . . . That the Play Is Far Too German': The Interplay of Institution and Dramaturgy in Shaping British Reactions to German Theatre," in *Cultural Impact in the German Context*, ed. Rebecca Braun and Lyn Marven (Rochester, NY: Camden House, 2010), 150–66.

[17] Fiona Copland and Angela Creese, *Linguistic Ethnography: Collecting, Analysing and Presenting Data* (London: Sage, 2015), 30.

[18] Copland and Creese, *Linguistic Ethnography*, 32.

[19] Michael Agar, cited in Copland and Creese, *Linguistic Ethnography*, 33.

[20] Copland and Creese, *Linguistic Ethnography*, 33.

[21] Beate Littig, "Interviewing the Elite—Interviewing Experts: Is There a Difference?" in *Interviewing Experts*, ed. Alexander Bogner, Beate Littig, and Wolfgang Menz (Basingstoke: Palgrave Macmillan, 2009), 99.

[22] L. A. Dexter, *Elite and Specialized Interviewing* (Evanston, IL: Northwestern University Press, 1969).

[23] Information on Arne Pohlmeier can be found at: www.twogentsproductions.co.uk, accessed February 1, 2019.

[24] Information on Tonderai Munyevu can be found at: www.twogentsproductions.co.uk, accessed February 1, 2019.

[25] Information on Caroline Steinbeis can be found at: www.carolinesteinbeis.com, accessed February 1, 2019.

[26] Information on Matt Steinberg can be found at: www.mattsteinberg.net, accessed February 1, 2019.

[27] Information on Andrew Dickson can be found at: www.andrewjdickson.com, accessed February 1, 2019.

[28] Copland and Creese, *Linguistic Ethnography*, 198.

[29] Bruno Latour, *Reassembling the Social: An Introduction to Actor-Network Theory* (Oxford: Oxford University Press, 2005), 11. For Braun's use of Latour, see Rebecca Braun, "The World Author Is in Us All: Conceptualising Fame and Agency in the Global Literary Market," *Celebrity Studies* 7, no. 4 (2016): 457–75.

[30] Latour, *Reassembling*, 45.

[31] Latour, *Reassembling*, 46.

[32] Latour, *Reassembling*, 10, 203.

[33] Adrian Peel, "German Director Getting to Grips with King of England," *Cambridge Independent*, February 7, 2017, n.p.

[34] Caroline Steinbeis, "Quite a Cliffhanger . . .," Twitter, February 3, 2017, https://twitter.com/csteinbeis/status/827605449155416066.

[35] Tim Cribb, *Bloomsbury and British Theatre: The Marlowe Story* (London: Salt, 2007), back-cover blurb.

[36] Interview with Caroline Steinbeis, held on July 16, 2018, ethical clearance reference MRA-17/18-6437. Future references are given contextually in the text.

[37] Sian Bradshaw, "Review: *Edward II*," *Varsity*, February 10, 2019, https://www.varsity.co.uk/theatre/12101.

[38] Hare, in Sweet, *Playwrights*, 69.

[39] Interview with Andrew Dickson, held on July 20, 2018, ethical clearance reference MRA-17/18-6437. Future references are given contextually in text.

[40] Interview with Matthew Steinberg, held on July 10, 2018, ethical clearance reference MRA-17/18-6437. Future references are given contextually in text.

[41] Lloyd Evans, "The Play's Design Is All Wrong: *Woyzeck* Reviewed," *Spectator*, June 3, 2017, https://www.spectator.co.uk/2017/06/the-plays-design-is-all-wrong-woyzeck-reviewed.

[42] John Willet, "Ups and Downs of British Brecht," in *Re-Interpreting Brecht: His Influence on Contemporary Drama and Film*, ed. Pia Kleber and Colin Visser (Cambridge: Cambridge University Press, 1990), 76.

[43] Huang, *Chinese Shakespeares*, 39.

[44] Latour, *Reassembling*, 45.

[45] Interview with Arne Pohlmeier, held on June 23, 2018, ethical clearance reference MRA-17/18-6437. Future references are given contextually in text.

[46] Holdsworth, *Theatre & Nation*, 6–7.

[47] Christin Essin, "An Aesthetic of Backstage Labour," *Theatre Topics* 21, no. 1 (2011): 33–48.

[48] Dennis Kennedy, *The Spectator and the Spectacle: Audiences in Modernity and Postmodernity* (Cambridge: Cambridge University Press, 2009), 116.

[49] Interview with Tonderai Munyevu, held on June 23, 2018, ethical clearance reference MRA-17/18-6437. Future references are given contextually in text.

[50] Barnett, "'I've Been Told,'" 151.

[51] Matt Trueman, "Meet the German Artists Revolutionizing UK Theatre Stage Design," *Stage*, February 4, 2019, https://www.thestage.co.uk/features/2019/meet-the-german-artists-revolutionising-uk-stage-design.

[52] Erika Fischer-Lichte, "Introduction: Interweaving Performance Cultures—Rethinking 'Intercultural Theatre': Towards an Experience and Theory of Performance Beyond Postcolonialism," in *The Politics of Interweaving Performance Cultures: Beyond Postcolonialism*, ed. Erika Fischer-Lichte, Torsten Jost, and Saskya Iris Jain (New York: Routledge, 2014), 2.

[53] Trueman, "Meet the German Artists."

[54] Mark Ravenhill, "Foreword," in Dan Rebellato, *Theatre & Globalisation* (Basingstoke: Palgrave Macmillan, 2009), xiii.

[55] Peter Boenisch, *Directing Scenes and Senses: The Thinking of Regie* (Manchester: Manchester University Press, 2015), 23.

[56] Latour, *Reassembling*, 46.

[57] See Peter Brook, *The Empty Space* (London: Penguin, 1990).

[58] See Barnett, "'I've Been Told,'" esp. 153–57.

[59] Barnett, "'I've Been Told,'" 157.

[60] Johannes Birgfeld and Ulrike Garde, "Falk Richter and Anouk van Dijk's *Complexity of Belonging*: Exploring Internationalisation in Contemporary Theatre," *German Life and Letters* 71, no. 3 (2018): 353–73 (357).

[61] Gerhard Jörder, *Ostermeier-Backstage* (Berlin: Theater der Zeit, 2014), 13.

[62] Peter Boenisch and Thomas Ostermeier, *The Theatre of Thomas Ostermeier* (New York: Routledge, 2016), 1.

[63] Jörder, *Ostermeier-Backstage*, 88, 124.

[64] Jörder, *Ostermeier-Backstage*, 8.

[65] Latour, *Reassembling*, 39.

12: Tuning in to Germany: The BBC German Service and the British Occupation

Emily Oliver

"Hier ist England! Hier ist England! Hier ist England!" This was the announcement Germans would hear if they happened to tune their radios to the BBC German Service during the Second World War. While technology enabled Britain to cross into enemy territory via the airwaves, actually speaking to Germans in a language they understood—in a tone to which they would respond favorably, about topics that interested them—required a complex combination of linguistic and cultural competence, knowledge, and creativity. It also required those working for the BBC German Service to consider carefully to whom and for whom they were speaking. Originally conceived as part of Britain's psychological warfare effort, the German Service continued to broadcast from Bush House in London well beyond the end of the Second World War, until its closure in 1999. What bodies of knowledge and intellectual insights did its employees draw on to maintain this transnational broadcasting effort? How did German listeners react to programs from the United Kingdom? What adjustments were necessary to transition from wartime to peacetime broadcasting? This chapter explores transnational exchange between Britain and Germany by focusing on the ways in which the BBC chose to address its German target audience in the 1940s.

Scholarship on the BBC German Service has focused primarily on the war years and neglected its role in subsequent periods of German history.[1] Drawing on hitherto unexamined archival sources, this chapter presents the first analysis of the German Service's role during the Allied occupation of Germany (1945–49)—a crucial period for the development of the German media landscape. The transition from war to peace in the mid-1940s saw a renewed negotiation between external, internal, and bilateral British and German voices on the BBC German Service, at a time when Britain was very directly involved in efforts to rebuild, control, and reshape the German media. Accessing and broadcasting authentic German voices became crucial to attracting and retaining listeners during this period, as did the question of how to position the German listener in relation to an extraterritorial speaker. In these ways, the BBC German Service's development during the immediate postwar years serves as a case study for two nations' attempts to redefine their position in the world after a period of embittered conflict. The chapter begins with a brief history of the German Service's development during the war, before analyzing its attempts at audience research during the Allied occupation to show how German listeners perceived Britain and the BBC, and the close links they made between these two entities.

Broadcasting during the Second World War

The BBC German Service was founded somewhat hastily during the Munich Crisis in 1938, and initially it drew at random on German-speaking journalists in London. For instance, its very first broadcast on September 27, 1938, Neville Chamberlain's live speech on his Munich talks with Hitler, was translated during the broadcast itself by Robert Lucas (born Robert Ehrenzweig, 1904–84), a Jewish Austrian émigré working as the London correspondent for a Viennese newspaper. The speaker tasked with delivering Chamberlain's speech in German had even less broadcasting experience than Lucas. Walter Goetz (1911–95) was a German-born cartoonist for the *Daily Express*, who found himself waiting desperately at the microphone for the next translated sentence to be fed through so he could read it out live on the air.[2] For a while, the German Service continued its ad hoc broadcasting at the Foreign Office's request, with news bulletins being written by BBC Overseas Service staff and translated into German in-house. In January 1939, a series of political talks and commentaries ("Sonderberichte") was added, before the German Service became a department in its own right in April 1939.[3]

In October 1940, a twenty-nine-year-old Englishman was placed in charge, who proceeded to restructure the Service. Hugh Carleton Greene (1910–87), brother of the novelist Graham Greene, was fluent in German, having previously worked as the *Daily Telegraph*'s Berlin correspondent. Under Greene's tenure, the Service gradually assembled a highly diverse workforce of German speakers. Some were British citizens with an excellent knowledge of German, such as Lindley Fraser (1904–63), a former economics professor from Edinburgh who was recruited as a personality speaker in the early 1940s. Taking on the "Sonderbericht" series throughout the war, Fraser became "the single most popular commentator" on the German Service.[4] The role of productions director was filled by the British actor Marius Goring (1912–98), who was fluent in German, having studied in Frankfurt, Vienna, and Munich.[5] Other English staff included Christina Ogilvy (later Christina Gibson, 1915–2005), formerly Secretary for the Relief Department of the International Student

Service, and Patrick Gordon Walker (1907–80), who had taught history at Oxford and would go on to become a Labour MP and cabinet minister after the war.

The main source of native German speakers was London's growing talent pool of Jewish émigrés. The BBC's émigré employees are too numerous to list here, but they included: Bruno Adler (1889–1968), an art historian and literature scholar from Prague; Carl Brinitzer (1907–74), who had practiced law in Germany before being forced to emigrate; the Hungarian-born director and dramatist Martin Esslin (born Julius Pereszlenyi, 1918–2002); the Austrian theater director Julius Gellner (1899–1983); the Berlin actresses Annemarie Hase (1900–1971) and Lucie Mannheim (1899–1976); and the German director and scriptwriter Fritz Wendhausen (1890–1962). Through chairing daily program meetings, Greene gradually turned this heterogeneous group of Brits, Germans, and Austrians into an efficient broadcasting team. A balance of British nationals and native German speakers was necessary since Germans and Austrians were banned from voicing opinions on the air during the war: all commentaries had to be delivered by British staff members, whereas native German speakers were only permitted to write scripts, voice particular parts in features, or read the news.[6] This also enabled the German Service to promote its identity as a *British* broadcaster for Germany, and to avoid the perception that it was run exclusively by Jewish émigrés.[7]

The main way in which the German Service aimed to attract listeners was its claim to be the voice of truth, which meant reporting British military setbacks as well as victories. The key element at the heart of all programming was accurate and up-to-date news, acting as "the magnet which attracted the audience."[8] Since accurate information on the progress of the war was what made Germans tune in, any attempts to influence the audience were restricted to non-news and fictional program items, which were to act as "a vehicle for propaganda."[9] In order to persuade its German audience to take the considerable risk of listening to enemy broadcasts, the BBC German Service judiciously differentiated between warmongering Nazis and supposedly peaceful, "ordinary" Germans.[10] As a 1943 report on the European Services' output stated: "We have always made a distinction between the German war machine and the German people."[11] The Service broadcast a number of satirical comedy features that used everyday German characters as their protagonists to critique the ruling Nazi elite. For instance, Adler scripted a series in which the garrulous Berlin housewife Frau Wernicke complained about the troubles caused to ordinary Germans by those at the top.[12] A series by Lucas featured the fictional Corporal Adolf Hirnschal writing letters to his beloved wife Amalia, in which he professed his support for the führer's ideals while inadvertently detailing the disastrous progress of

Germany's Russian campaign from an ordinary soldier's perspective.[13] The German Service continued to differentiate between Nazis and ordinary Germans throughout the rest of the war, for instance expressing sympathy with German civilian victims of Allied bombing raids while placing the blame for these measures squarely among the higher echelons of the ruling Nazi elite.[14]

Listening to Listeners

The end of the Second World War brought significant changes for the BBC German Service: on the one hand, it could no longer lay claim to its monopoly on truthful, independent broadcasting in Germany, as listening to foreign stations was no longer a crime and the German media were gradually rebuilt. On the other hand, from spring 1945 onward, for the first time the BBC had direct access to its German listeners. Christina Gibson was one of the first German Service correspondents to follow British forces into the liberated territories in early 1945. Wherever she went, Gibson was astonished at how many people recognized the names of German Service contributors and were familiar with their regular wartime broadcasts.[15] Once lines of postal communication were open, the BBC received thousands of letters from Germany detailing just how important its broadcasts had been to particular individuals during the darkest days of Nazi rule.

In August 1945, the German Service received more than a thousand letters, rising to over 2,500 in the following month.[16] This trend continued, with over 25,000 letters from Germany arriving in the first ten months of 1946:[17] "Many letters still begin with the expression of gratitude for BBC wartime broadcasts and the encouragement they brought to Anti-Nazi listeners. Several listeners say Lindley Fraser and Hugh Carlton Greene literally saved them from suicide which they would otherwise have committed."[18] Although the evidence was anecdotal rather than statistical in nature, Gibson, now in charge of sifting the post and writing listener research reports, stressed the importance of these letters: "For the BBC, handicapped by long distance from the German scene, it is invaluable to have this constant contact by correspondence. It provides the possibility of gauging the impact of our broadcasts, of adjusting the tone and methods of approach to the changing moods of our listeners and above all it gives us the 'feel' of the audience in a way which cannot be done by statistical surveys."[19]

Although all German Service employees were "in tune" with Germany to the extent that they had gained significant knowledge and experience of the country and its language before 1933, this transnational exchange had been almost entirely cut off through the war, turning the short geographical distance between the two countries into an ever-widening cultural divide. In this context, the listener letters provided a vital link to the target country. For the first time since the German Service's inception, communication between the BBC and Germany went both ways, enabling the Service to get an accurate impression of its listenership: a year after war's end, the German Service estimated its audience at about two million, of which roughly half lived in the British zone of occupation.[20]

Correspondence from Germany was so enthusiastic that the German Service created a letter-box program. Premiering on July 4, 1945, the "Funkbriefkasten" quickly became one of the most popular programs on the German Service. The initial "vague plan of . . . helping the formation of German public opinion by providing a platform for free discussion" proved a resounding success: a year after its creation, Gibson reported that "the original fortnightly quarter hour has now expanded to a twice weekly half hour programme," and proudly claimed that "the Funkbriefkasten has a much larger audience in Germany than any other BBC programme."[21] Germans, it seems, were keen to air their opinions and fascinated by the opportunity of hearing them broadcast freely on the radio. In her summary of listener responses, Gibson surmised that:

> twelve years of spiritual repression and of Nazi standardisation in the field of ideas have given very many Germans of all types and classes a longing to unburden themselves, to thrash out their own ideas and to hear what their compatriots really think. What the BBC has done has been simply to provide a medium for debate between Germans, the debate taking the form of broadcast letters from . . . every section of the German community.[22]

The German Service was now able to broadcast a diverse range of authentic German voices instead of using British speakers to ventriloquize scripts by German exiles. In order to prove the letters' authenticity and to demonstrate that democratic debate could tolerate criticism, the editors also diligently included letters voicing Anglophobic or Nazi views.[23]

Through providing a forum for letters from Germany, the BBC enabled Germans to set the agenda and to communicate with one another—indeed, letter writers often responded to opinions that had been broadcast in previous episodes. Although the "Funkbriefkasten" was heavily curated, with BBC staff selecting which letters to quote, how to present them, and whom to cast as readers, it nevertheless offered the BBC a rare opportunity of speaking with a German voice instead of being perceived as the mouthpiece for official British policy: "The Funkbriefkasten provides the BBC with an invaluable vehicle for saying to Germans through the mouths of Germans many things which would not come well from Englishmen to Germans."[24] This made it an anomaly among the German Service's postwar programs, which frequently struggled to capture their listeners' mood and position themselves favorably in relation to the rapidly shifting sands of German public opinion under Allied occupation.

From War to Peace: Redefining the German Service's Role

At Bush House, the war was followed by important staff changes. Several of the stalwart British wartime broadcasters left to take up other opportunities: Patrick Gordon Walker, who as assistant director of the German Service had been one of the first to report from the liberated Bergen-Belsen concentration camp, was elected to Parliament. Marius Goring resumed his successful acting career, frequently playing Nazi officers in British films. Many of the native German speakers remained with the German Service, but the BBC gradually came to fear that a decade-long absence might have rendered these employees out of touch with the postwar German population. The Controller of European Services, Sir Ian Jacob, suggested that the BBC recruit new, younger staff from Germany:

> It is necessary that our new recruits should be Germans with recent experience of life in Germany—either during the war or since, or preferably both. It is essential in the German Service . . . that . . . those who broadcast should have been going through the same kind of experience as the people to whom they talk. To some extent we can make good deficiencies by sending people to visit their countries, . . . but it is far better if we can draw our talent directly from the country and renew it from time to time.[25]

In Jacob's view, linguistic proficiency and detailed cultural and political knowledge were no longer enough to guarantee the quality of broadcasts to Germany. Whereas during the war it had been important to broadcast external voices representing an alternative Germany outside the country's physical borders, the BBC now wanted to recruit some "ordinary" Germans to speak for themselves.

In order to avoid sounding disconnected from German audiences, presenters needed to demonstrate a sense of shared experience. This effectively marginalized anyone who hadn't experienced the war and its aftermath in Germany—a blow to the émigré staff. Aside from their age (most German and Austrian employees had been born around the turn of the century), the émigrés' "otherness" seems to have been a significant factor, as Jacob's memo betrayed: "The point which should not be overlooked is that in general our recruits should not be Jews. For obvious reasons we have a large number of these in our German Service now, and I am anxious to reduce the proportion."[26] Since their religious or ethnic background had nothing to do with these employees' broadcasting credentials, Jacob's comments suggest that during the postwar years, the BBC was anxious to employ "typical" Germans on its staff, who would represent a broad listenership rather than a recently decimated minority within German society.

In the late 1940s, the BBC started reserving a proportion of all posts on its External Services for employees from abroad on three-year contracts. The German Service initially struggled to find suitable candidates, but eventually employed a series of young German journalists, many of whom went on to become leading figures in the German media and continued to attribute their success to the BBC's excellent journalistic training.[27] Among the first German postwar staff were Franz Wördemann (1923–92), head of West German Television during the 1960s and chief editor of the *Münchener Merkur* from 1973; and Conrad Ahlers (1922–80), who would publish the article triggering the *Spiegel* affair in 1962 and later became the spokesman for Willy Brandt's government. Training future leading media personalities was to be the German Service's most significant impact on postwar Germany. The journalist Rudolf Walter Leonhardt (1921–2003) called the BBC German Service "die beste Journalistenschule der Welt" (the best journalism school in the world), concluding that "in der täglichen Arbeitsroutine von Bush House ... haben mehr Ausländer England und englischen Journalismus verstehen gelernt, als irgendeine andere einzelne Institution das für sich in Anspruch nehmen kann" (more foreigners learned to understand England and English journalism in the daily work routine of Bush House than any other single institution can lay claim to).[28] This meant that even German journalists working within the domestic German media after the Second World War were significantly influenced by British journalism, be it through style, ethics, or choice of content.

The BBC's other major impact on the postwar German media landscape was Hugh Carleton Greene's departure for Hamburg in 1946 to rebuild German broadcasting in the British zone. Greene became head of the Nordwestdeutscher Rundfunk (NWDR), and was replaced by Lindley Fraser as head of the German Service.[29] Greene's project of building up the Nordwestdeutscher Rundfunk as a German version of the BBC Home Service was so successful that the NWDR and the BBC German Service quickly found themselves stepping on each other's toes in providing Germans with news. In November 1945 a document was drawn up to differentiate between the roles the two services were to play in the future German broadcasting landscape. It was agreed that the NWDR should fulfill "the function of providing for the British Zone of Germany a Home Service," while the BBC would provide "for Germany as a whole a London service speaking with 'the voice of Britain.'"[30] A subsequent policy document stated unambiguously that "the reeducation of the

German people is the direct concern of the B.B.C. German Service."[31] Since the NWDR's task was to build a new tradition of German broadcasting and attract new listeners, it was felt that "excessive attention by N.W.D.R. to the political and historical reeducation of Germans [would] destroy its credibility."[32] Consequently, the reeducation of Germans and the "projection of Britain" became the BBC German Service's chief postwar tasks.[33]

While the term "reeducation" remained notoriously ill-defined throughout the British occupation, the "projection of Britain" entailed "explaining to the Germans . . . the policy, work, problems and achievements of the Control Commission" as well as "Britain, the Commonwealth, British policy . . . and democratic conceptions."[34] This constituted a clear mandate for the German Service to act as a kind of didactic public-relations agency for the United Kingdom. Just when it had gained the ability to attract new listeners through broadcasting authentic German voices, the BBC German Service was forced to focus on British institutions and to promote British government policy to its German listeners.

The effects of these decisions could clearly be seen in programming on the German Service over the next few years. In addition to a daily report on the Nuremberg trials, the BBC introduced features detailing Hitler's rise to power,[35] a long series called "How Democracy Works,"[36] and talks explaining British rule in different parts of the empire.[37] In July 1945 alone, Lindley Fraser authored six talks on "The Work of Military Government," covering industry, food, transport, communications, justice, education, and public health.[38] Although these items contained important information for German listeners, several of Fraser's predictions turned out to be inaccurate, for instance his assurance "dass die Lebensmittellage des Jahres 46/47 besser sein wird als sie im Augenblick ist" (that the food situation in 1946/47 will be better than it is at present).[39] In fact, the winter of 1946/47 saw a worsening of food provision, with Germans in the British zone receiving only half the daily calories deemed necessary for subsistence by the United Nations.[40] By making such erroneous claims, Fraser risked sounding out of touch and somewhat condescending to German listeners suffering food shortages under British occupation.

Richard O'Rorke, who joined the German Service in 1948, later criticized "the need which the Service along with every other British institution felt to try to 'reeducate' the German people," recalling that "there were a whole range of programmes describing parliamentary democracy, the British legal system and British methods of education. I cannot imagine that this schoolmasterly approach did much to encourage listening."[41]

Contemporary listener responses suggest that O'Rorke was right. Several listeners rejected top-down attempts at reeducation via radio, particularly where these concerned the recent German past: "Fritz Ruhnke writes from Hagen in Westfalen to tell us that he is sick and tired of hearing about German crimes and thinks it time the B.B.C. dropped this unsavoury subject. What about Britain's crimes? Britain is to blame for the fuel and food shortage."[42] Although this kind of reaction to reeducation efforts was to be expected in certain quarters, it seems that even some loyal BBC listeners gradually began to adopt this view. In March 1946, a female listener from Bremen reported a conversation with a leading figure at a German radio station, which had initially revolved around their shared positive memories of wartime BBC broadcasts. When asked what he made of more recent German Service programs, the listener reported that this man had answered:

> "Auch ich höre London nicht mehr, kein Mensch hört sie mehr, sie haben sich vollkommen um allen Kredit gebracht. Nach Kriegsende haben sie nichts als Konzentrationslager-Greuelgeschichten gebracht, das hat niemand mehr anhören können." Auf meinen Einwand, dass die Konzentrationslagernachrichten doch gerade damals völlig neu waren für jedermann, sagte er: "Ach was, das habe ich im Krieg genau so gut gewusst wie die BBC auch, aber damals hat sie kein Wörtchen davon gesagt. Hinterher hatte sie es nicht mehr nötig, taktvoll und freundschaftlich zu sein. Deshalb hat man auch genug von ihr."
>
> ["I don't listen to London anymore either; no-one listens to them anymore; they have completely discredited themselves. At the end of the war they broadcast nothing but concentration camp horror stories; no-one could bear to listen to that anymore." At my objection that news of the concentration camps was completely unknown to everyone, particularly at that time, he said: "Rubbish! I already knew that during the war just as well as the BBC did, but back then they never breathed a word of it. Afterwards they no longer needed to be tactful and friendly. That's why everyone's had enough of them."][43]

The listener's admission of a shared secret knowledge of Nazi genocide before 1945 is coupled with the expectation that the BBC would nevertheless maintain a tactful silence about this once the war was over.[44] Both in terms of content and tone, some German listeners expected the BBC German Service to demonstrate that it was clearly on their side.

Lindley Fraser's popularity in particular began to decline in proportion to the changing view of Britain as a poor occupier. Several listeners felt betrayed, contrasting Fraser's wartime promises of a fair British occupation with his harsh postwar criticism of Germans. A listener from Hamburg claimed that "everybody switches off when Lindley Fraser begins to talk," citing conversations with anti-Nazi acquaintances in which "the name of Lindley Fraser recurred whenever they voiced their disappointment at the difference between wartime and present-day broadcasts."[45] Many accused Fraser of not knowing enough about the volatility of daily life in occupied Germany, and of an about-turn in his professed views of Germany since the end of the war. By April 1946 these complaints had multiplied, with Gibson noting that "quite a large number of listeners accuse BBC speakers in general and Lindley Fraser by name of Deutschenhass [hatred of Germans] and of singing a Hassgesang [song of hatred] in broadcasts from London."[46] Whereas during the war the BBC had walked a fine line between truthful reporting and not alienating or offending German listeners, it showed no such qualms in its zealous pursuit of reeducation during the early postwar period. The German Service was in danger of becoming tone-deaf.

Germans' sense of having been betrayed by the German Service only worsened as the general provision for the population in the British zone deteriorated. Many listeners saw the BBC as a direct representative of the British government, and consequently blamed it for government failures:

> The writers are very much disappointed, particularly by Lindley Fraser, whom they frequently heard during the war telling them "Wir werden eine Völkerfamilie sein!" (We will be a family of nations!). "Sie führen das ganze deutsche Volk langsam, aber sicher dem Hungertode entgegen. . . . Was kann der unschuldige einzelne Deutsche dafür, was seine Führer verbockt haben? . . . Ihr treibt das deutsche Volk dem Kommunismus in die Hände!"
>
> [You are slowly but surely leading the entire German people towards starvation. . . . What can the innocent individual German do about the things his leaders got up to? . . . You are driving the German people towards communism!][47]

The distinction between the "innocent individual German" and "his leaders" was one that the German Service had actively encouraged throughout the war in order to win over listeners and convince them that Britain had their best interests at heart. This policy now backfired: German listeners felt wrongly accused of crimes committed not by them but by their leaders, and in turn accused the BBC of hypocrisy in pointing out these crimes.

By July 1946, Anglo-German relations in the British zone had soured so considerably that Gibson concluded in her monthly report:

> At present the most important single factor to be considered in planning output in the light of audience reaction is the very significant rise in the curve of anti-British feeling. . . . Increasing numbers of hostile anonymous letters are addressed to the BBC. They have usually little to do with the BBC—beyond occasional vague assertions that its broadcasts are lies and its speakers hypocrites—and

they are in the main violent anti-British outbursts written by people near despair.[48]

Having built up a reputation as the "voice of truth" during the war, the German Service's postwar policy of casting itself as the "voice of Britain" made it an obvious target for anti-British attacks. In January 1947, Gibson concluded that "the single factor which has probably lost us more valuable listeners than any other is what is felt to be the widening gulf between British policy in theory as expounded by the BBC and British policy in practice as put into effect by Military Government."[49]

Although the BBC was unable to exert direct influence on government policy, it was not entirely powerless, nor indeed blameless, in this situation. Whereas its wartime reputation for telling the truth had been achieved partly through reporting British setbacks and failures, in the immediate postwar period the German Service neglected to include any criticism of British occupation policy in its output, and consequently risked alienating its audience.

During the war, the Service had consistently pursued a strategy of finding "hooks" and "bait" for new audiences in order to get them to listen to less palatable content. By abandoning this strategy the BBC risked losing its core audience: although the Nazi threat had disappeared, the Service was nevertheless competing with other (Allied, and increasingly, German) broadcasters. Audience research showed that listeners missed the humorous features that had characterized the BBC's German output during the war: "It is much lamented that the gaps created by the demise of Gefreiter Hirnschal . . . and Frau Gertrud Wernicke remain unfilled; our most successful post-war innovations . . . are very admirable, but they are seldom funny. If we could occasionally make our audience laugh it would add to the attractiveness of listening to London and perhaps help to clear the political atmosphere."[50] The loss of these features not only represented a missed opportunity for entertaining the Germans: it also meant that the German Service no longer included any programs that adopted the ordinary German's perspective. The BBC's newly recruited young German staff members could not compensate for this, since there were still too few of them in the late 1940s and they had yet to receive adequate training. During the Allied occupation, the German Service thus spoke to the Germans from a British perspective, and occasionally allowed Germans to speak through broadcast letters, but it no longer attempted to speak from a German point of view about everyday worries, or to make fun of those in power—since those in power were now the Allied occupiers.

As the occupation progressed, there seems to have been some gradual recognition of this tonal shift within the BBC: in June 1947, a new policy for the German Service noted that "the 'tone' of B.B.C. broadcasts to

Germany needs constant review. It should move gradually from that of the victor speaking to the defeated to that of normal relations."[51] Two years later, when restructuring radio output, Fritz Beer, who had been in charge of the German Workers' Programme throughout the war, made this critique: "Today, when we have at our disposal newspapers, news bulletins, eye-witness accounts and personal experiences from Germany, our knowledge—at least in detail—is far more superficial than during the war. This is partly due to the fact that our commentaries on events in Germany have yielded pride of place to the projection of British policy and of the Western world."[52]

Both the German Service's inside knowledge of Germany and its ability to speak to Germans as equals suffered from its attempts to fulfill its assigned role in the projection of Britain. These efforts also adversely affected its listenership and reputation. It was not until the BBC refocused its efforts on combating communist propaganda in the eastern zone from 1949 onward that it began to claw back its wartime reputation as the voice of truth.

Positive Reeducation: Language and Literature

The predominantly negative reactions to the BBC's political output might easily give the impression that this was its only contribution to postwar German broadcasting. However, this is far from the truth: while the majority of airtime (23 percent) was still devoted to news, documentary features and plays formed the second-largest proportion of output (21 percent).[53] Since broadcasts no longer had to contend with interference from jamming, scriptwriters could tackle substantial works of literature. A survey of features scripts from the immediate postwar period indicates an astonishing array of literary adaptations, ranging from early modern English drama, through Dickens and other nineteenth-century novelists, to modern classics by authors such as D. H. Lawrence and George Orwell. The first postwar cultural feature was a program on Shakespeare by Marius Goring in June 1945, followed by a further twelve literary and cultural programs before the end of that year.[54] The annual number of cultural features steadily rose during the occupation period, reaching eighty-two by 1949, which is remarkable given that almost all features required adapting and translating into German, followed by rehearsals and recording, sometimes with a large cast.

In addition to several Shakespeare plays, the writers adapted such classics as Ben Jonson's *Volpone* or Christopher Marlowe's *Edward II* and *Faustus* for radio. In an effort to reintroduce cosmopolitan cultural programming after years of Nazi *Gleichschaltung* (the enforced standardization of political, social, economic, and cultural institutions under fascism), the BBC also presented features on Enlightenment and Jewish writers, such as Gotthold Ephraim Lessing and Heinrich Heine, adapted Hugo von Hofmannsthal's *Jedermann* (Everyman), and contributed a number of Goethe features during the bicentenary of the writer's birth in 1949. However, not all literary features were necessarily highbrow in content. Realizing that English crime writing could be a popular cultural export, in 1949 the German Service introduced the "Bibliothek des Horrors" (Library of Horror), a crime club on the airwaves, featuring stories by Arthur Conan Doyle, Agatha Christie, Edgar Allan Poe, Dorothy L. Sayers, H. G. Wells, and others. In contrast to its monophonic political output after the war, the German Service's cultural programming struck a balance between education and entertainment, giving its listeners access to classical and popular Anglo-American literature in their own language.

Another important addition to postwar programming was the inclusion of English lessons by radio. "Lernt Englisch im Londoner Rundfunk" (Learn English with Radio London) had been introduced under Hugh Greene's directorship very soon after the end of the war.[55] The two staff members responsible for this program were the Welshman Alaric Arengo-Jones, who had worked as a translator in prewar Vienna and now broadcast under the pseudonym Seton Anderson, and Carl-Heinz Jaffé (1902–74), a German émigré actor. The ten-minute program was broadcast every morning and evening, presenting very short introductions to English grammar and vocabulary as well as exercises for listeners. In contrast to several other programs at the time, listener response to the English lessons was overwhelmingly positive:

> At a time when anti-British feeling is so noticeably on the increase in Germany it is perhaps remarkable that this programme should be swamped with the friendliest possible letters: letters . . . of gratitude and of congratulation for the teacher or self-congratulation for the pupil; letters of unbounded enthusiasm for the English language and all things English; Christmas cards, Easter greetings, drawings of the BBC family, poems, pressed flowers—all the paraphernalia of our flourishing fan-mail.[56]

With the sudden urgent need for Germans (particularly in the British and American zones) to learn English, it was a clever tactical decision to offer free language tuition, open to anyone with access to a radio set. Language learning played a crucial role in Anglo-German relations at a time of tension on many other fronts. Through the inclusion of language lessons immediately after the Second World War, the BBC offered Germans an opportunity to acquire an essential skill, while also introducing them to British culture and customs, thus fostering transnational exchange.

Having gained considerable prestige among Germans through its objective reporting during the Second World War, the BBC German Service clearly struggled to adjust to a new role during peacetime. In some ways, this process mirrored Germans' struggles to find their place in the world and figure out how to interact with former enemies. The BBC's efforts to find the right voice were hampered on the one hand by its responsibility for explaining British policy to Germans, and on the other hand by German listeners' failure to differentiate between the corporation and the British government. However, the extremely positive perception of language and literature programs at a time of great tension between Britain and Germany serves as a reminder of soft power's value in shaping interactions between people of formerly hostile nations. At a time when Britain's military and political representatives faced resistance on the ground in Germany, its cultural ambassadors were nevertheless enthusiastically received by Germans keen to redefine their place in the world.

Notes

Uncredited translations are my own.

[1] See Asa Briggs, *The War of Words* (London: Oxford University Press, 1970); Gerard Mansell, *Let Truth Be Told: 50 Years of BBC External Broadcasting* (London: Weidenfeld and Nicolson, 1982); Kristina Meier, "The German Service of the BBC during the Second World War: Attitudes towards Satire as a Weapon of War," in *World War II & the Media: A Collection of Original Essays*, ed. Christopher Hart, Guy Hodgson, and Simon Gwyn Roberts (Chester: University of Chester, 2014), 61–84; Stephanie Seul, "The Representation of the Holocaust in the British Propaganda Campaign Directed at the German Public, 1938–1945," *Leo Baeck Year Book* 52 (2007): 267–306; Seul, "'Plain, Unvarnished News'?: The BBC German Service and Chamberlain's Propaganda Campaign Directed at Nazi Germany, 1938–1940," *Media History* 21 (2015): 378–96; Jennifer Taylor, "The 'Endsieg' as Ever-Receding Goal: Literary Propaganda by Bruno Adler and Robert Lucas for BBC Radio," *Yearbook of the Research Centre for German and Austrian Exile Studies* 1 (1999): 43–57; and Rhys W. Williams, "'Frau Wernicke' at the BBC: Wartime Satire and Propaganda," in *Diasporas and Diplomacy: Cosmopolitan Contact Zones at the BBC World Service (1932–2012)*, ed. Marie Gillespie and Alban Webb (London: Routledge, 2013), 57–69. Exceptions to this trend are Charmian Brinson and Richard Dove, eds., *"Stimme der Wahrheit": German-Language Broadcasting by the BBC* (Amsterdam: Rodopi, 2003); and Patrick Major, "Listening behind the Curtain: BBC Broadcasting to East Germany and Its Cold War Echo," *Cold War History* 13 (2013): 255–75.

[2] Robert Lucas, "The German Service of the BBC" [typescript], May 7, 1983, 35, RLU 3/1/55, Robert Lucas Papers, Institute of Modern Languages Research, Senate House, University of London.

[3] See Seul, "Plain, Unvarnished News," 382.

[4] BBC German Section, "Listening and Reaction in Germany," October 10, 1945, 8, E3/275/1, BBC Written Archives Centre (henceforth WAC).

[5] See Goring's obituary in *The Telegraph*, October 10, 1998, http://www.powell-pressburger.org/Obits/Marius/Telegraph.html (accessed September 18, 2018).

[6] See Gunda Cannon, ed., *"Hier ist England"—"Live aus London": Das deutsche Programm der British Broadcasting Corporation 1938–1988* (London: BBC External Services, 1988), 6. The only exception to this rule was Thomas Mann, whose direct appeals to German listeners were considered of such great value that the BBC went to great lengths to record them in California and transfer them to the United Kingdom via New York. See Thomas Mann, *Deutsche Hörer! Fünfundfünfzig Radiosendungen nach Deutschland* (Frankfurt: Fischer, 1965).

[7] See Richard O'Rorke, "Sendungen für Deutschland—der Deutsche Dienst der BBC 1945–1955," *Rundfunk und Geschichte* 5, no. 4 (1979): 180.

[8] "BBC German Service," March 25, 1942, E1/758/2, BBC WAC.

[9] "Layout of BBC Broadcasts in German," September 3, 1940, 4, E1/758/1, BBC WAC.

[10] See Seul, "Plain, Unvarnished News," 385.

[11] "Extract from Output Report of B.B.C. European Services dated January 10–16, 1942" [corrected to: 1943], E1/758/2, BBC WAC.

[12] For an edited collection of all scripts in the "Frau Wernicke" series, see Bruno Adler, *Frau Wernicke: Kommentare einer "Volksjenossin,"* ed. Uwe Naumann (Mannheim: Persona Verlag, 1990).

[13] See Robert Lucas, *"Teure Amalia, vielgeliebtes Weib!" Die Briefe des Gefreiten Adolf Hirnschal an seine Frau in Zwieselsdorf* (Frankfurt am Main: Fischer Taschenbuch, 1984).

[14] See Emily Oliver, "Inventing a New Kind of German: The BBC German Service and the Bombing War," in *Allied Communication to the Public during the Second World War: National and Transnational Networks*, ed. Simon Eliot and Marc Wiggam (London: Bloomsbury, 2019), 149–66.

[15] See Christina Ogilvy, interviewed by Wolfgang Labuhn, "'Hier ist England!': The German Language Service of the BBC during WW II," prod. Peter Schaufler, May 8, 1985 (BBC German Service), A33/164, Deutsches Runfunkarchiv (DRA), Frankfurt am Main.

[16] BBC German Section, "Listening and Reaction in Germany," October 10, 1945, 1, E3/275/1, BBC WAC.

[17] Christina Gibson, "Evidence on the German Audience for British Broadcasts," November 6, 1946, 7, E3/275/1, BBC WAC.

[18] BBC German Section, "Listening and Reaction in Germany," October 10, 1945, 7, E3/275/1, BBC WAC.

[19] Christina Gibson, "Evidence of the German Audience for British Broadcasts," December 14, 1946, 2, E3/275/1, BBC WAC.

[20] Christina Gibson, "Evidence on the German Audience for British Broadcasts," August 31, 1946, 1, E3/275/1, BBC WAC.

[21] Christina Gibson, "Evidence on the German Audience for British Broadcasts," July 6, 1946, 3, E3/275/1, BBC WAC.

[22] Christina Gibson, "Evidence on the German Audience for British Broadcasts," July 6, 1946, 4.

23 See Patrick Major, "Listening behind the Curtain: BBC Broadcasting to East Germany and Its Cold War Echo," *Cold War History* 13 (2013): 258.

24 Christina Gibson, "Evidence on the German Audience for British Broadcasts," July 6, 1946, 6.

25 Memo from Ian Jacob, "Recruitment of Germans for the German Service," June 3, 1947, R13/148/4, BBC WAC.

26 Memo from Ian Jacob, "Recruitment of Germans for the German Service," June 3, 1947.

27 See Richard O'Rorke, "Der Deutsche Dienst der BBC 1948–75: Vom Krieg zum Frieden," in Cannon, *"Hier ist England"—"Live aus London,"* 37.

28 Rudolf Walter Leonhardt, "Die beste Journalistenschule der Welt," *Die Zeit*, May 9, 1975, https://www.zeit.de/1975/20/die-beste-journalistenschule-der-welt (accessed September 23, 2018).

29 See Florian Huber, *Re-education durch Rundfunk: Die Umerziehungspolitik der britischen Besatzungsmacht am Beispiel des NWDR 1945–1948*, ed. Peter von Rüden and Hans-Ulrich Wagner (Hamburg: Verlag Hans-Bredow-Institut, 2006); and Michael Tracey, *Das unerreichbare Wunschbild: Ein Versuch über Hugh Greene und die Neugründung des Rundfunks in Westdeutschland nach 1945* (Cologne: Kohlhammer-Grote, 1982).

30 "Minutes of Meeting Held in the Conference Room, Bush House," November 21, 1945, E1/757, BBC WAC.

31 "Respective Functions of B.B.C. German Service and N.W.D.R. Statement of Policy," November 24, 1945, E1/757, BBC WAC.

32 "Respective Functions of B.B.C. German Service and N.W.D.R. Statement of Policy."

33 "Respective Functions of B.B.C. German Service and N.W.D.R. Statement of Policy."

34 Memo from Gauntlett (Chief of Public Relations/Information Services Control Group, Berlin) to Military Governor, "Public Relations/Information Services Control," March 23, 1948, PRO/FO 1056/124, National Archives, Kew.

35 See, for example, Martin Esslin, "Voices from the Past No. 2: The End of the Weimar Republic," prod. Fritz Wendhausen, August 18, 1947, "German Features: Scripts" (August 1947), BBC WAC; and Carl Brinitzer, "Voices from the Past No. 10: Autoritäre oder parlamentarische Staatsform," prod. K. Schloessingk, July 3, 1948, "German Features: Scripts" (July 1948), BBC WAC.

36 See, for example, Edmund Wolf, "How Democracy Works No. 17," prod. Fritz Wendhausen, June 2, 1947, "German Features: Scripts" (June 1947), BBC WAC.

37 See, for example, Edmund Wolf, "Palestine—The Background," prod. Julius Gellner, May 23, 1946, "German Features: Scripts" (May 1946), BBC WAC; Edmund Wolf, "Report on India," prod. Walter Hertner, November 5, 1946, "German Features: Scripts" (November 1946), BBC WAC; H. W. Privin, "Southern Rhodesia: The Land of the Future," ed. Edmund Wolf, prod. Julius Gellner, November 21 and 25, 1947, "German Features: Scripts" (November 1947), BBC

WAC; and Robert Lucas, "Entdeckungsreise—Colonial Journey," prod. Walter Hertner, July 21, 1949, "German Features: Scripts" (July 1949), BBC WAC.

[38] Lindley Fraser, "The Work of Military Government No. 1: Industry," July 16, 1945; "The Work of Military Government No. 2: Food," July 19, 1945; "The Work of Military Government No. 3: Transport and Communications," July 21, 1945; "The Work of Military Government No. 4: Law and Justice," July 19, 1945; "The Work of Military Government No. 5: Education," July 24, 1945; "The Work of Military Government No. 6: Public Health," July 28, 1945, "German Service—Lindley Fraser: Talks and Features (Sonderbericht) 1945," BBC WAC.

[39] Lindley Fraser, "The Work of Military Government No. 2: Food," July 19, 1945, 3.

[40] See Giles MacDonogh, *After the Reich: From the Liberation of Vienna to the Berlin Airlift* (London: John Murray, 2007), 363.

[41] O'Rorke, "Der Deutsche Dienst der BBC 1948–75," 37.

[42] Christina Gibson, "Random Notes from the Mail—15th Edition," March 26, 1946, 4, E3/275/1, BBC WAC.

[43] Gibson, "Random Notes from the Mail."

[44] For more on the BBC German Service's selective reporting on the persecution of the Jews during the Second World War, see Seul, "The Representation of the Holocaust in the British Propaganda Campaign."

[45] BBC German Section, "Listening and Reaction in Germany," October 10, 1945, 8, E3/275/1, BBC WAC.

[46] Christina Gibson, "Random Notes from the Mail—16th Edition," April 29, 1946, 2, E3/275/1, BBC WAC.

[47] Christina Gibson, "Random Notes from the Mail—21st Edition," July 25, 1946, E3/275/1, BBC WAC.

[48] Christina Gibson, "Evidence on the German Audience for British Broadcasts," July 6, 1946, 2–3.

[49] Christina Gibson, "Evidence on the German Audience for British Broadcasts," January 14, 1947, 6, Countries: Germany, "German Service: Audience Research Reports" (1947), E3/275/2, BBC WAC.

[50] Christina Gibson, "Evidence on the German Audience for British Broadcasts," January 14, 1947, 5–6.

[51] E. I. C. Jacob, Controller European Services, "Statement of Policy for the German Service," June 6, 1947, 2, E1/758/2, BBC WAC.

[52] Memo from Fritz Beer to Lindley Fraser, "Eastern Germany Programme," February 24, 1949, 5, E1/756, BBC WAC.

[53] Lindley Fraser, "Report on BBC German Service," October 28, 1946, 3, E1/758/2, BBC WAC.

[54] See Andreas Höfele, "Reeducating Germany: BBC Shakespeare 1945," in *Shakespeare and European Politics*, ed. Dirk Delabastita, Jozef De Vos, and Paul Franssen (Newark: University of Delaware Press, 2008), 255–77.

[55] See the four-volume printed companion to the series: Carl Heinz Jaffé, Seton Anderson, and Henry English, *Lernt Englisch im Londoner Rundfunk: Ein Helfer für Hörer der von der BBC gesendeten deutsch-englischen Unterrichtsstunden* (Hamburg: Hammerich und Lesser, 1947).

[56] Christina Gibson, "Evidence on the German Audience for British Broadcasts," June 6, 1946, 5–6, E3/275/1, BBC WAC.

13: Reterritorializing German Pop: Kraftwerk's *Industrielle Volksmusik* as a Transnational Phenomenon

Uwe Schütte

IN THIS CHAPTER I will focus on the Düsseldorf pioneers of electronic pop music Kraftwerk, using their work as a case study on the transnational influence exerted by the German pop music movement known retrospectively as *Krautrock*. The term is problematic, but less so because of the offensive potential often attributed to it by British scholars; David Stubbs has noted that the word "retains the condescension of the British music press, who found the very fact that these groups were German inherently amusing."[1] Germans, however, have readily accepted it as a generic title, though only retrospectively; when the *Krautrock* bands were active, there was little self-perception on part of the musicians that they were part of a movement, as there were different centers and scenes across Germany (most important in West Berlin, Munich, and Düsseldorf/Cologne). For example, Michael Rother of *Neu!* (New!) has stated: "Any box or label that is attached to our music tries to neglect the fact that we weren't a 'family' of German musicians, we had no common goals or identity."[2]

In describing German experimental music from about 1968 to the mid-1970s, but also beyond, so-called *Krautrock* constituted a hugely heterogeneous body of musical approaches and styles. Ulrich Adelt rightly hesitates in representing *Krautrock* as a unified genre or countercultural movement, rather arguing that it constitutes "a field of cultural production,"[3] and defining the term as "an all-encompassing name for the music of various German performers from roughly 1968 to 1974."[4] What is undisputed, however, is that the music retrospectively called *Krautrock* proved to have a massive impact beyond Germany on the development of music styles. In the field of *Krautrock*, Kraftwerk stands out not least because artistically it is arguably the most successful and influential German group and because the group continues to perform live to great acclaim. As such, their work offers a rich case study for exploring the impact of German pop music in the United Kingdom and the United States.

Kraftwerk, founded in 1970, became internationally famous with its 1974 release of the epochal track *Autobahn* (Motorway), which became a top-ten hit in the United States. The group's main body of work appeared between 1974 and 1981, and thus belongs more to the aftermath of *Krautrock*. The Kraftwerk project is very much a *Gesamtkunstwerk* (total work of art, or unified aesthetic) of sound and vision, which incorporated important influences from countries such as France, Italy, and Russia, and had, in turn, a great influence in Britain and the United States, but also Japan and Slovenia. As such, Kraftwerk problematizes the popular notion that only bands and pop music styles developed in the anglophone world are cited as being globally influential.

Their groundbreaking album, *Trans Europa Express* (Trans-Europe Express), from 1977 explored transnational and cosmopolitan themes and aesthetics, and functions very much as the companion piece to *Autobahn*, an album that was concerned with the conceptual idea of expressing a specifically German identity. As Ralf Hütter, a founding member of Kraftwerk, explained: "*Autobahn* was about finding our artistic situation: Where are we? What is the sound of the German *Bundesrepublik* (Federal Republic)? Because at this time German bands were having English names and not using the German language."[5] This provocative dichotomy of both musically defining and overcoming Germanness was mirrored in the early transnational reception of Kraftwerk, which was either reduced to being stereotypically German or seen to represent an utter "otherness."

This chapter will first provide a research overview on the engagement of German studies with German pop music, building the case for using Kraftwerk as a case study for examining the transnational reach of German pop music. The discussion then analyses the musical style that the band itself termed *industrielle Volksmusik* (a challenging term to translate, as detailed below), and discusses how and in what form Kraftwerk's music traveled to the United Kingdom and the United States. For, interestingly, the reception in the two countries differed considerably: in the United Kingdom, Kraftwerk found wide reception among groups who would dominate the charts and who gave rise to the mainstream movement of synth-pop (for instance, groups like Depeche Mode and Orchestral Manoeuvres in The Dark). It also influenced post-punk bands (like The Fall) or local movements like the London-based New Romantics-scene, as well as proved inspiration to artists like David Bowie. Yet, as this chapter will reveal, in contrast to this British reception, Kraftwerk's electronic sound attracted the attention of urban African American communities in New York, Detroit, and, to a lesser degree, the entire East Coast, helping to spark the minimalist sounds of underground styles such as electro, techno, and house.

(Re)Mapping German Pop

German pop music has recently become the focus of greater attention in anglophone German studies, both in the United States and, particularly, the United Kingdom and Ireland. This follows developments in Germany: over the last ten years *Germanistik* has begun to address research into German pop music and pop culture in the context of an increasing turn from traditional philology to cultural studies– and media studies–oriented approaches. Initially, particular attention was afforded to the short-lived trend of *Popliteratur* (pop literature), but the focus of investigation was gradually broadened to include all forms of popular culture, even advertisements and fashion. A paradigmatic example of this development is the establishment of the interdisciplinary journal *POP: Kultur & Kritik* (POP: Culture & Criticism) in 2012; its board of editors includes a number of scholars holding chairs in German literature, but also independent scholars and junior academics.

Ironically, it was the pioneering work of British academics and theoreticians working outside of German studies—from the initial work of the Birmingham Centre for Cultural Studies, up to contemporary scholars working in a gray zone between academia and music journalism (like Mark Fisher, Steve Goodmann, or Kodwo Eshun)—from which German researchers took their inspiration. A number of introductory volumes and readers were published that aimed to "translate" the state of anglophone theory of popular culture for the newly emerging German discipline of *Poptheorie* (pop theory)—for example, Thomas Hecken's *Pop: Geschichte eines Konzepts* (Pop: History of a Concept, 2009), or Christoph Jacke, Jens Ruchatz, and Martin Zierold's edited volume *Pop, Populäres und Theorien* (Pop, the Popular, and Theories, 2011). A major achievement and milestone of German-language pop music research was presented in Diedrich Diederichsen's extensive study *Über Pop-Musik* (On Pop Music, 2014). His densely written and comprehensive study develops a strongly trans-medially oriented theory of pop music for which he coined the term, or rather the notation or spelling, *Pop-Musik* (differentiating it thereby from the uncritically used description of the genre as *Popmusik*).

The lack of serious engagement with German pop music in German studies in Britain until recently is thus quite ironic given the fact that Britain represents the birthplace of cultural studies. There have only been very isolated and not necessarily prominent examples, such as Jennifer Shryane's monograph *Blixa Bargeld and Einstürzende Neubauten: German Experimental Music* (2011) and David Robb's edited volume *Protest Song in East and West Germany since the 1960s* (2007). Indeed, many of the academic treatments of German pop music emerging from the United Kingdom during the same period of time were scattered across other disciplines such as musicology, cultural studies, theater and performance studies, and sociology, and were often by researchers with no command of German and hence no access to German-language sources. This might also explain why in many cases German pop music has only ever been dealt with tangentially or in isolation.[6]

This situation, however, began to change in Britain and the United States when German music from the late 1960s to the mid-to-late 1970s was not so much "rediscovered" as properly acknowledged as a vital source of continuous musical inspiration for anglophone bands. With English-language pop music entering into a phase called "retro-mania" by the music critic Simon Reynolds in 2011, there was a remarkable upswing in media interest in *Krautrock*. Pertinent examples are provided by BBC programs such as *Krautrock: The Rebirth of Germany* (BBC Four TV, 2009) or *The Man Machine: Kraftwerk, Krautrock and the German Electronic Revolution* (BBC Radio Six, 2012). Journalistic publications such as David Buckley's *Kraftwerk Publikation: A Biography* (2012), David Stubbs's *Future Days: Krautrock and the Building of Modern Germany* (2014), or Rob Young's *All Gates Open: The Story of CAN* (2018) not only demonstrate the remarkable revival of popular interest of the British public in German pop music since 2010 but also underline the fact that this interest is mainly focused on the *Krautrock* movement and the most important protagonist of German electronic pop music, the Düsseldorf band Kraftwerk.[7]

It is important to note, however, that the increased academic focus on *Krautrock* and Kraftwerk by anglophone scholars can be described as a transatlantic effort, mimicking the transnational repercussions of German (electronic) pop music. Thus while British scholars Sean Albiez and David Pattie published the edited volume *Kraftwerk: Music Nonstop* (2011), containing contributions from mainly UK scholars, a special *Krautrock* issue of the journal *Popular Music and Society* appeared in December 2009, containing five articles by US researchers and German contributors. By the mid-2010s, the research landscape for German pop music looked very different from a decade earlier. It could be argued that the transnational turn in scholarship not only provided a sound theoretical basis for research into German pop music but actually encouraged researchers to examine *Krautrock* (and related musical styles) within a new theoretical framework. The importance of a transnational perspective on German music from the late 1960s was demonstrated in particular by two studies that are firmly based on the approach.

First, there is Alexander Simmeth's *Krautrock Transnational: Die Neuerfindung der Popmusik in der BRD, 1968–1978* (Krautrock Transnational: The Reinvention of Pop Music in the FRG, 1968–1978, 2016), which originated from a PhD thesis in history and examines the transnational quality of *Krautrock*, particularly from a cultural-historical perspective. It demonstrates that pop musical cultural exchange takes place in both directions, and along multiple pathways:

> Dabei ist der Kulturtransfer aus den USA und Großbritannien nach Westdeutschland ebenso von Interesse wie die umgekehrte Transferrichtung, für die der Begriff "Krautrock" überhaupt erst geprägt worden ist—von wem und wo sei dahingestellt. Es geraten Transfers von Ideen, Praktiken, Symbolen, Personen und Objekten in den Blick, aber auch die Wahrnehmungen und diskursiven Rückwirkungen dieser Transfers in den verschiedenen nationalen Kontexten.[8]

> [In this way, the cultural transfer from the United States and Great Britain to West Germany is of just as much interest as the reverse direction of transfer, for which the term "Krautrock" had been actually coined—by whom and where is another matter. Transfers of ideas, practices, symbols, people, and objects come into view, but also the perceptions and the discursive feedbacks of these transfers in the various national contexts.]

Second, Ulrich Adelt's important study *Krautrock: German Music in the Seventies* (2016) includes many groundbreaking chapters examining, for example, the musical contributions made by *Krautrock* bands to the soundtracks of New German Films. "Although it emerged with an emphasis on a specific white West German counterculture, *Krautrock*'s expressions of sonic identity proved to be varied and conflicted," as Adelt stresses.[9] The music only retrospectively dubbed *Krautrock* was thus far too heterogeneous to constitute a clearly defined movement. Henceforth, argues Adelt, *Krautrock* should rather be understood as a diverse field of cultural production occurring within differing specific social contexts. What united the various musicians and bands, however, was the need to redefine, through music, a post-Holocaust German national identity that sought to break with the nationalist aberrations of the past while also rejecting the Anglo-American pop-cultural hegemony of their present.

The common cultural and ideological impetus behind *Krautrock*, in all its diverse forms, was therefore a reterritorialization of German culture in the changed context of a post-fascist, consumerist culture that, to some considerable degree, rejected any real atonement for its recent crimes. As a cultural phenomenon, it strongly paralleled the political protest movement known as the *68er Bewegung* (68 Movement), which positioned itself as a "transnationale 'Gegenkultur' besonders scharf gegen den Konsum als Lebensform, besonders in seiner popkulturellen Ausprägung" (transnational "counterculture," particularly strongly against consumerism as a way of life, especially in its pop-cultural forms).[10]

The common aesthetic quality uniting *Krautrock* was the emphasis it placed on experimentation with sound and song structures. Through these musical means the bands constructed what can be described, using Josh Kun's notion of the "audiotopia," as an alternative utopian space. This aesthetic space, constructed from experimental sounds, marked less an attempt to create a German-sounding pop music, as so much of this music already included non-German elements and influences, and thus sought to create a hybridized version of Germanness that challenged essentialist and fixed notions of what it meant to be German. As such, it also strongly resonated with musicians outside Germany who also felt political dissatisfaction with their own culture and its pop music. As Kun puts it, "Music can be of a nation, but it is never exclusively national; it always overflows, spills out, sneaks through, reaches an ear on the other side of the border line."[11]

Why Kraftwerk?

Numerous individual artists from Germany have had isolated, surprise international successes over these four decades, but these were mostly linked to individual singles or to a short period of international fame. For example, Nena's catchy pop tune "99 Luftballons" (99 Balloons, in English as 99 Red Balloons) from 1983 was a huge success in Germany and internationally, despite the fact that, initially, there was no English-language version released.[12] A little earlier, Falco also enjoyed success in the European charts with the international version of "Der Kommissar" (The Inspector), which was based on the original version, mixing his strongly Austrian-inflected German with English. The case of Falco serves as a reminder about the problematic classification of artists as "German": the use of the German language works a marker of artistic identity. There are many different ways in which artists from the German-speaking countries avoided using their language to mask their background, or use it playfully to enrich the predominant use of English. Pertinent examples are provided by the Münster-based Alphaville, or the German-speaking Swiss duo Yello, or, indeed, the London-based band Propaganda, originally from Düsseldorf, all of whom scored massive hits in English across Europe and beyond. A German-born musician like the Hollywood composer Hans Zimmer would also not necessarily be considered as belonging to the realm of German pop music, for various reasons. Another poignant case is the deceased Velvet Underground *diseuse* Christa Päffgen, a.k.a. Nico, whose artistic trademark was her heavily cultivated German accent.

Currently, Neue Deutsche Härte (new German hardness)[13] forerunners Rammstein and the techno pop act Scooter represent the two most internationally successful German bands commercially, both shifting millions of units and selling out major stadiums. But while Scooter aims to obscure its German roots, Rammstein makes a beguiling spectacle out of amplified stereotypes of Germanness. Their aim of provoking by toying with images of perverted sexuality or fascist imagery has to be considered problematic and is overall probably more a matter of taste than of morals.[14]

Kraftwerk, too, did play ironically with its Germanness in media interviews after the group's international breakthrough. However, they increasingly also introduced a European dimension to their work, for instance through their use of French, English, and Spanish for song lyrics. Therefore, they represent the example of a band that performs its Germanness overtly but not exclusively in their music, while at the same time they enjoyed international success and had a transnational impact on the music made in other countries. This complex situation makes them ideally suited to serve as a case study for this chapter. The reach and cultural complexity of this ostensibly German band is reflected in the most recent scholarship. The year 2011 saw the appearance of the first academic anthology on Kraftwerk. Entitled *Kraftwerk: Music Nonstop* (2011), and edited by Sean Albiez and David Pattie, it collected contributions by British, Finnish, Norwegian, and German researchers that examined the Kraftwerk oeuvre from various perspectives. The international composition of the group of contributors to the volume demonstrates the transnational range of interest in Kraftwerk, which clearly constitutes the most influential band to have emerged from Germany.

Kraftwerk lends itself to a paradigmatic consideration of the transnational influence of German pop music owing to both the pioneering nature of its music and its longevity as a band, operating now for nearly fifty years. With concerts played at leading international cultural institutions such as the Vienna Burgtheater, but also the London Tate Modern and the Sydney Opera House, Kraftwerk has gained recognition for its multimedia *Gesamtkunstwerk* beyond the field of pop music, as it has raised, inter alia, the interests of museum curators, scholars in the field of art history, literary writers, and art journalists.

A watershed moment in this process was the retrospective of the eight studio albums that define their (self-determined) canon—ranging from *Autobahn* (1974) to *Tour de France* (2003)—which they performed over eight evenings at the Museum of Modern Art in April 2012. Dubbed *The Catalogue—12345678*, these concerts acted as showcases for the *Catalogue* box set released in 2009, which contained so-called digital remasters of their oeuvre. In 2017 a similar box set, now called *3-D The Catalogue*, provided an update, documenting the albums in live recordings of concerts played between 2012 and 2016.

This constant process of musically revising and sonically upgrading their "music data,"[15] which began in the early 1990s and continues to date, has made the Kraftwerk oeuvre a work in progress, and contrasts sharply with the earlier period from 1974 to 1981, in which the main body of their "catalogue" consisted of the release of five groundbreaking albums within the short time frame of just seven years. Arguably, while it was the short release time that actually made them internationally important, the very process of constant revision and live performance of the music, which now stretches well over three decades, made sure that Kraftwerk would not disappear from the music scene.

In this combination, Kraftwerk exerted a major influence on the development of electronic (dance) music, first by influencing British synth-pop of the 1980s, then by inspiring the producers at the forefront of techno and house music in the United States. The revolutionary music that developed in the United States then filtered back to Europe, thus closing the transnational loop of mutual influences. And while it is impossible to ascertain the exact degree of influence that Kraftwerk's sound had on electronic pop music, in a journalistic context their influence on the course of pop music was often compared to that of The Beatles. It seems more advisable though to follow Neil Straus, who phrased the issue as follows: "What the Beatles are to rock music, Kraftwerk is to electronic dance music."[16]

Ethnic Sounds from the Rhein-Ruhr Region—*Industrielle Volksmusik*

In line with their *Krautrock* peers, Kraftwerk's music very much originated from the desire to define a new national identify for themselves as young Germans in the aftermath of the fascist catastrophe and the Holocaust. Though identification with Anglo-American popular culture offered a viable alternative to the "tainted" cultural tradition as represented by the band's parental generation, members of their own generation, like Ralf Hütter and Florian Schneider, were not fully satisfied by this situation: "There was really no German culture after the war. Everyone was rebuilding their homes and getting their little Volkswagens. In the clubs when we first started playing, you never heard a German record, you switched on the radio and all you heard was Anglo-American music, you went to the cinema and all the films were Italian and French. That's okay but we needed our own cultural identity."[17]

Unlike bands such as their Cologne-based peers Can, Kraftwerk eschewed the world music approach taken by many bands, as well as the otherworldly "kosmische Musik" (cosmic music) escape route favored by their Berlin-based peers and the synthesizer pioneers Tangerine Dream— both of which arguably ducked the issue of exploring German identity through pop music. They worked instead with a notion of "Heimatklänge" ("Sounds From Home," the title of a track on their 1973 album *Ralf & Florian*), an approach to sound rooted in the sonic culture of their immediate *Heimat* (homeland)—that is to say, the heavily industrialized

Rhineland and the elegant city of Düsseldorf, where they had founded their Kling Klang studio in the seedy area around the main station.

While it took three successive albums, released from 1970 to 1973, to develop their musical style and define their artistic identity as an emerging *Gesamtkunstwerk* in the area of pop music, their fourth album, *Autobahn*, indeed proved to be a watershed moment for German music. The title track, occupying the entire A-side and running just short of 23 minutes, was the first fully formed example of their musical concept: "Our music is electronic, but we like to think of it as ethnic music from the German industrial area—*industrielle Volksmusik*. On our end, it has to do with a fascination with what we see all around us, trying to incorporate the industrial environment into our music."[18] It is difficult, if not impossible, to render the term *industrielle Volksmusik* into adequate English. David Bowie did a fairly good job by transposing it as "folk music of the factories."[19] Literal translations of the term yield confusing results due to false semantic links to the musical genres "industrial" and "folk," respectively. In fact, the notion of *industrielle Volksmusik* needs to be translated contextually and understood as an ambitious term that was revolutionary at the time yet has become commonplace today: electronic pop music.

Autobahn was released in November 1974 and was often mistaken for the first fully electronically produced album in pop history: in fact, Florian Schneider played flute and Eberhard Kranemann contributed guitar on the title track. Nevertheless, the album proved to be a turning point in the history of German pop music and can certainly be thought of as inaugurating the era of electronic pop music. In the mid-1970s the extensive *Autobahn* network that covered West Germany, and the state of Nordrhein-Westfalen (North Rhine Westphalia, NRW) in particular, represented something of an ambivalent national symbol, as it signified the infrastructural achievements of both the Nazi era and the so-called economic miracle of the postwar years. In addition, in economic terms, car manufacturing provided the backbone of the postwar economy, while automobile engineering, paradigmatically conveyed in the marketing slogan *Vorsprung durch Technik* (progress through technology), was considered a hallmark of German industry.

The cover painting by Emil Schult, which featured an uncannily empty motorway with only a black Mercedes Benz driving towards the onlooker while a white Volkswagen Beetle could be seen driving away from view, can be read as an allegory for the simultaneity of (a dark Nazi) past and (an optimistic, non-nationalist) future in a difficult present, which is characterized by potential tensions—the empty motorway alludes to the *Fahrverbote* (ban on driving) issued in the wake of the oil crisis of the early 1970s. Therefore it has been argued that in a complex way, *Autobahn* "reflects upon the state of German cultural, artistic, and musical identity" and "explicitly addressed aspects of German identity loaded with references to the Nazi era and beyond."[20]

The monotonous lyrics "Wir fahr'n fahr'n fahr'n auf der Autobahn" (We drive, drive, drive on the motorway), also by Schult, imitated the monotonous rhythm of the long track, which in turn emulated the monotonous experience of a car journey on the motorway. It can be further argued that such monotony mirrored the repetitious nature of work at a car assembly line, or indeed the very principle of the industrial production process. Against this background, it is illuminating to consider the following statement by Ralf Hütter on the Kraftwerk concept of *industrielle Volksmusik*: "It has always interested us to make industrial music. Assembly line music. Production processes, which are all around us in the industrial world."[21]

This definition expediently links up Kraftwerk's "ethnic music" from Düsseldorf with that of the musical tradition of Detroit—another city characterized by heavy industrialization, which had forged its own musical styles from Motown to the electronic dance music "techno" as artistic derivations of technological processes. Kraftwerk made a direct lyrical reference to Detroit on its *Expo2000* EP from 1999: "Detroit / Germany / We're so electro."[22] In 2000, the productive connection between *industrielle Volksmusik* from the NRW and the pioneering techno scene in Detroit was cemented by the release of a follow-on EP called *Expo Remix*, which contained remixes by Underground Resistance artists. The fact that this EP is the only official release containing remixes in the tightly curated, sparse Kraftwerk catalogue signals the importance they assign to the kinship with African American techno producers. To be clear, however, not all Detroit techno artists feel a great debt to Kraftwerk, and the birth of the techno style can certainly not be attributed in a monocausal way to the Kraftwerk influence. The release of the *Expo Remix* EP should rather be understood as an artistic acknowledgement between the two cities of Detroit and Düsseldorf.

The single largest factor driving Kraftwerk's influence on British and American musicians (though not limited to the anglophone world, as Kraftwerk also had a considerable impact on Japanese pop music) was the abandonment of the traditional instrumentation of rock bands. The band's total embrace of electronic instruments not only mirrored the industrialized economy of West Germany but also became a key thematic and aesthetic template for their recorded music and live on-stage performances. As early as 1975, at the concerts played during a triumphant first tour of the United States, the band was announced, in German, as "Kraftwerk—Die Mensch-Maschine" (Kraftwerk—the Man Machine)

The artistic notion of the "man machine" hence conceptually underpinned Kraftwerk's run of groundbreaking albums in the second half of the 1970s, even before the release of the *Mensch-Maschine* album in 1978.

Indeed, as studio technology became more advanced and more accessible during the late 1970s, Kraftwerk exploited these developments to assure that the sound of their machine music stayed ahead of any competition. Noteworthy in the development of electronic music was in particular the pioneering research that Florian Schneider undertook in the area of speech synthesis and its integration into the format of the pop song.

In interview statements, Hütter developed an unsystematic theory of the "man-machine" concept that underpinned Kraftwerk's musical production. Hütter explained in 1978: "The machines are part of us and we are part of the machines . . . They play with us and we play with them. We are brothers. They are not our slaves. We work together, helping each other to create."[23] Their "android doo-wop," according to Simon Reynolds, was also "a conscious, deliberately constructed aesthetic offence to traditional rock values . . . where a sense of unbuttoned maleness, of hair and heart and emotive authenticity was paramount."[24] Instead of the live spectacle of male rock-star bodies performing on stage, then, Kraftwerk members stood still behind their consoles and refused to interact with the audience by way of eye contact or announcements. Even more so, the *Mensch-Maschine* album inaugurated the use of lookalike dummies acting as "robot" doppelgängers of the musicians, both on stage during the performance of the key tune "Die Roboter" (The Robots) and for promotional purposes.

It is this emancipative potential of the musical "man-machine" concept and the robot iconography that enabled the surprising transnational "Atlanticultural" axis between Düsseldorf and Detroit, which is encapsulated in the techno track "Afrogermanic" by an African American producer called Chaos, released on the Underground Resistance label in 1998. But before we can progress to this stage of development in the 1990s, we need to examine how the Kraftwerk sound first greatly influenced bands in the United Kingdom.

Kraftwerk's Invasion of Britain

The transnational *Wirkungsgeschichte* (reception history) of the Düsseldorf electronic sound first began in the United Kingdom, stimulating the rise of British synth-pop in the late 1970s. The band's acceptance and popularity in the United Kingdom was certainly enhanced by the fact that after *Autobahn* they provided English versions of their lyrics, while some songs on *Radio-Aktivität* featured bilingual lyrics—even though they do not necessarily constitute literal or complete translations and sometimes offer variations. The key albums from *Trans Europa Express* (Trans-Europe Express, 1977) to *Computerwelt* (Computerworld, 1981) were issued in parallel German- and English-language versions. Several singles also appeared in idioms other than German and English—for example, "Dentaku" (1981), the Japanese version of "Taschenrechner" (Pocket Calculator), or "Les Mannequins" (1977), as the French version of "Schaufensterpuppen" (Showroom Dummies). *Electric Cafe* (1986), renamed *Techno Pop* in 2009, featured a mix of German, English, and Spanish, while *Tour de France* (2003) is near exclusively sung in French.

Kraftwerk's utopian vision of "Europa Endlos" (Europe Endless), the German opening track of *Trans Europa Express*, was matched by the development of increasingly using other European languages on later albums. In his reflective piece on the Kraftwerk UK tour of 2017, "Europe, Endless?: On Watching Kraftwerk Live, a Year after Brexit," Luke Turner asks polemically if Britons no longer deserve to partake in the transnational spirit of European culture: "An idealized sense of the European is distilled in every vibration of every note and tonight that feels like another world. The culture they came from has its flaws but seems to progress, evolve, recover all those words of human and holistic positivity. Meanwhile, Britain scrabbles around in our sandpit, the castles of our national certainty crumbling, paper flags soggy in the summer rain."[25]

Interestingly, Kraftwerk initially faced a cautious, if not hostile, reception in the United Kingdom. The infamous "Kraftwerkfeature" interview by Lester Bangs, which appeared in the music magazine *Creem* in September 1975, was emblazoned with an illustration showing a large Nazi-style eagle holding a big swastika in his claws, making the piece look like a Nazi propaganda publication from the 1930s. In the United Kingdom, it was reprinted by *New Musical Express* on September 6, 1975. *New Musical Express* chose "Kraftwerk—the Final Solution for the Music Problem?" as the title; the accompanying illustration showed a band photo inserted into an image of the *Reichsparteitagsgelände* (Party Rally Grounds) in Nuremberg, insinuating once more that Kraftwerk members were bona fide Nazis. Karl Bartos asks in his autobiography: "War das also der britische Humor? Ob das englische Publikum die Botschaft des *NME* verstanden hatte oder nicht—es blieb zu Hause. Wir spielten vor leeren Sälen in Newcastle, Hampstead, Bournemouth, Bath, Cardiff, Birmingham und schließlich am 11. September in Liverpool."[26] (Was this then the famed British humor? Whether or not the English readership had understood the message of the *NME*—they stayed at home. We played to empty venues in Newcastle, Hampstead, Bournemouth, Bath, Cardiff, Birmingham, and, finally on September 11, Liverpool). Present at the latter concert was the teenage Andy McCluskey, who would be so inspired that he formed Orchestral Manoeuvres in The Dark (OMD) with Paul Humphreys. They paid homage to their musical mentors by calling their 1980 album *Organisation*, the name of the band Hütter and Schneider were in before they founded Kraftwerk. OMD's album *Sugar Tax* (1991) contained a cover version of "Neonlicht" (Neon Lights), while their

1980 hit single "Electricity" imitated Kraftwerk's track "Radioaktivität" (Radioactivity) in sound and lyrical content.

Alongside OMD, bands like Depeche Mode, Ultravox, Soft Cell, and the Human League adapted in various ways the synthetic sound aesthetics of Kraftwerk. For example, the furious drumming patterns on Depeche Mode's "Master and Servant" from their 1984 album *Some Great Reward* bear an evident proximity to "Metall auf Metall" (Metal on Metal) by Kraftwerk, while the video shows black-and-white newsreel footage from the Bonn *Bundestag* (federal parliament) featuring leading German politicians Willy Brandt, Franz Josef Strauss, Rainer Barzel, and Walter Scheel. Another obvious case in point is Gary Numan, whose hits "Cars" and "Are 'Friends' Electric?" betray an obvious debt to Kraftwerk's aesthetics. Like other synthesizer musicians Numan adopted an artificial, androgynous look with uniforms and makeup, which borrowed from Kraftwerk's self-image on *Die Mensch-Maschine*.

Through the Covent Garden Blitz Club and its resident DJ Rusty Egan, the Kraftwerk sound also impacted the United Kingdom's New Romantic movement, inspiring the musical duo Visage, whose self-titled debut album from 1980 contained the international hit "Fade to Grey."[27] Another important conduit for Kraftwerk's influence in the United Kingdom in the 1980s was the Manchester music scene based around the Factory Records label. The hugely influential graphic designer Peter Saville stated: "I am very influenced by Kraftwerk: they shaped my understanding of the possibilities of contemporary music, and that shapes my understanding of the visual language that can be associated with it. . . . The culture of Factory is highly informed by Kraftwerk: and it's Factory that pretty much defines Manchester culturally in the late 20th century."[28] David Buckley describes New Order's "Blue Monday" (1983) as "perhaps the most Kraftwerkian single of all time."[29] However, Kraftwerk's influence on New Order stretches back to much earlier in the band's history, to a time when they were known as Joy Division. That influence, though, was less musical and more to do with visual aesthetics. In postindustrial Manchester, Kraftwerk represented a sort of sleek European modernity that Joy Division copied by dressing more informally (wearing narrow ties), and adopting a distanced attitude towards the media.[30]

The industrial band Cabaret Voltaire from Sheffield, to name one last example, sounded nothing like the more popular UK synth-pop bands but were aptly described by Ralf Hütter as "Brüder der industriellen Volksmusik" (brothers in electronic pop music) owing to the experimental nature of their Dada-influenced avant-garde music, coupled with video-tape loops.[31] The original trio of Stephen Mallinder, Richard H. Kirk, and Chris Watson were raised in the bleak, postindustrial environment of southern Yorkshire. Unlike Kraftwerk, who artistically refined the notion of the industrial noises produced by factories and machines into a "clean" sound, Cabaret Voltaire sought to emulate them in their noisy, rough, and "dirty" sounding music. They chose to work from their own studio, dubbed Western Works, in a former derelict industrial building, paralleling Kraftwerk's establishment of the Kling Klang studio.

What gave the Cabaret Voltaire project its special profile in the formative exploratory years between 1973 and 1978, as well as during their acclaimed phase between 1978 and 1982 on the Rough Trade label, was their strongly experimental interest in sound creation and processing, which matched Kraftwerk's ambitions. Cabaret Voltaire evidenced a strong interest in the radical politics of the German left, notably the Red Army faction, or Baader-Meinhof group. Around 1977, they recorded the track "Baader Meinhof," a chilling collage that combined distorted samples from news speakers in German with vocals in English, interspersed with piecing sounds. The radical musical ethos of Cabaret Voltaire was thus connected to the political extremism in Germany, infusing the British music scene with outside influences that accompanied the political tensions during the punk revolution—though this was an artistic statement rather than a call to political violence. From 1982, Cabaret Voltaire chose to take a more commercial, dance-oriented route with their releases on the Virgin label. The British DJ and producer Andrew Weatherall describes their formative influence on the UK dance scene by placing them in a transnational trio of acts: "Alongside Kraftwerk and Donna Summer, Cabaret Voltaire taught me the joys of machine funk."[32]

David Bowie and Kraftwerk

Another significant conduit between German and British pop music was David Bowie—and *Kraftwerk* was the key to that link. Bowie told *Playboy* magazine in 1976: "My favorite group is a German band called Kraftwerk—it plays noise music to 'increase productivity.' I like the idea, if you have to play music."[33] Kraftwerk, in an exceptional gesture, namechecked him (and Iggy Pop) on the lyrics to "Trans Europa Express": "Wir laufen ein in Düsseldorf City / und treffen Iggy Pop und David Bowie" (We arrive at Düsseldorf city station / and meet Iggy Pop and David Bowie).[34] Attracted to the music by Düsseldorf bands like *Neu!* and *Kraftwerk*, Bowie had moved from Los Angeles to West Berlin in August 1976, where he stayed until February 1978. Apart from these musical influences, he was strongly attracted by the early twentieth-century avant-garde art, notably Expressionist painting and cinema, and the decadent culture of the Weimar republic, as imaged in the film *Cabaret* (1966), based on the novel *Goodbye to Berlin* (1939) by Christopher Isherwood.[35]

The albums of his so-called Berlin trilogy were recorded largely, though not exclusively, in the legendary Hansa Studios located near the

Berlin Wall. As Adelt writes, Bowie's Berlin trilogy, especially *Low* (1977) and *"Heroes"* (1978), radically broke with the musical conventions of anglophone rock music "in similar ways krautrock had done."[36] The Kraftwerk model was central for his approach: "Like Kraftwerk, Bowie abandoned blues scales and harmonic structures in favour of more monotone minimalism and electronic instrumentation and espoused a distinctly European sensibility as well as a conceptualization of a self-referential *Gesamtkunstwerk* that included music, clothes, album covers, concerts, and interviews."[37]

Though bands like Faust, Harmonia, and Cluster certainly left a musical imprint on the new sound that Bowie was developing in cooperation with Brian Eno, it was Kraftwerk's conceptual ideas that he adopted for his own means. For instance, their notion of music as a man-machine product appealed to Bowie, who had previously presented himself as an alien on stage and on film. Speaking on his album *Station to Station*, he stated: "I think the biggest influence on that album was the work of Kraftwerk and the new German sound. I tried to apply some of the randomness and I utilized a lot of that feeling for especially the title track."[38] Rather than directly imitating the sound of Kraftwerk, Bowie thus took from Kraftwerk an artistic tool set for musical production. And yet—just as with Michael Jackson—Hütter and Schneider turned him down when it came to collaborations, in order to preserve the integrity of the Kraftwerk project. While Kraftwerk name-checked him on the title song of *Trans-Europe Express*, Bowie had "one complete side of *Radio-Activity* played over the PA at full volume as a kind of support act, before taking the stage"[39] during his *Isolar* tour in support of *Station to Station* in 1976. The tour of sixty-four performances helped to popularize Kraftwerk to a large international audience that may not have been familiar with them before.

Another, albeit more indirect, way of establishing a transnational dialogue with Bowie was the song "Spiegelsaal" (Hall of Mirrors) on *Trans Europa Express*. It tells the story of a young man in a hall of mirrors who, confronted with his own reflection, experiences an identity crisis. This lyrical scenario is enriched with various cultural allusions (from Oscar Wilde's antihero Dorian Gray to the myths of Narcissus and Echo). The reference to "sogar die größten Stars" (even the greatest stars), repeated fourteen times, strongly suggests, however, that David Bowie is the real addressee of this song, which states about the protagonist: "Er schuf die Person die er sein wollte / und wechselte in eine neue Persönlichkeit" (He made up the person he wanted to be / and changed into a new personality).

These words represent an evident allusion to Bowie's various role changes at the time—from the playful *Hunky Dory* era, to Ziggy Stardust, and later the Thin White Duke persona. In view of the fact that Bowie had left his Californian exile for Germany to escape the drug problems that his stardom had created, Kraftwerk saw in him an example of the narcissistic trials and tribulations that came with fame as a major pop star: "Sogar die größten Stars / verändern sich im Spiegelglas. / Der Künstler lebt im Spiegel / mit dem Echo seines Selbst" (Even the greatest stars / change themselves in the looking glass. / The artist is living in the mirror / with the echoes of himself). The song "Spiegelsaal" hence represents an example of an indirect transnational dialogue between two major musical acts that were evidently mutually influential yet maintained a personal and artistic distance from each other.

Sonic Repercussions across the Atlantic

A witness to testify to the ready reception of Kraftwerk's "indigenous" electronic sound in the context of an entirely different local, social, and cultural context can be found in Run DMC's Jam Master Jay. He stated: "These guys proved to me you don't have to be where I'm from to get the music. That beat came from Germany all the way to the 'hoods of New York City."[40] Kraftwerk's reception history in the United States begins in 1982 with the "Planet Rock" EP by Afrika Bambaataa & The Soulsonic Force. It fused the *industrielle Volksmusik* from Düsseldorf with the emerging black hip-hop and electro music cultures in New York. Sampling the brutal drum pattern of "Nummern" (Numbers) and the distinctive melody of "Trans Europa Express," the white producer Arthur Baker created, according to Robert Fink, a funky futurist fantasy in which "European art music is cast, consciously or not, in the role of an ancient, alien power source."[41]

The Detroit techno producer Carl Craig recalls the moment he first heard "Taschenrechner" on the radio: "I was twelve years old when I heard Kraftwerk for the first time. . . . It was mind-warping! I found out what it was and went down to the record store to buy the single. It had a clear sleeve with the band's faces on it and some Japanese type. I thought they were from Japan and dreamed about what they might be like."[42] The reception of Kraftwerk among the African American community hence greatly differed from the group's reception in the United Kingdom (and Europe), as it was devoid of any Nazi clichés or German stereotypes. Rather, it constituted a sort of sonic cannibalism of a sound that possessed no evident reference points.

What has been largely overlooked hitherto is the pivotal role that *Mensch-Maschine* played in the transnational and transcultural hybridization processes that contributed to the development of techno. The cultural interface that allowed music developed in the prosperous NRW to find considerable appeal in deprived inner-city areas in New York and Detroit was the transhuman notion governing Kraftwerk's man-machine aesthetics. Christoph Schaub observes: "For the politics involved in early Detroit techno, musical aesthetics and narratives that allowed an imagination of identity formation beyond race and ethnicity were crucial."[43] From the perspective of socially and culturally underprivileged African Americans, then, to portray oneself as a robot, as Kraftwerk did on the *Mensch-Maschine* cover, was understood as a political move that consciously rejected a definition of identity along the (arbitrary) lines of nationality and skin color.

The musical man-machine as embodied by Kraftwerk's visual image but equally by their minimalist electronic sound was perceived as transcending even the transnational; the robot iconography was perceived as a universal representative of a future race beyond the confines of social division and racial discrimination. In the very same way that Kraftwerk sought to reflect a specifically German identity (against the global dominance of Anglo-American rock music) through its *industrielle Volksmusik*, the African American communities in the United States in a parallel move developed their own styles of music in opposition to the rock mainstream of white America, and the concurrence and structural similarity of these two developments made for a perhaps unexpected cultural interface.

Once Hütter and Schneider had sensed the surprising interest in their music in the context of the disco explosion, they aimed to make further inroads into this market. To this end, the African American mixing engineer Leanard Jackson from Detroit was asked to help with the production of *Mensch-Maschine*. According to Bussy, he "had arrived from America fully expecting to be assisting with an album made by four black guys from Düsseldorf. Having listened to their music he was convinced that the basic rhythm tracks had to have been produced by black musicians."[44]

Unsurprisingly, therefore, the minimalist, rhythmically orientated electronic music pioneered by Kraftwerk fell on particularly fertile musical soil with African American producers in the Michigan industrial belt area. The emergence of "the new sound of Detroit" occurred in the early 1980s, coincidentally around the same time when Kraftwerk's run of great albums came to a halt with *Computerwelt* in 1981.[45] Cybotron's seminal "Clear" from 1983, for instance, did not simply sound as if it had emerged straight from the Kling Klang studio, though the band name owed a debt to Kraftwerk's robot stylings. Juan Atkins adapted the sound from Düsseldorf without hesitation, "sometimes clearly referencing Kraftwerk tunes such as 'Computer World' (on the track 'Industrial Lies')."[46] Atkins would later continue with the Model 500 project and became largely recognized as one of the forward thinkers of the Detroit techno scene.

The musical collective Underground Resistance (UR), who belong to the so-called second wave of Detroit techno, similarly found inspiration in Kraftwerk's artistic strategy of near-refusal to communicate with the outside world, forcing listeners and journalists to focus on the music itself.[47]

"UR" refers to both an independent record label and the pseudonym of a group composed of Mike Banks and Jeff Mills founded at the end of the 1980s. In the same vein that Public Enemy politicized rap, Banks and Mills politically radicalized techno music. UR's "creed," according to its manifesto, is centered on the need to liberate oneself from the cultural and social boundaries imposed on "the inhabitants of Earth" by "the programmers" (in other words, the record industry, mass media, and politicians, etc.). "By using the untapped energy potential of sound, we are going to destroy this wall [between races] much the same as certain frequencies shatter glass. Techno is a music based in experimentation; it is music for the future of the human race."[48]

The manifesto bears evident links to Kraftwerk's own futurist concerns and the techno optimism that largely, though surely not exclusively, characterizes their work. Kraftwerk's futurist orientation proved instrumental in allowing their music to be recodified in an entirely different cultural and social context in the United States because of the phenomenon of "Afro-futurism." Though this term was coined only in 1993 by the cultural critic Mark Dery, it refers to a literary and cultural aesthetic rooted in the 1960s. In terms of music, reference points cited often mention the explicitly extraterrestrial myths of Sun Ra and his Arkestra, as well as George Clinton with Parliament-Funkadelic.

Dery first defined Afro-futurism as: "Speculative fiction that treats African themes and addresses African American concerns in the context of twentieth-century techno culture—and more generally, African American signification that appropriates images of technology and a prosthetically enhanced future."[49] Critics have attributed the wider fascination with science fiction among the Afro-American community to the fact that African Americans had their heritage erased as a consequence of the crimes of the slave trade. As their cultural past is therefore obscured and tainted with the collective trauma of their ancestors' forceful removal from their homelands, they are as a result forced to look forward towards a better future.

Structurally, this cultural mechanism parallels the situation in which the generation of Germans to which Hütter and Schneider belonged found itself in: in the same way that the Germano-futurism of Kraftwerk offered a cultural perspective to deal with the moral dilemma of belonging to the perpetrator's side, Afro-futurism addressed the concerns of the descendants of the victims of the slave trade. A perfect example for a techno music-based take on Afro-futurism is the production duo Drexciya. Drexciya was active during the 1990s and operated with extreme levels of secrecy regarding the identity of its members (as was later revealed to be James Stinson, who died in 2002, and Gerald Donald). Drexciya's musical output constitutes a politically charged *Gesamtkunstwerk* based on the Afro-futurist legend of a hidden land called "Drexciya" on the seabed of the Atlantic.

According to Drexciya myth, the subaquatic civilization was founded by the children of African women who drowned in the Atlantic during the Middle Passage. (It was a common practice during the slave trade to throw pregnant women overboard, as they could not be sold.) Their babies, however, continued to breathe underwater: first through amniotic fluid, then through lungs better suited to their aquatic world. Later grown into a marine warrior race called Drexciyans, the offspring of the victims wanted to take revenge for what was done to them. The record releases by Drexciya pretended to represent messages from these underwater creatures, encoded in the universal language of techno music. Track titles referred to elements of the Drexciyan mythology, while the cover artwork of their 1999 album *Neptune's Lair* depicts the metropolis of the subaquatic realm.

After the death of Stinson, Gerald Donald released music under various aliases and project names. Liberated from the conceptual restraints of the Drexciya project, Kraftwerk's considerable influence on the producer openly came to the fore. His most well-known project is the duo Dopplereffekt, founded in 1995, which features numerous German references in an unmistakable nod to Kraftwerk. For instance, *Gesamtkunstwerk* was chosen for the title of their 1999 compilation of tracks that betray such evident allusions to the Kraftwerk sound that they occasionally come across as a persiflage of the original.

Donald, who now lives in a Bavarian village near Lake Starnberg, has even been accused of covertly promoting (or trivializing) fascist ideology because of his use of the pseudonym Heinrich Müller, which is suspected to refer to the infamous Nazi *Schreibtischtäter* (desk-based perpetrator) of the same name who ran the Gestapo from October 1939. Heinrich Müller is, of course, such a common name in Germany that a certain link cannot be established. As such, the problematic cultural construction of a perceived link between Nazism (or fascist traits) and electronic music, underwritten by a certain definition of "Germanness," finds an expression that mirrors the attribution of Nazi traits that Kraftwerk was subject to in its early anglophone reception.

Conclusion

The patterns of musical transmission that were unknowingly started when Kraftwerk began to work on an electronic form of pop music led to one of the most remarkable transnational processes of cultural hybridization and exchange in the history of pop music. In the context of British pop of the 1980s, Kraftwerk served as trailblazers, as models and blueprints for synth-pop's top forty hits. Synth-pop's performance of "Germanness" was perceived as an ambivalent gesture that mixed the deeply engrained xenophobic clichés about Germany with an admiration for the musical achievements of Kraftwerk's key albums, from *Autobahn* from 1974 to the 1986 album *Electric Cafe*. In musical terms, the synth-pop bands from the United Kingdom successfully managed to develop further the sonic characteristics of Kraftwerk's electronic pop songs, infusing them, as it were, with British pop sensibilities. The Germanness of Kraftwerk was mapped against the existing cultural framework that governed the perception of Germany—that is, *Autobahn* was referenced to the Nazi past and the achievements of German car engineering. The Germanness that Kraftwerk embodied may have contradicted certain stereotypes and expectations, but it did not challenge any self-perception of Britishness.

The situation in the United States was markedly different. The *Gesamtkunstwerk* of Kraftwerk's "techno pop,"[50] with its man-machine aesthetics and retro-futurist style, connected differently with an urban minority group. Kraftwerk members were not so much Germans as exotic "others," the complete antithesis to the white rock'n'roll aesthetics that governed US mainstream music. In their search for an entirely different musical language, black producers from Detroit saw Kraftwerk as a source of inspiration and a resource to develop their own identity- and politics-charged aesthetics. Explaining this particular and lasting form of transnational reach, Mike Banks described the fascination exerted by Kraftwerk on so many Detroit techno artists not in terms of their national-cultural origins but in terms of their transhuman universality: "In the early days, I never heard anybody say anything about their race. They weren't Germans, they weren't white, in fact we thought they were robots."[51]

Notes

Uncredited translations are my own.

[1] David Stubbs, "Introduction," in *Krautrock: Cosmic Rock and Its Legacy*, ed. Nikolaos Kotsopoulos (London: Black Dog, 2009), 4.

[2] Quoted in Mark Pilkington, "Harmonia," in Kotsopoulos, *Krautrock*, 103.

[3] See Ulrich Adelt, *Krautrock: German Music in the Seventies* (Ann Arbor: University of Michigan Press, 2016), 3. Adelt provides some pointers to the stylistic diversity of *Krautrock*, citing the electronic music of Klaus Schulze and the jazz rock of Kraan, the political songs of Floh de Cologne, the folk rock of Witthäuser & Westrupp, as well as bands that are harder to classify, such as Faust, Cluster, or Popol Vuh.

[4] Ulrich Adelt, "Machines with a Heart: German Identity in the Music of Can and Kraftwerk," *Popular Music and Society* 35, no. 3 (2012): 359–74 (360).

[5] Quoted in Stephen Dalton, "Album by Album: Kraftwerk," *Uncut* (2009): 68.

[6] Representative of early examples of British research outside German Studies are Stephen Biddle, "Vox Electronica: Nostalgia, Irony and Cyborgian Vocalities in Kraftwerk's *Radioaktivität* and *Autobahn*," *Twentieth Century Music* 1, no. 1 (2004): 81–100; and Alex Seago, "The 'Kraftwerk-Effekt': Transatlantic

Circulation, Global Networks and Contemporary Pop Music," *Atlantic Studies* 1, no. 1 (2004): 85–106.

[7] In addition to a *Krautrock*/Kraftwerk focus, there was also increasingly thriving work undertaken in rap and techno music, with questions of identity formation through pop music as a frequent feature in relevant research.

[8] Alexander Simmeth, *Krautrock Transnational: Die Neuerfindung der Popmusik in der BRD, 1968–1978* (Berlin: Transcript Verlag, 2006), 29.

[9] Adelt, *Krautrock*, 1.

[10] Simmeth, *Krautrock Transnational*, 4.

[11] Josh Kun, *Audiotopias: Music, Race and America* (Berkeley: University of California Press, 2005), 20.

[12] Sean Albiez and Kyrre Tromm Lindvig, "Autobahn and Heimatklänge: Soundtracking the FRG," in *Kraftwerk: Music Non-Stop*, ed. Sean Albiez and David Pattie (New York: Continuum, 2011), 19.

[13] This term is most strongly associated with Rammstein and its crossover style of metal, industrial, and electronica backed up by carnivalesque stage show. "The 'hardness' of Neue Deutsche Härte stems from musical tropes borrowed from thrash metal and groove metal, namely tightly-orchestrated, minor-mode guitar riffs synchronized with steady, four-on-the-floor, unsyncopated drumming (often using a double-bass drum to emphasize the rhythm), with the guitars and bass playing below their normal ranges." In Alexander Carpenter, "Einstürzende Neubauten to Rammstein: Mapping the Industrial Continuum in German Pop Music," in *German Pop Music: A Companion*, ed. Uwe Schütte (Berlin: de Gruyter, 2017), 163.

[14] The year 2013 saw the publication of the first dedicated volume on Rammstein by US scholars. See John Littlejohn and Michael Putnam, *Rammstein on Fire: New Perspectives on the Music and Performances* (Jefferson, NC: McFarland & Company, 2013). The book deals with both the band's music and their stage practice.

[15] The term to be found on the artwork of their albums when referring to their music.

[16] Neil Straus, "Call Them the Beatles of Electronic Dance Music," *New York Times*, June 15, 1997.

[17] Quoted in Tim Barr, *Kraftwerk: From Dusseldorf to the Future (with Love)* (London: Ebury, 1999), 64.

[18] Mark Dery, "Interview with Ralf Hütter," *Keyboard Magazine* 10 (1991).

[19] Quoted in David Buckley, *Kraftwerk Publikation: A Biography* (London, Omnibus, 2012), 89.

[20] Melanie Schiller, "'Fun, Fun, Fun on the Autobahn': Kraftwerk Challenging Germanness," *Popular Music and Society* 37, no. 5 (2014): 618–37 (623).

[21] Willi Andresen, "Computer Liebe. Interview with Ralf Hütter," *Tip* 22 (1991): 202.

[22] In performance, Hütter sings "Detroit / Germany / We're so electric." It is of course conspicuous that the US city is not paired with its German counterpart

Düsseldorf, but the country as a whole. It appears that Kraftwerk wanted to circumvent naming Berlin as Germany's techno capital.

[23] "Interview with Ralf Hütter," *Future* 5 (1978): 24.

[24] Simon Reynolds, quoted in David Stubbs, *Future Days: Krautrock and the Building of Modern Germany* (London: Faber & Faber, 2014), 194.

[25] Luke Turner, "Europe, Endless?: On Watching Kraftwerk Live, a Year after Brexit," *The Quietus*, June 22, 2017, http://thequietus.com/articles/22676-kraftwerk-live-review-brexit (accessed November 29, 2019).

[26] Karl Bartos, *Der Klang der Maschine: Autobiografie* (Cologne: Bastei, 2017), 170.

[27] The New Romantics were a flamboyant music and fashion movement of the early 1980s that originated in London's Blitz night club. DJ Rusty Egan mixed British glam music by David Bowie, Marc Bolan, or Roxy Music with Kraftwerk tracks.

[28] Quoted in Buckley, *Kraftwerk Publikation*, 161.

[29] Buckley, *Kraftwerk Publikation*, 199.

[30] Buckley, *Kraftwerk Publikation*, 160.

[31] Booklet accompanying the *Conform to Deform '82/'90* compilation (Virgin, 2001).

[32] Booklet accompanying the *Conform to Deform '82/'90* compilation.

[33] Cameron Crowe, "David Bowie: An Outrageous Conversation with the Actor, Rock Singer and Sexual Switch-Hitter," *Playboy* 9 (September 1976).

[34] In the desire to eliminate any elements that make them sound dated, Kraftwerk no longer sings these lines. Interestingly, Bowie also paid tribute to Kraftwerk by naming one track on the *"Heroes"* album "V-2 Schneider," an allusion to Florian Schneider.

[35] See the excellent book by Tobias Rüther, *Helden: David Bowie und Berlin* (Berlin: Roger & Bernhard, 2008).

[36] Adelt, *Krautrock*, 129.

[37] Hugo Wilcken, *Low* (New York: Continuum, 2005), 35.

[38] Quoted in *David Bowie: Five Years*, dir. Francis Whately (BBC, 2013).

[39] Ralf Dörper, quoted in Rudi Esch, *Electri_City: The Düsseldorf School of Electronic Music* (London: Omnibus Press, 2016), 127.

[40] Barr, *Kraftwerk*, 172.

[41] Robert Fink, "The Story of ORCH5, or, the Classical Ghost in the Hip-Hop Machine," *Popular Music* 24, no. 3 (2005): 352.

[42] Quoted in Barr, *Kraftwerk*, 152.

[43] Christoph Schaub, "Beyond the Hood?: Detroit Techno, Underground Resistance, and African American Metropolitan Identity Politics," *Forum for Inter-American Research* 2, no. 2 (2008): 2–3.

[44] Pascal Bussy, *Kraftwerk: Man, Machine, and Music* (Middlesex, UK: SAF, 2001), 94.

[45] *Techno! The New Sound of Detroit* was the title of a compilation released in 1988 that is largely credited as providing the name of the new genre.

[46] Barr, *Kraftwerk*, 19.

[47] Underground Resistance infamously refuses to communicate with the media and does not have a press officer or public relations department; the only information available on its website is the group's manifesto.

[48] Underground Resistance, "Manifesto," http://www.undergroundresistance.com (accessed November 29, 2019).

[49] Mark Dery, ed., *Flame Wars: The Discourse of Cyberculture* (Durham, NC: Duke University Press, 1994), 180.

[50] This term refers to the working title of *Electric Cafe*; the original album title was restored for the digital reissue in 2009.

[51] Quoted in Mark Fisher, "Interview with Mike Banks," *Wire* 285 (2007).

Contributors

SAI BHATAWADEKAR is Associate Professor of Hindi-Urdu and Director of the Center for South Asian Studies at the University of Hawai'i, Manoa. She writes on Hegel's and Schopenhauer's interpretations of Hinduism, Buddhism, and Islam. Her current group project is on "Apophasis, or Negative Theology" in five major world religions. She has also worked on film adaptations of literature in German cinema and on Bollywood's global orientation. After teaching German for a few years, she created Hindi-Urdu language programs at The Ohio State University and the University of Hawai'i that feature performance-based learning, including Indian classical and folk dances and student documentary films.

TOBIAS BOES is Associate Professor of German Language and Literature at the University of Notre Dame. He is the author of *Formative Fictions: Nationalism, Cosmopolitanism, and the Bildungsroman* (2012), and *Thomas Mann's War: Literature, Politics, and the World Republic of Letters* (2019).

DIRK GÖTTSCHE is Professor of German at the University of Nottingham, Member of the Academia Europaea, and Honorary President of the International Raabe Society. His research and publications range from German literature of the long nineteenth century and Realism through to Austrian Modernism and its legacies in comparative and contemporary German literature. This includes modernist short prose; research on time, history, and memory in German literature; and German postcolonial and cross-cultural studies. He has published widely in German postcolonial studies, including his monograph *Remembering Africa: The Rediscovery of Colonialism in Contemporary German Literature* (Camden House, 2013), the co-edited volume *(Post-)Colonialism across Europe: Transcultural History and National Memory* (2014) and the co-edited *Handbuch Postkolonialismus und Literatur* (2017). He is currently the principle investigator of the Leverhulme International Research Network in Comparative Literature ("Landscapes of Realism: Rethinking Literary Realism(s) in Global Comparative Perspective") and is working on a monograph on German literature and the politics of memory with regard to the anti-Napoleonic wars.

JAMES HODKINSON is Reader in German at Warwick University. He is currently working on the monograph *Ambivalent Similarities: Islam in*

German-Speaking Culture of the Long Nineteenth Century and leading a public engagement project, funded by Warwick University, examining the value of historical German cultural sources on Islam in driving community projects, public debate, and educational policy in the United Kingdom today. He is the author of *Women and Writing in the Works of Novalis: Transformation beyond Measure?* (Camden House, 2007); and co-editor of *Deploying Orientalism in Culture and History: From Germany to Central and Eastern Europe* (Camden House, 2013) and *Encounters with Islam in German Literature and Culture*, ed. with Jeff Morrison (Camden House, 2009), as well as numerous journal articles and book chapters on German Romanticism, Orientalism and Islam, nineteenth-century literature, travel writing, fine art, and contemporary music.

CARLOTTA VON MALTZAN is Professor of German at Stellenbosch University in South Africa. She is editor of *Acta Germanica: German Studies in Africa*, and co-editor of *Jahrbuch für Internationale Germanistik*. She has published widely on exile and contemporary German literature, intercultural German studies, and postcolonial studies. Her current research focuses on Africa in the imaginary and writing Africa in German fiction.

FRAUKE MATTHES is Senior Lecturer in German at the University of Edinburgh. Her research focuses on contemporary German-language literature, particularly by authors of non-German origins; transcultural literature and culture; and masculinity studies. She is the author of *Writing and Muslim Identity: Representations of Islam in German and English Transcultural Literature, 1990–2006* (2011), and the coeditor, with Emily Jeremiah, of *Ethical Approaches in Contemporary German-Language Literature and Culture* (*Edinburgh German Yearbook* 7, 2013), and, with Lizzie Stewart, of *Emine Sevgi Özdamar at 70* (special issue of *Oxford German Studies*, 2016). Her current monograph project, which was funded by the Leverhulme Trust with an Early Career Fellowship, examines "new masculinities" in contemporary German literature.

BEN MORGAN is Fellow and Tutor in German at Worcester College, Associate Professor of German, and Co-Convenor of the Oxford Comparative Criticism and Translation Programme at the University of Oxford. He is the author of *On Becoming God: Late Medieval Mysticism and the Modern Western Self* (2013) and articles on modernist literature, film, and philosophy in the German-speaking world (Trakl, Kafka and Kierkegaard, Benjamin and Heidegger, Fritz Lang, Leni Riefenstahl, the Frankfurt School). He is also co-editor, with Carolin Duttlinger and Anthony Phelan, of *Walter Benjamins anthropologisches Denken* (2012), and with

Sowon Park and Ellen Spolsky, of a special issue of *Poetics Today* titled "Situated Cognition and the Study of Culture" (2017).

JOHN K. NOYES has been Professor of German at the University of Toronto since 2001, where he was Chair of the Department of Germanic Languages and Literatures from 2002 to 2007. Before that, he was Professor of German and Theory of Literature at the University of Cape Town. He has published on the cultural history of colonialism, postcolonial theory, and the history of sexuality. He is the author of *Colonial Space: Spatiality in the Discourse of German Southwest Africa, 1884–1915* (1992), *The Mastery of Submission: Inventions of Masochism* (1997), and *Herder: Aesthetics against Imperialism* (2015). He edited the volume *Herder's "Essay on Being": A Translation and Critical Approaches* (Camden House, 2018). Noyes's current research is on the legacy of the Enlightenment concept of "common humanity" in post-apartheid South Africa.

EMILY OLIVER is Senior Instructor in German at the University of Oxford. Her research focuses on Anglo-German cultural relations and media in the twentieth century. After earning a PhD at the University of Birmingham, she worked as a postdoctoral research associate at King's College London on the European Research Council project "Beyond Enemy Lines: Literature and Film in the British and American Zones of Occupied Germany." In 2016, she was awarded a Leverhulme Early Career Fellowship to pursue her research project "Broadcasting Nations: A History of the BBC German Service (1938–1999)" at the University of Warwick. Emily's work on the BBC German Service has been featured on BBC Radio 4, the BBC World Service, and in a TV documentary on BBC 4. Her first book, *Shakespeare and German Reunification: The Interface of Politics and Performance*, was published in 2017.

KATE RIGBY is Director of the Research Centre for Environmental Humanities at Bath Spa University and Adjunct Professor at Monash University (Melbourne). Her research lies at the intersection of environmental, literary, philosophical, historical, and religious studies, with a specialist interest in European Romanticism, ecopoetics, and ecocatastrophe. She is co-editor of the University of Virginia Press's series Under the Sign of Nature, and her books include *Topographies of the Sacred: The Poetics of Place in European Romanticism* (2004), *Ecocritical Theory: New European Approaches* (co-edited, 2011) and *Dancing with Disaster: Environmental Histories, Narratives, and Ethics for Perilous Times* (2015). A key researcher with the Humanities for the Environment Mellon Australia-Pacific Observatory, she was the inaugural President of the Association for the Study of Literature, Environment and Culture (Australia-New

Zealand), and the founding Director of the Australia-Pacific Forum on Religion and Ecology.

BENEDICT SCHOFIELD is Reader in German and Director of the Centre for Modern Literature and Culture at King's College London. He is currently working on the monograph *A Moral Compass*, which considers the depiction of Germany and Austria in contemporary American and Japanese fiction, and is the co-editor (with Rebecca Braun) of *Transnational German Studies*, the German volume in Liverpool University Press's Transnationalizing Modern Languages series. He is the author of *Private Lives and Collective Destinies: Class, Nation and Folk in the Works of Gustav Freytag* (2012), and co-edited (with Charlotte Woodford) *The German Bestseller in the Late Nineteenth Century* (Camden House, 2012) and *The Racehorse of Genius: Literary and Cultural Comparisons* (with Martin Liebscher and Godela Weiss-Sussex, 2009), as well as numerous journal articles and book chapters on nineteenth-century German culture, German-language theater and performance, German Shakespeare, and twentieth-century US-German relations.

UWE SCHÜTTE earned his PhD in German literature at the University of East Anglia, Norwich. Since 1999, he has worked at Aston University, Birmingham, where he is a Reader in German. He is the author of thirteen monographs and has edited six volumes. His latest publications include *Urzeit, Traumzeit, Endzeit—Versuch über Heiner Müller* (2012), *Unterwelten: Zu Leben und Werk von Gerhard Roth* (2013), *Interventionen: Literaturkritik als Widerspruch bei W. G. Sebald* (2015), *German Pop Music: A Companion* (2017), and *Mensch-Maschinen-Musik: Das Gesamtkunstwerk Kraftwerk* (2017).

CAROL TULLY is Professor of German at Bangor University. She earned her PhD at Queen Mary University of London (1996). Since then, she has established an international reputation as a scholar in the area of European cultural exchange in the nineteenth century with a primary focus on Germany and Spain. She has published a number of books, scholarly editions, translations, and journal articles. She was Head of the School of Modern Languages at Bangor from 2005 to 2011 and also Deputy Head of the College of Arts and Humanities. She took up the role of Pro-Vice Chancellor for Students in 2011. Professor Tully has been active in a number of subject associations, in particular as the Welsh representative on the University Council for Modern Languages, and she fulfills a number of roles for the AHRC.

Index

academia. *See* academy, the
academy, the, 7, 8, 9–11, 109, 110, 111, 126, 139, 155, 184, 189, 191–93, 194, 198, 199, 216, 220, 259
Ackermann, Rolf, works by: *Die weiße Jägerin*, 119
Acta Germanica, journal, 114, 144
actor-network theory, 192, 223, 225, 229, 232, 233
Adelbert von Chamisso Prize, 92, 102
Adelt, Ulrich, 257, 261, 271
Adler, Bruno, 241
Adorno, Theodor, 160, 161, 163
Advaita Vedanta, 181
aesthetics, 26, 46, 117, 127, 155, 160, 164–65, 183, 193, 228–30, 258, 269, 272–73, 276
African American culture, 193, 258, 266, 267, 272–75; in postwar West Germany, 126
African continent, 58, 110, 112–13, 114–15, 116, 117–22, 123–26, 135–36, 138–39, 139–45, 145–46, 148–50, 150–52, 196, 198, 200
African diaspora, 20, 110, 122–26
African migrants' writing, in German, 20, 110, 122–26
African National Congress (ANC), 138
Afrika Bambaataa & The Soulsonic Force, US band, 272
Afro-futurism, movement and concept of, 274
Afro-Germanic popular music, 193. *See also* African American culture
Agar, Michael, 222
Ahlers, Conrad, 245
Ahmed, Sara, 100–101

Alberto, Ibraimo, works by: *Ich wollte leben wie die Götter*, 124
Albiez, Sean, 260, 263
Ali, Mohammed, contemporary UK artist, 191, 215, 216
Ali, Mohammed, works by: *The Art of Empathy*, 213–15
alienation effect (Brecht), 179
allies, incl. allied forces of World War II, 59, 239–40, 242, 244, 249
Alphaville, German band, 262
Alternative für Deutschland, political party, 2
America, North: comparative literature as discipline in, 103; contemporary poetry of, 165; feminism and, 162; German studies as discipline in, 2, 136, 198; landscape of, 48; politics and history of, 2, 44; pop music of, 264; response to Germany and Germans, 66, 68, 70. *See also* African American culture
Andersch, Alfred, works by: *Weltreise auf deutsche Art*, 117
Anglo-German relations, 74–75, 82, 85, 86, 88–89, 221, 234–35, 248, 251
anthropocene, 163, 166
Apartheid, 123; German Studies in the era of, 136, 138–39, 140–42, 144, 145–49, 151
Applegate, Celia, 3–4
Apter, Emily, 23–24
Archenholz, Johann W., works by: *Litteratur- und Völkerkunde/Neue Litteratur und Völkerkunde*, 24
Arendt, Hannah, 117
Arengo-Jones, Alaric, 251
Aristotle, 49

Arnold, Matthew, 82
arts and humanities, as subject area, 1, 3, 10, 109, 111
Arts and Humanities Research Council (ARHC), 10
Arts Council England (ACE), 212
Asia-Pacific, region, 136, 170–71, 173, 184
Asmal, Kader, 146
Assmann, Aleida, 99
Athenaeum, The, 88
Atkins, Juan, 273
audience: for literary works, 87; for public engagement activities, 194–95, 199–201, 204, 205, 207, 210, 211–15, 216; for radio audiences (*see* listeners); response to art, 49; and the theatre, 179, 180, 220, 224–26, 228, 230–31
Auerbach, Erich, 23, 35, 35–37, 43
Aukongo, Stefanie-Lahya, works by: *Kalungas Kind*, 124
Austin, Sarah, 87
Australia: colonization and decolonization in, 157, 162, 166; emigres in, 158, 159; Environmental humanities in, 156, 160, 162–65; German Studies in, 136; research funding in, 10
Austria: country, 197; emigres from, 142, 240, 241, 244; environmentalism in, 155; relationship to colonialism and postcolonialism, 20, 109, 114, 117, 121, 135, 126–27; university disciplines in, 77
Austria-Hungarian Empire, 201, 121
avant-garde theater, 233
Ayim, May, 124

Baader-Meinhof group, 270
Bachmann, Ingeborg, works by: *Malina*, 177–78
Bala, Welsh town of and lake, 83, 88
Baker, Arthur, 272
Bangor, Welsh town of, 78
Bangs, Lester, 268
Banks, Mike, 274, 276
Barbican theater, 225
Barnett, David, 221, 228, 230
Bartos, Karl, 268
Barzel, Rainer, 269
BBC (British Broadcasting Corporation) German Service, 192–93, 239–52
Bechhaus-Gerst, Marianne, works by: *Treu bis in den Tod*, 126
Beck, Ulrich, 4, 6
Becker, Carl Heinrich, 199–200
Beebee, Thomas O., 7
Beer, Fritz, 250
Beetz, Dietmar, works by: *Flucht vom Waterberg*, 117
Beinssen-Hesse, Silke, 161
Bell, Rudolf Duala Manga, 123
belle lettres, 25
Benjamin, Walter, 36, 164
Bennewitz, Fritz, 180
Berlin, Isaiah, 62
Berlin, theatrical culture of, 192, 229, 231–34
Berliner Ensemble, German theater, 225
Berman, Russell, 4, 111
Bertuch, Friedrich J., editor: *Allgemeine Literatur Zeitung*, 24
Bhabha, Homi, 39, 109, 111–12
Bhatti, Anil, 197
Biendarra, Anke S., 6
Bildung, concept of, 27, 35, 52, 62, 66, 142
Bildungsreise, 137
Bildungsroman, 35, 117, 118
Biller, Maxim, 95
Bin Hamed, Muhammed, 120
Black German literature, 20, 110, 117, 122–26
Blaeulich, Max, works by: *Menschenfresser*, 121
Bollywood, 171, 173, 176, 177, 180
brahman, 181
Brandt, Willy, 245, 269
Brexit, 1, 219, 221, 234, 268
Bridgetower, George August Polgreen, 125

Brinitzer, Carl von, 241
Bodi, Leslie, 159
Bodrožić, Marica, 92
Boehmer, Elleke, 34–35, 37, 49
Boenisch, Peter, 229, 233
Bohnenkamp, Anne, 25
Borchmeyer, Dieter, 59, 63–64
Bower, Jaco, 151
Bowie, David, 258, 265, 270–72
Bowie, David, works by: *"Heroes,"* 271; *Low*, 271; *Station to Station*, 271
Braun, Rebecca, 92, 94, 223
Brecht, Bertolt, 179–80, 224
Britain: interfaith relations in, 200–201; nation-centered politics of, 2; projection of, 192, 239–40, 245–48, 250, 252
British Empire, 58, 139
British Isles. *See* Britain
British theater, 219–20, 230
broadcasting, 193, 239, 240–41, 242, 245–46, 250
Brook, Peter, 230
Brooks, Mel, 177
Buch, Hans Christoph, works by: *Sansibar Blues oder Wie ich Livingstone fand*, 120
Büchner, Georg, productions of: *Woyzeck* (dir. Joe Murphy, 2017), 225
Buckley, David, 260, 269
Buddhism, 181–82
Bülow, Frieda von, 119
Burton, Richard, 120

Cabaret Voltaire, 269–70
Caernarfon, 83–84
Caillé, René-Auguste, 122
Cambridge Arts Theatre, 223
Cambridge Independent, UK newspaper, 223
Cameron, James, works by: *Titanic*, 177
Cameroon, 118, 123
Cameroon, theatre of, 222, 226–67
Can, German band, 260

canon, the, 1, 5, 7, 8, 17, 20, 23, 36, 59, 80, 91, 94, 114, 135, 142, 179, 180, 230, 263
Capel Curig, 80
Capus, Alex, 117
Capus, Alex, works by: *Eine Frage der Zeit*, 120–21
Carlson, Marvin, 220
Carlyle, Thomas, 39, 74
Casanova, Pascale, 4
Cassin, Barbara, 22
celtic, 19, 85
celtomania, 77
Césaire, Aimé, 111
Chamberlain, Neville, 240
Cheah, Pheng, 26, 30
Chekhov, Anton, 229
Chinese Theater, circulation of, 220
Christianity, 200, 204, 205
Christie, Agatha, 251
Churchill, Caryl, productions of: *Love and Information* (dir. Caroline Steinbeis, 2018), 231
cinema: European, 264; Expressionist, 270; German, 6, 17; Indian, 171, 178; representation of colonialism in, 155
climate change, 165
Clingman, Steven, 9
Clinton, George, 274
Cluster, German band, 271
coauthorship, concept and practice of, 196
colonial gaze, 171
colonialism: Australian, 157, 163, 166; British, 149; Dutch, 136, 138, 139–40, 145; European, 142, 152, 174, 183, 196; German, 4, 58, 109–27, 136, 150, 197, 200; relation to theatre practice, 227
colonization. *See* colonialism
comedy, 40, 176, 184
communicative approach, in language learning, 176–77
communism, 248
community arts, outreach and impact in, 191–92, 201–15
comparative linguistics, 175

comparative literature, 35, 43, 103, 109, 136, 159–60, 165, 166
comparative methods, 173, 174, 177–78, 180–83. *See also* comparative literature
Conrad, Joseph, works by: *Heart of Darkness*, 110
Contrapuntal reading, Said's concept of, 114
Cooper, James Fenimore, 37, 52
Cooper, James Fenimore, works by: *The Last of the Mohicans*, 42, 48–49; *The Pilot*, 42; *The Pioneers*, 42, 48; *The Spy*, 42
Copland, Fiona, 222
Cosmopolitanism, theories of, 62–64, 68–69, 110, 127. *See also Weltbürger(tum)*; world citizenship
Costabile-Heming, Carol Anne, 2
craftsmanship, literary, 41–44, 50
Craig, Carl, 272
Creese, Angela, 222
crime fiction, 20, 116–22, 126
cultural studies, discipline of, 2, 74, 109, 111, 113, 144, 159–60, 197, 259–60
culture industry, 23
Czernin, Monika, works by: *Jenes herrliche Gefühl der Freiheit*, 119

D'Alembert, Jean, works by: *Encyclopédie*, 24
Damrosch, David, 7, 34, 36–37, 97
Darwin, Charles, 182
decline, historical concept of, 26, 29. *See also Niedergang*
decolonization, concept of in academia, 1, 23, 112–13, 152; political, 152, 163
democracy, 246
Denham, Scott, 2
Department of Business, Energy and Industrial Strategy (BEIS), 10
Depeche Mode, 258
Depeche Mode, works by: *Some Great Reward*, 269
Derrida, Jacques, 98, 160
Dery, Mark, 274

deterritorialization, of German language and culture, 135. *See also* reterritorialization
Detroit, pop music scene, 258, 266–67, 272–73, 276
Deutsch als Fremdsprache. *See* German language, study of
Deutsch Na Klar, textbook, 176
Deutsche Demokratische Republik (DDR). *See* German Democratic Republic (GDR)
Deutscher Akademischer Austauschdienst (DAAD). *See* German Academic Exchange Service
Deutsches Ausland-Institut, 68
Devlin, Es, 225
dialogic approaches, 146, 198
diaspora, African, 20, 110, 122–25; literature of, 5
Dickens, Charles, 250
Dickson, Andrew, 222, 224–25, 228–31, 232–33, 234
Diderot, Denis, 29
Diderot, Denis, works by: *Encyclopédie*, 24
Diederichsen, Diedrich, 259
director's theatre. *See Regietheater*
discourse, in Goethe, 24–25, 30
diversity, in Goethe, 28
divinity, 25
Döblin, Alfred, 95
Döblin, Alfred, works by: *Amazonas*, 114
Doctrine of Maya, 181
Dolbadarn Castle, Wales, 81
Donald, Gerald, 274–75
Dos Passos, John, 95
Doyle, Arthur Conan, 251
Dunker, Axel, 114
Duperron, Anquetil, 181
Dürrenmatt, Friedrich, works by: *Die Panne*, 180
Düsseldorf, 257, 260, 262, 265–67, 270, 272–73

east-west cross-cultural relations, 171, 181

eastern turn, in German literature, 92
Ecker, Gisela, 161
Eckermann, Johann Peter, 18, 34–35, 39–40, 41, 47, 50, 70
ecocide, 166
ecocriticism, 155, 166
ecofeminism, 161
economics, study of, 25, 174
education, higher education, 9, 136, 142, 148–50, 157; in policy, 139, 142, 145–50; in schools, 10, 205–6, 210, 216. *See also Bildung*, concept of; reeducation
Egan, Rusty, 269
Ehrenzweig, Robert. *See Lucas*, Robert
Eisteddfod, Welsh cultural festival, 83
El Loko, works by: *Der Blues in mir*, 124
émigrés, 23, 156, 157, 158, 159, 166, 240, 241, 244, 251
empire, 20, 59–64, 68–69, 74, 111–13, 116, 138, 197, 200, 201, 246. *See also* colonialism; imperial
England, 19, 75–78, 85–89, 155, 157, 159, 175, 207, 220, 223, 239, 245
English people, the, 85–86
English language, the, 251
English studies, discipline of, 4, 155
Engombe, Lucia, works by: *Kind Nr. 95*, 124
enlightenment, 62, 66, 143, 159–60, 160–61, 200, 201, 250
environmental humanities, discipline of, 136, 155–56, 162–63, 165
Eshun, Kodwo, 259
Essin, Christin, 227
Esslin, Martin, 241
Europe, region and culture, 26, 36, 44, 58, 59, 64, 66, 69, 74, 76, 78, 80, 82, 92, 99–101, 103, 152, 156, 164, 171, 182–83, 196, 198, 199, 200, 202, 216, 219–21, 228, 229, 230, 234–35. *See also* colonialism, European
European theater, concept and circulation of, 219–21, 224, 228, 229–30, 234
European Union, 1, 10, 219

Evans, Lloyd, 225
Excellence in Research Australia (ERA), 10
exhibitions, use of in public engagement work, 191, 199–203, 207
exile, 5, 69–70, 243, 271
experience, concept of, 18, 22–23, 29, 45, 71
exploration, 4, 27, 121, 122, 171
Expressionism, German, 213

Falco, Austrian musician, 262
family novel, 20, 110, 116–22, 126
Fanon, Frantz, 111
Faust, German band, 271
Fichte, Hubert, 64, 67, 69, 70, 110
Fichte, Johann Gottlieb, works by: *Reden an die deutsche Nation*, 19, 61–63
financial crisis, of 2008, 1
Fisher, Mark, 259
Fokus Deutsch, textbook, 176
France, 4, 58, 59, 82, 258
Francophonie, 4
Frankfurt School, 161
friendship, 22
Foreign and Commonwealth Office (UK), 240
Forster, Georg, 74
Fortschritt, German concept of, 26–27. *See also* progress
Fraser, Lindley, 240, 242, 245, 246–48
French studies, discipline of, 4
Friedrich, Caspar David, 171, 172
Fuchs, Anne, 97
Funkbriefkasten, radio programme, 243
fusion, 66, 70, 173, 179, 180, 184

Gadamer, Hans-Georg, 182
Gardner, Lyn, 219, 220, 221
Gastarbeiterliteratur, 91
Gellner, Julius, 241
German Academic Exchange Service (DAAD), 148, 158
German Book Prize, 20, 92, 102

German Democratic Republic (GDR), 123, 124, 159
German freedom, concept of, 61–64
German greatness, concept of, 19, 59–61, 71
German language, study of, incl. *Deutsch als Fremdsprache*, 1, 113, 143, 193, 230; grammar-translation method, 174–75
German reunification, 6, 118, 123, 124, 232
German Studies Association, USA, 3
German unification, of 1989. *See* German reunification
Germanistik: Germanophone tradition of, 3, 111, 113, 155, 166, 259; *interkulturell(e)*, 113, 143
Germanness, concept of, 8, 19, 66, 92–94, 102, 191, 192, 193, 221, 223–28, 258, 262, 263, 275–76
Germany: British zone of, 243, 245–46, 258; media landscape of, 239, 242, 245; occupation of, 239–40, 243–44, 246–27, 249–50
Gerunde, Harald, works by: *Eine von uns*, 126
Gesamtkunstwerk, total work of art, 258, 263, 265, 274–75, 276
Gibson, Christina. *See* Ogilvy, Christina
Gilman, Sander, 150
Ginzkey, Franz Karl, 201, 217
global, the, 1–3, 3–7, 8–9, 9–10, 20, 26–27, 34, 36–37, 38, 51, 51–52, 59, 74, 91, 94, 101, 111, 135–36, 220
global history, discipline of, 4
global literature. *See* world literature
global trade, 6, 23, 27, 115, 122, 123
globalization, 1, 3, 4, 5–6, 71, 110, 117, 120, 122, 126, 139, 149
Glötzner, Johann, works by: *Der Mohr*, 125
Goede, Christian August Gottlieb, 19, 78, 84, 85–86
Goede, Christian August Gottlieb, works by: *England, Wales, Irland und Schottland: Erinnerungen an Natur und Kunst aus einer Reise in den Jahren 1802 und 1803*, 75, 77
Goethe, Johann Wolfgang von, 7, 17–19, 22–30, 34–52, 68, 70, 74, 80, 87, 164, 175–76, 178, 191, 204–7, 211–12, 251
Goethe, Johann Wolfgang von; works by: *Egmont*, 29; *Farbenlehre*, 22, 28, 35, 40; *Faust*, 17–18, 22, 25, 27, 29, 30, 178–79; *Götz von Berlichingen*, 29; *Heidenröslein*, 176; *Hermann und Dorothea*, 29, 39, 42; *Jenaische Allgemeine Literatur-Zeitung*, 24; "Metamorphose der Pflanzen," 25; *Novelle*, 18, 34–35, 42–52; *Propyläen*, 26; *Torquato Tasso*, 18; *Über Kunst und Althertum*, 18, 34, 38, 40, 49; *Wahlverwandtschaften*, 25, 44; *West-östlicher Divan*, 25, 191, 204, 211, 212; *Wilhelm Meisters Lehrjahre*, 35, 52; *Wilhelm Meisters Wanderjahre*, 25, 35, 41, 44; *Xenien*, 25
Goethe Institut, 175, 227
Goetz, Walter, 240
Goldziher, Ignaz, 199
Goodbody, Axel, 155, 164
Goodman, Steve, 259
Goring, Marius, 240, 244, 250
Götting, Michael, works by: *Contrapunctus*, 125
Gramling, David, 5
Grant, James, 87
Great Britain. *See* Britain
Great Trek, the, 140
Greene, Graham, 240
Greene, Hugh Carleton, 240–42, 245, 251
Grimm, Jakob and Wilhelm, works by: *Grimms Wörterbuch*, 24
Grosz, Elizabeth, 160
Grünewald, Hildemarie, 140
Guardian, UK newspaper, 219, 222, 224, 231
Guthke, Karl S., 27

Habeck, Robert, works by: *Der Schrei der Hyänen*, 118–19
Hafez, of Shiraz (Khwāja Shams-ud-Dīn Muḥammad Ḥāfeẓ-e Shīrāzī), 191, 204, 207, 212. *See also Hafis*
Hafez-Goethe Monument (Hafis-Goethe Denkmal), 191, 204, 205, 206
Hafis, 205
Hahn-Hahn, Ida von, 74
Haines, Brigid, 5
Halbfass, Wilhelm, 182
Halle, Randall, 6
Halverson, Rachel J., 2
Hamann, Christof, works by: *Fester*, 119; *Usambara*, 122
Handke, Peter, works by: *Die Angst des Tormanns beim Elfmeter*, 177, 185
Hannerz, Ulf, 6, 8
Hardenberg, Friedrich von. *See Novalis*
Hare, David, 219–21, 224, 228, 229, 231, 234–35
Harmonia, German band, 271
Harms, Ludwig (Louis), 140
Hartmannm, Lukas, 117
Hartmannm, Lukas, works by: *Abschied von Sansibar*, 120; *Die Mohrin*, 125
Hase, Annemarie, 241
Hawai'i, 136, 170–71
Hecken, Thomas, 259
Hegel, G. W. F., 171, 181–84; concept of *Geist* (Spirit), 181
Heidegger, Martin, 158, 164
Heidelberg, 81–82
Heimat, 76, 80, 93, 98–100, 264
Heine, Heinrich, 74, 251
Herbert, Jeremy, 225
Herder, Johann Gottfried, 26, 64, 178, 181
Hermand Jost, 155
Hermannsburg Mission Society, 140
hermeneutics, 183
Hermes, Stefan, 114
Herrmann, Elisabeth, 5–6
Hesse, Hermann, 121

Hesse, Hermann, works by: *Siddhartha*, 179
higher education. *See* education, higher education
Hill-Gibbins, Joe, 225, 228
Hilliges, Ilona Maria, works by: *Ein Kind Afrikas*, 122; *Sterne über Afrika*, 122
Hindi, language and culture, 136, 145, 171, 175, 176–77, 180, 183
Hinduism, 173, 175, 181–82
Hispanic studies, discipline of, 4
historical linguistics, discipline of, 175
historical novel, the, 41, 117, 118, 120, 121, 125
historiography, 19, 122–13
history, discipline of, 3–4, 109, 111, 121, 155, 157, 200
Hitler, Adolf, 66, 112, 121, 240, 246
Hoffmann, Giselher W., works by: *Die schweigenden Feuer*, 118
Hofmannsthal, Hugo von, works by: *Jedermann*, 251
Hohendahl, Peter Uwe, 2
Holdsworth, Nadine, 221, 227
Holocaust, 20, 115–16, 117, 119, 151, 157, 164, 166, 261, 264
Honold, Alexander, 114
Hoppe, Felicitas, 5
Horkheimer, Max, 160–61
Horn, Peter, 144
Horne, Thomas, 85–86
Hove, Ivo von, 225
Huang, Alexa, 220, 225
human development, 27
Human League, The, UK band, 269
Humboldt, Friedrich Wilhelm Christian Karl Ferdinand von, 74, 175, 178
Humboldt, Friedrich Wilhelm Heinrich Alexander von, 67, 74
Humphreys, Paul, 268
Hütter, Ralf, 258, 264, 266, 267, 268, 269, 271, 273, 274
hybridity, 5, 121, 179
Hytner, Nicholas, 230

Ibsen, Henrik, 229

identity formation, 75
identity politics, 152
impact, as measure of research, 91, 194–95, 198–204, 205, 210–15, 216
imperial, 19, 58–59, 60, 64, 66, 69, 89, 109–10, 111–13, 115–16, 117, 120–21, 123, 200
India: cinema and theatre, of, 171, 176, 177–80; interaction with German culture, 177–80, 180–83; interaction with German language, 174–77
Indo-Pacific languages, 136
Ingeborg Bachmann Prize, 92
intercultural theatre, 229
interfaith relations, 196, 200–201, 206; community work, 199
intertextuality, 7
Iovino, Serenella, 155
Ireland, 76, 85, 259
Islam: binary treatment of, 196, 212; in contemporary media, 194, 199, 200; in the history of German-speaking culture, 194, 195–98, 199–201, 207
Islamophobia, 2, 194

Jackson, Leanard, 273
Jackson, Michael, 271
Jacob, Sir Ian, 244–45
Jaffé, Carl-Heinz, 251
Jarausch, Konrad H., 3
Jaumann, Bernhard, works by: *Der lange Schatten*, 119; *Steinland*, 119; *Die Stunde des Schakals*, 119
Jay, Paul, 4
Jeremiah, Emily, 94
Jerome, Jerome K., works by: *Three Men on the Bummel*, 88
Jews, 43, 78, 95, 112, 157, 162, 199, 224, 240, 241, 250
Jones, William, 181
Jonson, Ben, 250
journalists, 240, 245, 268, 273
Joy Division, UK band, 269. *See also* New Order, UK band
Judaism, 199

Kacandes, Irene, 2
Kafka, Franz, 158
Kafka, Franz, works by: *In der Strafkolonie*, 114; *Der Prozess*, 177
Kālidāsa, 175, 178
Kampmann, Bärbel, 126
Kant, Immanuel, 28, 180–81
Karnad, Girish, works by: *Hayavadana*, 179–80
Kathakali, 179
Kaya, Nevzat, 155
Kehlmann, Daniel, 5
Keiany, Mohsen, 192, 212–14
Keiany, Mohsen, works by: *The Desensitized Artist*, 212–14; *Meeting Point*, 212–14; *Soon After*, 212–13
Keltomanie. *See* celtomania
Kennedy, Dennis, 227
Kimmich, Dorothee, 197
Kittler, Friedrich, 158
Kleist, Heinrich von, works by: *Die Marquise von O.*, 177; *Der Prinz von Homburg*, 158; *Die Verlobung in St. Domingo*, 114
Klewitz, Andreas von, works by: *Kegilé oder die seltsame Reise des Kammerdieners Jeremias Grobschmied von Brandenburg nach Afrika*, 118
Kling Klang, recording studio, 265, 270, 273
Knauss, Sibylle, works by: *Die Missionarin*, 122
Kohl, Johann Georg, 19, 84
Kohl, Johann Georg, works by: *Reisen in England und Wales*, 75–76, 77, 87
Kolonialwaren, 115
Koselleck, Reinhart, 26–27
Kracht, Christian, 5, 117
Kracht, Christian, works by: *Ich werde hier sein im Sonnenschein und im Schatten*, 121; *Imperium*, 121
Kraftwerk, 193, 257–76
Kraftwerk, works by: *Autobahn*, 258, 263, 265–66, 267, 276; *The*

Catalogue, 263; *Computerwelt*, 267, 273; *Expo 2000*, 266; *Expo Remix*, 266; *Mensch-Maschine*, 266, 267, 269, 272–73; *Ralf & Florian*, 264; *Die Roboter*, 267; *Techno Pop*, 209; *Tour de France*, 263, 268; *Trans Europa Express*, 258, 267–68, 270, 271, 272
Kramer, Johannes, works by: *Das Delta*, 122; *Die Stadt unter den Steinen*, 122
Kranemann, Eberhard, 265
Krautrock, 257–58, 260–61, 264, 271. See also pop music, German
Kruger, Paul, 141
Kruse, Cornelia, works by: *Preußischer Liebesglück*, 126
Kühn, Dieter, works by: *Beethoven und der schwarze Geiger*, 125
Kulke, Christine, 161
Kun, Josh, 262

labor, 27, 43, 51, 139–40, 227
Laing, Alexander Gordon, 122
Lan, David, 231
Langer-Löw, Christa, works by: *Antonio Congo*, 125
language, pedagogy of, 136, 173, 174–77, 175–76. See also German language, study of
Latour, Bruno, 192, 223, 225, 227, 229, 232, 233, 234
Laurien, Ingrid, 145
Lawrence, D. H., 250
le Carré, John, 138, 152
Lebensraum, concept of, 112
Leibniz, Gottfried W., 28
Leipzig Book Fair Prize, 92
Leonhardt, Rudolf Walter, 245
less commonly taught languages (LCTL), 176–77
Lessing, Gotthold Ephraim, 251
Levine, Caroline, 94
libraries, 76
Library of Congress, 19, 59, 68
Liebig, Justus von, 83
Lied(er), 75, 79, 82
Lieskounig, Jürgen, 144

Lionnet, Françoise, 9
listeners, radio: letters from, 193, 239–40, 242–44, 246–50, 251–52; research into, 240, 242, 249
literary marketplace, 24
Litteratur, as defined by Goethe, 24–25
Liverpool, 80–81, 268
local, the, concept of, 2, 8, 101, 116, 135
London, 61, 74, 77, 120, 138, 202, 207, 212, 224–25, 229, 239, 240, 241, 245, 247–48, 249, 251, 258, 262, 263
Longfellow, Henry Wadsworth, 82
Lucas, Robert, 240, 241
Lützeler, Paul Michael, 110, 111

Mabinogion, Welsh literary collection, 79
Malkmus, Bernhard, 155, 169
Mancewicz, Aneta, 220, 235
Manchester, UK city, 269–70
Mani, B. Venkat, 30, 94, 103–8
Mann, Heinrich, works by: *Professor Unrat*, 178
Mann, Thomas, 19, 58–73, 121, 179, 253, 281
Mann, Thomas, works by: "Essay on Schiller," 71; "Germany and the Germans," 68–69, 72–73; "Germany's Guilt and Mission," 71, 73; *Lotte in Weimar*, 68; *Die vertauschten Köpfe*, 179
Marcil, Yasmine, 84
Marlowe, Christopher, 223–24, 236, 250
Marlowe, Christopher, productions of: *Edward II* (dir. Caroline Steinbeis, 2017), 223–24
Marlowe Society, The, 223–24
Marquard, Leopold, 142
Martin, Alison, 84, 90
März, Ursula, 93, 103, 106
Max Mueller Bhavan, Indian branch of the Goethe Institut, 175, 177
May, Ferdinand, works by: *Sturm über Südwest-Afrika*, 116–17

May, Theresa, 1
McCluskey, Andy, singer, 268–69
media, artistic, 111, 116, 135, 197, 211, 214
media, press and news media, 194, 197, 199, 200, 239–56. *See also* BBC
media studies, 111, 259–60
Mehta, Vijaya, 180
Meinecke, Friedrich, works by: *Weltbürgertum und Nationalstaat*, 64–67, 73
Meister, Jan Christoph, 144–45, 153
Memmi, Albert, 111
memory studies, 71, 96–107
Mepin, Daniel, works by: *Die Weissagung der Ahnen*, 123, 132
metafiction, 20, 116–26
Métissage, 23
Meusel, Johann G., works by: *Historisch-Litterarisches Magazin*, 24
Meyer, Hans, 122
Mies, Maria, 161
migrant writer, 91–107, 110, 122–26
Migrantenliteratur, migrant literature, 20, 132, 91–107, 110, 122–26
migration, 1–9, 20, 91–107, 110–12, 113, 116, 124, 126, 128
migration studies, discipline of, 5, 6, 20, 110–16
Mills, Jeff, 274
Misipo, Dualla, works by: *Der Junge aus Duala*, 123
Mitchell, Katie, 225
modern (foreign) languages, discipline of, 3–4, 111, 145
modernism, 114, 155, 281
modernity, in thought, culture and literature, 19–20, 26, 30, 31, 32, 56, 165, 233, 237, 260, 263, 269; as epoch, 6–7, 22–24, 31, 64, 65, 71, 73, 77, 107, 110, 112, 113, 118, 130, 131, 132, 161, 163, 167, 175, 179, 200, 237, 269
Monty Python's "Philosophers' Football," 184, 185, 188
Mora, Terézia, 92

morphology, 25–28, 32
Müller, Ray, works by: *Ein Traum von Afrika*, 119
multicultural(ism), 2, 20, 71, 115, 117, 125–26, 128, 179, 205
multidirectional(ity), as concept, 5, 116, 131, 221
multilingualism, 5, 12, 108, 136, 145–47
Munyevu, Tonderai, 222
Murphy, Joe, 225
music, and literature, 20, 32, 40, 44, 48, 49, 84, 96, 104, 158, 176, 178, 179, 193; electronic, 156, 257–79
Muslim(s): in German and Austrian culture, 195–210; media representations of in the UK, 194–218
mythology, 27, 158, 179, 275

Nadj Abonji, Melinda, works by: *Tauben fliegen auf*, 91, 105
Namibia, 118, 119, 124, 131, 138, 144
Napoleon (Bonaparte), 66, 76, 281
National Theatre, the, UK, 230
nationalism, 2, 4, 5, 59–64, 66, 68, 71, 84, 102, 109, 110, 119, 127, 194, 216, 261, 265
nation(ality), concept of, 1–13, 17, 19, 23, 26, 39, 43, 59, 61, 58–73, 74–90, 94, 96, 102, 109, 110, 111, 123, 135, 138, 157, 163, 176, 179, 183, 193–94, 199, 216, 220, 221, 224–27, 230, 235, 240, 246, 248, 252, 261, 262, 268, 273, 276
Nazism, incl. National Socialism, 68, 70, 108, 113, 115, 116, 117, 121, 125, 131, 241–42, 243, 244, 247, 249, 250, 265–66, 268, 272, 275–76
Ndumbe III, Kum'a, works by: *Ach Kamerun! Unsere alte deutsche Kolonie*, 123
Nena, German singer, 262
network theory, 192, 223, 232, 236
Neu!, German band, 257, 270

New Order, UK band, including Joy Division, 269–70
New Romantics, The, UK pop musical sub-culture, 251, 269, 278
news, reporting of, 23, 68, 93, 99, 201, 223, 224, 240, 241, 245, 250, 269, 270
Nico, German singer and musician, 262
Niedergang, German historical concept of, 26–27. *See also* decline
Nietzsche, Friedrich, 37, 54, 158, 182
Nietzsche, Friedrich, works by: *The Genealogy of Morals*, 37, 54
Nigeria, 122
Nirvana, Buddhist notion of, 181
Nordwestdeutscher Rundfunk (NWDR), 245
Norris, Rufus, 225
Novalis (Georg Philipp Friedrich Freiherr von Hardenberg), 30
Novalis, works by: *Die Christenheit oder Europa*, 61; *Heinrich von Ofterdingen*, 32, 156, 158, 163, 167, 195–98
Numan, Gary, singer, 269

Oberprieler, Gudrun, 144, 153
occident(al), 23, 197, 198, 217
Ogilvy, Christina, 240, 253
Old Vic, theatre, 225
Orchestral Manoeuvres in The Dark, UK band, 258, 268–69
Orchestral Manoeuvres in The Dark, works by: *Sugar Tax* (LP), 268–69
orientalism, 58, 71, 108, 109, 111–12, 120, 127, 186, 187, 196–97, 217. *See also* Said, Edward
O'Rorke, Richard, 246, 253, 254
Orsini, Francesca, 102, 108
Orwell, George, 250
Osborne, Dora, 98, 107
Ostermeier, Thomas, 229, 232–34, 237, 238
other(ness), concept of, 39, 54, 74, 100, 102, 177, 194, 244, 258
Outside Edge, UK theater company, 222

Pakendorf, Gunther, 144, 152, 153, 154

Paluch, Andrea, works by: *Der Schrei der Hyänen*, 118–19
Pan African Language Board (PanSALB), 145
Pappelbaum, Jan, 228
paracolonial, concept of, 136, 139
Pattie, David, 260, 263, 277
pennillion, Welsh musical tradition, 79
Pereszlenyi, Julius. *See* Esslin, Martin
performance, in theater, performing arts, 173, 177, 192, 193, 207–9, 218, 222, 227, 229, 231–32, 237, 260, 264, 267, 271, 275, 277; dialogue within, 173, 184; interpretation in, 173, 231; interweaving concept of, 229, 232, 237
performance based teaching and learning, 177
periphery, geographical, 19, 75; cultural, 5, 19, 37, 75, 77, 87–89
Peters, George F., 12
Petropoulos, Jonathan, 2, 12
philology, methods of, 8, 35, 36, 37, 84, 259
philo-selfie, concept of, 170–88
Pickford, Susan, 84, 90
Pieken, Gorch, works by: *Preußischer Liebesglück*, 126
Plato, 180–81
Poe, Edgar Allan, 251
Pohlmeier, Arne, 222, 225–27, 228, 229, 231, 233, 236
Pohlmeier, Arne, productions by: *Angaboko!-Brigands!*, 227
politics: and the alt-right, 211; of the Cold War, 50; cosmopolitan politics, 66; as distinct from culture, 61, 63, 69; and egoism, 66; in the Federal Republic of Germany, 85, 113; in the GDR, 113; global politics, 180; and imperialism, 117; nation-centered, 61, 112; politics of memory, 20, 116, 119, 123; in South Africa, 146, 152, 154; in the theater, 228–30, 237; in the UK, 1, 194, 219, 221, 234; in the US, 1–2, 44; world politics, 197

polyperspectivism, 118
polyphony: of discourse: 32, 195–96; in literature, 28–29, 32, 44, 120, 195–96
Pop, Iggy, singer, 270
pop music, German, 156, 193, 257–79
populism, 2, 211
porosity, concept of, 9–11, 192, 194–95, 221, 223, 227, 228, 229, 231, 232, 234
Portuguese studies, discipline of, 4, 144, 147
postcolonial amnesia, concept of, 113
postcolonial cultural and literary production, 3–5, 116–26
postcolonial gaze, 110, 112, 116, 117, 123
postcolonialism, theory and study of, 3, 5, 11, 23, 34, 53, 58, 109–32
postmemory, 122, 123, 131
postmodernism, 6, 122, 167, 237
Pratt, Mary Louise, 75, 90
process based teaching and learning, 177
progress, historical, 26–30, 31, 62. *See also Fortschritt*
progressive thought and politics, 5, 8, 59, 181, 182, 197, 199
project based teaching learning, 177
Propaganda, German band, 262
propaganda, in media and politics, 138, 201, 241, 250, 252, 255, 268
provincialism, 37, 91–95, 114, 130
psychological warfare, 239
public engagement, by academics and artists, 9–11, 14, 97, 194–218, 258
Puchner, Martin, 51, 57
Pückler-Muskau, Hermann von, 19, 75, 77, 84, 87, 89, 90
Pückler-Muskau, Hermann von, works by: *Briefe eines Verstorbenen: Ein fragmentarisches Tagebuch aus England, Wales, Irland und Frankreich; geschrieben in den Jahren 1828 und 1829*, 75, 77, 87; *Tour in England, Ireland and France in the years 1828 and 1829; with remarks on the manners and customs of the inhabitants, and anecdotes of distinguished public characters; in a series of letters by a German Prince*, 87, 90
Puranas, The, 181
Pwllheli, Welsh town, 8

Raabe, Wilhelm, 114, 130
Rammstein, German band, 262–63, 277
Ravenhill, Mark, 229, 237
Rebellato, Dan, 220, 235, 237
reeducation, 245–48, 250–52
Research Excellence Framework (REF), UK, 9–11, 13
Regietheater (director's theatre), 192, 220–21, 225, 228–31, 233, 234, 237
regionalism, 91–105
regionality, 93, 95
rehearsal practice, 226, 227, 250
relativism, 173, 182
representation: aesthetic practice of, 18, 23–26, 27–30, 46–47, 56, 77, 173, 181, 194, 195–96, 197–98, 199–200, 202, 204, 214, 216; political, 182, 196
Respublica literaria, 26
reterritorialization of German culture, 257–79
revolution, concept of, 27, 32, 66, 151, 180; in the arts, 151, 260, 264, 265, 270
Reynolds, Simon, 260, 278
Rhodes, Cecil John, 149, 151, 153
Rickson, Ian, 225
Riebeeck, Jan van, 139
Riordan, Colin, 155
Ritz, ManuEla, works by: *Die Farbe meiner Haut*, 125
Robb, David, 259
Roberts, David, 159–60
Rodenberg, Julius, 78–79, 84, 85
Rodenberg, Julius, works by: *An Autumn in Wales (1856). Country and People, Tales and Songs*, 75, 90; *Deutsche Rundschau*, 78; *Ein*

Herbst in Wales: Land und Leute, Märchen und Lieder, 75, 78–82, 89, 90; *Insel der Heiligen*, 85
Rohmer, Eric, 177, 186
Romantic, thought, writing, 76, 78, 79, 84, 88, 155, 158, 164–65, 168, 169, 171, 175, 181, 195–96, 201
Romanticism, German, 57, 165, 169, 171, 195–96, 201
Roscoe, Thomas, 87
Rothberg, Michael, 116, 131
Royal Court, theater, 222
Ruete, Emily, 120
Ruete, Emily, works by: *Memoiren einer arabischen Prinzessin*, 120
Run DMC, US band, 272

Said, Edward, 21, 58–59, 71, 109–12, 114, 120, 127, 129, 196–98. *See also* orientalism
Śākuntala, 175, 178, 179, 186
Sanskrit, 174, 183
Sapir Whorf Hypothesis, 175
Sayers, Dorothy L., 251
Schaub, Christoph, 272, 278
Schaubühne, German theater, 231–34
Scheel, Walter, 269
Scheich, Elvira, 161
Schiller, Friedrich, 19, 39, 58–64, 67, 69, 70, 71, 72, 227
Schiller, Friedrich, works by: "Deutsche Größe," 19, 59–64; *Die Räuber*, 227
Schlegel, Karl Wilhelm Friedrich von, works by: *Über die Sprache und Weisheit der Indier*, 175, 185
Schlegel brothers (Karl Wilhelm Friedrich von and August Wilhelm von), 76, 175, 178, 181, 185
Schneider, Florian, 265–68, 271, 273, 274, 278
Schopenhauer, Arthur, 173, 175, 180–82, 187
schools, secondary, academic engagement with, 9–10, 139, 140–47, 173–74, 178, 191–93, 199, 202–18
Schroeter, Werner, 178

Schubert, Franz, 176, 179
Schuchardt, Hugo, works by: "Keltische Briefe," 75, 88, 89, 90
Schult, Emil, 265–66
Schulz, Gerhard, 158
Schulz, Hermann, works by: *Auf dem Strom*, 122
science(s), natural, 25–29, 30, 31; and literature, 25–29, 31, 53, 162–63
sciences, social, 3, 6, 109, 111, 158–59, 161, 260
Scott, Walter, 37, 41–47, 55, 56, 74
Scutt, Tom, 225
self-reflexivity: of academic discourse, 20; in literary practice, 19, 118, 173, 183, 184, 222; in pedagogy, 173–75
Shakespeare, William, 39, 40, 186, 231, 235, 237, 250, 255
Shakespeare, William, productions of: *Hamlet* (dir. Ian Rickson, 2011), 225; *Hamlet* (dir. Lyndsey Turner, 2015), 225
Shakespeare, William, works by: *A Midsummer Night's Dream*, 180; *Romeo and Juliet*, 177, 186
Shakespeare's Globe, UK theatre, 231
Shantaram, V., works by: *Pinjra*, 178, 180, 186
Sheffield, UK city, 202, 222, 269
Sheffield Theatres, UK, 222
Shi, Shu-mei, 9, 12
Shryane, Jennifer, 259
similarity, concept of, 197, 199, 201, 216
Simmeth, Alexander, 260, 277
Simpsons, The, TV show, 177
Siskind, Mariano, 102, 108
Skorge, Silvia, 143
slave(ry), 27, 69, 120, 123, 125, 139, 140, 196, 267, 274, 275
Smith-Prei, Carrie, 5, 13
Snowdon, Mount, in Wales, 81, 87
So Einfach, textbook, 175
social sciences, discipline of. *See* sciences, social
Soft Cell, UK band, 269
soft power, 193, 196, 252

South Africa, 135–36, 138–54
South West Africa, incl. *Südwestafrika*, 110, 111, 113, 114, 115, 117, 118, 130, 138, 144. *See also* Namibia
sovereignty, political, concept of, 27
Sow, Noah, works by: *Deutschland Schwarz Weiß*, 125
Soweto, student uprising of, 143, 146, 152
spatial, concept of, 24, 26, 27, 28, 29, 283
spatio-temporal, concept of, 26–27
Spain, 76
Spanish studies, discipline of. *See* Hispanic studies
Spiker, Samuel Heinrich, works by: *Reise durch England, Wales und Schottland im Jahre 1816*, 75, 77, 86, 87, 89, 90; *Travels through England, Wales and Scotland in the year 1816 by Dr S. H. Spiker, Librarian to his Majesty the King of Prussia, dedicated to the Friends of England*, 86–87
Spivak, Gayatri Chakravorty, 24, 31, 96, 103, 106, 108, 111, 159, 198, 217
Spurensuche, historical method, 112, 124–25, 129
Stangl, Thomas, works by: *Der einzige Ort*, 122
Stanišić, Saša, works by: "Fallensteller," 103–4, 108; *Herkunft*, 102, 108; *Vor dem Fest*, 20, 91–108; *Wie der Soldat das Grammofon repariert*, 92, 104, 105
Steinaecker, Thomas von, works by: *Schutzgebiet*, 118
Steinbeis, Caroline, 222–31, 236
Steinberg, Matt, 222–33, 236, 237
Steiner, Nicola, 96–97, 106
Sternberg, Josef von, works by: *Der blaue Engel*, 178
Stinson, James, 274–75
Strauss, Franz Josef, 269
Stubbs, David, 257, 260, 276, 278

subjectivity, in philosophy and literature, 18, 24, 27, 53
Südafrikanischer Germanistenverband (SAGV), 144, 152, 153
Sullivan, Heather, 155, 164, 169
Summer, Donna, 270
Sun Ra and his Arkestra, US band, 274
Sweet, Jeffrey, 219, 235, 236

Taberner, Stuart, 5, 13, 101, 105, 107, 108
Tait's Edinburgh Magazine, 87, 90
Telford, Thomas, 77, 86
temporality, 3, 7, 8, 24–30, 58
Tendulkar, Vijay, 180, 186
theater: as artistic medium, 29, 30, 74, 75, 136, 151, 171, 173, 177, 178, 179, 180, 181, 183, 192, 207, 209, 210, 219–38; national cultures of in UK and Germany, 219–38
Theatertreffen, festival, 232
Theaterzentrum OTHNI Yaoundé, theater, 227
Thomsen, Mads Rosendahl, 101, 107
Tieck, Ludwig, 76
Timm, Uwe, 110, 117, 131, 150
Timm, Uwe, works by: *Morenga*, 110, 117, 150
Tip, Tippu. *See* Bin Hamed, Muhammed
Togo, 118, 120, 123, 124
translation, 4, 7, 23–24, 35, 39–41, 50, 71, 74, 76, 82, 84–89, 97, 106, 120, 160, 162, 174–75, 192, 234–35, 265–67
translingualism, 12
transnational(ism), 1–14, 17, 18, 20, 21, 39, 50, 64, 70, 91, 93–95, 99, 100–104, 105, 107, 111, 123, 135–36, 166, 191, 193, 195, 198, 215, 219, 220–21, 223, 225, 229, 232–34, 239, 251, 253, 257, 258, 260, 261, 263, 267, 268, 270–73, 275, 277, 284
travel writing, 19, 74–90
Trojanow, Illija, 5–6, 120, 131

Trojanow, Ilija, works by: *Die Weltensammler*, 120, 131
Trommler, Frank, 3, 4, 12
Trueman, Matt, 228, 229, 237
Trump, Donald, 1
Turner, Luke, 268, 278
Turner, Lyndsey, 225
Twitter, 223, 236
Two Gents, theater company, 222, 226, 236

Uckermark, 92, 93, 100–103, 105, 106
Uerlings, Herbert, 114, 129, 130, 132
UK Research and Innovation (UKRI), 10, 13, 14, 217
Ultravox, UK band, 269
Underground Resistance, techno artists/record label, 266, 267, 273, 278, 279
United Kingdom, incl. academy, cultural life, education system, politics, 1, 10, 136, 166, 192, 193, 194, 195, 199, 201, 205, 210, 211, 212, 219–23, 225, 227, 228, 229–31, 232, 234, 239, 246, 253, 257, 259, 267, 268, 269, 276
United States, incl. German culture and German studies in, 2, 12, 19, 44, 73, 136, 144, 150, 155, 171, 176, 193, 222, 257–64, 266, 272–76
universalism, concept of, 23, 28, 64, 66–70, 173, 182
universality, 23, 31, 276
university, 24, 76, 82, 111, 125, 136, 141–43, 147, 148, 149, 151, 157, 158, 159, 160, 164–66, 170, 176, 177, 198, 200–202, 204, 206, 223
Upaniṣads, The, 173
Urdu, language and culture, 136, 171, 177

Valentin, Veit, works by: *Deutschlands Außenpolitik von Bismarck bis zum Ende des Weltkrieges*, 67, 73
Vedas, The, 181
Velvet Underground, US band, 262
Vereenigde Oost-Indische Compagnie (VOC, or Dutch East India Company), 139
Versailles, Treaty of, 113
Vertovec, Steven, 6, 13
Visage, UK band, 269
voice(s), acoustic, figurative, and narrative, 5, 32, 38, 40, 45, 95–96, 101, 102, 115, 116, 117, 195, 196, 198, 202, 204, 210–11, 212–15, 239, 241, 243, 244, 245, 246, 249, 250–52
Völkerschauen, 115, 130
Volksbühne, German theater, 231–33
Volkslied, incl. folksong, 75, 79–80, 82, 196
Volksmusik, industrielle, 264–67
Voltaire, 29
Vyleta, Dan, 6

Wackwitz, Stephan, works by: *Ein unsichtbares Land*, 119
Wagner, Richard, work by: *Die Meistersinger von Nürnberg*, 63, 72, 182
Wales, 19, 74–90
Walker, Patrick Gordon, 241, 244
Walter, Ferdinand, 82, 90
war: Bosnian, 92; Cold, 59, 252, 254; Colonial, in South West Africa, 114, 117, 118. See also World War I; World War II
Weatherall, Andrew, 270
Weimar, German city of, 191, 204, 205, 212, 216
Weimar classicism, incl. *Weimarer Klassik*, 32, 56, 59, 72
Weimar Republic, the, 67, 113, 115, 126, 130, 254, 270
Weiss, Peter, 151, 154
Weißhaupt, Brigitte, 161
Weissmann, Dirk, 5, 12
Welles, Orson, works by: *The Trial*, 177
Wells, H. G., 251
Welsh, language, people and culture, 72, 82–88

Welt, 17, 22, 24, 25, 27, 30. *See also specific* compound nouns derived from *Welt* and world
Weltbürger(tum), 25, 31, 64, 66, 67, 73. *See also* world citizenship
Weltdeutschtum, 8, 19, 58–73
Weltengarten, journal, 114, 132
Weltenschöpfer, 25
Weltensumpf, 25
Weltgeist, 67
Weltgeschichte, 25
Welthistorie, 25
Weltliteratur, 7, 13, 17, 18, 22–23, 24, 25, 30, 31, 34–35, 38, 51–52, 53, 55, 68, 70, 91–94, 102. *See also* world literature(s)
Weltregiment, 25
Weltseele, 25
Weltwirrwesen, 25
Wenders, Wim, films by: *Die Angst des Tormanns beim Elfmeter*, 177, 185
Wendhausen, Fritz, 241, 254
Widmer, Urs, works by: *Im Kongo*, 110
Wierlacher, Alois, 113, 143
Wilke, Sabine, 155
will, faculty of, 44, 180–82, 187; negation of, 181
Willet, John, 225, 237
Willi, Magda, 229
Wördemann, Franz, 245
world: as abstract, 1–14, 17–21, 22–23, 30; as economic, 6, 10, 14, 17, 19, 23, 25, 26, 31, 36, 46, 59, 70, 71, 89, 102, 111, 122; multi-layered concept of, 18, 19, 22, 30, 45; nonacademic world, 9–11, 192–93, 194, 195, 215; as progress, 26–28; representation of, 27–28; spatio-temporal, concept of, 24, 26–7; territorial concept of, 2, 19, 21, 59, 135

world belonging, concept of, 17, 23, 62, 64, 67, 100
world citizenship, concept of, 1, 25, 26, 31, 56. *See also Weltbürger(tum)*
world consciousness, concept of, 17, 18, 26, 163, 181
world culture, concept of, 36, 37, 38, 44, 52, 179
world history, 25–30, 182, 187. *See also Weltgeschichte*
world literature(s), concept of, 4–8, 13, 17–20, 22–26, 30, 31, 34–44, 45, 47, 49, 51, 52, 53–57, 70, 92–95, 97, 102–4, 105, 106, 108, 135–36, 180, 236. *See also Weltliteratur*
World War I, 64, 67–68, 113, 117, 121, 123
World War II, 100, 113, 138, 150–51, 156, 158, 193, 239, 240, 242, 245, 250, 252, 255, 264
worlding, process of, 6, 123, 124, 193
worldly, quality of, 17, 21, 114, 130, 135

Yello, Swiss band, 262
Yildiz, Yasmin, 5, 12
Young, Rob, 260
Young Vic, UK theater, 225, 231

Zaimoglu, Feridun, 105
Zaimoglu, Feridun, works by: *Ruß* (Soot), 93, 106
Zantop, Susanne, 111, 128
Zedler, Johann H, works by: *Zedlers Universal-Lexicon*, 24
Zeh, Juli, works by: *Unterleuten*, 93, 106
Zimmer, Hans, 262
Zuma, Jacob, 149

Printed in the United States
By Bookmasters